Thomistic Existentialism
& Cosmological Reasoning

Thomistic Existentialism
& Cosmological Reasoning

JOHN F. X. KNASAS

The Catholic University of America Press
Washington, D.C.

Copyright © 2019
The Catholic University of America Press
All rights reserved

Cataloging-in-Publication Data available from the Library of Congress
ISBN 978-0-8132-3710-7

To

Rev. Victor B. Brezik, CSB

Founder

Center for Thomistic Studies

CONTENTS

Acknowledgments ix
List of Abbreviations xi

Introduction 1

Part 1. Aquinas's *De Ente* Reasoning and the Cosmological Argument

1. Thomistic Reflections on Leibniz's *a posteriori* Reasonings 9
2. Existence and a Proof for God in Aquinas 31
3. Neo-Thomist Discussion of the *De Ente* Reasoning 68
4. *Actus essendi* and Analytic Thomism 106
5. The *De Ente* Reasoning and Objections to Cosmological Reasoning 131

Part 2. The *De Ente* Reasoning and Aquinas's Proofs for God

6. Aquinas's Metaphysics and Our Knowledge of God's Existence 173
7. A More Robust Version of the *De Ente* Reasoning 189
8. *Viae* for God: *Summa contra Gentiles* 216

9. The *viae* of the *Summa Theologiae* and the
   Compendium Theologiae 248
10. Other Possible *viae* 276
11. Questions and Replies 290

Conclusion: Does Aquinas Contribute to Cosmological
Reasoning? 305

Selected Bibliography 315
Index 325

ACKNOWLEDGMENTS

Chapter 2, sections 1–5, and chapter 3, sections 2–4, were originally published as "The Intellectual Phenomenology of *De Ente et Essentia*, Chapter Four" by *The Review of Metaphysics* 68, no. 1 (2014): 107–54.

Chapter 3, section 1, and chapter 4, section 2, are republished from *Being and Some Twentieth-Century Thomists* (New York: Fordham University Press, 2003), 202–7 and 224–36.

Chapter 4, section 1, and chapter 5, section 1, appeared in "Haldane's Analytic Thomism and Aquinas' *Actus Essendi*," published in *Analytical Thomism: Traditions in Dialogue*, edited by Craig Paterson and Matthew S. Pugh (Burlington, Vt.: Ashgate, 2006), 233–52.

Chapter 4, section 3, is from "Existential Thomist Reflections on Kenny: The Incompatibility of the Phoenix and Subsistent Existence," *Proceedings of the American Catholic Philosophical Association* 89 (2015): 195–208.

ABBREVIATIONS

Works of Aquinas

Comp. Theol.	*Compendium Theologiae*
De Ente	*De Ente et Essentia*
De Pot.	*Quaestiones Disputatae de Potentia Dei*
De Ver.	*Quaestiones Disputatae de Veritate*
In de An.	Commentary on the *De Anima* of Aristotle
In de Trin.	Commentary on the *De Trinitate* of Boethius
In Meta.	Commentary on the *Metaphysics* of Aristotle
In Phys.	Commentary on the *Physics* of Aristotle
In Sent.	Commentary on the *Sentences* of Peter Lombard
De Malo	*Quaestiones Disputatae de Malo*
Quodl.	*Quaestiones de quodlibet*
SCG	*Summa contra Gentiles*
ST	*Summa Theologiae*

Other Terms

PNC	Principle of Noncontradiction
PSR	Principle of Sufficient Reason

Thomistic Existentialism
& Cosmological Reasoning

Introduction

Classic Cosmological Reasoning

I would like to introduce my book by explaining the parts of the title. By "cosmological reasoning" I mean classic cosmological reasoning. By "classic" I mean the *a posteriori* proofs found in Leibniz. I call the Leibnizian proofs classic because they were the proofs Kant had in mind when Kant coined the phrase "cosmological argument." Since Kant "cosmological reasoning" has assumed a wider sense. It means any theistic reasoning from a feature of the world more obvious than teleology. Accordingly, Plato's and Aristotle's proofs from motion and Kalam's reasoning from the world's temporal inception count as cosmological arguments.

Nevertheless, there is a wisdom in keeping to the classic version. If I read Leibniz correctly, his proofs possess the virtue of forcing us to reflect on what is meant by the existence, or being, of the thing. In the proofs existence does seem to be an item distinct from the thing as another item, and both thing and existence appear to be in a contingent relation. Both are "touching" like one book does another on a shelf or one hat does another on a rack. Beginning with Kant, these points and others have provoked intense grumbling among philosophers. Fundamentally, is existence distinct from the thing or is it just the thing?

Perhaps the debates would have far less volume and longevity if the stakes were not so high. I remember as an undergraduate first hearing of the possibility of proving the existence of God. I had a strong faith in God and was content with that. Yet I had already experienced the power of proof. The new idea of applying proof to God's existence loomed before me as the Mt. Everest of the intellectual life. If you could prove anything, would it not be that? I did not know if it could be done, but I wanted to hear what philosophers had to say about it. If my listening brought me into the discussions about existence, then I would have to hear them.

Also, it may be precipitous to discount the metaphysical proclivities of the human mind. I recall still earlier catching the stark difference between saying "I" versus "I am." "Am" gave the second expression additional meaning. Moreover, that additional meaning was most important for without it I was nothing. Granted, this insight occurred in a philosophy class, but I was still a non-major and the class was only a second core course. Evidently, ordinary people can undergo philosophical experiences.

Leibniz's proofs connect with those experiences but offer, of course, stupendous implications. Unfortunately, Leibniz's thinking about existence in these proofs is, as I will explain, remarkably shallow. Hence, Kant and others could easily raise objections to the proofs. The remedy to that shallowness brings me to Thomistic Existentialism. My thesis is that among proponents of Thomistic Existentialism one can find a more nuanced understanding of existence that avoids the debilities found in Leibniz's understanding. In other words, it makes cosmological reasoning cogent. An ironic acknowledgment of this thesis is found in the consistent mention of Aquinas among debunkers of cosmological reasoning.

"Thomistic Existentialism"

Thomistic Existentialism became popular in the 1950s. Jacques Maritain suggested it in his *Existence and the Existent* (1948), where he compared Thomism to Sartre's existentialism as the true existentialism that not only exalts existence but also preserves essence.[1] Broadly speaking, the phrase means the

---

1. Jacques Maritain, *Existence and the Existent*, trans. Lewis Galantiere and Gerald B. Phelan (New York: Vintage, 1966), 3. In the 1950 Marquette University Aquinas Lecture, Robert Henle uses the term "existential Thomism": "The metaphysics to which I refer is existential Thomism, the metaphysics of being (*ens*) and existential act (*esse*)." *Method in Metaphysics* (Milwaukee, Wis.: Marquette University Press, 1980), 6. Also, Joseph Owens explicitly answers the question "What is an existential Thomist?" in his 1957 Marquette University Aquinas Lecture, *The Future of Thomistic Metaphysics* (Milwaukee, Wis.: Marquette University Press, 1973), 36–48. Owens provides abundant textual references. Gerald A. McCool, *From Unity to Pluralism: The Internal Evolution of Thomism* (New York:

interpretation of Aquinas that sees as central to his metaphysics the act of being, or of existence: *esse* or *actus essendi*. Hence, to be a being, or an existent (*ens* or *existens*) is to be a possessor of *esse*. In his *Summa contra Gentiles* (hereafter "*SCG*") II.54, Aquinas describes the Aristotelian hylomorphic substance as a composition still needing to be composed with *esse* in order to be a being. Aquinas indicates that natural reason accesses *actus essendi* in a variation of what Aristotle called the second operation of the intellect and which the Scholastic tradition called judgment. It is the judgmental apprehension of *esse* that makes the metaphysician. In virtue of the judgmental apprehension of *esse* and in reasoning set out in *De Ente et Essentia* (hereafter "*De Ente*"), chap. 4, the metaphysician reaches a subsistent instance of *esse* that Aquinas can identify with the God who mentioned his name as *Ego sum qui sum*. Consequently, insofar as Aquinas intends his God proofs to be philosophically cogent, then these *viae* are understandable only by this metaphysics of *actus essendi*.

Aquinas's doctrine of *esse* has some obvious advantages over the notion of existence often found in cosmological argument debate. First, as an act, or *actus*, *esse* is naturally dependent, at least upon its subject. No need exists to appeal to the principle of sufficient reason to initiate explanation. Known through judgment, *esse* is the act of all form and consequently a nonformal act. *Esse* can be added to the thing so that we do not ruin the identity between the possible and the actual, as Kant claimed would happen. Also, the priority of *esse* to its subject will allow one to say without redundancy, "Socrates exists." No problems are created that would force one to regard this positive existential proposition as a second-order proposition translatable into a nonexistential proposition. Finally, because *esse* is originally encountered in judgment, then our formed concepts of existence can express it but fail to present it. These concepts will allow God to be a logically necessary being with no commitment to ontological reasoning and will allow Aquinas to say that "God exists" is self-evident in itself but not to us.

The most persistent critics of Existential Thomism are other Thomists.

Fordham University Press, 1999), 182–86, and Benedict Ashley, *The Way toward Wisdom: An Interdisciplinary and Intercultural Introduction to Metaphysics* (Notre Dame, Ind.: University of Notre Dame Press, 2006), 49–50, continue the terminology. In deference to Aquinas's ascription of a knowledge of *esse* to Aristotle, Ralph McInerny, *Praeambula Fidei: Thomism and the God of the Philosophers* (Washington, D.C.: The Catholic University of America Press, 2006), chap. 13, speaks of "Aristotelian existentialism."

Their most persistent criticism is that if the doctrine of *esse* is central, then certainly Aquinas's *viae* are also central. The doctrine of *esse*, however, seems to be conspicuously absent from the *viae*. Hence, the doctrine cannot be as central and as important as Existential Thomists think. For generations Thomists have considered their existential brothers as torturing the *viae* by placing them on a Procrustean bed.

In reply to this criticism I present two arguments that, as far as I can tell, are new. First, no Existential Thomist has defended an interpretation of the *viae* from a previous determination of where and when Aquinas believes that the philosopher proves God's existence. In his rejection of Anselmian reasoning for God, Aquinas makes it quite clear that he wants *viae* that will pass philosophical muster. Moreover, Aquinas has a definite understanding of philosophy with its divisions and the accomplishments of those divisions. If one can determine if Aquinas assigns a knowledge of God to one of those divisions, then should not the division become a hermeneutical key for reading the *viae*? Is it sensible to think that if Aquinas held that in philosophy the metaphysician proves God's existence, that the Common Doctor would place that opinion aside when he wrote what he wanted to be philosophically cogent arguments?

Second, the Existential Thomist approach to God from *esse* has been done a disservice by identifying it with the proof in the fourth chapter of *De Ente*. The *De Ente* reasoning far from exhausts the metaphysician's causal reflections on *esse*. The argument shows what can be done beginning from the priority of *esse* to its subject. Emphasizing the priority of *esse* enables the metaphysician to quickly reach *esse subsistens* as the only adequate cause of *esse*. Judgment, however, does more than give *esse* as prior. Judgment also portrays *esse* as the act *of the thing*. In that respect a modicum of dependency upon the thing is also part of the story about judgmentally grasped existence. Hence, any causes of the thing become causes of the *esse*. If the thing is a changeable thing, then the causes will first involve hylomorphic principles of matter and form and then extrinsic conditions of efficient and final causes for the form in matter, etc. Eventually, from this direction the metaphysician will come to *esse subsistens*. In other words, Existential Thomist reflections on *esse* can borrow reflections from other divisions of philosophy without ceasing to be metaphysical. This acknowledgment would explain how thinking about *esse* could be so camouflaged in the *viae*. In sum, to deal with the apparent absence of the metaphysics of *esse* in Aquinas's *viae*, Existential Thomism needs to acknowledge a more robust version of the *De Ente* reasoning.

Hence, the book has two divisions. The first presents a reading of the fourth chapter of *De Ente* for the purpose of portraying Aquinas's more nuanced understanding of existence than the understanding found in Leibniz's proofs. Aquinas's understanding is then brought into the secular discussion of cosmological reasoning in its classic form, especially as the discussion bears upon the existence of things. In chapter 1 I show that Leibniz's proofs are hobbled by an unnuanced understanding of the existence of a thing. Hence, the Kantian critique of Leibniz quickly devolved into issues of ontological reasoning and whether existence is a predicate. Subsequent debate continued those issues and others: the validity of the principle of sufficient reason and the idea of logically necessary existential propositions. In chapters 2 to 4, I argue my interpretation of the *De Ente* reasoning with other Thomists. In chapter 5 I use my interpretation to address the above issues in cosmological argument debate. Other objections are also considered: sense realism, the problem of evil, and Heidegger's ontotheology. In sum, part 1 argues that unlike Leibniz's notion of existence in his *a posteriori* proofs. Aquinas's thesis of *esse* is sufficiently nuanced to provide in the *De Ente* cosmological reasoning that stands the test of the cosmological argument debate.

The second division presents new reasons for realizing that far from being an interesting and perhaps valid argument, the *De Ente* reasoning is at the heart of Aquinas's *viae*. In chapter 6 I investigate if Aquinas ever assigns knowledge of God to a specific division of philosophy. I conclude that Aquinas gives that prerogative to metaphysics. In chapter 7 I show that the *De Ente* reasoning far from exhausts the metaphysician's reflections on *esse*. The *De Ente* reasoning is a much fuller and robust argument. In that more robust guise the *De Ente* reasoning proves to be the hermeneutical tool for understanding the many *viae* for God throughout Aquinas's writings. Chapters 8–10 make good that claim by canvasing each of the many *viae*.

Among younger scholars of Aquinas there is some renewed interest in the *De Ente* reasoning and the notion of *esse* that it contains. By illustrating the value of Aquinas's understanding of the thing's existence as a *sui generis actus* or attribute of its own for classic cosmological reasoning, I hope to contribute to this momentum by reopening a path of Thomistic interpretation that flourished in the 1950s—Thomistic Existentialism.

PART I

Aquinas's *De Ente* Reasoning and the Cosmological Argument

[1]

Thomistic Reflections on Leibniz's *a posteriori* Reasonings

It is appropriate to begin with Leibniz. Immanuel Kant coined the phrase "cosmological proof" with Leibniz's proof *a contingentia mundi* expressly in mind.[1] Also, there are philosophical lessons to be learned from Leibniz's proofs that create an opening for Aquinas's metaphysics. In his *Critique of Pure Reason*, Kant summarizes the reasoning this way:

It runs thus: If anything exists, an absolutely necessary being must also exist. Now I, at least, exist. Therefore an absolutely necessary being exists. The minor premise contains an experience, the major premise the inference from there being any experience at all to the existence of the necessary. The proof therefore really begins with experience, and is not wholly *a priori* or ontological. For this reason, and because the object of all possible experience is called the world, it is entitled the *cosmological* proof. Since, in dealing with the objects of experience, the proof abstracts from all special properties through which this world may differ from any other possible world, the title also serves to distinguish it from the physico-theological proof, which is based upon observations of the particular properties of the world disclosed to us by our senses.

The proof then proceeds as follows: The necessary being can be determined in one way only, that is, by one out of each possible pair of opposed predicates. It must

[1]. Immanuel Kant, *Critique of Pure Reason*, trans. Norman Kemp Smith (New York: St. Martin's Press, 1965), A604/B632 (508).

therefore be *completely* determined through its own concept. Now there is only one possible concept which determines a thing completely *a priori*, namely, the concept of *ens realissimum*. The concept of the *ens realissimum* is therefore the only concept through which a necessary being can be thought. In other words, a supreme being necessarily exists.[2]

Kant divides the argument into two stages. The first stage proceeds from some existent to an absolutely necessary being. The second stage goes on to specify necessary being as most real or as a supreme being, an *ens realissimum*. Concerning this second stage, Kant remarks, "The cosmological proof, which we are now about to examine, retains the connection of absolute necessity with the highest reality, but instead of reasoning, like [the ontological argument], from the highest reality to necessity of existence, it reasons from the previously given unconditioned necessity of some being to the unlimited reality of that being."[3] The "retained connection" is a significant feature in cosmological reasoning. For Kant it is the argument's Achilles' heel, as we will see. How, though, does this Kantian summary compare with Leibniz's proof *a contingentia mundi*?

Leibniz's Arguments

Expressed Leibnizian arguments for God from contingency are as follows:

Selection A

God is the first reason for things: for such things as are bounded, as all that which we see and experience, are contingent and have nothing in them to render their existence necessary, it being plain that time, space and matter, united and uniform in themselves and indifferent to everything, might have received entirely other motions and shapes, and in another order. Therefore, one must seek the reason for the existence of the world, which is the whole assemblage of *contingent* things, and seek it in the substance which carries with it the reason for its existence, and which in consequence is *necessary* and eternal.[4]

---

2. Ibid., A605/B633–A606/B634 (508–9).
3. Ibid., A604/B632 (508).
4. G. W. Leibniz, *Theodicy* (1710), as quoted by William Lane Craig, *The Cosmological Argument from Plato to Leibniz* (London: MacMillan Press, 1980), 269.

Selection B

But there must also be a *sufficient reason* for *contingent truths*, or those *of fact*,—that is, for the sequence of things diffused through the universe of created objects—where the resolution into particular reasons might run into a detail without limits, on account of the immense variety of the things in nature and the division of bodies *ad infinitum*. There is an infinity of figures and of movements, present and past, which enter into the efficient cause of my present writing, and there is an infinity of slight inclinations and dispositions, past and present, of my soul, which enter into the final cause.

And as all this *detail* only involves other contingents, anterior or more detailed, each one of which needs like analysis for its explanation, we make no advance: and the sufficient or final reason must be outside of the sequence or *series* of this detail of contingencies, however infinite it may be.

And thus it is that the final reason of things must be found in a necessary substance, in which the detail of changes exists only eminently, as in their source; and this is what we call God.

Now this substance, being a sufficient reason of this detail, which also is linked together throughout, *there is but one God, and this God is sufficient.*

We may also conclude that this supreme substance, which is unique, universal and necessary, having nothing outside of itself which is independent of it, and being a pure consequence of possible being, must be incapable of limitations and must contain as much of reality as is possible.

Whence it follows that God is absolutely perfect, *perfection* being only the magnitude of positive reality taken in its strictest meaning, setting aside the limits or bounds in things which have them. And where there are no limits, that is, in God, perfection is absolutely infinite.[5]

Selection C

Thus far we have spoken as simple *physicists*: now we must advance to *metaphysics*, making use of the great principle, little employed in general, which teaches that *nothing happens without a sufficient reason*; that is to say, that nothing happens without its being possible for him who should sufficiently understand things, to give a reason sufficient to determine why it is so and not otherwise. This principle laid down, the

---

5. G. W. Leibniz, *Monadology* (1714), ed. Philip P. Weiner, in *Leibniz Selections* (New York: Charles Scribner's Sons, 1951), nos. 36–41 (540–41).

first question which should rightly be asked, will be, *Why is there something rather than nothing?* For nothing is simpler and easier than something. Further, supposing that things must exist, we must be able to give a reason why they must exist so and not otherwise.

Now this sufficient reason for the existence of the universe cannot be found *in the series of contingent things*, that is, of bodies and of their representations in souls; for matter being indifferent in itself to motion and to rest, and to this or another motion, we cannot find the reason of motion in it, and still less of a certain motion. And although the present motion which is in matter comes from the preceding motion, and that from still another preceding, yet in this way we make no progress, go as far as we may; for the same question always remains. Thus it must be that the sufficient reason, which has no need of another reason, be outside this series of contingent things and be found in a substance which is its cause, or which is a necessary being, carrying the reason of its existence within itself; otherwise we should still not have a sufficient reason in which we could rest. And this final reason of things is called *God*.

This primitive simple substance must contain in itself eminently the perfections contained in the derivative substances which are its effects; thus it will have perfect power, knowledge and will: that is, it will have supreme omnipotence, omniscience and goodness.[6]

Finally, a text earlier than the above does not mention contingency, yet it is obviously parallel to the above texts.

Selection D

In addition to the world or aggregate of finite things, there is some unity which dominates, not only like the soul in me, or rather like the Ego itself in my body, but in a much higher sense. For the unity dominating the universe, not only rules the world but creates and fashions it, is superior to the world, and, so to speak, extramundane, and is thus the ultimate reason of things. For the sufficient reason of existence can not be found either in any particular thing or in the whole aggregate or series. Suppose a book on the elements of geometry to have been eternal and that others had been successively copied from it, it is evident that, although we might account for the present book by the book which was its model, we could nevertheless never, by assuming any number of books whatever, reach a perfect reason for them; for we may always wonder why such books have existed from all time; that is, why books exist at all and why they are thus written. What is true of books is also true of the different

---

6. G. W. Leibniz, *The Principles of Nature and Grace* (1714), in *Leibniz Selections* (ed. Weiner), nos. 7–9 (527–28).

states of the world, for in spite of certain laws of change a succeeding state is in a certain way only a copy of the preceding, and to whatever anterior state you may go back you will never find there a complete reason why there is any world at all, and why this world rather than some other. And even if you imagine the world eternal, nevertheless since you posit nothing but a succession of states, and as you find a sufficient reason for them in none of them whatsoever, and as any number of them whatever does not aid you in giving a reason for them, it is evident that the reason must be sought elsewhere. For in eternal things even where there is no cause there must be a reason which, in permanent things, is necessity itself or essence, but in the series of changing things, if it were supposed that they succeed each other eternally, this reason would be as will soon be seen, the prevailing of inclinations where the reasons are not necessitating (i.e., of an absolute or metaphysical necessity the opposite of which would imply contradiction), but inclining. From which it follows that even by supposing the eternity of the world, an ultimate extramundane reason of things, or God, cannot be escaped.

The reasons of the world, therefore, lie hidden in something extramundane different from the chain of states or series of things, the aggregate of which constitutes the world. We must therefore pass from physical or hypothetical necessity, which determines the later states of the world by the prior, to something which is of absolute or metaphysical necessity, the reason for which cannot be given. For the present world is necessary, physically or hypothetically, but not absolutely or metaphysically. It being granted, indeed, that the world such as it is, is to be, it follows that things must happen in it just as they do. But as the ultimate origin must be in something which is metaphysically necessary, and as the reason of the existing can only be from the existing, there must exist some one being metaphysically necessary, or whose essence is existence; and thus there exists something which differs from the plurality of beings or from the world, which, as we have recognized and shown, is not metaphysically necessary.[7]

I want to make five initial observations on these selections. First, the starting point is contingent being. But "contingent being" quickly becomes ambiguous. On the one hand, Leibniz understands the contingent as an existing thing that could quite well be not existing. This sense of "contingent" seems operative in (C) when Leibniz asks why there is something rather than nothing. On the other hand, the contingent is a thing existent in one way but could quite well be existent in another fashion. Both (A) and (C) provide ex-

[7]. G. W. Leibniz, *On the Ultimate Origin of Things* (1697), in *Leibniz Selections* (ed. Weiner), 345–47.

amples of this second sense of the contingent: time, space, and matter as they are indifferent to various motions, shapes, and orders. Interestingly, Leibniz mentions these two senses almost in the same breath. In (C) he juxtaposes the issues of why there is something rather than nothing and why things are so and not so, and in (D) he insists upon a cause for "why there is any world at all, and why this world rather than some other." Leibniz glides from one to the other.

This ambiguity is troubling because in (B) and (D) Leibniz intends to reach a necessary being that is a creator. But as starting points he employs the second sense of contingent where he writes of the "infinity of figures and of movements, present and past" in (B) and "states of the world" in (D). Hence, it is unclear how the necessary being is anything more than a mover. Characteristic of a mover is that it works on something presupposed, a material cause, and fashions it. A creator causes without presupposing something to fashion. By causing matter, for example, to have this shape rather than that or this motion rather than that, the necessary being looks to be a mover and not a creator.

Nevertheless, because the proofs conclude to a being necessary in the existential sense, a reader can assume that the first sense of contingent must be operative somewhere earlier in the argument; however, it is debatable precisely where this happens. Is the existential sense invoked after the need for an overarching mover of the states of the world so that each thing essentially contingent is also existentially contingent? Or is the existential sense invoked simultaneously with the second sense so that things are initially recognized as contingent in both senses?

Second, the proofs proceed by trying to find a reason for a thing being one way when it could quite well be another way, for example, matter with this shape, when it could quite well have another shape. In my opinion, Leibniz's contingent could be modeled as the point of a "V" with the end points of the lines being the alternatives. But given the alternatives, it is intolerable that matter in fact have this shape without a reason. *De facto* togetherness, or brute contingency, is unacceptable. It is in this context of simply *de facto* togetherness that Leibniz expresses in selection (C) the "great principle, little employed in general, which teaches that *nothing happens without a sufficient reason.*" Just how the "V" model of the contingent drives the mind to a reason will have to be studied. Also, its applicability or not to existential contingency is another issue. For are existing or not existing alternatives like having this shape or that shape?

Third, the selections consider the possibility of explaining the initial contingent by a temporally antecedent contingent. For example, a first piece of matter is moving this way because it was antecedently struck by a second matter moving that way. Yet as the second matter is like the first, we do not yet have a full explanation of the first. It becomes obvious that if one appeals to a third like the first two, then explanation is still being delayed. In other words, before the second can explain the first, the second must be explained by the third. But the third does not have an explanation yet. If the antecedent contingents are let go to infinity, then each is looking for a full explanation that is never forthcoming in the infinite series. In this respect, Leibniz's reasoning seems to echo Aristotle's reasoning in *Physics* VIII.6 that the endless series of generation of self-movers is explained neither by one of them nor by all of them together.[8] If the initial contingent being needs a reason for its existence also, then the full explanation of the first is still lacking. This deficiency in explanation remains even if we go into an infinite temporal regress of contingent beings.

Fourth, Leibniz concludes that the sufficient reason for any contingent thing, and so for the entire series, must be found outside the series in a being "which is its cause, or which is a necessary being, carrying the reason for its existence within itself" (C) or "whose essence is existence" (D). It seems clear that Leibniz is concluding to the existentially necessary and so the existentially contingent should have been involved previously. Given the two descriptions of necessary being in selections (C) and (D), one might wonder if necessary being has or is existence. Leibniz is clear, however, that he thinks that at the point of necessary being, his reasoning (B, C, D) has reached God. In this respect Leibniz's argumentation takes exception to Kant's summary description with its two stages.

---

8. For more on Aristotle's reasoning, see chapters 7 and 8 below. The analogy between the geometry book and the states of the world that Leibniz places in selection (D) may seem puzzling. The selection speaks of an individual eternal geometry book which is the original from which all others are copied. But there is no individual eternal state of the world that is somehow original for the others. In fact the eternal book is the conclusion of the reasoning that no one book in the series fully explains another. Likewise, Aristotle argued in *Physics* VIII.6 that an eternal series of generables requires outside of itself something not generable neither *per se* nor *per accidens*.

Fifth and finally, to complete the schema it should be noted that Leibniz also argues the infinity of the necessary being. Leibniz argues the divine infinity in two ways. First, in selections (B, C) God is perfect because God is the unique cause of all else. God at least eminently contains the perfections of all other things. But second, in selection (B) God "must contain as much reality as is possible" because he is a "pure consequence of possible being." What does this mean?

At first glance, the remark would seem to be a veiled reference to one of Leibniz's *a priori* proofs for God. In this *a priori* proof necessary being is a being "in whom essence involves existence, or with whom it is sufficient to be possible to be actual."[9] Against such a reading is the realization that by inserting an *a priori* proof for God within an *a posteriori* proof, Leibniz would render the *a posteriori* proof otiose. It could be that Leibniz made such an unseemly move. But in light of other possibilities, I doubt that he did. One other possibility is that "possible being" refers to contingent being, the starting point of selection (B). Leibniz's reiteration of the starting point would be a reminder to the reader that the proof has reached necessary being. But why the reminder?

The answer could be that in the rationalist tradition, a necessary being was *ipso facto* an infinite, or all-perfect, being. This connection of necessary being with the infinite is not elaborated upon by Leibniz. But it was a familiar one in the rationalist tradition. For example, for Descartes I could not cause my own existence because if I did, I would not be finite but infinite. A self-caused being is an infinite being. Descartes writes:

But if I [were independent of every other, and] were I myself the author of my being, I should doubt of nothing and I should desire nothing, and finally no perfection would be lacking to me; for I should have bestowed upon myself every perfection of which I possessed any idea and should thus be God. And it must not be imagined that those things that are lacking to me are perhaps more difficult of attainment than those which I already possess; for, on the contrary, it is quite evident that it was a matter of much greater difficulty to bring to pass that I, that is to say, a thing or substance that thinks, should emerge out of nothing, than it would be to attain to the knowledge of many things of which I am ignorant, and which are only the accidents of this thinking substance. But it is clear that if I had of myself possessed

---

9. G. W. Leibniz, *Monadology*, no. 44 (541).

this greater perfection of which I have just spoken [that is to say, if I had been the author of my own existence], I should not at least have denied myself things which are the more easy to acquire [to wit many branches of knowledge of, which my nature is destitute].[10]

By way of comment, what is surprising is that Descartes sees nothing incongruous in a self-caused being, a *causa sui*. What he regards as anomalous is a *causa sui* being finite. After all, if something has performed the awesome feat of producing its own existence then surely it can give itself every other perfection as well.

Finally, Spinoza seems to glide easily from the idea of substance as self-caused to its infinity. To do the first is identical with doing the second. In *Ethics* I, prop. VIII, after arguing in prop. VII that existence necessarily pertains to substance, Spinoza remarks that no substance is finite because "it would then be limited by something else." The idea is that without a limit to itself, self-caused substance actualizes every perfection. In going from necessary being to infinite being, Leibniz seems to be an heir to this rationalist tradition.

---

10. René Descartes, *Mediations on First Philosophy* III, trans. Elizabeth S. Haldane and G. R. T. Ross in *The Philosophical Works of Descartes* (Mineola, N.Y.: Dover, 1955), 1:168. By the example of the author, Descartes implies that he is thinking of himself as an efficient cause of his existence. Later in the context of proving God by way of efficient causality, Arnauld criticized Descartes for conceiving God as self-derived in the sense of efficient causality. Descartes tried to meet this criticism by claiming that he was speaking only analogously. There is an analogy between a formal cause and its effects, for example, the triangle and its properties, and an efficient cause and its effects. The basis for the analogy is that the effects of a formal cause are not really distinct from it. Descartes says, "[We] should reply to the question as to why God exists, not indeed by assigning an efficient cause in the proper sense, but only by giving the essence of the thing or formal cause, which, owing to the very fact that in God existence is not distinguished from essence, has a strong analogy with the efficient cause, and may on this ground be called similar to an efficient cause" (*Works*, 2:113). For Aquinas all real properties are also efficiently caused by the nature of the thing; see below, note 29 in chapter 2. Also, Thomistically speaking, Descartes's revised position about God as self-derived would still involve the conception of something prior to *esse*. But there is nothing conceivably prior. *Esse* is the actuality of all acts. Again, see the comment of William Norris Clarke below at note 2 in chapter 5. The conceptual irreducibility of *esse* will always be a stumbling block for the Existential Thomist to affirm the Principle of Sufficient Reason: "Whatever exists has either in itself or in another the reason for its existence."

Background in Kant's Critique of the Ontological Argument

Kant's main problem with the cosmological argument is that in its second stage it necessarily turns into the ontological argument. To appreciate Kant's problem, it is necessary to look at his handling of the ontological argument.

The form of the ontological argument that Kant criticizes is that of Descartes. Descartes presents the argument in the fifth book of his *Meditations*. According to Kant's summary, the argument goes as follows. Just as a triangle must have three sides, so too existence must belong to an all-perfect being. Hence, God exists. On the other hand, here is Descartes's actual argument:

> But now if just because I can draw the idea of something from my thought, it follows that all which I know clearly and distinctly as pertaining to this object does really belong to it, may I not derive from this an argument demonstrating the existence of God? It is certain that I no less find the idea of God, that is to say, the idea of a supremely perfect Being, in me, than that of any figure or number whatever it is; and I do not know any less clearly and distinctly that an [actual and] eternal existence pertains to this nature than I know that all that which I am able to demonstrate of some figure or number truly pertains to the nature of this figure or number, and therefore, although all that I concluded in the preceding Meditations were found to be false, the existence of God would pass with me as at least as certain as I have ever held the truths of mathematics (which concern only numbers and figures) to be.
>
> This indeed is not at first manifest, since it would seem to present some appearance of being a sophism. For being accustomed in all other things to make a distinction between existence and essence, I easily persuade myself that the existence can be separated from the essence of God, and that we can thus conceive God as not actually existing. But, nevertheless, when I think of it with more attention, I clearly see that existence can no more be separated from the essence of God than can its having its three angles equal to two right angles be separated from the essence of a [rectilinear] triangle, or the idea of a mountain from the idea of a valley.[11]

What is especially noteworthy is the ambiguity on how existence relates to the all-perfect being. In the Kantian summary existence is an "internal property" as having three lines is an internal property of triangle. The other internal property would be "intersecting." Likewise "rational" is an internal

---

11. *Works*, 1:180–81.

part of the definition of human nature, namely, "rational animal." In Descartes's argument existence is an "external property." As Descartes says, God's existence is like the equaling of the triangle's three angles to two right angles. This equaling does not belong to the essence of triangle but follows upon it. Likewise, God's existence is like the valley produced by the mountains. The valley is not the mountains but follows upon them. In other words, understood as an external property, existence is like a property in the Aristotelian and Scholastic sense. An Aristotelian property is something not identical with the essence of the thing though necessarily connected with it. The property flows from the thing's essence. Consider risibility and mortality as they follow upon human nature.

In sum, existence seems to be understood differently in Kant's summary of ontological reasoning and in Descartes's actual argument. In the summary existence is construed as an internal property. In the Cartesian argument existence is an external property. Yet, as will be seen, Kant's critique would seem to hold in either case.

Kant's Critique of Ontological Reasoning

What is Kant's critique? In sum, existence is not a predicate, and hence it is not something that could be placed into another concept so as to be unpacked later. For Kant the meaning of existence simply is the thing with all its *bona fide* internal and external properties coming to be in itself. Kant says, "'Being' is obviously not a real predicate; that is, it is not a concept of something which could be added to the concept of a thing. It is merely the positing of a thing, or of certain determinations, as existing in themselves."[12] In other words, for Kant a thing's coming to exist makes as little intrinsic difference to the thing as a thing's change of state. For example, the picture's coming to exist means simply the picture's going from the mind of the artist to the canvas. The picture goes from being in the artist to being in itself. Existence is simply this change of state and nothing more. As such, existence seems to lack the definiteness needed to be a predicate.

Kant backs these reflections up by demonstrating that existence is not a

---

12. Kant, *Critique of Pure Reason*, A598/B626 (504).

predicate. If existence is a predicate then either (1) existence adds something determinate to the subject or (2) it adds something indeterminate to the subject. But both are absurd. Hence, existence is not a predicate. The first alternative is absurd because my thinking of the possible would always be wrong. My thinking of the possible would be wrong because the thinking would always leave something out about the possible. In other words, if becoming actual adds something to the thing about which I was thinking, then I was not thinking of that thing. There will be a difference between the thing as thought and the thing as existing, and so thought will always be inadequate *vis-à-vis* the real. Kant says,

[the thing as thought] would not be exactly the same thing that exists, but something more than we had thought in the concept; and we could not, therefore, say that the exact object of my concept exists. If we think in a thing every feature of reality except one, the missing reality is not added by my saying that this defective thing exists. On the contrary, it exists with the same defect with which I have thought it, since otherwise what exists would be something different from what I thought.[13]

Kant's thinking here is similar to this. If I go to a Starbucks and ask for a coffee but keep getting a coffee with cream, then I am not getting what I want. Likewise, if what I want actualized always comes with an addition, then I am not getting what I want. Finally, the second alternative is absurd because it reduces existence to nothingness. If nothing determinate is added, nothing is added.

Kant concludes with his famous remark that there is no difference between a hundred possible thalers and a hundred actual thalers. The actual is just the possible considered as being in itself. "Otherwise stated, the real contains no more than the merely possible. A hundred real thalers do not contain the least coin more than a hundred possible thalers." So the ontological argument is wrong for thinking that existence is a predicate, that is, a determinate something that could be unpacked from the content of a concept or *a fortiori* that could follow upon the content of a concept.

---

13. Ibid., A600/B628 (505).

Kant's Critique of the Cosmological Argument

According to Kant, the cosmological argument goes wrong in its second stage. At that point the argument identifies the necessary being reached in the first stage with the *ens realissimum*, the most real or perfect being. What is wrong can best be described by citing Kant.

Fallacious and misleading arguments are most easily detected if set out in correct syllogistic form. This we now proceed to do in the instance under discussion.

If the proposition, that every absolutely necessary being is likewise the most real of all beings, is correct (and this is the *nervus probandi* of the cosmological proof), it must, like all affirmative judgments, be convertible, at least *per accidens*. It therefore follows that some *entia realissima* are likewise absolutely necessary beings. But one *ens realissimum* is in no respect different from another, and what is true of some under this concept is true also of all. In this case, therefore, I can convert the proposition *simpliciter*, not only *per accidens*, and say that every *ens realissimum is* a necessary being. But since this proposition is determined from its *a priori* concepts alone, the mere concept of the *ens realissimum* must carry with it the absolute necessity of that being; and this is precisely what the ontological proof has asserted and what the cosmological proof has refused to admit, although the conclusions of the latter are indeed covertly based on it.[14]

Kant's problem is the convertibility issue. (1) "Necessary being is an all-perfect being" converts to (2) "Some all-perfect beings are necessary being." But insofar as there can be only one all-perfect being, then (3) "The all-perfect being is a necessary being." Kant evidently considers asserting (3) to be asserting the ontological argument, *viz.*, "The all-perfect must exist." The ontological argument, though, wrongly considered existence as a property. So, because the cosmological argument can be contorted to affirm the truth of (3), then the cosmological argument can be tarred with the same brush as the ontological argument. Only if the cosmological argument avoided affirming the truth of "The all-perfect is a necessary being" could it be a cogent argument. But the argument cannot avoid it.

---

14. Ibid., A608/B636–A609/B637 (510–11).

Smart's Rejoinder to Kant's Critique and a Reconstituted Critique

Kant's critique has proved to be a puzzle both to proponents and opponents of cosmological reasoning. J. J. C. Smart, an opponent, expresses most clearly the problem with Kant's critique. In his "The Existence of God" Smart says that no convertibility problem exists because necessary being has been demonstrated.[15] There is nothing wrong with converting a proposition in which the subject is dealing with an existent. For example, from "Humans are rational" I can at least say "Some rational beings are human." Where you get into problems is converting propositions whose subjects do not deal with existents. For example, "Trespassers will be prosecuted." This proposition need not assert the existence of trespassers. With that in mind its conversion to "Some of the prosecuted are trespassers" is wrong.

What then is Kant's mistake? Kant's error is that by the time he has reached (3), he has forgotten that he has done it on the basis of (1). A slip in memory has occurred. Recalling that (1) has been demonstrated, anyone can see that converting (1) to (3) is as legitimate as converting "Humans are rational" to "Some rational beings are human." If you grant the first proposition, as Kant forgot that he had done, why quarrel with the second?

Smart's criticism is echoed by others like Frederick Copleston, Jacques Maritain, James Collins, and Bruce Reichenbach.[16] Yet Smart, and also Terence Penelhum, go on to argue that Kant's critique is valid but misplaced.[17] Kant's claim that the cosmological argument lapses into ontological reasoning is true at the first stage of the cosmological argument. The error of the ontological proof is to regard existence as a property. This understanding is wrong because it would make existence a predicate, which it is not. According to the reconstituted Kantian critique, this error is already in the conclusion of

---

15. J. J. C. Smart, "The Existence of God," in *The Cosmological Arguments, A Spectrum of Opinion*, ed. Donald R. Burrill (Garden City, N.Y.: Doubleday, 1967), 266–67.

16. Jacques Maritain, *The Dream of Descartes*, trans. Mabelle L. Andison (New York: Philosophical Library, 1944), 139–40; Fredrick Copleston, *A History of Philosophy* (Westminster, Md.: Newman Press, 1960), 6:298–99; James Collins, *A History of Modern European Philosophy* (Milwaukee, Wis.: Bruce Publishing, 1954), 502–3; Bruce R. Reichenbach, *The Cosmological Argument: A Reassessment* (Springfield, Ill.: Charles C. Thomas, 1972), 129.

17. Terence M. Penelhum, "Divine Necessity," in *The Cosmological Arguments* (ed. Burrill), 143–64. For a discussion of Penelhum, see chapter 5, below.

the cosmological argument's first stage. The conclusion is necessary being—a thing that is understood to involve its own existence. Again, existence is being regarded as a property, hence as a predicate. But existence is not a predicate for it does not characterize. Existence is an indeterminate something, and hence is nothing predicative.

Further Reflections

However, I wonder if Smart and others have taken Kant's objection back far enough. Is not Leibniz taking existence as a real predicate when the existential sense of contingency is introduced? I mentioned that it is unclear whether this sense of the contingent is simultaneous with the essential sense of contingent or brought in some time later. In any case it is brought in before the conclusion of necessary being. As I also mentioned, when it is introduced, existential contingency construes the existence of the thing using the "V" model that Leibniz has already used to speak about the contingency of motion in matter or the contingency of this shape in matter rather than that shape. In the "V" model matter is the point of the "V" and this motion or that, this shape or that, are distinct terms at the end of the lines. According to the same model, Leibniz should be understanding the existence of some thing in the world as a distinct term that the thing can have. The existential construal of the "V" should have at the end of the lines existence and nonexistence, or real existence and some other existence. In any case, existence seems to be distinct enough to be a real predicate, just as this motion or this shape or that. So, even though Smart raises the existence as predicate objection only in respect to necessary being, I do not believe that Smart's focus means that existence is not treated as a predicate even earlier. At least Leibniz appears to treat existence as a predicate in respect to contingent being.

In his *Leibniz: Determinist, Theist, Idealist*, Robert Merrihew Adams notes that in late 1670s correspondence with Arnold Eckhard, Leibniz seems to concede Kant's subsequent thesis that existence is not a predicate.[18] In that correspondence Leibniz denies that existence is a perfection in the manner of a quality of its own. Rather, existence is a perfection of essence in the sense

---

18. Robert Merrihew Adams, *Leibniz: Determinist, Theist, Idealist* (Oxford: Oxford University Press, 1994), 158–60.

of a certain status for essence. This status interpretation of the perfection of existence is close to Kant's idea of existence as the positing or occurrence of the possible. Adams mentions a number of reasons for Leibniz's shifts in thinking about existence. One reason is that the status view of existence avoids the standard objection to ontological reasoning as it is based upon the idea that existence is an essential quality of God. The standard objection is that propositions in which the predicate is contained in the subject are only conditionally true. Accordingly, "The angles of a triangle are equal to two right angles" is really saying "If a triangle exists, its angles are equal to two right angles." Hence, "God exists necessarily" is reducible to "If God exists, then God exists necessarily."[19] Instead Leibniz would have the ontological argument say something like "Since God is the best, then God occurs." In this version of ontological reasoning no need exists to speak about existence as a perfective quality of its own.

Adams quotes another reason that Leibniz entertained for jettisoning the interpretation that existence is a simple perfection and quality of its own: "If Existence were something other than an essence's demand [*exigentia*], it would follow that it has some essence or superadds something new to things, about which it could be asked again whether this essence exists, and why this one rather than another."[20] If an essence is existent by reason of existence added to it, then because existence is in some manner an essence, one can ask again why the essence of existence exists.[21]

Consequently, Adams describes and critically discusses Leibniz's attempts to understand more precisely the status of essences when existing. For example, the status of things when existing is their inclusion in the best possible world. Adams notes that this certainly seems to be a cumbersome way of knowing that something, even ourselves, exists. Also, when one thinks about

---

19. Ibid., 161–62.
20. Ibid., 158.
21. Leibniz's criticism is remarkably similar to Averroes's and Aquinas's critique of Avicenna. As Aquinas gives it: "If being and one are predicated of the substance of each thing by reason of something added to it [i.e., accidentally], being would have to be predicated also of the thing added, because anything at all is one and a being. But then there would be the question whether being is predicated of this thing (the one added) either essentially or by reason of some other thing that is added to it in turn. And if the latter were the case then the same question would arise once again regarding the last thing added, and so on to infinity. But this is impossible." Commentary on the *Metaphysics* of Aristotle [hereafter "*In Meta.*"], IV, l. 2, n. 555; taken from *Thomas Aquinas: Commentary on Aristotle's Metaphysics*, trans. John P. Rowan (Notre Dame, Ind.: Dumb Ox Books, 1995), 204. For Averroes, see *Des. Destructionum*, disp. 5, ed. Juntas (1574), 78A.

it, this first Leibnizian description of existence might make the existence of things and the existence of the best possible world independent of God.[22] If the best exists, then the best world exists. Similarly problematic is Leibniz's description of existence as what would please God if God existed.[23] Finally, anticipating Berkeley's thesis of being as being perceived, Leibniz also describes the status of things as existent in these terms: "to Exist is nothing other than to be Sensed [*Sentiri*] – to be sensed however, if not by us, then at least by the Author of things." Here the problem is a lack of conversion. To be sensed implies existence but does existence imply to be sensed?[24]

Setting aside necessary existence, what is one to think about Leibniz on contingent existence? Should it be understood as a property, quality, perfection of its own of the thing or should it be thought of as some kind of status for the thing? For example, should one think of existence as the essence's occurrence as a member of the best possible world? As far as the application of that question to Leibniz's thought in general, I must plead excuse. I ask the question only in regard to the God arguments *a contingentia mundi*. In that respect, what seems decisive is the noted parallel of existence to the motions and shapes of matter. The various motions and shapes are definitely properties and perfections of their own and so they can be predicates. This construal of the motions and shapes seems to point in the same direction for what is called the existence of things. The thing's existence also will be something, like a motion or shape, that matter can have or not. So whatever the case may be with Leibniz in his larger discussion of existence, in the context of his cosmological arguments, he regards existence as a predicate not only in the case of necessary being but also in the case of contingent beings.[25]

22. Adams, *Leibniz*, 167.
23. Ibid., 169.
24. Ibid., 170.
25. E. M. Curley holds that in contingent beings existence is a predicate but only in the sense of an extrinsic denomination: "This does not, however, mean that existence is not a predicate. It is an extrinsic denomination, but not one which is wholly extrinsic. There is always some basis in the nature of the thing for the correct predication of existence, a basis which consists of the fact that the thing enters into the best possible world." "The Root of Contingency," in *Leibniz: A Collection of Critical Essays*, ed. Harry G. Frankfurt (Notre Dame, Ind.: University of Notre Dame Press, 1976), 90. Likewise, as I mentioned, Merrihew Adams argues on the basis of correspondence with Eckhard that Leibniz came to understand the perfection of existence in terms of "a degree or quantity of reality or essence." In my opinion, these realization views of existence do not agree with the mentioned "V" model that Leibniz is using in his contingency arguments.

Obviously, this understanding of existence in Leibniz's proof is wide open to Kant's critique that existence is not a predicate. From a Thomistic background, however, a reply is possible. The proponent of the contingency form of the cosmological argument could retort that existence is a unique property and hence a unique predicate. To claim, as Kant does, that existence does not add anything determinate is *not* to say that existence does not add anything at all. Kant is assuming that anything, if it is anything, is a *determinate* something. But saying that "something exists" seems to be saying something more than just saying "something." If Kant is correct in saying that existence is not a determinate something, then existence will be an indeterminate something and as such a unique property. Likewise, for Aquinas, *esse* is the act of all form. *Esse* could not be that and be a form itself. Also, *esse* is the perfection of all perfections. Again, *esse* could not be such if "perfection" is taken in the same sense. So, there may be the possibility of recasting the contingency argument in terms of this more nuanced understanding of existence.

But that is only one problem and a possible reply. At the start of the arguments what grabs Leibniz's attention is the sheer logical unconnectedness of matter and its present shape, motion, or existence. Intolerable to Leibniz's mind is their merely *de facto* togetherness. What makes this *de facto* togetherness intolerable is, as selection (C) notes, "the great principle ... that nothing happens without a sufficient reason," that is, the principle of sufficient reason (hereafter "PSR"). Whether the PSR is philosophically defensible remains a question.[26] With the strong existential sense of the PSR

---

26. John Gurr, *The Principle of Sufficient Reason in Some Scholastic Systems 1750–1900* (Milwaukee, Wis.: Marquette University Press, 1959), 42–43, says that the PSR and of identity are "more intuitional than deductive, they are the given of the rationalistic mind generating its own data and starting points." D. J. B. Hawkins, "Sufficient Reason, Principle of," *New Catholic Encyclopedia* (New York: McGraw-Hill, 1967), 3:777–78, sees the PSR as intuitive for Leibniz and demonstrative from the principle of identity for Wolff. Craig, *The Cosmological Argument from Plato to Leibniz*, 263, understands Leibniz to provide both *a priori* and *a posteriori* demonstrations of the PSR. In their "A New Cosmological Argument," *Religious Studies* 35, no. 4 (1999): 463, Richard M. Gale and Alexander R. Pruss use a weak form of the PSR to argue for God. In plain speech this weak form asserts some possible world in which the contingent has an ultimate explanation. They argue (464) that if there is some possible world in which what is actually contingent has an explanation, then the actually contingent both does and does not have an explanation in that possible world. If the actually contingent not having an explanation leads to that contradiction, then the actually contingent must have an explanation. Two comments. First, one could argue the opposite. If there is some possible world in which what is actually contingent has no explanation, then the actually contingent both does not and does have an explanation in that possible world. If the actually contingent having an explanation leads to that

in mind—that is, whatever exists has either in itself or in something else a reason for its existence—William Rowe incisively finds a string of defenses wanting.[27]

First, the PSR is not demonstrated *a priori*. Such an attempted demonstration takes two forms. Both are *reductio ad absurdum*. In the first form, denial of the principle leads to a denial of the principle of noncontradiction. In the second, the denial of the PSR involves the absurdity of implicitly affirming the PSR. On the first form, the demonstration proceeds as follows. If something exists without a sufficient reason, then it has no sufficient reason and so should both exist and not exist at the same time. The problem here is that the reasoning seems to assume the PSR while trying to prove it. For without the PSR, that something exists without a sufficient reason does not entail that this something does not exist. It only entails that the thing is a brute fact. Neither is the PSR demonstrated *a priori* by showing that the denial is self-contradictory. By itself the fact that we cannot deny the principle without affirming it may only be bringing out a way we have to think and not a way that reality is constituted.

Second, the PSR is not demonstrated *a posteriori* or from experience. As Rowe points out, at best experience would lead us to formulate only a weak form of the PSR in which what happens has a reason. Perhaps, though, this weak sense claims too much. Hume's critique of causality must be faced.

---

contradiction, then the actually contingent must have no explanation. Second, the authors admit that their weak form of the PSR still begs the question that the contingent has an explanation, but they insist (474) that no good grounds exist to question it. Yet why should the notion of an explainer for the contingent be brought in even as a possibility? In other words, some confront the contingent, for example, the two books next to each other on a shelf, and no thought of an explanation occurs. One might as well think of hobbits when one thinks of battleships. I do not think the authors' weak PSR does justice to the brute fact view. I do not understand that view to be that something is without an explanation but that something just is. Explanation is not a part of the picture, even to be denied. I believe Aquinas would agree with this. Aquinas's claim will be "What belongs to a thing is caused." So, only when the contingent is analyzed into a subject/determination situation will concerns for explanation arise. Pruss offers other arguments in behalf of the PSR. I comment on some of them in later chapters. My second comment would apply also to Robert C. Koons, who begins his version of cosmological reasoning with the observation that his pencil could quite well have an even number of molecules instead of the present odd number. Robert C. Koons, "A New Look at the Cosmological Argument," *American Philosophical Quarterly* 34, no. 2 (1997): 197.

27. William Rowe, *The Cosmological Argument* (Princeton, N.J.: Princeton University Press, 1975), 75–83. The strong existential sense of the PSR seems implied by the "Why is there something rather than nothing" question in selection (C).

Hume strongly argued that in our experience of happenings we neither perceive causality nor anything that would allow it to be demonstrated.[28]

Third and finally, the PSR does not seem to be intuitively true. Intuition fails to perceive either an analytic link or a synthetic link between an existent and explanation. An analytic link is found when the meaning of the predicate is contained in the subject. For example, "All bachelors are male." A synthetic link is found when the two are necessarily together though not on the basis of containment nor experience. Now there is no analytic link because there is no containment of the notion of explanation in the notion of being. "A being is something to be explained" is not analytically true. There is no synthetic link because we can think a being without thinking of explanation.

But perhaps Rowe has missed something and understandably so because Leibniz himself seems hardly to notice it. The missed detail is that there is a stratification between the merely *de facto* together items. In other words, the shape is an attribute of the matter, as well as the motion and existence. But attributes are *ipso facto* dependent items. They at least require a subject of which to be attributes. Their essential dependence would be what sparks the desire for explanation. The logical unconnectedness of the attribute with the subject would not be what initiates the need for explanation but would be what directs the need for explanation to something other than the subject.

So it may be that the need for a reason for the logically unconnected items implicitly depends upon a subject/attribute stratification of the items. Unfortunately, the proofs give the impression that any situation of logically unconnected items is intolerable. In other words, our curiosity should be evoked by two equal items *de facto* together, for example, two books on a shelf or two beads on a string. But without stratification, a brute fact attitude seems to be well in place.

In fairness to Leibniz, he does appear to stratify. For example, in selections (A) and (D), Leibniz speaks about things and *their* existence and about the existence *of* the world. Such thinking is also indicated by the PSR itself: "nothing happens without it being possible for him who would sufficiently

---

28. For a discussion of Hume's critique of the proposition, "What happens has a cause," see John F. X. Knasas, *Being and Some Twentieth-Century Thomists* (New York: Fordham University Press, 2003), 216–21.

understand things, to give a reason sufficient to determine why it is so and not otherwise." The thing is possessor and the existence, for example, is the possession. Nevertheless, I still believe that to the benefit of the critics of the PSR, like Rowe, the subject/attribute logic behind the language is not taken seriously. What Leibniz does take seriously is the logical unconnectedness of the items.

But finally even if the stratification of the items is taken seriously there are still issues. In the case of matter's motion or shape, no one would hesitate to stratify them subsequent and posterior to the matter. Would one want to stratify the *sui generis* item of existence in the same way? Obviously not, for matter is still matter without some motion or shape but what is matter without its existence? This radical need for existence seems to lead to a situation in which existence is basic and fundamental to the thing. But in that prior position is existence still an attribute?[29] Despite the above talk of things and *their* existence and the existence *of* the world, perhaps the thing is in the genitive and is like an attribute to existence. Also, if, because of its priority, existence is less like an attribute, can it still be an essentially dependent item? Without a probing clarifying metaphysical analysis to resolve these questions, it seems that reasoning *a contingentia mundi* comes to a dead end in a thing whose existence is considered fundamental to it. That result is well short of God as God is usually understood.

Conclusion

The value of reflecting upon Leibniz's argument for God *a contingentia mundi* is that it forces us to begin thinking through what we mean by the thing's existence. Surely, it is more than the occurrence of the thing. Intuitively we seem to catch an inequality of meaning between "something" and "something exists." Kant may be correct to claim that existence is not a determinate property. Existence seems, nevertheless, to be a property; if necessary,

---

29. In his *Aquinas's Way to God: The Proof in the De Ente et Essentia* (Oxford: Oxford University Press, 2015), 103, Gaven Kerr remarks, "But if this [that *esse* is absolutely primary] is the case, then the fact seems built into Aquinas's metaphysics of *esse* that when it comes to the esse of a thing, one must stop and cannot proceed any further." Kerr goes on to argue against uncaused non-intrinsic properties.

existence is an indeterminate one. We, however, cannot stop there. For the PSR to have force, the items *de facto* together must be stratified according to subject/attribute categories, but that emendation might cause the PSR to lose its status as the basic principle in the reasoning. Yet even if stratification is introduced, it is still not clear why we cannot settle for a situation in which the thing is explained by its prior existence. If one is to save anything of the contingency form of reasoning, that rescue lies in a more carefully wrought understanding of existence.

[2]

Existence and a Proof for God in Aquinas

At first glance Aquinas's texts appear to contain a proof for God from existence understood as some kind of act or perfection of a thing. I am thinking especially of a passage in chapter 4 of the *De Ente*, where Aquinas discusses how essence is found in substances separate from matter. Here is a translation of the text with my numbered divisions.

[1] Whatever belongs to a thing is caused [2] either by the principles of its nature (as the capacity for laughter in man) or comes to it from an extrinsic principle (as light in the air from the influence of the sun). [3 and 4] Now being itself [*ipsum esse*] cannot be [5] caused by the form or quiddity of a thing (by "caused" I mean by an efficient cause), because that thing would then be its own cause and it would bring itself into being, which is impossible. It follows that everything whose being is distinct from its nature [*aliud a natura sua*] must have being from another. [6] And because everything that exists through another is reduced to that which exists through itself as to its first cause, there must be a reality that is the cause of being for all other things, because it is pure being [*esse tantum*]. [7] If this were not so, we would go on to infinity in causes, for everything that is not pure being has a cause of its being, as has been said. It is evident, then, that an intelligence is form and being, and that it holds its being from the first being, which is being in all its purity; and this is the first cause, or God.[1]

---

1. As translated by Armand Maurer in *On Being and Essence* (Toronto: Pontifical Institute of Mediaeval Studies, 1963), 56–57.

As I analyze it, the text has seven indicated points falling into two major divisions. The first major division creates a general framework. Points (1) and (2) fall into this first division. The second major division applies the general framework to *esse*. There we find points (3) to (7).

The passage opens with (1) the decisive claim: everything that belongs to something is caused (*Omnis autem quod convenit alicui ... est causatum*). From the cited examples of the ability to laugh and light in the air, it is clear that what "belongs to a thing" is an Aristotelian accident. Moreover, the mentioned causality appears to be efficient. So, what belongs to a thing is efficiently caused.[2] Later I will further unpack Aquinas's arresting opening remark. What is significant now is to note that in the next lines Aquinas goes on to speak about a thing's existence (*esse*) as falling in the category of what belongs to a thing. Consequently, the thing's existence is caused. In the case of *esse*, the first cause is a thing that does not have *esse* but is it (*esse tantum*). Aquinas concludes the passage by identifying *esse tantum* with *Deus*.

Aquinas will continue to utilize this reasoning. One can find it in the *Summa contra Gentiles* and the *Summa Theologiae* (hereafter "*ST*").[3] Even though the reasoning never explicitly occurs in the context of proving God's existence, an anomaly that I address in part 2 of this book, the reasoning does contain the conclusion that God exists. As such it seems similar to Leibniz's contingency proofs in which the existence of things, like their motion and shape, is treated as an act or perfection of things. In this chapter I will argue that while this is true, in his doctrine of *esse*, or *actus essendi*, Aquinas offers a more philosophically nuanced view of the thing's existence than is found in Leibniz's proofs. To that end, I will provide a description of Aquinas's understanding of the *esse* of a thing, his understanding of the philosophical access to *esse*, and the causal reduction to *esse tantum*. In chapter 3 I will address some Thomistic points of discussion about the *De Ente*. In subsequent chap-

---

2. That the sun is an efficient cause is obvious. That human nature is the efficient cause of the ability to laugh is less obvious. But as point (5) indicates, Aquinas intends to consider efficient causality for accidents like risibility. Elsewhere, it is Aquinas's view that not only are extraneous accidents efficiently caused but also proper and *per se* accidents of which risibility is an example. See *ST* I, q. 77, a. 6, co. At *Questiones Disputate de Anima*, q. 12, ad 7, Aquinas refers to risibility as a proper accident: "For some [accidents] are caused from the principles of the species and are called proper accidents [*propria*], just as risible for man.... The powers of the soul are accidents as properties [*proprietates*]." Only in mathematics do we have proper accidents that are not efficiently caused.

3. Other instances of the reasoning are *SCG* I.22, *Amplius. Si*, and *ST* I, q. 3, a. 4, co.

ters of part 1, I will weigh Aquinas's *De Ente* reasoning against some prominent arguments against cosmological reasoning.

Aquinas's Understanding of *esse*

Many of Aquinas's remarks on *esse* occur within his remarks on the notion of being, the *ratio entis*. Aquinas says that something is called a being in virtue of possessing its *esse* or *actus essendi*. Consequently, a being is a *quasi habens esse*, that is, a being is "as if a haver, or possessor, of *esse*."[4] Just why Aquinas

---

4. That *esse*, *actus essendi*, is the defining note of the *ratio entis* is a thesis that spans Aquinas's theological career. "Since in the thing there is its quiddity and its being [*esse*], truth is based on the being of the thing more than on the quiddity, just as the name of being [*nomen entis*] is imposed from the being [*esse*]." Commentary on the Sentences of Peter Lombard [hereafter "*In Sent.*"], I, d. 19, q. 5, a. 1, co. "Just as motion [*motus*] is the act of the mobile insomuch as it is mobile; so too being [*esse*] is the act of the existing thing [*actus existentis*], insomuch as it is a being [*ens*]" (*In I Sent.*, d. 19, q. 2, a. 2, co.). "In the statement, 'To be [*esse*] is other than that which is,' the act of being [*actus essendi*] is distinguished from that to which that act belongs. But the name of being [*ratio entis*] is taken from the act of existence [*ab actu essendi*], not from that whose act it is." *De Ver.*, q. 1, a. 1, ad 3, second set; trans. Robert W. Mulligan, *The Disputed Questions on Truth* (Chicago: Henry Regnery, 1952), 1:8. "For no creature is its being [*esse*], but is a possessor of being [*habens esse*]." *Quaestiones de quodlibet* [hereafter "*Quodl.*"] II, q. 2, a. 2, co.). "Being [*esse*] is called the act of a being insomuch as it is a being [*actus entis in quantum est ens*], that is, by which something is named a being [*ens*] in act in the nature of things. And so being [*esse*] is not attributed except to things which are contained in the ten categories; whence being [*ens*] by such being [*esse*] is divided by the ten genera" (*Quodl.* IX, q. 2, a. 3, co.). "Yet we signify one thing through that which we call being [*esse*], and another thing through that which we call that which exists [*id quod est*]; just as we signify one thing when we say running [*currere*], and another through that which is called a runner [*currens*]. For running and being [*currere et esse*] are signified in the abstract, just as white; but what is, that is a being and a runner [*ens et currens*], are signified in the concrete, just as a white thing [*album*]" (*In de Hebd.*, chap. II). "Then, too, because being [*esse*] is compared even to the form itself as act. For in things composed of matter and form, the form is said to be the principle of being [*principium essendi*], for this reason: that it is the complement of the substance, whose act is being [*esse*]. Thus, transparency is in relation to the air the principle of illumination, in that it makes the air the proper subject of light. Accordingly, in things composed of matter and form, neither the matter nor the form nor even being [*esse*] itself can be termed that which is. Yet the form can be called *that by which it is*, inasmuch as it is the principle of being; the whole substance itself, however, is *that which is*. And being [*esse*] itself is that by which the substance is called a being [*ens*].... On the other hand, in substances composed of matter and form there is a twofold composition of act and potentiality: the first, of the substance itself which is composed of matter and form; the second, of the substance thus composed, and being [*esse*]; and this composition also can be said to be of *that which is* and being, or of *that which is* and *that by which a thing is*." *SCG* II.54, *Deinde*; trans. James Anderson, *Summa Contra Gentiles* (Notre Dame, Ind.: University of Notre Dame Press, 1975), 2:157–58. "Then others advanced further and raised themselves to the consideration of being as being [*ens inquantum est ens*], and who assigned a cause to things, not only according as they are *these*

makes a qualification here, I will explain later. Now I want to describe generally what Aquinas means by *esse* or *actus essendi*. Neo-Thomists have rendered these phrases into English as "the existence of a thing." This translation is unfortunate because we can begin thinking about *esse* or *actus essendi* as if it were just the fact of a thing. In ordinary talk, "the existence of a thing" means just the fact of the thing. For example, if we ask, "Does so-and-so exist?," all that we want to know is whether so-and-so is a fact, is in the world. One can regard Aristotle, Averroes, Kant, and contemporary logicians as philosophically reiterating the existence-as-fact understanding. Also, Etienne Gilson observed that even some contemporary Thomists favor an Averroistic interpretation of being. These Thomists could emphasize Aquinas's repeated assertions that a substance is essentially a being.[5] This could not be true if a substance were a being by its distinct act of existence. When a thing is denominated as something on the basis of something distinct from it, the denomination is always accidental. For example, my being called a pianist is an accidental denomination because its basis is an act distinct from me, *viz.*, my acquired habit of being able to play the piano. These Thomists also point out that the only other sense of being about which Aquinas speaks is being in the sense of the truth of a proposition.

---

or *such*, but according as they are *beings* [*entia*]. Therefore, whatever is the cause of things considered as beings, must be the cause of things, not only according as they are *such* by accidental forms, nor according as they are *these* by substantial forms, but also according to all that belongs to their being [*esse*] in any way whatever. And thus it is necessary to say that also primary matter is created by the universal cause of things." *ST* I, q. 44, a. 2, co., in *The Basic Writings of St. Thomas Aquinas*, ed. and trans. Anton C. Pegis (New York: Random House, 1945), 1:429. "Nam ens dicitur quasi esse habens, hoc autem solum est substantia, quae subsistit" (For a being is called as if a possessor of being, this is substance alone which subsists) (*In XII Meta.*, l. 1, n. 2419). "Et ideo hoc nomen *Ens* quod imponitur ab ipso *esse*" (And so this name being which is imposed from the being itself) (*In IV Meta.*, l. 2, n. 558). Finally, in *In VI Meta.*, l. 3, n. 1215, God is a cause to "omnia inquantum sunt entia" because he is an "agens per modum dantis esse."

5. "We must realize (with the Philosopher) that the term 'a being' [*ens*] in itself has two meanings. Taken one way it is divided by the ten categories." *De Ente*, chap. 1 (trans. Maurer, 28). "Now as Avicenna says, that which the intellect first conceives as, in a way the most evident, and to which it reduces all its concepts, is being [*ens*]. Consequently, all the other conceptions [*conceptiones*] of the intellect are had by additions to being. But nothing can be added to being as though it were something not included in being—in the way what a difference is added to a genus or an accident to a subject—for every reality [*natura*] is essentially a being [*ens*]." *De Ver.* q. 1, a. 1, co. (trans. Mulligan, 1:5). Repeating Averroes *contra* Avicenna, Aquinas argues at *In IV Meta.*, l. 2, n. 555, that "being [*ens*] and one [*unum*] are predicated of the substance of every thing through itself [*per se*] and not according to an accident [*secundum accidens*]."

But other assertions of Aquinas exclude for him the merely fact-sense of the existence of a thing. I have already mentioned Aquinas's notion of *ens* as *habens esse*. In still other passages exemplified in note 4, Aquinas regards existence as a distinct principle composed with the individual substance to render the substance a being (*ens*), an existent. In fact, *esse* is sufficiently distinct to compare its composition with a substance to form's composition with matter within the substance. Moreover, he compares the meaning of *ens* and *esse* to those of *currens* and *currere*. Just as a runner is a man plus his act of running, so too a being is something plus its act of existing. But the act of running is something distinct from the man, and hence a thing's act of existing should also be distinct from it. The same thinking is revealed in a most famous remark on *esse*. Both in *Quaestiones Disputatae de Potentia Dei* (hereafter "*De Pot.*") and *Summa Theologiae*, Aquinas says that he understands by *esse* the act or actuality of all acts and the perfection of all perfections.[6] But as an act or actuality, substantial and accidental forms are distinct items composed with another item that is in potency to the act. Hence, calling *esse* an act and an actuality should indicate on Aquinas's part similar thinking. Aquinas will also be considering *esse* as a distinct item composed with another item that is in potency to the act. Finally, Aquinas also uses the infinitive *esse* as a noun or substantive in the context of referring

---

6. "Being [*Esse*], furthermore, is the name of an act [*actum quondam*], for a thing is not said to be because it is in potency but because it is in act. Everything, however, that has an act diverse from it is related to that act as potency to act; for potency and act are said relatively to one another." *SCG* I.22, *Amplius. Esse* (trans. Pegis, 1:120). "Being [*esse*], as we understand it here, signifies the highest perfection of all: and the proof is that act is always more perfect than potentiality. Now no signate form is understood to be in act unless it be supposed to have being. Thus we may take human nature or fiery nature as existing potentially in matter, or as existing in the power of an agent, or even as in the mind: but when it has being it becomes actually existent [*sed hoc quod habet esse, efficitur actu existens*]. Wherefore it is clear that being as we understand it here is the actuality of all acts [*actualitas omnium actuum*], and therefore the perfection of all perfections [*perfectio omnium perfectionum*]." *Quaestiones Disputatae de Potentia Dei*, q. 7, a. 2, ad 9; trans. English Dominican Fathers (London: Burns Oates and Washbourne, 1934), 3:12. "Being itself [*ipsum esse*] is the most perfect of all things, for it is compared to all things as that which is act [*actus*]: for nothing has actuality except so far as it is. Hence being is the actuality of all things, even of forms themselves." *ST* I, q. 4, a. 1, ad 3 (trans. Pegis, 1:38). "Now all the perfections of all things pertain to the perfection of being [*perfectio essendi*]; for things are perfect precisely so far as they have being after some fashion." *ST* I, q. 4, a. 2, co. (trans. Pegis, 1:39). In reading these texts it is important to not lose sight of the fact that *esse* is the act in virtue of which the thing is a fact or actuality. *Esse* is not just the actuality of the thing but it is the act by which the thing is an actuality. For further discussion, see below, my section "Other Interpretations of the *Secunda Operatio*."

to the individual generable and corruptible thing as *possibile esse et non esse*.⁷

In sum, it is not so much that Aquinas disagrees with the fact-sense of the thing's existence, but rather that Aquinas insists that the fact-sense be deepened to include the act in virtue of which the thing is a fact. A thing is a fact in virtue of its *actus essendi*. The relation of this act to the substance with which it is composed also bears mention. In respect to the substance rendered a being by composition with *esse*, *esse* is prior (*prius*),⁸ first (*primus*),⁹ most profound (*profundius*) and most intimate (*magis intimum*).¹⁰ *Esse* is the core around which the thing revolves. It is like the hole of a doughnut. Just as the hole is outside the doughnut yet "inside" the doughnut, so too *esse* is an act distinct from the thing but for all its distinctness *esse* is most intrinsic to the thing. We are accustomed to conceiving acts of a thing as items subsequent and posterior to a thing. So the notion of an act basic and fundamental to its thing is strange. But for reasons yet to be given, if one is to correctly appreciate *esse*, usual ways of thinking must be suspended. Here is how one Neo-Thomist metaphysician explains the relation of *esse* to the thing:

---

7. "We find in the world, furthermore, certain beings, those namely that are subject to generation and corruption, which can be and not-be. But what can be has a cause because, since it is equally [*de se aequaliter*] related to two contraries, namely, being and non-being [*esse et non esse*]." *SCG* I.15, *Amplius* (trans. Pegis, 1:98–99). "Again, everything that can be and not-be has a cause; for considered in itself [*in se consideratum*] it is indifferent to either, so that something else must exist which determines it to one." *SCG* II.15, *Praeterea* (trans. Anderson, 2:48).

8. "It follows that something is the cause of its own being [*causa essendi*]. This is impossible, because, in their notions the existence of the cause is prior [*prius*] to that of the effect. If, then, something were its own cause of being [*causa essendi*], it would be understood to be before it had being [*haberet esse*]—which is impossible." *SCG* I.22, *Amplius. Si* (trans. Pegis, 1:119). Even though the cause is called *prius*, clearly the *esse* is also. The thing cannot trump the priority of its own *esse* to be a cause of it.

9. "Now the first [*primus*] of all effects is being [*ipsum esse*], which is presupposed to all other effects, and does not presuppose any other effect." *De Pot.*, q. 3, a. 4, co. The primacy of *esse* is implied in further texts. See *ST* I, q. 4, a. 1, ad 3, cited above in note 6, as well as: "From the very fact that being [*esse*] is ascribed to a quiddity, not only is the quiddity said to be but also to be created; since before it had being [*esse*] it was nothing, except perhaps in the intellect of the creator, where it is not a creature but the creating essence." *De Pot.*, q. 3, a. 5, ad 2 (trans. Dominican Fathers, 110). See also: "God at the same time gives being [*esse*] and produces that which receives being [*esse*], so that it does not follow that his action requires something already in existence." *De Pot.*, q. 3, a. 1, ad 17 (trans. Dominican Fathers, 88).

10. "But being [*esse*] is innermost [*magis intimum*] in each thing and most fundamentally present [*profundius*] within all things, since it is formal in respect of everything found in a thing." *ST* I, q. 8, a. 1, co. (trans. Pegis, 1:64).

The notion that there is an accident prior to substance in sensible things is repellent to the ingrained human way of thinking. Yet the effort has to be made for the metaphysical understanding of existence. Not substance, but an accident, being, is absolutely basic in sensible things. This has to be understood, however, in a way that does not make being function as the substance. Strictly, it is not the being that is there, but the substance that has the being. The nature cannot take on an adverbial relation to its being. Man cannot be regarded as basically a certain portion of being that exists humanly, or a horse as another portion of being that exists equinely. The man and the horse are not portions of being, but substances that have being. They, and not their being, have to be expressed substantively, even though their being is prior to their natures. Not the subject, but the predicate, is absolutely basic.[11]

The priority of *actus essendi* to the thing that it actuates seems to explain Aquinas's earlier mentioned qualification in describing the *ratio entis* as *quasi habens esse*. Usually what is possessed by a thing is regarded as subsequent and posterior to the thing. For example, if I have a tan, I have an item distinct from me, yet posterior and subsequent to me. We come to understand the tan as distinct and posterior because I can be found without it. This manner of verification obviously fails for *esse*. Without the *esse*, I am not found at all. So, if we can cogently come to distinguish *esse* from the thing, we should not be surprised to find that *esse* is an act of the thing that does not fit the familiar parameters of an act of the thing.[12]

Priority also enables one to understand how being (*ens*) can on the basis of *esse* be essentially predicated. As mentioned, predication on the basis of an act distinct from a thing is usually an accidental, not essential, predication. However, the radical priority of *esse* not only distinguishes *esse* from the thing, but in its own manner the priority places the *esse in* the thing. By being *prius*, *esse* is *magis intimum*. Somewhat similarly by its central location the hole of the

---

11. Joseph Owens, *An Elementary Christian Metaphysics* (Houston, Tex.: Center for Thomistic Studies, 1985), 75. He continues, "Given what I have been saying, Aquinas's teaching on *esse* is decidedly matter of fact and even pedestrian." Brian Davies, "Aquinas, God, and Being," *The Monist* 80, no. 4 (1997): 514. For references to Neo-Thomists who appear to regard the nature as taking on an adverbial relation to its *esse*, see Knasas, *Being and Some Twentieth-Century Thomists*, chap. 9, n20.

12. Unlike the thing's other "possessions" that are all posterior and subsequent to the thing, the *esse* "had" by the thing is prior and fundamental to the thing. Hence, "esse est accidens, non quasi per accidens se habens, sed quasi actualitas cuiuslibet substantiae" (*Quodl*. II, q. 2, a. 1, ad 2). At *Quodl*. XII, q. 5, a. 1, the priority of angelic *esse* to the angel itself is used to deny that *esse* is an ordinary accident: "quia accidens intelligitur inesse alicui praeexistenti. Angelus autem non praeexistit ipsi esse."

doughnut is not just outside but also inside the doughnut. Hence, predication on the basis of *esse* is not simply accidental but also essential.[13] Along with analogy understood as sameness-in-difference, the dual status of *esse* as both accidental and essential is guaranteed to drive analytical minds mad. Some ideas cannot be perfectly isolated from other ideas.

The Intellect's Twofold Operation

What philosophical case does Aquinas make for his unique *esse* understanding of the existence of a thing? Obviously, the answer to this question is, for my purposes, a central one. Unfortunately, a full answer never made it to the written page. Aquinas's texts contain remarks of a definitive character but they are never fleshed out as a philosopher would desire. In other words, for an elucidation of the notions of matter and form, a philosopher can turn to Aquinas's commentary on Aristotle's *Physics* or to Aquinas's own short work, *De Principiis Naturae*. The closest Thomistic exposition on *ens* and *esse* is the *De Ente et Essentia*, but, as is evident from the very title, the *De Ente* remains oblique to my present concerns. Given what I have said at the beginning of this chapter, I do not mean that the *De Ente* is bereft of *esse*-talk. I mean that the *esse*-talk is always subordinate and tangential to talk about *essentia*. This situation means that the student of Aquinas will have to piece together patently and carefully the philosophical access to *esse* that certainly existed in Aquinas's mind just as there certainly existed in Aquinas's mind the science of mathematics as is evident from the few but profound remarks he made about number and figure.

The preceding lines of my *De Ente* selection contain an assertion that, I believe, opens up Aquinas's mind on the topic of the philosophical access to *esse*. The remark is the famous "possum enim intelligere quid est homo vel phoenix, et tamen ignorare an esse habeant in rerum natura" (I can know what a man or a phoenix is and still be ignorant whether it has being in reality). This remark reiterates a conclusion made in the prior chapter about the absolute consideration of essence. There the conclusion was that the absolute consideration of essence abstracts from *every esse*, without prescinding

---

13. This point escapes Brian Davies who remarks, "['is a being'] does not tell us anything about anything.... It cannot serve to tell us what something is." "Aquinas, God, and Being," 510.

from *esse*: "natura hominis abstrahit a quolibet esse, ita quod non fiat praecisio alicuius eorum." The correlating of the phoenix remark with absolute consideration is important because it allows us to locate the phoenix remark within the context of the *duplex operatio intellectus*. In various reiterations of this doctrine from the *De Anima* of Aristotle,[14] Aquinas says that the first intellectual operation apprehends (*apprehendit*) or looks upon (*respicit*) the essence of the thing, while the second operation comprehends (*comprehendit*) or looks at (*respicit*) the existence of the thing, the *esse rei*. Again, Aquinas asserts but does not elucidate. Even the *De Anima* commentary adds little or nothing to Aquinas's claim. But there is an interpretive gain. One knows the direction in which to head. A philosopher interested in knowing how to access the notion of *esse* as it appears in my *De Ente* selection would be led to the twofold operation of the intellect.

I would like to provide a phenomenology of the two intellectual operations. By "phenomenology" I simply mean offering claims relentlessly cued by what we are observing in our own mental life.[15] For example, Joseph Owens has performed the inestimable service of distinguishing between the second operation that grasps the *esse* of the thing and the activity of forming propositions. In the writings of many other Thomists, this second operation appears

14. "There is a twofold operation of the intellect. One of these is called by some the 'imaginatio intellectus.' In the third book of his *De Anima*, the Philosopher names it the understanding of indivisibles [*intelligentiam indivisibilium*]. It consists in the apprehension of the simple quiddity. By another this operation is called by the name '*formatio*.' The other of these [operations] is what they call '*fidem*,' which consists in the composition or division of the proposition [*propositionis*]. The first operation looks on the quiddity of the thing; the second looks upon its being [*esse*]. And because the notion [*ratio*] of truth is based on being [*esse*] and not on quiddity, ... so truth and falsity are properly found in the second operation and in its sign which is the enunciation [*enuntiatio*], and not in the first or in its sign which is the definition." *In I Sent.*, d. 19, q. 5, a. 1, ad 7. See also d. 38, q. 1, a. 3, co., and his commentary on the *De Trinitate* of Boethius [hereafter "*In de Trin.*"], q. 5, a. 3, co.

15. Here "phenomenology" simply refers to an investigation without prejudice to what appears. In his *Elementary Christian Metaphysics*, 214, Owens employs the term that way: "But even elementary scientific procedure requires that [the contents of human cognition] be investigated without prejudice as 'what appears,' as *phainomena*. If what 'appears' in sensible things actually seen and touched is that the things exist externally to the cognition, the fact that they are perceived to exist in reality has to be numbered among the contents distinguished by the phenomenology." Hence, here one should not assume that Husserl's categories are to be employed. Those categories themselves must be justified by the investigation. In fact, echoing the previous Owens quotation, in note 39 below I dispute Husserl's analysis of perceptual intentionality in which things are present through perspectives. In my investigation, things are immediately present, though inexactly.

to be identified with forming propositions.[16] Owens differentiates the two. The proposition is only the expression of what the second operation is already grasping. The proposition is related to the second operation, but not by way of identity. It is an effect of the second operation rather than the operation itself.[17] Owens's distinction leaves as the more exciting philosophical issue, not the investigation of the proposition, but the description of the second operation. What is it? As far as I can tell, however, Owens fails to provide that description. Rather, he appears content to insist that the second act is a grasping, even an intuiting,[18] of the thing's act of existence. Likewise, he calls

---

16. "Existential judgments are meaningless unless they are meant to be true. If the proposition 'Peter is,' means anything, it means that a certain man, Peter by name, actually is, or exists." Etienne Gilson, *Being and Some Philosophers* (Toronto: Pontifical Institute of Mediaeval Studies, 1952), 201. Also, "Assuredly, the actual existence of what the terms of judgment signify is directly or indirectly required for the truth of any predication, for the formal correctness of such a judgment as all swans are white is independent of its truth" (ibid., 196). "The proper function of judgment is to say existence" (ibid., 202). "The formula in which this composition is expressed is precisely the proposition or judgment." Etienne Gilson, *The Christian Philosophy of St. Thomas Aquinas*, trans. Lawrence K. Shook, CSB (Notre Dame, Ind.: University of Notre Dame Press, 1994), 41. "All this becomes evident in the case of a judgment of existence, for example: *Socrates is*. Such a proposition clearly expresses by its very composition the composition of the substance Socrates and its existence in reality" (ibid.). Also Gerald Phelan, "Suppose I should say, 'this paper is blue'; I make a judgment in regard to a fact." *"Verum sequitur Esse Rerum,"* in *G. B. Phelan: Selected Papers*, ed. Arthur G. Kirn (Toronto: Pontifical Institute of Mediaeval Studies, 1967), 139. "The judgment thus essentially consists in affirming the existence (in the unity of real existence) of a thing in which two concepts united by the mind (in a unity of intentional existence) are actually or possibly realized. This is the composition and division effected by the judgment" (ibid., 148). Finally, Robert J. Henle: "Yet, in order to form the judgment 'Socrates is a man,' intellectual knowledge of the individual is necessary" (*Method in Metaphysics*, 69). "A judgment concerning a material individual (e.g. 'Socrates is a man.') is possible only through an intellectual awareness of and an operational unity with the sense powers in which the individual is presented" (ibid., 71).

17. "'Judgment' has two meanings that require careful distinction. In one meaning it is the dynamic intellective act by which synthesizing existence is being grasped. In the other meaning, it is the static, frozen representation of that action's cognitional form. In the first meaning, it denotes the 'second operation' of the intellect.... In the first meaning, the object of the cognition is an actual existential synthesizing that is taking place before its gaze. In the other meaning, the object is a static representation of that synthesizing, even though that synthesizing is no longer taking place." Joseph Owens, "Judgment and Truth in Aquinas," in *St. Thomas Aquinas on the Existence of God: Collected Papers of Joseph Owens*, ed. John R. Catan (Albany: State University of New York Press, 1980), 47. Also, "Accordingly, 'judgment,' in its technical sense of knowing existence, is a different activity from the constructing of propositions." Joseph Owens, *An Interpretation of Existence* (Houston, Tex.: Center for Thomistic Studies, 1985), 22. "What is known dynamically through judgment is represented statically in a proposition" (ibid., 24).

18. Owens, *Interpretation*, 24.

the second act dynamic, synthesizing, and conditioned by time.[19] But we never have this grasping, intuiting, dynamic, synthesizing further described. My "phenomenology" will attempt to describe this grasping. In chapter 3 I apply the results to other interpreters of the fourth chapter of *De Ente*.

For my phenomenology of the first operation I want to focus on the *De Ente*'s doctrine of absolute consideration of essence. As I mentioned above, the first operation's looking at the essence of the thing and the absolute consideration of essence seem to be one and the same. Aquinas presents both as considering the essence of the thing but missing the *esse* of the thing. Aquinas reserves to its second operation the intellect's looking at the thing's *esse*. This identification is important because while Aquinas does not elaborate upon his claim that the first operation looks at the thing's essence, he does elaborate upon the absolute consideration of essence. I will take his account of absolute consideration, then, as his elaboration of the *prima operatio intellectus*.

Aquinas says that the absolute consideration of essence considers what is true of the essence as such. Hence, to "human" as such belongs rational and animal, but not white or black nor one or many. Why are the features of black and white and one and many placed aside? The following lines give an answer:

If someone should ask, then, whether a nature understood in this way can be called one or many, we should reply that it is neither, because both are outside the concept of humanity, and it can happen to be both. If plurality belonged to its concept, it could never be one, though it is one when present in Socrates. So, too, if oneness belonged to its concept, the nature of Socrates and of Plato would be identical, and it could not be multiplied in many individuals.[20]

The concern is whether any definite number is part and parcel of the meaning of the word "man." The text answers no. The argument is that if "man" included in its meaning being six, then any one man would be six men. Likewise, if "man" included in its meaning being one, then every man would be identical with every other. Hence, any definite number is not part and parcel of what "man" means. To be noted is that a factual situation is what prompts one to the absolute consideration of essence. In this case the facts

---

19. Ibid., 25, and Owens, *Elementary Christian Metaphysics*, 49–52.
20. Aquinas, *On Being and Essence* (trans. Maurer, 46).

are man being one in Socrates, but being many in Socrates, Plato, and Aristotle. White and black should have been set aside for the same reasons. Man is white in Plato and black in Socrates; hence, it must not include either under pain of making all men black or white.

Likewise, Aquinas says elsewhere that essence itself is neither composite nor simple. The given reason is that we know essence to be simple in God but composite in men.[21] Also, finger, foot, and hand and other parts of this kind are outside the definition of man because whether or not one has these parts, one will still be a man.[22] Finally, the nature of animal is abstracted from reason because it is known to be in brutes.[23]

What do these descriptions indicate about absolute consideration? Among other things, they indicate that absolute consideration takes place presupposing a presentation of a multiplicity of instances. These instances seem to control and guide the focusing action of the mind upon the essence as such. For example, the meaning of animal is presented in the multiplicity of Tom the man and Fido the dog, and these facts steer the intellect to abstract the meaning without including reason. If I am correct that absolute consideration is just another way of speaking of the first intellectual operation, then what I have just described will be the case for the first operation as it looks upon the essence of the thing.

It should be noted that Aquinas says in *Quaestiones Disputatae de Veritate* (hereafter "*De Ver.*") that the first operation is fittingly called *intellectus*.[24] *Intellectus* derives from the combination of *intus* and *legere*, which means "to read into." Such is what the absolute consideration also does when it attains

---

21. "Concerning the notion of quiddity insomuch as it is quiddity [*De ratione autem quidditatis inquantum est quidditas*], is not that it is composite; because a simple nature would never be found, which at least in God is false: nor is it concerning its notion that it is simple, since certain [natures] are found that are composite, as humanity." *In II Sent.*, d. 3, q. 1, a. 1, co.; ed. Mandonnet (Paris: P. Lethielleux, 1929), 2:87.

22. "But finger, foot, and hand, and other parts of this kind are outside the definition of man; and thus the essential nature of man does not depend on them and he can be understood without them. For whether or not he has feet, as long as he is constituted of a rational soul and a body composed of elements in the proper mixture required by this sort of form, he will be a man." *In de Trin.*, q. 5, a. 3, co.; trans. Armand A. Maurer, *On the Division and Methods of the Sciences* (Toronto: Pontifical Institute of Mediaeval Studies, 1963), 32.

23. "... as animal abstracts from reason, although some animals are rational." *In de Trin.*, q. 5, a. 4, ad 5 (trans. Maurer, 49).

24. *De Ver.*, q. 1, a. 12, co.; see also q. 15, a. 1, co.

essence. These remarks appear to be phenomenologically correct. We start with a multiplicity. As we focus on essence, our attention penetrates into the data. The visual terms for the first operation should be noted. The first operation *respicit*, it is a *consideratio*; it "reads" the essence like the eye reads a word.

We need not think that Aquinas is Platonizing here. In fact, later he argues that the absolutely considered essence abstracts from every *esse*. Hence, it would not be a being, an *ens*, and so not independently known. Phenomenologically it is known through the data in which it exists. Sometimes we know something not by its own existence but by the existence of something else. It is the existing data that sustains the absolute consideration of the essence. In conclusion, the general character of the first operation, phenomenologically speaking, is a penetrative movement of attention into a multiplicity in order to achieve an awareness of a commonality.

Two caveats are appropriate here. First, the initial consideration of essence from its presence in some multiplicity should not be confused with a definitional consideration. In other words, even though we may be certain that the essence of man includes no definite complexion and so is what I will call complexion-neutral, and that an understanding of man in terms of its genus and difference may take some time to achieve, if it is ever achieved. For example, if the definitional notes are animal as the genus and rational as the difference, then obviously a juxtaposition of man to mule, for example, is further required to make the genus and the difference of man stand out. These notes are in the initial apprehension of the commonality, but they are not yet appreciated. Accordingly, Aquinas describes the first operation as the understanding of indivisibles and as simple apprehension. The same phenomenon of knowing a commonality but not knowing how to describe it is found at *ST* I, q. 44, a. 2. Aquinas presents the history of philosophy in terms of a threefold consideration of being. Being is the commonality that philosophers have always been contemplating but only in the third phase of philosophy's history do philosophers succeed in pinning down what it means to be a being (*ens*). For Aquinas, that definitive understanding is for a substance to have *esse*.[25]

---

25. "One of the first things we know with certitude is that being is, that it is what it is, and that it cannot be anything else, but to know what being is is a very different matter. It has been discussed for almost twenty-five centuries, and even Martin Heidegger has not yet discovered the answer." Etienne Gilson, *Christian Philosophy of St. Thomas*, trans. Armand Maurer (Toronto: Pontifical Institute of

Second, again, the absolutely considered essence is considered in the data. Elsewhere at *SCG* I.53, Aquinas describes how having been informed by the species of the thing, the intellect goes on to form an intention of the thing understood.[26] This formed intention is distinct from the intelligible species that actualizes the intellect and is the principle of intellectual operation. Such a formed intention is necessary because the intellect, like the imagination, understands both a present and absent thing and because the intellect "understands a thing as separated from material conditions, without which a thing does not exist in reality." This text suggests two contrasting views of essence. One view of essence is the more original. It follows the intellect's actualization by the species of the thing. Another view is subsequent and follows the intellect forming an intention of the essence. The latter results in a view of essence separated from material conditions. Hence, the original view of essence should be a view of essence still immersed within the material data. And the second view should be of essence more independent from the data.

That absolute consideration is intention-free also seems to be phenomenologically verified. While absolutely considering the essence, we are aware that on the side of the considering we are fashioning a likeness of the essence. This likeness can be taken up to entertain the essence in a more data-free manner. The importance of this distinction of views will become evident as I go along, especially when I discuss (in chapter 4) the views of Anthony Kenny. Important for my current phenomenology of the two operations is the original apprehension of the essence in the rich context of the data. With that view maintained I now proceed to a phenomenology of the intellect's second operation.

In the texts on the *duplex operatio intellectus* referenced above in note 14, the intellect's second operation that grasps the *esse* of the thing is described as consisting in the composition or division of the proposition. This description sounds strange. Propositions may express the existence of something, for example, *Socrates est*. But does simply formulating a proposition grasp the

---

Mediaeval Studies, 1993), 51. Gilson's discussion of the history of philosophical discussion about being in his *Being and Some Philosophers* could also be mentioned here.

26. For the text see below chapter 4, note 38. See also Aquinas, *Quodl.* V, q. 5, a. 2, co. For a current discussion about the fundamental role of formal signs, see John O'Callaghan, "Concepts, Mirrors, and Signification: Response to Deely," *American Catholic Philosophical Quarterly* 84, no. 1 (2010): 133–62.

existence being expressed? Obviously not. It is clear that one can form the proposition "The weather is sunny" in the midst of a thunder storm. Though the second operation may involve the construction of a proposition, which Aquinas calls a *signum* of the second operation, the second operation is something more than that. As I have previously noted, Owens has driven this distinction home.

The richness of the second operation is most easily indicated by a study of its presentation in Aquinas's mature work, the *Summa Theologiae*. The text that I have in mind is the following:

> The human intellect must of necessity understand by composition and division. For since the intellect passes from potentiality to act, it has a likeness to generable things, which do not attain to perfection all at once but acquire it by degrees. In the same way, the human intellect does not acquire perfect knowledge of a thing by the first apprehension; but it first apprehends something of the thing, such as its quiddity, which is the first and proper object of the intellect; and then it understands the properties, accidents, and various dispositions affecting the essence. Thus it necessarily relates one thing with another by composition or division.[27]

The above text clearly parallels the texts on the intellect's twofold activity. What help does the text provide in understanding the intellect's second operation? The composing of the intellect is said to bear upon the accidents of the quiddity. These are found in the singular thing. Aquinas discusses how the intellect knows singular things: "Hence our intellect knows directly only universals. But indirectly, however, and as it were by a kind of reflexion [*quasi per quandam reflexionem*], it can know the singular, because, as we have said above [q. 84, a. 7], even after abstracting the intelligible species, the intellect, in order to understand actually, needs to turn to the phantasms in which it understands the species."[28] The nature of the composing activity of the intellect's second act is clear. The composing is the intellect's reintegrating of its awareness of the quiddity with its awareness of the individual. The intellect can always perform this act of reintegrating because abstraction must always begin with the phantasm. As a result of this com-

---

27. *ST* I, q. 85, a. 5, co. (trans. Pegis, 1:823). For earlier expressions of the *secunda operatio* in the *Sentences* commentary, *De Veritate*, and *SCG*, see Knasas, *Being and Some Twentieth-Century Thomists*, 189–91.

28. *ST* I, q. 86, a. 1, co. (trans. Pegis, 1:830–31).

posing, the object of our awareness is now no longer just the quiddity but the quiddity-in-the-individual. This is a complex object of consciousness. Hence, it can only be expressed in the complex way of a proposition. It is no surprise, then, that interpreting this composing of the intellect in terms of the above reflection, Aquinas says that the intellect forms the proposition "Socrates is a man." Forming a proposition does not constitute the intellect's second act; it crowns that act. The act itself is the above reflective composition.[29]

In summary and phenomenologically considered, the general character of the intellect's twofold operation is a seesawing or an ebb and flow in our cognitive attention. In the first operation there is a narrowing of one's attention upon the commonality in some multiplicity, upon the one in the many. We are going, attentively speaking, into the data, leaving other things, the *accidentia*, behind. In the second act of the mind, our attention regains its original perspective but without the loss of what it had spied in its first act. The intellect's second operation of composing is evidently like a "rebounding" of one's attention back off the commonality to the particular instances in which it was spied.

Aquinas's Philosophical Case for *esse*

So far my description of the *duplex operatio intellectus* has yet to appear in the context of Thomistic Existentialism. Hence, it is important to note that the *De Ente* text on absolute consideration of essence goes on to describe the essence as abstracting, but not prescinding, from all *esse*.[30] This remark should

---

29. "Therefore it understands the universal directly through the intelligible species, and indirectly the singular represented by the phantasm. And thus it forms the proposition, '*Socrates is a man*.'" *ST* I, q. 86, a. 1, co. (trans. Pegis, 1:830–31). For a suggestion about how the division of the second operation is also a form of composition because it applies negation to a previous conception, see Knasas, *Being and Some Twentieth-Century Thomists*, 242–44.

30. "This nature has a twofold being [*duplex esse*]: one in individual things and the other in the soul, and accidents follow upon the nature because of both beings. In individuals, moreover, the nature has a multiple being [*esse*] corresponding to the diversity of individuals; but none of these beings [*esse*] belongs to the nature from the first point of view, that is to say, when it is considered absolutely. It is false to say that the essence of man as such has being in this individual: if it belonged to man as man to be in this individual it would never exist outside the individual. On the other hand, if it belonged to man as man not to exist in this individual, human nature would never exist in it. It is true to say, however, that it does not belong to man as man to exist in this or that individual, or in the soul. So it is clear that the nature of man, considered absolutely, abstracts from every being [*abstrahit a*

imply that essence can be set up in an existential multiplicity. For as noted, essence abstracts from black and white because we find essence in a color multiplicity; from one or many, because we find it in a number multiplicity. In fact the *De Ente* assigns to essence a twofold *esse*: an *esse* in singulars (*in singularibus*) and one in the soul (*in anima*). Aquinas argues that neither *esse* belongs to the nature or essence when absolutely considered, though the nature prescinds from neither. His argument is as follows. First, if it belonged to the nature of man to be in Socrates, then the nature of man would not be found in any other man. Second, if not to exist in Socrates belonged to man as man, man as man would never exist in Socrates.

What interests me is the first premise. Two objections could be raised. First, Aquinas concludes to essence abstracting from every *esse* (*a quolibet esse*) from a consideration just of its *esse* in singulars. Should he not have concluded to an existential neutrality of essence simply in respect to *esse* in singulars? But a reflection upon the absolute essence of man in respect to black and white reveals that Aquinas's argument begins from data sufficient for its conclusion. A total color neutrality for man is reached just from man as black and white. One easily sees from Aquinas's consideration of man as black or white that if any color, say red or yellow, is proper to man than all men would be that color and the races would be denied. So even though the data sample is small, it permits an absolute conclusion that is unaffected by problems with induction. The same is true for the reasoning from existence in a multiplicity of individuals in Aquinas's above first premise. One sees that any existence considered proper to the absolute essence would rivet the essence to it and prevent it from being found existing elsewhere. So Aquinas is not hesitant to conclude that a nature with a multiple *esse* in singulars abstracts not only from that *esse* but also from an *esse in anima*.

The second objection appears to be more intractable. Some have understood the *esse in singularibus* terminology as just second-order talk for the designated matter of the essence, for example, this flesh and these bones of Socrates. In an earlier chapter Aquinas had mentioned the essence of man as abstracting from designated matter, though without precision. For these Thomists it suffices to have an existent when the essence is singularized with

---

quolibet esse], but in such a way that it prescinds from no one of them." Aquinas, *On Being and Essence* (trans. Maurer, 47).

the addition of designated matter. In other words, is not to have an individual to have a being? Hence, *esse* talk is just talk about the fact of some thing as a result of adding designated matter. Could Aquinas be understanding the *esse in singularibus* from which essence abstracts to be just the fact of these singulars? It is doubtful. As mentioned, in chapter 4 Aquinas goes on to talk about *esse* as "belonging" (*convenit*) to the essence and he compares *esse* to the accidents of risibility and illumination. But facts do not "belong" to something. Also, *esse* is obviously not designated matter which like all matter is potential. So how does a reader understand the remarks on absolute consideration of essence as abstracting from all *esse* in the Thomistic sense of the word?

Perhaps the consideration of a similar, but not identical, situation and its resolution will help. As Aquinas himself remarks, if "animal" exists, it will be as rational or not.[31] Hence, someone might think that the existence of animal is simply the fact of the composition of animal and rational. Others will insist that for the existence of animal one has to go further. Animal exists not if just rational is added but only if designated matter is added. In other words, though it is true that animal exists as rational or not, it is not true that a rational animal is an existent. There is a lack of conversion here.

How is one to make evident the need to go further than just the addition of rational or not? Will not one elaborate a multiplicity of individual men with their designated matters from which man is abstracted? That prior abstraction of man will show that though "animal" will exist only as rational or not, a rational animal is still not an existent. There is the further ground to cover that has been created by the previous abstraction of man.

My point is that to those who think that the abstraction of man from *esse in singularibus* is just an abstraction from the fact of some men, one should rather argue that there is a proto-abstraction of the individual men from *esse*. In the light of this abstraction man clearly abstracts both from *esse* and from designated matter. One would never confuse the two. Similarly, but not identically, there is a proto-abstraction of man from the designated matter of the individuals, so that animal clearly abstracts both from designated matter and from being rational or not. In other words, from a multiplicity of existential

---

31. "Thus, there cannot be an actual animal unless it be a rational or an irrational animal." Aquinas, *SCG* I.24 (trans. Pegis, 1:124). Also, "For *rational* added to animal gains for *animal* being in act" (ibid. [1:125]).

instances of the same individual there is an absolute consideration of the individual itself as abstracting from every *esse*, or as existence-neutral.

This will strike many as absurd. For is not to have an individual *ipso facto* to have an existent? For example, is not to say "This room exists" to utter a tautology? Does not speaking of "this room" automatically indicate that you are speaking of an existent and so you should go on to say something other than "exists"?[32] But Aquinas regularly speaks this way. To have an existent is to have an individual, but to have an individual is not *ipso facto* to have an existent. Aquinas juxtaposes the individual substance to its *esse*. For example, at *SCG* I.15 and II.15, Aquinas uses the phrase *possibile esse et non esse* for the individual generable and corruptible thing in relation to its *esse*.[33] Later in II.54, Aquinas considers the individual substance made up of matter and form to be composed with *esse* as a potency with its act. These texts suggest that Aquinas can carry out what *De Ente* calls an *absolute consideratio* not just on a universal essence but also on an individual. The strongest confirmation of an absolute consideration of the individual is *SCG* I.65. In one argument for God's knowledge of singulars, Aquinas speaks both of the universal essence (*essentia univeralis*) and the singular essence (*essentia singularis*).[34] This can be

32. D. F. Pears and J. F. Thomson, *Is Existence a Predicate?* (London: Aquin Press, 1963), 4, state that some existential propositions can be so constructed that the subject alone referentially implies existence, e.g., "This room exists," and so these propositions are tautologies. The only way to avoid tautology is to have the subject referring to an existence different from the existence asserted by "exists."

33. "We find in the world, furthermore, certain beings, those namely that are subject to generation and corruption, which can be and not-be. But what can be has a cause because, since it is equally [*de se aequaliter*] related to two contraries, namely, being and non-being [*esse et non esse*]." *SCG* I.15, *Amplius* (trans. Pegis, 1:98–99). "Again, everything that can be and not-be has a cause; for considered in itself [*in se consideratum*] it is indifferent to either, so that something else must exist which determines it to one." *SCG* II.15, *Praeterea* (trans. Anderson, 2:48). See Lonergan: "You will see that the notion of existence emerged with the question whether the particularized concept, *this thing*, was anything more than a mere object of thought." Bernard J. F. Lonergan, "*Insight*: Preface to a Discussion," *Proceedings of the American Catholic Philosophical Association* 32 (1958): 80.

34. "Again by knowing the principles of which the essence of a thing is composed, we necessarily know that thing itself. Thus, by knowing a rational soul and a certain sort of body, we know man. Now, the singular essence [*singularis essentia*] is composed of designated matter and individuated form. Thus, the essence of Socrates is composed of this body and this soul, just as the universal essence [*essentia hominis universalis*] of man is composed of soul and body, as may be seen in *Metaphysics* VII. Hence, just as the latter principles fall within the definition of universal man, so the former principles would fall in the definition of Socrates if he could be defined. Hence, whoever has a knowledge of matter and of what designates matter, and also of form individuated in matter, must have a knowledge of the singular. But the knowledge of God extends to matter and to individuating accidents and

described in terms of, for example, the universal essence of man as composed of soul and body and the essence of Socrates as composed of this body and this soul. Aquinas goes on to explain that insofar as *esse* is had by individuals, and insofar as God is the universal principle of being, then God in knowing his essence knows singulars. So Aquinas does not understand the potency to *esse* that is essence simply as the universal. Potential essence is also the singular and individual. Without that admission the previous argument for God's knowledge of singulars would be impossible to understand.

If this proto-abstraction is an absolute consideration, then it must presuppose a presenting of a thing in an existential multiplicity. What could that multiplicity be? Does not the thing only really exist? Surprisingly not. Aquinas understands sense cognition, for example, what one is doing right now as one looks this way, realistically. By "realistically" I mean that some real thing is the direct and immediate object of the sensory awareness. By denominating the object as real, I mean that one is aware that the object would continue to exist even if one closed one's eyes. The object is not existent only in the awareness and so is perhaps a picture or representation of the reality. The immediate sense realism means that some reality also exists cognitionally. As Aquinas says, cognition is the existing perfection of one thing brought to be in another.[35] A multiplicity of reality juxtaposed to itself cognitionally

---

forms. For, since His understanding is His essence, He must understand all things that in any way are in His essence. Now within His essence, as within the first source, there are virtually present all things that in any way have being [*esse*]. Matter and accidents are not absent from among these things, since matter is a being [*ens*] in potency and an accident is a being [*ens*] in another. Therefore, the knowledge of singulars is not lacking to God" (trans. Pegis, 1:211–12). Also, "Quaelibet autem forma signata non intelligitur in actu nisi per hoc quod esse ponitur." *De Pot.*, q. 7, a. 2, ad 9. To be noted is that *De Ente*, chap. 1, speaks of essence as that by which a thing falls into a category. Hence, essence can stand for what a thing is and for its definition. This is the reason for also referring to essence as quiddity. Interestingly, then, the discussion of essence in *De Ente* is not exhaustive. It omits the singular essence which does not have a definition. Lamentation about *De Ente* not including much elaboration of *esse* should be coupled with lamentation about *De Ente* not featuring the *singularis essentia*. Anthony Kenny's talk of the universal and individual essence, *Aquinas on Being* (Oxford: Clarendon Press, 2002), 14, should not be equated with Aquinas's remarks in *SCG* I.65. For Aquinas the individual *is* the individual essence; for Kenny Socrates *has* an individual essence. Also, Kenny insists that there is "no individuation without actualization (only what actually exists can be identified, individuated, counted)" (46).

35. *De Ver.*, q. 2, a. 5, ad 15; also q. 2, a. 2, co. "The sense-objects which actuate sensitive activities—the visible, the audible, etc.—exist outside the soul; the reason being that actual sensation attains to the individual things which exist externally." *In II de An.*, l. 12, n. 375; trans. Kenelm Foster and Silvester Humphries (Notre Dame, Ind.: Dumb Ox Books, 1994), 249. "For what is seen is color which exists in an exterior body." *In III de An.*, l. 8, n. 718 (trans. Foster and Humphries, 419).

existing is tailor-made for an absolute consideration of some individual precisely as existentially neutral. In other words, if reality also genuinely cognitionally exists, then reality cannot be real of itself. It must contain a factor that of itself exists in no way and so can be open to multiple ways of existence. Somewhat similarly but not completely, if the hot coffee is to take on another temperature, then the hot coffee cannot of itself be hot. Of course, the difference between the two cases is that the individual thing has two existences at the same time while the coffee, when cold, is not hot. Again, the simultaneity of real and cognitional existence requires this difference. Evidently acquiring cognitional existence is not like acquiring a physical attribute.[36] But that concession has no effect on the reasoning. The mind is still driven by the facts to something as existence-neutral in the reality present in sensory awareness.

The above makes Aquinas's sense realism more than a jumping off point of his philosophy. Rather, it is something important for the philosopher to linger upon.[37] It seems to imply that the real items of sensation are of themselves ontologically hollow. For all their *de facto* realness, they are not *de jure* real. It would also explain the recurrence of Leibniz's wonder of why there is something rather than nothing. Aquinas's immediate realist understanding of sense cognition has been discussed elsewhere and will be discussed further in chapter 5.[38] In its defense, for now it will suffice to observe that a reflective sweep of current sensation fails to find any ideas, or expressed species, in and through which that cognition is basically occurring. Such ideas are the reflexively discernible fact with acts of imagining and remembering. To observe that my current sensation is an idea-free zone suffices to know that I am not dreaming or hallucinating.

Likewise, relativities in sense cognition—for example, the straight stick as bent, the square towers from a distance as round, the circular coin as ellip-

---

36. That the change involved in cognition precisely as cognition does not fall under the umbrella of *ens mobile*, see Aquinas, *In III de An.*, l. 12.

37. "In fact, one may claim that it is exactly this double existence of the same thing, say the Parthenon or a man or a horse, that enables metaphysics after Avicenna to get off the ground. The one thing is found to exist in two different ways. This shows that the thing itself is not the same as either existence, thereby setting up the basic problem of metaphysics, namely being *qua* being in contradistinction to the things that have being." Joseph Owens, "The Range of Existence," in *Proceedings of the Seventh Inter-American Congress of Philosophy* (Québec: Les Presses de L'Université Laval, 1967), 57.

38. See the discussion described in Knasas, *Being and Some Twentieth-Century Thomists*, chap. 3, "Sensation: The Invasion of the Real."

tical, the cube as three-sided—all presuppose that cognitional presence cannot immediately present a reality inexactly. In other words, the philosopher assumes that cognitional presence is like physical presence in which things are found with all of their exact qualities. But why make that assumption? In the above cases, something real is directly present to me albeit inexactly. Why should direct cognitional presence mean exactness?[39]

My point is that to understand Aquinas's text on the absolute consideration of universal essence that abstracts from every *esse* (so that *esse* retains Aquinas's unique *actus* sense of the word), one has to assume a proto-abstraction in which some individual man (i.e., singular essence) is abstracted from existence. Otherwise one will continually interpret the *esse* from which the universal essence abstracts as just the fact of some individual.[40] At most, the philosopher could fatten up this fact understanding with a reference to designated matter which of course is still not what Aquinas intends by *esse*. My remarks on immediate sense realism are intended to establish the data from which the proto-abstraction would proceed.

---

39. In *Ideas: General Introduction to Pure Phenomenology* (New York: Collier Books, 1972), Edmund Husserl employs the perspectival character of sense perception to justify bracketing all judgments about the existence of things made in the natural attitude. In other words, as perspectival the sense datum cannot be the spatial thing. Moreover, as a perspectival affair perception cannot ever have the thing, or its real qualities, "immanent" to perception: "the sensory data which exercise the function of presenting colour, smoothness, shape and so forth perspectivally ... differ wholly and in principle from colour, smoothness, shape *simpliciter*, ... *The perspective variation ('Abschattung'), though verbally similar to the perspected variable (the 'Abgeschattetes'), differs from it generically and in principle*" (119). The spatial thing and its qualities are all necessarily "transcendent" (120). These thoughts illustrate that Husserl is also assuming that every direct presence of a spatial thing must involve the spatial thing exactly. If exactness is not there, neither is the thing there. But evidently direct cognitional presence does not demand exactness as does direct physical presence. When I am looking at the bent stick, I do not have directly present before me in my cognition an inexact *Abschattung*; I have an inexact reality. For an exposition of how an Aristotelian would account for the unique fact that something can be directly present but inexactly, see Joseph Owens, *Cognition: An Epistemological Inquiry* (Houston, Tex.: Center for Thomistic Studies), 43–46. Owens explains that because real form is ultimately formally, in contrast to materially, received by the sense power, then it is the very form of the real thing that is received and the sensor becomes that real thing. If in the process leading to formal reception of form, other real factors impact on the form, then the form is received inexactly and the sensor becomes that real thing inexactly. In his *Introduction to Phenomenology* (Cambridge: Cambridge University Press, 2000), 19, Robert Sokolowski says that at bottom we perceive "profiles" and that these are "private and subjective."

40. Such is my reply to David Twetten's Aristotelian objection to the *intellectus essentiae* argument that to get a matter/form composition is to get the *esse rei*. For the objection and another existential Thomist reply, see Kerr, *Aquinas's Way to God*, 30–34. For further permutations of the objection and replies, see Knasas, *Being and Some Twentieth-Century Thomists*, 196–202.

Finally, an absolute consideration of the individual, and not just the specific nature, as existence-neutral will be an adjustment for some Thomists. To readers of classic cosmological reasoning, however, such a consideration is front and center. For Leibniz it is this matter that is indifferent to this or that shape, this or that motion. For Kant the possible is some individual thing with all of its determination not yet in itself. What is able to be is not just some universal in an individual instance but the individual instance itself. Reflection upon cosmological reasoning may help the Thomist to rediscover something in Aquinas's thought itself.

In sum, absolute consideration is astonishing. It amounts to doing the *prima facie* oxymoronic task of considering what in itself is nothing. This would be permanently unintelligible if one lost the bigger picture. To sustain an object of consideration, it is not necessary to backtrack and attribute to the absolutely considered essence some existence in virtue of which it can be considered. Sufficient for such essence to be considered is the existence of the data from which the essence is considered. There is nothing impossible with knowing something from the existence of something else. Once known from the data, the intellect can form, as I mentioned above, a concept of the essence and so know it in a more isolated manner. But here again, our consideration of the essence is based upon the existence of the formed concept in our mind.[41]

If the existence-neutral individual is juxtaposed to other such individuals, further multiplicities can be formed from which further absolute considerations can be prompted. Instead of continuing down that line of conceptualization, I would now like to commence the second operation from the absolute consideration of the individual as existence-neutral. Also, in light of my topic, I would like to conduct this rebound of the intellect's attention to the instance which is the individual really existing. What object forms before the mind's eye when one's attentive movement bottoms out at that instance? Does not one see that something has been added to the individual such that it is now more than existence-neutral? Similarly, does not moving the mind's

---

41. Kerr, *Aquinas's Way to God*, 13n9, argues that the absolute consideration of essence is the consideration of a second intention. His reason is that the "consideration" is a consideration of the mind. So, the essence is in the mind. Kerr does not mention, however, that Aquinas has absolute consideration abstracting even from *esse in anima*. So "consideration" in absolute consideration does not mean a second intention existing in the mind.

attention from the temperature-neutral coffee to the coffee as hot bring forth the hot temperature as a distinct addition to the coffee? The same kind of acquaintance with an addition, or attribute, is occurring when the second operation moves from the thing as existence-neutral to the thing as really existing. Real existence is now the addition, or attribute. I believe that this is the moment to which Aquinas referred when he remarked in his *Sentences* commentary that the *secunda operatio respicit esse rei*. From now on I will use the term *esse* to refer to this addition to the individual that renders the individual a fact or existent.

Also, does not this existential addition manifest a peculiar relation to the individual? In the combination of individual and *esse*, the *esse* stands forth as basic and fundamental. As mentioned, Aquinas denominates *esse* as *prius*, *primus*, *profundius*, and *magis intimum*. These characterizations make sense in what we have seen so far. The reason is apparent. The subject of itself is nothing. Our awareness of the subject in absolute consideration should not make us forget that we are considering something that of itself is nothing. Hence, the absolutely considered subject as existence-neutral is not "there" to have the second operation reintegrate with the individual *esse* as a posterior and subsequent item. In contrast, the hot temperature of the coffee is reintegrated as an item posterior and subsequent to the coffee. The reason for this difference is found in the fact that the absolute consideration of the coffee as temperature-neutral was attained from the coffee really existing in both temperature instances.

Other Interpretations of the *secunda operatio*

In the beginning of the previous section, I mentioned how a reader might be puzzled by Aquinas's claim that absolute consideration of essence abstracts from *esse*. Why not say that essence abstracts from designated matter? Consequently, the second operation would reintegrate the abstracted essence with its designated matter. But designated matter is not *esse*. So how is Aquinas understanding the *duplex operatio* such that it provides a view of the thing's composition with its *esse*? I went on to offer my answer to that problem, but other Thomists use similar difficulties to argue that the *duplex operatio intellectus* is not Aquinas's philosophical access to his metaphysical principle of *actus essendi*.

John M. Quinn does not regard *In de Trin.*, q. 5, a. 3, co., nor the other passages like it, as speaking of the very act of being. In this passage, Aquinas speaks of the *esse rei* as "result[ing] from the union of the principles of a thing in composite substances." Quinn's expressed reason is: "Not being composed, the actuality of actualities cannot issue from prior principles. Rather, since a whole being derives from the composition of its principles, *ipsum esse rei* here must denote the concrete reality."[42] Siger of Brabant said something similar when he remarked: "Also if being [*esse*] in created beings is something constituted through the principles of the essence, and what is constituted through the principles of the essence is the thing itself, it follows that the being of the thing [*esse rei*] is the thing itself. Therefore, it is not something added."[43]

In reply, in my opinion, it should be especially noted that at *SCG* II.54 Aquinas briefly but clearly states how form is a *principium essendi*. I will speak about this text more at length at the end of chapter 4. Now let it suffice for me to repeat Aquinas's words that form is the *principium essendi* by being the *complementum* of the substance whose act is *esse*. In other words, form sets up the potency whose act is *esse*. Aquinas's statement makes perfect sense within my previous presentation of the *duplex operatio*. The absolutely considered substance is the potency for *esse* that will be grasped by judgment. If the *secunda operatio* grasps *esse*, as I have explained, then *esse* is presented as the act *of the thing*. Hence, any conditions for the thing, such as form, become conditions for the *esse*. So to Quinn I would point out that the principles of the thing first constitute the thing as potency. The principles do not yet constitute a being (*ens*). The principles can be said, however, to constitute the *esse* of the thing because they render the thing an appropriate potency for *esse*. All of these observations can be made with the context of the *duplex operatio* as it is bottoming out with the *actus essendi* of the thing.

Finally, if one takes a look at Aquinas's *responsio* from which *In I Sent.*, d. 19, q. 5, a. 1, ad 7 (cited in note 14), is taken, any doubt that the *secunda operatio intellectus* refers to *esse* in the *actus essendi* sense vanishes. In the *responsio*, the *esse* that founds truth is the same *esse* from which the name of *ens* is taken. This *esse* is *actus essendi*, not the concrete reality. The concrete reality

---

42. John M. Quinn, *The Thomism of Etienne Gilson* (Villanova, Penn.: Villanova University Press, 1971), 66.

43. Siger de Brabant, *Quaestiones in Metaphysicam*, ed. Armand Maurer (Louvain-La-Neuve: Éditions de l'Institut Supérieur de Philosophie, 1983), 33.95–97.

is *ens*, not *esse*. The two opening quotations from the *Sentences* commentary cited in my note 4 illustrate this distinction between *ens* and *esse*. I know of no text in which Aquinas identifies *esse* with *ens*.[44] Aquinas may have a philosophical problem clearly explaining how judgment *respicit esse rei* in the sense of a metaphysical principle, but the texts assert that thesis. One should not try to change the expressed meaning of the texts to solve the problem.

John Wippel agrees with Quinn. In the context of the two operations, Wippel asks, "Does [Aquinas] simply intend to signify by *esse* the fact that something actually exists (its facticity)? Or does he also have in mind the thing's distinct intrinsic act of being (*actus essendi*)?"[45] Wippel's answer to these questions is that he "prefers to take" *esse* in the first sense.[46] Even though Wippel will go on to cite texts, he hints that this issue is more of his own making. Indeed as I replied to Quinn, as far as I know, Aquinas never used *esse* for *ens*. In my opinion, then, the task should not be answering Wippel's questions so much as figuring out how the *secunda operatio* should be construed to *respicit esse rei* in the sense of *actus essendi*.

By my count Wippel offers four reasons for taking the *esse rei* grasped in the second operation as the fact of the thing.[47] First, in the fourth chapter of *De Ente*, Aquinas argues to the *actus* sense of *esse*, and thus he is not beginning from it. Second, a reader could interpret the texts on the *duplex operatio intellectus* as considering the *actus essendi* sense of *esse* as already given. Third, at *ST* I, q. 3, a. 4, and *De Pot.* q. 7, a. 2, ad 9, Aquinas names *esse* as the *actualitas* of every act or form. This actuality talk for *esse* dovetails with the facticity sense of *esse*. Wippel interprets the *habens esse* sense of *ens* in the same facticity fashion. "To have *esse*" means to have actuality. Fourth, in Aquinas's commentary on Aristotle's *Peri Hermeneias* I, 5, Thomas says that *est* principally signifies "actuality."

In my philosophical estimation, my metaphysical interpretation of the *duplex operatio* is left intact. First, understanding judgment as providing an

---

44. Aquinas famously describes *esse* in a threefold way at *In I Sent.*, d. 33, q. 1, a. 1, ad 1. *Esse* can signify either the essence, the act of the essence, and the truth of propositions. There is no mention of the "concrete reality."

45. John F. Wippel, *The Metaphysical Thought of Thomas Aquinas: From Finite Being to Uncreated Being* (Washington, D.C.: The Catholic University of America Press, 2000), 31.

46. Ibid., 34.

47. Ibid., 32–34.

actus sense of *esse* does not preclude development in the understanding of this *actus*. Beginning from the existential multiplicity of things both really and cognitionally existing, the *duplex operatio* will give a grasp of *esse* as a distinct *actus*. Still unclear is the precise nature of the borderline between this *actus* and its subject. The judgmental rebounding of attention from the thing as existence-neutral to the thing as real is not able to discern if *esse* actuates the thing by a *de facto* merging with it or actuates the thing by remaining distinct from it. That the second alternative is true is known only after the proof of subsistent *esse*. To be the proper effect of subsistent *esse*, caused *esse* must not be merged. Also, as I have just briefly mentioned but will develop, judgment's grasp of *esse* as a distinct act brings out not only the priority of *esse* to its subject but also a dependency of *esse* upon its subject. Hence, conditions for the thing become conditions for the *esse*. In that light, too, the *De Ente* reasoning is not the metaphysician's full view on *esse*.

Second, Wippel's claim that the *Sentences* texts on the *duplex operatio* could be presuming a previous acquaintance with *esse* makes sense hermeneutically if one is already convinced that for Aquinas *esse* could mean facticity. In other words, *esse* means to be a fact or, in Aquinas's terminology, to be a being (*ens*). As I noted with Quinn, however, in my reading, I never find Aquinas using *esse* for *ens*. Aquinas famously describes *esse* in a threefold way at *In I Sent.*, d. 33, q. 1, a. 1, ad 1, where *esse* can signify either the quiddity or nature, the act of the essence, or the truth of propositions. There is no mention of the "concrete reality."[48] So, in my opinion, the issue is not to stray from Aquinas's sense of *esse* as an *actus* but to attempt to understand, philosophically difficult as it is, how the *secunda operatio* can *respicit esse rei*.

Third, it is true that the texts do not catch Aquinas using *ens* for *esse*, but sometimes we find the texts using *actualitas* for *esse*. In English we use "actuality" for the fact of a thing. For example, "Brexit is now an actuality." So,

---

48. In his probing and extensive "The Accidental and Essential Nature in the Doctrine of St. Thomas Aquinas," in *St. Thomas and the Existence of God* (ed. Catan), 67, Owens identifies the first sense with the nature that exists and so "It seems to correspond to what was expressed by the participle in the sense in which being is wrapped in nature, ... It signifies the subject of being, being as taken in the concrete." At *In III Sent.*, d. 6, q. 1, a. 2, co., however, and in a noncommittal way, Aquinas says that sometimes (*aliquando*) *esse* is used for the essence because principles able to be designated by their acts, "quia per actus consueverunt significari eorum principia, ut potentia vel habitus." This second text, in my opinion, indicates that in the first text Aquinas was not speaking of quiddity or nature in the concrete. Owens also tries to argue that sometimes Aquinas uses *ens* for *esse* in the *actus* sense (65).

from this angle could we say that there is in Aquinas's text a facticity sense of *esse*? Before looking at the texts, it should be noted that sometimes in English "actuality" is used not for the fact of the thing itself but for the act that makes the fact. For example, "The actuality of distrust is what led to their defeat." When Aquinas is referring to *esse* as *actualitas*, does he mean the fact of some thing or does he mean some act of the thing?

The paradigmatic case of Aquinas doing this is *De Pot.*, q. 7, a. 2, ad 9: "quod dico esse est actualitas omnium actuum, et propter hoc est perfectio omnium perfectionum" (what I call *esse* is the actuality of all acts and on account of this is the perfection of all perfections). If Aquinas had said that *esse* is the "act of all acts" that would have settled the matter. But the use of the word *actualitas* creates the possibility that *esse* means not an act itself but just the fact of these other acts. Nevertheless, in at least four ways the text itself makes plain that by *actualitas* Aquinas means the second use of "actuality."

First, the ninth reply begins by placing *esse* into a context of act and potency. It says "actus est semper perfectio potentia" (act is always the perfection of potency). Can the relation of facticity to non-facticity capture the act/potency relation? The first pair is two different considerations of one thing. The second pair stands for two different items. Hence, at *SCG* II.54, Aquinas can speak of a twofold composition of act and potency in sensible things. One is of form and matter; the other is of that composition with *esse*. Would one ever speak of a substance being composed with its facticity, or with itself as a fact? Second, the text immediately goes on to speak of being in act by the positing of *esse*: "quaelibet autem forma signata non intelligitur in actu nisi per hoc quod esse ponitur." Here facticity, *in actu*, is distinguished from *esse* like an effect from its cause.

Third, the same manner of thinking about *esse* is continued a few lines down: "hoc quod habet esse, efficitur actu existens" (that which has *esse* is caused [to be] existing in act). Then there follows Aquinas's famous statement about what he means by *esse*. In light of the three remarks leading up to this famous statement, *actualitas* could not mean facticity. It clearly means the act by which the thing is a fact. Fourth, the ninth reply ends by distinguishing this *esse* from that *esse* by the nature that it is of. The nature is described as a potency whose act is *esse*. The very last line compares *esse* to *vita*. Hence, to me it is clear that when *esse* is mentioned as Aquinas wants to understand it, *esse* means *actualitas* in the sense of an *actus*.

Finally, the same analysis can be made of Aquinas's commentary on Aristotle's *Peri Hermeneias* I, 5. Aquinas says that as employed in propositions "'*est*' principally signifies the actuality of every form commonly, whether substantial or accidental."[49] Does "actuality" mean facticity? Two paragraphs earlier this actuality is the *esse* composed with the thing in what is meant by being, *ens*. "This is indeed most clearly seen in saying 'being' [*ens*], because *being* is nothing other than *that which is*. And thus we see that it signifies both a thing, when I say 'that which,' and existence [*esse*] when I say 'is' [*est*]."[50] Facticity is present here but as *ens*, not *esse*.

Finally, Anthony Kenny disputes the existential sense of *est* insofar as "existential statements are only a tiny fraction of the number of sentences that we compose and employ."[51] It is true that for Aquinas not every assertion expresses *esse*. Armand Maurer shows that the "is" in "eternal" truths corresponds to no *esse* proper to the truth itself.[52] For Aquinas, just as essences considered in themselves abstract from every being, so too do truths when considered in themselves. Using terminology taken from John of St. Thomas, Maurer says that at best these truths can be said to have a "negative" eternity in that in themselves they abstract from any subject in and through which they can come and go in being.[53] As so entertained, the "eternal" truth is not being envisaged with any existence at all.

The Cause of *esse*

The previous is my best understanding of how Aquinas philosophically accesses the *esse rei*. In chapters 3 and 4, I will defend it against some fellow Thomists. Now I want to explain how Aquinas uses the results of the *duplex operatio* to make the causal conclusion in my opening *De Ente* text.

It is the mentioned stratification of the thing and its existence that prompts points (3) and (4) of the *De Ente* text quoted at the beginning of this chapter. As distinguished from one another, the thing and *esse* are not

---

49. *Aristotle: On Interpretation, Commentary by St. Thomas and Cajetan*, trans. Jean T. Oesterle (Milwaukee, Wis.: Marquette University Press, 1962), Book I, l. 5, n. 22 (53).
50. Ibid. (52).
51. Kenny, *Aquinas on Being*, 56.
52. Armand Maurer, "St. Thomas and Eternal Truths," *Mediaeval Studies* 32 (1970): 91–107.
53. Ibid., 101.

equal. They are stratified in the manner of thing as subject and *esse* as attribute. Point (3) is the characterization of *esse* as an attribute. This situation is ripe for causal reasoning. Point (4) is the notion that the attribute of *esse* is efficiently caused. The implied thinking is that the attribute is *ipso facto* dependent, at least upon its subject as material cause. But as a material cause, the subject lacks the actuality to account for the characterizing attribute. This insight shifts the full explanation of the attribute either to the subject in some other respect than subject or to another subject.

Of these two alternatives, only the second will fit *esse*. Point (5) indicates a problem in viewing the *esse* as efficiently caused by its subject. Subjects that account for their attributes are in some other respect already in act.[54] For example, I can move myself locally because one leg is actually in a place while the other leg is moving to a place. The problem with applying this model to the subject and its *esse* is that we know that apart from the *esse* the subject is not at all actual. As the phenomenological analysis showed, judgment proceeded from the subject as existence-neutral. As existence-neutral, the subject possesses no resources to be in some other respect the cause of *esse*.

What then is the identity of this something else that completes the explanation of the attribute of *esse*? Point (6) answers that question. The something else must be a thing whose *esse* is intellectually included in it. Otherwise, as point (7) explains, an unacceptable infinite regress is generated. In that regress each thing would be asking for a cause of its *esse* that no other thing in the regress would be able to be. One would be trying to explain the unexplained by more of the unexplained.

At this point a reader could ask the question if *esse tantum* is known before the elimination of the infinite regress or only after its elimination. Textually it is possible to read the remark about the impossibility of an infinite regress as an afterthought. What would the logic of the text indicate? As what exists through another (*per aliud*) is a thing to which *esse* belongs, or to which *esse* is an accident albeit *sui generis*, then the explainer of the explained has to be a thing that is its *esse*. If one keeps a focus on the priority of the *esse* to the thing, one would never think of a regress, infinite or otherwise. Why?

---

54. "The actuality of the accidental form is caused by the actuality of the subject. So the subject, inasmuch as it is in potentiality, is receptive of the accidental form; but inasmuch as it is in act, it produces it. This I say of the proper and per se accident." *ST* I, q. 77, a. 6, co.

The answer is that *esse* when considered in its priority cannot be explained by something that is not *esse*. In the supposed regress, anything is something that of itself is existence-neutral. To conceive the *aliud* as this kind of thing is patently absurd. How can something that is of itself existence-neutral be the direct cause of *esse*? This reflection suffices to understand the *aliud* as something that is its *esse*. In light of the priority of *esse*, that is the only way left to configure the *esse* in the *aliud* so that the *aliud* is not something that of itself is existence-neutral.[55]

Consequently, the infinite regress is fanciful and merits the simple mention that Aquinas gives it. The regress is not so fanciful, however, that it would never occur to someone. If one's attention wanders from the priority of the *esse*, one could start thinking of the *aliud* in terms of things of a quite different nature that are causes of accidents in other things? Suffice it to recall Anthony Kenny's example of the moving hands producing heat. Hence, why could there not be a thing that has *esse* that produces *esse*? The reason for a negative answer is the necessary existence-neutrality of the thing that has *esse*. Such a thing cannot form another line of causality that has *esse* as an accidental offshoot just like the motion of the hands to a place incidentally produces heat.

To say that the envisaged regress at (7) is fanciful is not to say absolutely that there cannot be regresses of caused causes. The characterization of fan-

---

55. Joseph Bobik, *Aquinas on Being and Essence* (Notre Dame, Ind.: University of Notre Dame Press, 1970), 177–79, argues the same point in a different way. If B is a cause of the existence of A, then B completely explains A. But if B is like A, then C will completely explain B. We then have the following contradiction: A is completely dependent upon B and A is not completely dependent upon B. Hence, for A to completely depend on B, B must not be like A. In other words, the *per aliud* must be explained by the *per se*. On the other hand, I argue that the only otherness left for the *aliud* is non-accidental *esse*. More accidental *esse* would involve the absurdity of the unexplained explaining, or of the not-caused causing. Accordingly, I agree with Bobik's characterizing of the role of the infinite regress: "it does not function as a premiss, it can nonetheless be claimed to be relevant to the proof of God's existence in the sense that it serves to point out something which does not in fact have the function of a premiss, although there are some who think it does" (181). This point of immediate regress to *esse tantum* will be important to appreciate a persistent disjunction in many of Aquinas's *viae*, namely either we immediately reach God or do not by denying an infinite regress. Hence, unlike Wippel, *Metaphysical Thought of Thomas Aquinas*, 409n25, I do not see a logical slip in claiming that if the existence of A completely depends upon B, then B is all that A depends on. Finally, Kerr (in *Aquinas's Way to God*, 125) uses *modus tollens* to claim that the denial of an infinite regress is necessary to know that *esse* is caused *per aliud*. I do not think that we have a strict *modus tollens*. I would argue that an infinite regress does not imply that *esse* is not through another but implies that there is no *esse*.

ciful is made from the perspective of the priority of *esse*. As I will explain in subsequent chapters, other perspectives on *esse* exist. Without contradicting the priority of *esse*, the form of the subject of *esse* can be given a role as a condition for *esse*. Hence, causes of form become causes of *esse*, and these causes may lie in a simultaneous regress. But in all these cases, fanciful or not, the elimination of infinity in the regress will be on the basis of something like (6). An infinite regress of things each with *esse* belonging to them dispenses with the *aliud* that the members of the regress need. Similarly Aquinas will argue against an infinite regress of moved movers because Aquinas has already proved that what is moved is moved by another. An infinite regress removes the *aliud* that Aquinas already knows that motion needs.[56]

Also, further thought sees that *esse* cannot be just intellectually included in this thing; *esse* must be identical with the thing. In other words, *esse* is all that this thing is. The reasoning would go as follows. Because a thing had already been appreciated as something common, the thought of *esse* intellectually merged with a thing becomes the thought of *esse* communized. Common *esse*, however, is the intelligible heart of the *ratio entis*.[57] So the infinite perfection that the *ratio entis* possesses as a transcendental intelligibility is more precisely located in its *esse commune* dimension. It is this infinity of perfection that is transferred to a thing that is its *esse*.

As so transferred, *esse* cannot then be a portion of the thing with something else as another portion. Why? Would not that scenario have something joined to the infinite that is outside the infinite? Would that not admit the oxymoronic situation of the infinite having some of its perfection outside itself? So, if *esse* is some thing of itself, then that thing is only *esse*. Because this cause is a subject intellectually identical with its *esse*, we can call this cause subsistent *esse*. A bit more reflection should bring the realization that subsistent *esse* is unique. Only by the addition of something would one instance of subsistent being be different from another. But having an addition is what has just been excluded for something that of itself is infinite.

Though unmentioned in the *De Ente* text, two other characterizations of subsistent being appear to be logically proximate. First, subsistent being would

---

56. See below chapter 8, note 11.
57. See my remarks on *SCG* I.26 in chapter 4, "Anthony Kenny: The Fatal Flaw in the Man/Phoenix Argument."

be a presently active cause. Attributes that only initially depend upon their cause are attributes in a posterior and subsequent relation to their subjects. Because of the priority of the subject as material cause, there is the chance that the attribute caused in the subject by something else continues at least for a time apart from its initiator. Because of the priority of the *esse* to its subject, however, there is no chance to explain the continuance of the *esse* on the subject. Rather, the something else that initiates *esse* must also maintain it. Second, subsistent being must also be a creator. A creator produces its effect without presupposing a material to work upon. Because subsistent being produces the thing by causing a thing's *esse* which is *profundius*, then it can be said to create the thing.[58]

Absolute Consideration and Modality

I want to conclude by indicating how absolute consideration provides modal propositions, some of which are involved in the *De Ente* reasoning. Aquinas acknowledges three kinds of possibility.[59] First, something can be possible because of what an agent can do, *secundum activam potentiam*. So, a building is possible in respect to the builder. Second, something can be possible because of what something can undergo, *secundum passivam potentiam*. So, burning is possible in respect to the wood. The third kind Aquinas calls the absolutely possible. This possibility is not according to any power. Something is absolutely possible when the terms of a proposition have no opposition to each other. The lack of a power for the absolutely possible indicates that by the terms of a proposition Aquinas means the absolutely considered natures of the *De Ente* that *abstrahit ad quodlibet esse*. The same doctrine is indicated by Aquinas's claim in *De Pot.*, q. 3, a. 14, that something diverse in substance and caused by God can exist eternally. Absolutely speaking (*loquendo absolute*), no opposition exists between the notions (*rationes*) *esse semper*, *esse ab alio*, and *diversum in substantia*. This way of speaking echoes the doctrine of absolute consideration in the *De Ente*.

---

58. Aquinas's reasoning about God as *esse subsistens* extends further to God's intellection and volition. For the references see my *Being and Some Twentieth-Century Thomists*, 247. For a discussion of some puzzles in Aquinas's position that God's creation of the world is free, see John F. X. Knasas, "*Contra* Spinoza: Aquinas on God's Free Will," *American Catholic Philosophical Quarterly* 76, no. 3 (2002): 417–30.

59. *De Pot.*, q. 3, a. 14; *SCG* II.37, *Ex hoc*; *ST* I, q. 46, a. 1, ad 1.

In the case of this illustration of the absolutely possible, Aquinas manifests the neutrality of *esse ab alio* to *esse semper* by showing that motion is not the only way something can have being from another. It is not necessary, however, that the instances of the multiplicity be set up by an argument. The instances can be provided by experience as they were in the *De Ente* absolute consideration of *ratio humanitatis* from black or white, one or many, *esse in re* or *esse in anima*. The instances are crucial, however, for properly leading the abstraction to the appropriate neutrality.

It is crucial to understand that Aquinas is speaking of the absolutely possible as such. He is not speaking of it in relation either to active or passive potency. Considered as such the absolutely possible leads to some curious subject areas. Two examples are the annihilation of the cosmos and/or spiritual creatures. Insofar as each is existence-neutral, then absolutely speaking their non-*esse* is possible. But in regard to God's active power which is not exercised apart from his intelligence, Aquinas says at *De Pot.*, q. 3, a. 14, that God will provide *esse* as is fitting these natures and so they will exist forever. Likewise, I could say that a cup of coffee at two thousand degrees Fahrenheit is absolutely possible as such. The coffee is temperature-neutral and so is not opposed to any temperature. But from the viewpoint of passive potency such coffee would never exist. Existing at that temperature would vaporize the coffee. So what is absolutely possible as such is not what is absolutely possible in relation to active or passive potency.

This point places a brake on the absolutely possible. What is absolutely possible is not something that could be found in some possible world. Nevertheless, the absolutely possible is wild enough to allow us to enjoy, for example, the nonhuman rational animals of dwarfs, ents, elves, and orcs of J. R. R. Tolkien's fictional masterpiece, *The Lord of the Rings*.[60]

The absolutely impossible should be determined on the basis of an in-

---

60. In his "The Leibnizian Cosmological Argument," in *The Blackwell Companion to Natural Theology*, ed. William Lane Craig and J. P. Moreland (Oxford: Wiley-Blackwell, 2009), Alexander R. Pruss critically discusses the Aristotelian-essentialist account of modality. In this case, essences determine what can be and not be. That focus seems to coincide with Aquinas's absolute consideration and his doctrine of the absolutely possible. One complaint of Pruss is that the essentialist account of modality cannot control itself: "The story we have so far is that something is possible provided its existing is not contradictory to the truths encoded in those essences that exist. This, however, seems to let in so many essences that a certain amount of skepticism is engendered" (41). I hope that the above distinction between the absolutely possible as such versus the absolutely possible considered in

compatibility of terms. The standard example is the principle of noncontradiction (hereafter "PNC"). To see the relevance of absolute consideration to the vindication of this principle, let me proceed gradually.[61] Let us begin by taking an expression like the PNC but more superficial: "A thing cannot be complected and not complected at the same time and in the same respect." What are we understanding by the terms here? First, the thing complected is (1) me as pale and me as tanned. Second, the thing as not complected is (2) me as able to be both. In other words, the thing as not complected is me picked out as the commonality in the instances of me as pale and me as tanned. In Thomistic terms (2) is an absolute consideration of an individual essence.

Now it is important to realize that (2), me as able to be both, means me as completely complexionless. If at (2) I am complected, then I will always be that complexion and me as pale and tanned would have to be illusions. But that is ridiculous. I really do become both tanned and pale. So to accommodate those evident facts, we say necessarily that (1) insofar as I am complected, (2) I am not not complected. We recognize an undeniable distinction between me as complected and me as complexion-neutral. It is not that there *is* a distinction between (1) and (2); rather it is the case that there *must* be a distinction between (1) and (2). Insofar as I am complected, I cannot be complexion-neutral, and insofar as I am complexion-neutral, I cannot be complected. From that realization comes the general remark with which I began: "A thing cannot be complected and not complected at the same time and in the same respect."

Some might want to state the impossibility of contradiction more particularly. Hence, "I cannot be tanned and be pale at the same time." How would I analyze that situation from the viewpoint of absolute consideration? My capacity to be pale now is found back in me considered as complexion-neutral. But there is a strict separation between me as tanned and me as complexion-neutral. So as tanned, I have no capacity for being pale. In other words, if my being tanned is identical with my capacity for being pale, then my previously established complexion-neutrality would be compromised. Note that

---

relation to active or passive potency places some control into the absolutely possible. In other words, Pruss's complaint seems more appropriate of the absolutely possible as such, but the absolutely possible as such is not what exists.

61. For comment on the nature of Aquinas's defense of the PNC in his commentary on Aristotle's *Metaphysics* IV, see Knasas, *Being and Some Twentieth-Century Thomists*, 126–28.

the statement is not based simply on the fact that every time you see me as tanned, you do not see me as pale. That would make the statement just an observation statement. The statement would lack the necessity expressed in the words "cannot be." The observation must be supplemented with some intellectual reflection. In the previous lines I have tried to do that. This intellection reflection is not avoided simply by claiming that I know that I cannot be tanned and pale at the same time because the complexions are opposites, or contraries, and opposites exclude one another. How do I know that they are opposites? Simple experience will not suffice. For example, to know that they are opposites, it is not sufficient that I have repeatedly seen that when something is tanned it is not pale and vice versa. Again, that experience is some indication of opposition but the issue remains of whether future experience will continue to witness this opposition. I do know the truth about opposites excluding each other, but I know it by the above intellectual reflection. Again, if my ability to be tanned while I am pale is identical with my being pale and my ability to be tanned is back in me as complexion-neutral, then I am not complexion-neutral. My capacity to be tanned would drag my being pale into me absolutely considered.[62]

Let us turn to the PNC: "A thing cannot exist and not exist at the same time." What are the terms here? First, the thing existing is, for example, (1) me really existing and me cognitively existing. Me cognitively existing is a reference to sense realism. Second, the thing not existing is (2) me as able to be both. It is important to realize that (2), me as able to be both really and cognitively existing, means me as existenceless. If as able to exist in these ways, I am in some sense existing, then I will always be existing just in that way and my really existing and my existing in your sensation would necessar-

---

62. This kind of reflection suffices to understand why a square circle is absolutely impossible. If the square while it is a square is able to be a circle, then that possibility has to be read back into the square absolutely considered. What would follow, however, is that every realization of the square would be a square circle. You would never have just squares. Similarly the absolute impossibility of a *causa sui* is clear. A subject can be the cause of its attributes if the subject is actual in some other respect than subject. But as apart from *esse*, we know that a thing is existence-neutral. The thing cannot be in any manner existence positive under pain of riveting itself to existing only in that way. So to be a *causa sui*, a thing in some other respect than subject would have to exist and not exist at the same time. On the other hand, "We have not exhausted all the objections to the Aristotelian-essentialist view. Consider truths that hold of all things no matter what essence they might have. No entity has a shape that is both a square and a circle (at the same time and in the same respect), and no entity is a cause of itself. What makes these be necessary truths?" Pruss, "The Leibnizian Cosmological Argument," 40.

ily be illusions. So it is a necessary truth that insofar as I am existing, then I am not not existing. There is an observed necessary logical divide between (1) and (2).[63]

These reflections refute the Humean claim that propositions about experience can never be necessarily true. Rather, these propositions are just recordings of what we have seen so far and wages about what future experience will be. Also, they refute the Kantian claims that no analytic proposition can be *a posteriori* or that all *a posteriori* propositions are only synthetic.[64]

---

63. Aquinas has another classic example of a necessary truth: "Every whole is greater than its part." It also is an *a posteriori* truth, for at *ST* I-II, q. 51, a. 1, co., Aquinas admits that what a whole and a part is is known through species taken from phantasms. So what would be the rational reflection in the case of this proposition that would show that the proposition is more than an observation statement about what we have seen of wholes and parts so far? I think the following can be offered in behalf of an answer to that question. First is the truth that C is composed of A and B. That would be just an observation statement. Second, we would also just see that C is greater than A or B. Why would we say, however, that C is "necessarily" greater than A or B? If C as truly composed of A and B were less than A or B, then C would not be composed of A and B. So to keep the truth that C is composed of A and B, we necessarily have to say that C is greater than A or B.

64. In his "The Leibnizian Cosmological Argument," 44, Pruss argues that the Aristotelian causal account of modality offers a powerful reason in support of the PSR. In this account something is possible if there is something that can cause it. This seems similar to Aquinas's notion of possibility according to active potency. I would paraphrase Pruss's argument as follows. If there is a possible world in which it is possible to have an uncaused contingent, then by the Aristotelian causal account of possibility, there is a cause of this contingent. Hence, the possible contingent will be both caused and uncaused. In light of this contradiction, there is no possible world in which an uncaused contingent is possible. In comment from a Thomistic perspective, the argument makes sense only if the possible world is confused with the possible *secundum passivam potentiam*. It is true that you cannot have real passive potency without real active potency somewhere in reality. I, however, take Pruss to be speaking about a possible world in the sense of the absolutely possible. For Aquinas such a world is existence-neutral. We do not have something that needs accounting.

[3]

Neo-Thomist Discussion of the *De Ente* Reasoning

Aquinas has already made an advance over Leibniz. At the end of chapter 1, I mentioned that the difficulty in Leibniz's use of the principle of sufficient reason stemmed from his focus on the *de facto* togetherness of items. Though Leibniz's talk about the thing and its existence betrayed a stratification in which the thing was the subject and the existence an attribute, his focus remained the *de facto* togetherness between them and what was said to be the intolerability of accepting it as a brute fact. But even if Leibniz widened his focus to include this stratification, he was still faced with a certain arbitrariness. Unlike matter which is still matter without the shape or the motion, the thing seems to be nothing without its existence. So why not regard the existence as basic and fundamental to the thing? In that position, however, is existence still an attribute? Does it not become the subject, with the thing now as the attribute? Also, without remaining an attribute, is there any discernable intellectual need to account for the existence? Causal reasoning would appear to come to an end.

Aquinas's approach to *esse* from the *duplex operatio intellectus* philosophically elucidates how the thing's existence can be a *sui generis* attribute. Unlike other attributes which are subsequent and posterior to their subjects, existence is an attribute prior and fundamental to its subject. The crucial move is the initial data to which the *duplex operatio* will be applied. Things are not only in temperature and complexion multiplicities but also in existential multiplicities. Because of Aquinas's immediate sense realism, the real thing also cognitionally exists. Every time we open our eyes, we double the existence of the world. This situation drives the first intellectual operation to understand the thing as existence-neutral just as complexion and temperature multiplicities for a thing drive the mind to understand the thing as neutral in those respects. Of course, there is a difference and it is significant. In the case of the temperature or complexion multiplicities, we are led to entertain a *real* thing as temperature- or complexion-neutral. Consequently, by rebounding back to a temperatured or complected instance, the second operation adds the particular temperature or complexion as subsequent to something already there. The existential multiplicity will not allow us to understand the thing as common to the instances to be existing in any way. Hence, by rebounding back to an existing instance, the second operation adds the existence as an attribute but as a prior and fundamental attribute. In this way, one sees nothing anomalous about there being an attribute that is basic and fundamental to its subject. As mentioned in my elaboration of point (6) of the *De Ente* reasoning, this *sui generis* status for the thing's attribute of existence, or *esse* for Aquinas, enables causal reasoning to proceed to a first cause in which existence is not at all an attribute.

So Aquinas's *De Ente* reasoning holds the promise of avoiding the standard objections to cosmological reasoning as they are prompted by Leibniz's reasoning or by arguments indebted to Leibniz. Before I can determine if the *De Ente* keeps that promise, I need to run a gauntlet of objections to the *De Ente* text raised by my fellow Thomists. I devote this chapter to that task.

The Denials of Gilson and Maurer

There are Thomists who seem to attack the very idea that Aquinas intends the *De Ente* text to be a God-proof. No less than Etienne Gilson, one of my heroes of Thomistic Existentialism, is chief among these Thomists. Repeatedly over many years, Gilson explained the reasons for his hesitancy.[1] Yet it will

---

1. Gilson, *The Christian Philosophy of St. Thomas Aquinas*, 82; "La preuve du '*De Ente et Essentia*,'" *Doctor Communis* 3, no. 2 (1950): 257–60; "Trois leçons sur le problème de l'existence de Dieu," *Divinitas* 1 (1961): 6–8; *Le Thomisme*, 6th ed. (Paris: J. Vrin, 1972 [1962]), 97.

be my contention that an analysis of Gilson's reasons shows that his dismissal of the text is more nuanced than supposed. A reader of Gilson can discern that Gilson's dismissal does not obliterate, even from Gilson's own mind, an understanding of the text as a metaphysical proof.

Gilson always observes that when the reasoning of the *De Ente* occurs in Aquinas's texts, Aquinas never presents it as a proof for God's existence. For instance, it occurs at *SCG* I.22 and *ST* I, q. 3, a. 4, co. In both cases, the issue is not God's existence but God's simplicity. In particular, no composition of essence and *esse* exists in God. Second, in *SCG*, *ST*, and the *Compendium Theologiae* (hereafter "*Comp. Theol.*"), when Aquinas deliberately presents proofs for God, the *De Ente* reasoning is not to be found. Gilson underlines the point by remarking that Aquinas's key notion of *esse* is not invoked in any of the *quinque viae*, especially the third.[2] So, if the *De Ente* reasoning is a theistic proof, how does one explain its absence from this array of discussions of God's existence?

With the fact seemingly established, Gilson ventures what he thinks is the reason for the fact. Essential to a Thomistic *via* is that it begin from sense experience. But the Thomistic understanding of the essence/existence distinction in which existence is not the fact of the thing but an act (*actus essendi*) of the thing is not available to sensation, "even taken in the wide sense of the term."[3] Why not? These lines of the fifth edition of *Le Thomisme* explain: "Now, to the best of our knowledge, Thomas Aquinas has never attempted such a demonstration [*viz.*, a metaphysical one from sense experience]. Nor does one see how the thing could be done. The distinction of essence and existence presupposes the very notion of the pure act of being which its alleged demonstrations are supposed to justify."[4] In other words, the essence/*actus essendi* proof cannot be grounded in sense experience because it involves a reference to an extrasensory item—the notion of the pure act of being.

What Gilson is talking about becomes clear, in my opinion, from a discussion in his *The Elements of Christian Philosophy* which falls in the middle of the tail-end of his remarks on the *De Ente* text. Gilson concedes that, even among Thomists, debate exists about whether the existence of a thing is a state or an act. He notes that Aquinas favored the "act view." Neverthe-

---

2. Gilson, "Le Preuve du '*De Ente et Essentia*,'" 258.
3. "Même au sens large du terme." Gilson, *Le Thomisme*, 97n85.
4. *The Christian Philosophy of St. Thomas*, 82.

less, he concedes: "No such disagreement would take place if the presence, in things themselves of an act in virtue of which they can be called 'being' were a conclusion susceptible of demonstration." Gilson then offers this suggestion: "The impasse is an invitation to us to give up the philosophical way—from creatures to God—and try the theological way—from God to creatures. Thomas Aquinas may well have first conceived the notion of an act of being (*esse*) in connection with God and then, starting from God made use of it in his analysis of the metaphysical structure of composite substances."[5] How does a theological reference to God lead to the *actus* notion of a thing's existence? Accepting the *Ego sum qui sum* revelation of Exodus 3:14 at face value, Aquinas understands the text to say that God is pure *esse*. This conception of God produces an understanding of the existence of things as God's proper effect. Gilson explains: "It is one and the same thing to conceive God as pure *Esse* and to conceive things, so far as they *are*, as including in their metaphysical structure a participated image of the pure Act of Being."[6] In sum, the *De Ente* text is not a proof for God because its argument for a first cause that is a pure act of being presupposes an acquaintance with the act view of a thing's existence. But that act view itself is tied up with a revealed understanding of God as *ipsum esse*. So because of its theological suppositions, the text is not a God proof. If this is in fact what Gilson is saying, has not Gilson thrown the baby out with the bathwater? The price of "theologizing" the *De Ente* reasoning is to "theologize" the grasp of *actus essendi* in things.

As a matter of fact, it is the impression of a number of Thomists that Gilson "theologizes" Thomistic metaphysics.[7] Yet surely it is not as simple as that. Concurrent with Gilson's remarks on the *De Ente* reasoning are his remarks on judgment as natural reason's access to *actus essendi*. In the sixth edition of *Le Thomisme* (1965), Gilson says, "These two distinct operations both see the real, but they do not penetrate it to the same depth: intellection attains the essence, which the definition formulates, judgment attains the very act of existing [*jugement atteint l'acte même d'exister*]."[8] Judgment

---

5. Etienne Gilson, *The Elements of Christian Philosophy* (New York: Doubleday, 1960), 131.
6. Ibid., 133.
7. These Thomists include Thomas C. O'Brien, John M. Quinn, and John Wippel. For their reasons see my "Does Gilson Theologize Thomistic Metaphysics?," in *Thomistic Papers V*, ed. Thomas A. Russman (Houston, Tex.: Center for Thomistic Studies, 1990), 3–6.
8. *Le Thomisme*, 184. Gilson insists that only judgment can attain *esse*: "Le jugement seul peut

is an act of the human intellect, an intellect common to believer and unbeliever. Furthermore, in *Le Thomisme*, Gilson squarely rests Aquinas's metaphysics upon the resources of judgment: "A metaphysics of being, insofar as being consignifies existence, does not signify existence unless it precisely uses the second operation of the understanding and employs all the resources of judgment. The feeling, so just in itself, that the universal concept of being is the contrary of an empty notion, finds justification here. Its richness consists, first, of all the judgments of existence it virtually comprises and connotes."[9] In this passage, Gilson is clearly not a theologizer. The metaphysical viewpoint is set up thanks to the judgments that reveal various things in the light of their respective *esse*.

But it is unlikely that *Le Thomisme* signals a change of Gilson's mind from his *Elements of Christian Philosophy*, for the latter reiterates the same doctrine of judgment.

The second operation, which is the composition or division of concepts—that is, the judgment—attains the thing in its very act of being.... This conclusion, so firmly asserted by Thomas Aquinas, has often been overlooked or intentionally rejected by many among his successors. And no wonder, since it is tied up with the Thomistic notion of the composition of essence and the act of being in created substances.[10]

Gilson even insists that the judgmental grasp of *esse* is a "natural" operation of the human intellect.[11] It is very improbable that our purported theologizing text means to rule out a philosophical approach through judgment to Aquinas's understanding of existence as *actus essendi*.

What, then, does our text mean? I believe Joseph Owens is right to in-

---

atteindre l'existence.... l'act de juger peut seul atteindre le réel dans sa racine" (185). Incidentally, the final paragraph of ibid., 183, enables one to see that Gilson is unopposed to a conceptualizing of existence. Once existence is grasped by judgment, the intellect does go on to conceptualize this object. This is the entire point in Gilson's citing Aquinas's *habens esse* understanding of *ens*. What Gilson opposes is conceptualization as the original grasp of *esse*. Judgment is the original intellectual grasp. See also "But surely to maintain that existence is originally grasped through judgment is a far cry from the stand that existence is not conceptualizable!" Owens, "The Range of Existence," 1:55. For the claim that Gilson is opposed to all conceptualizing of existence, see Quinn, *The Thomism of Etienne Gilson*, 54–59.

9. Gilson, *Le Thomisme*, 188.
10. Gilson, *Elements*, 232.
11. "The human intellect thus reaches, even in its most natural operations, a layer of being more deeply seated than essences" (ibid.).

terpret it as Gilson surmising how revelation led Aquinas to a conception of existence that the latter went on to elaborate in straight philosophical fashion.

The tenet that the being of a thing is originally grasped through judgment and not through conceptualization seems introduced in the theological method of St. Thomas as the necessary epistemological support for an already accepted notion of God. If such be the case, it is entirely possible that St. Thomas was led to his metaphysical starting point by meditating on a scriptural notion of God, interpreted against a Neoplatonic background. It may be the case, likewise, that to appreciate the philosophical force and understand the full metaphysical significance of this tenet, the easiest way—perhaps, one might insist, the psychologically indicated way—is to retrace the steps by which it emerged out of its original historic setting at a definite epoch of Christian theology. It also may be possible to take the stand that other thinkers have missed this apparently obvious starting point because they did not use the theological approach. But with all this stated and weighed, the simple fact remains that the tenet is presented by St. Thomas as something immediately observable. Not the slightest indication is given that it is meant as a conclusion from other premises, or that any religious authority is being appealed to for its acceptance.[12]

Indeed, Gilson is speaking not of the only way to acknowledge *esse*. His professed intent is to explain how Aquinas "first" came by the notion. As he also remarks: "The problem under discussion now is: how did Thomas Aquinas achieve the awareness of the very possibility of this notion."[13]

It is no objection to Owens's interpretation to recall Gilson's claim: "No such disagreement would take place if the presence, in things themselves, of an act in virtue of which they can be called 'being' were a conclusion susceptible of demonstration." A reading of the previous pages shows that the open-ended demonstration that Gilson has in mind is the Avicennian argumentation reiterated by Aquinas in his *De Ente*.

Whatever does not belong to the notion of an essence or quiddity comes from without and enters into composition with the essence, for no essence is intelligible without is parts. Now, every essence or quiddity can be understood without anything being known of its existing. I can know what a man or a phoenix is and still be ignorant

---

12. Owens, *An Interpretation of Existence*, 132. In a footnote, Owens's quotation refers to Gilson, *Elements*, 131–33.
13. Gilson, *Elements*, 131.

whether it exists in reality. From this it is clear that the act of existing is other than essence or quiddity.[14]

Gilson's comment on this argument is that it fails to prove the distinction between essence and existence in concrete substances. Why? Gilson explains:

> The argument proves only that, in a created universe, existence must come to essences from outside and, therefore, be superadded to them. Any metaphysics or theology that recognizes the notion of creation necessarily agrees on this point. All Christian theologies in particular expressly teach that no finite being is the cause of its own existence, but this does not imply that existence is created in the finite substance as a distinct "act of being" (*esse*) added by God to its essence and composing the substance with it.[15]

In other words, the reasoning is open-ended because the word "existence" can be taken either in the *fact* sense or the Thomistic *act* sense. Consequently, the conclusion could mean either that the fact of existing is other than the essence or that the act of existing is other than the essence. Instead of demonstrating the Thomistic sense of existence, the reasoning presupposes it. Used as an approach to Thomistic *esse*, it understandably leads to the stalemate that Gilson describes a few pages later in our purported theologizing text.

In sum, Gilson's insistence that the Thomistic notion of *esse* is not susceptible to demonstration concerns the above Avicennian/Thomistic text. He is not making any absolute claim, namely, that *actus essendi* is philosophically unknowable. Rather, Gilson's words leave the way open for the presentation of judgment as the original philosophical apprehension of *esse*.

So, if one accepts Owens's interpretation of Gilson, and I see no reason not to, in Exodus 3:14, the Christian philosopher has a theological prompt to regard the existence of a thing as a distinct act of the thing, all of which the Christian philosopher can philosophically elaborate *via* the *secunda operatio intellectus*. Now because the *De Ente* text employs *esse* in the *actus essendi* sense, then the text should be essentially a philosophical text working out the implications of judgmentally grasped *esse*. Gilson's disavowal of the text as a metaphysical proof of God would not be *de jure*, or in principle. Given Gilson's remarks on natural reason's access to *actus essendi*, Gilson could not be saying

---

14. Quoted by Gilson, *Elements*, 127.
15. Ibid., 128.

that. Rather, the root of Gilson's disavowal lies in his exaggerated view of Exodus 3:14 as a psychological prerequisite for interpreting a thing's existence as a unique act of the thing. Despite his magisterial presentation of the judgmental grasp of existence in the sixth chapter of *Being and Some Philosophers*, Gilson may have felt it to be inadequate and himself incapable of improving it. Hence, to give others some sense of Aquinas's understanding of *esse*, he, perfectly within his rights, weighed the theological prompt quite heavily.

As I think is evident from my previous chapter, setting up judgment so that it *respicit esse rei* requires some finesse. The cognitional existence that real things can have simultaneously in sensation can go unnoticed and cause us to miss the existential multiplicity for things. Hence, Gilson is also perfectly within his rights to let his weighing impact his understanding of the *De Ente* text. Understood as a psychological requirement for metaphysics, theology is still a requirement. Hence, the required psychological reference to theology could lead one, as it did Gilson, to say that the essence/existence distinction is not given in sensation "even in a wide sense" at least as far as Gilson could tell. Consequently, the distinction could not be used in a Thomistic *via*, as far as Gilson could attempt a philosophical commentary. Weighing so heavily the psychological reference to theology could also lead one to say: "To the best of our knowledge, Thomas Aquinas has never attempted [a metaphysical] demonstration. Nor does one see how it could be done."[16] The same would make sense of "Le *De ente et essentia* ne contient aucune preuve de l'existence de Dieu."[17] I understand Gilson to mean that there is no proof for God in the *De Ente* that he feels confident to be able to explain philosophically to philosophers.

Gilson is also within his rights to interpret Aquinas in the same fashion. Hence for Gilson, Aquinas could have felt that his work in theology never permitted him to present the philosophical case for *esse*. Because of commitments to theological tasks, Aquinas left the philosophical elaboration of the judgmental grasp of *esse* in abeyance. That omission would render the *De Ente* text inconclusive, practically speaking. The lack of conclusive standing would also explain Gilson's observations of the text's absence in Thomistic contexts devoted to proving God.

16. Gilson, *Christian Philosophy of St. Thomas*, 82.
17. Gilson, *Le Thomisme*, 97n85.

Yet, others can feel free to disagree. Psychological requirements can become unnecessary. The detective who solves a case on the basis of a hunch, ends up with a body of evidence that has a life of its own so that in court the evidence will convince others who never shared the hunch of the detective. Why cannot this dynamic also be true of the development of Aquinas's metaphysical ideas? The burden will be to see if judgment's grasp of *actus essendi* can be provided sufficient philosophical luster to so stand on its own that even those philosophers of good will who do not share the theological prompt can be made to understand the thesis. Because of what I said in chapter 2, I am obviously of this opinion, and I also am of the opinion that such was also Aquinas's mind.

That last remark brings me into confrontation with Gilson's opening observations on the *De Ente* text. First, the text and its parallel passages never occur in a context of proving God's existence. It is difficult to understand why Gilson found this observation so persuasive, as in *Elements of Christian Philosophy*, Gilson himself admits that utilization of proofs for God in varied contexts is not foreign to the works of Aquinas.[18] Hence, absent the use of other reasons, Gilson's first observation is interesting but indecisive. Second, Gilson notes that when Aquinas *ex professo* sets out to prove God, Aquinas never includes the *De Ente* reasoning. Yet, again absent other reasons, the possibility remains that the *De Ente* thinking is present implicitly in the *viae*. As I will argue in part 2, the *viae* are open to interpretation by the *De Ente* text. Nothing in the wording of the *viae* excludes the *De Ente* reasoning. Further, as I will explain more fully, Aquinas has definite views about where and when the philosopher proves God's existence. The philosopher does this in metaphysics. Also, Aquinas has definite views about metaphysics. It is a *scientia* with an intelligible subject matter containing causal implications. The key note in Aquinas's understanding of the subject matter is *esse*. Should not Aquinas's views on how and where God falls in philosophy have some bearing on how to understand Aquinas's God proofs? Is it plausible to think that when Aquinas sets out to show how natural reason proves God's existence,

---

18. "Lastly, what serves as proof of the existence of God in one of Aquinas's works can very well become a proof of one of His attributes in another one. To quote only one striking instance, the admirable Disputed Question *De Potentia*, q. 3, a. 5, establishes that there can be nothing that is not created by God. Obviously, to prove such a conclusion is tantamount to proving that there is a God." Gilson, *Elements*, 56.

he sets aside these other positions? I do not think so. And thus a reader of Aquinas not only can read the *viae* according to the *De Ente* text, but ought to do so.[19]

Gilson's opening observations should not have so troubled him to the point that he was compelled to somehow construe the *De Ente* reasoning as nonprobative, at least practically speaking. In sum, my interpretation of Gilson on the *De Ente* is that because *esse* is naturally grasped through judgment, then the reasoning is essentially philosophical. Yet, as the existential interpretation of judgment is psychologically so heavily dependent upon a theological prompt, an understandable reservation exists about the probity of the argument with unbelievers. That background explains, for Gilson, Aquinas's apparent reluctance to give the *De Ente* reasoning as a God proof.

If I understand him, Armand Maurer, a well-known protégé of Gilson, sees Gilson's position more starkly. Throughout the various editions of his translation of the *De Ente*, Maurer continues Gilson's opinion that the *De Ente* text is not a God proof. Maurer reiterates the reasons of Gilson that I have already considered. Unfortunately, Maurer makes no mention of Gilson's insistence that judgment is natural reason's access to *actus essendi*. That omission is singularly unfortunate. It leaves the reader with the definite impression that Gilson has theologized other passages in addition to the *De Ente* text. The Exodus 3:14 revelation is the logical, rather than the psychological, *sine qua non* of Thomistic philosophy. As Maurer tells the tale, minus the judgmental grasp of *esse*, the reader is genuinely at a loss regarding the philosophical development of the fourth chapter of *De Ente*.

Recently, Maurer further elaborated his interpretation of Gilson's rejection of the *De Ente* text.[20] Maurer notes that Gilson labels the proofs of the essence/*actus essendi* distinction as "dialectical." Gilson's remarks occur in his *Introduction à la philosophie chrétienne*. By "dialectical" Gilson appears to mean: to begin with "nominal definitions."[21] This short book is signifi-

---

19. On metaphysics as the division that proves God, see chapter 6.

20. Armand Maurer, "Dialectic in the *De Ente et Essentia* of St. Thomas Aquinas," in *Mélanges offerts au Père L. E. Boyle à l'occasion de son 75e anniversaire*, ed. J. Hamesse (Louvain-le-Neuve: F.I.D.E.M. Publications, 1998), 573–83.

21. "The facility enjoyed by the dialectician is his greatest danger. It is always possible to begin with nominal definitions of being, substance, and cause in order to deduce their consequences with the help of the first principle." Gilson, *Christian Philosophy of St. Thomas*, 68.

cant for its relentless consideration of *actus essendi*, and Maurer has my esteem for making it available to English-speaking readers. The work does not mention judgment. But the book does occur between other works by Gilson that continue to mention judgment and its grasp of *actus essendi*. In fact, in his translator's introduction, Maurer mentions that *Christian Philosophy* is "*Elements* in tabloids."[22] It is true that Gilson asks how Aquinas justifies the essence/*actus essendi* distinction and answers his questions with "No reply is forthcoming."[23] But it is plain here that the issue is one of providing a demonstration or proof. Just as the phoenix argument is not a proof because *esse* could be taken either as fact or act, other "arguments" are affected by a similar ambiguity. To dispel that ambiguity in Aquinas's texts, the notion of pure being (*ipsum purum esse*) must be taken for granted and this is "only because, for the theologian, it is the proper name of God. To think pure *esse* is to think God."[24] We have already heard Gilson make this point in *Elements* in which, I would remind my reader, Gilson affirms natural reason's access to *esse* through judgment. Hence, in my opinion, when Gilson calls the reasoning "dialectical," he is not intending to preempt the essentially philosophical character of the reasoning. The reasoning is essentially philosophical because it relies on the resources of judgment. But it is in fact dialectical because the judgmental grasp of *esse* relies so heavily on a theological prompt. Absent that prompt, Aquinas's definition of *esse* as *actus essendi* would strike a philosopher as a "nominal" definition.

But Maurer presents Gilson as understanding the phoenix argument to be dialectical *essentially*. If I understand Maurer, Maurer gives three reasons for this claim. First, "Thomas's purpose in explaining what the terms being and essence mean, how they are found in the different orders of things, and how they are related to logical notions, can be achieved without considering beings in their real existence. The reasoning to the distinction between essence and existence and to the existence of God can be understood as dialectical, subserving the stated purpose of the treatise."[25] For Maurer, Aquinas's *De Ente* describes a mental landscape. It describes how the notions of being and essence break down in the mind. But because the mental breakdown

22. Ibid., xi.
23. Ibid., 62.
24. Ibid., 60.
25. Maurer, "Dialectic in the *De Ente*," 581.

could be different from the real breakdown, everything is dialectical, or provisional. Aquinas could not be claiming to know with certitude the truth of things.

Second, turning to the phoenix argument, Maurer remarks:

> The reasoning in chapter 4 is likewise dialectical, beginning with the premise: <<Now every essence or quiddity can be understood without knowing anything about its existence.>> This is derived from the Aristotelian logical dictum that knowing what a thing is is different from knowing that it is; that the answer to the question what a thing is differs from the answer to the question that it is. On this logical dictum depends Thomas's whole argumentation for the distinction between essence and existence in creatures and for the existence of God as pure *esse*; and it ensures that the whole argument is dialectical.[26]

In other words, again, just because the mind asks particular questions is no guarantee that there is a corresponding distinction in reality.

Third, jumping to the fifth chapter of the *De Ente*, Maurer cites a text that he claims presents a dialectical argument for the distinction between essence and existence. Here is Maurer's translation of the text: "Everything in a genus must have a quiddity that is other than existence. This is because the quiddity or nature of a genus or species does not differ, as regards the notion of the nature, in the individuals in the genus or species, whereas different individuals have difference [*sic*] existences."[27] Maurer's comment is: "The argument is dialectical, for it is based on the logical notions of genus and species—a common source of dialectical reasoning."[28]

None of these reasons, in my opinion, withstand scrutiny. First, by Aquinas's very first words in the *De Ente*, a reader knows that his purpose is more than just explaining the meaning of terms. Aquinas's opening remark that a small error in the beginning is a large one in the end makes clear that he is preoccupied with truth. Any subsequent descriptions of meanings must be taken as descriptions of *true* meanings. Moreover, in his *Sentences* commentary Aquinas is already on record with a definite idea of truth. Truth is the adequation of the intellect to the thing. More particularly, truth is achieved by the intellect conforming itself to the *esse* of the thing and so lies in the

26. Ibid., 582–83.
27. Ibid., 582n26.
28. Ibid., 583.

intellect's second operation.[29] Hence, with the maintaining of the intellect in truth as Aquinas's purpose in the *De Ente*, I would not say that Aquinas could achieve his purpose "without considering things in their real existence."

Also dialectical reasoning begins from only probable premises. The reason is that the dialectician deals with beings of reason that are extrinsic to reality.[30] In contrast, the philosopher deals with things and his demonstrations achieve certitude. How, then, could Aquinas be expressly intending to avoid even a slight initial error and also be proceeding dialectically? Initiating the *De Ente* with something only probably true does not accord with the author's purpose of avoiding a slight error so as to avoid a larger one in the end.

What of Maurer's observation that the phoenix argument is based on the logical dictum that knowing what a thing is is different from knowing that it is "thus ensuring that the whole argument is dialectical"? Maurer's observation comes too fast. Before flying to the logical works, should not one first try to interpret the remark that one can know what a phoenix is and not know that a phoenix exists within its own context of the *De Ente*? I think such a move is only fair. When a reader does study the remark's larger context, the reader is brought back to the intellect's absolute consideration of essence that *abstrahit ad quodlibet esse*. Such a consideration initially takes in not only the nature's *esse in anima* but also the nature's *esse in singularibus*. Further, as abstracting from all *esse*, the absolutely considered nature is not yet even an *ens rationis*, or a second intention. Hence, neither in its beginning nor in its end is absolute consideration dialectical. Rather, the intellect's apprehension of the cold hard facts drives the implications. In my opinion, within the ambit of the *De Ente*, the phoenix argument makes no appeal to what may be only the idiosyncratic questioning of the mind. Rather, it makes better interpretive sense to regard the argument as appealing to the previous delineation of absolute consideration with its presumption of Aquinas's realist epistemology.

Finally, is Maurer's cited text from the fifth chapter of *De Ente* "based on the logical notions of genus and species—a common source of dialectical reasoning"? A rereading of the text fails to confirm a basis in logic. The given

---

29. For the texts, see my "Transcendental Thomism and *De Veritate* I, 9," in *Thomistic Papers VI*, ed. Knasas (Houston, Tex.: Center for Thomistic Studies, 1994), 229–50.

30. "But the dialectician proceeds to consider [the common accidents of real being] from the conceptions of reason, which are extrinsic to reality [*extranea a natura rerum*]." *In IV Meta.*, l. 4, n. 574 (trans. Rowan, 212).

reason for the assertion of the first line is "because the quiddity or nature of a genus or species does not differ, as regards the notion of the nature." In other words, the basis is not logical intentions, *viz.*, the genus as genus or species as species. By mentioning "the nature of a genus" Aquinas is not talking about what a genus is. Rather, Aquinas is referring to the absolutely considered nature that when given an *esse in anima* can be either a genus or a species. This "notion of the nature" is what is the same in individuals that are in the genus or species. Aquinas's description of absolute consideration of a nature has the nature existing not only in the soul but also *in singularibus*. Though Maurer's cited text is talking about something in logic, *viz.*, things in a genus or species, the text is not speaking about these things based on "logical" terms.

The Character of the Distinction

Another great debate exists among Thomists. The issue is the nature of the distinction between the thing and its *esse* at point (1) of the *De Ente* text. In other words, is the distinction a real distinction or a conceptual distinction? Earlier I noted that at *SCG* II.54 Aquinas compares the substance/*esse* composition to the matter/form composition such that in a being there is at least these two compositions. So, Aquinas intends that the first composition involves real distinction like the second.[31] The philosophical evidence for a real distinction between matter and form is found in the matter's independence in reality from any one form. While matter is always found with some form, matter does not have to be found with some one form.

The previous general description of absolute consideration provides an understanding of what is meant by a conceptual distinction. So given the multiplicity of a European and an African, we can see that what we mean by human does not also involve the notions of some one complexion. That a real distinction exists between human nature and a complexion would be known by supplementing absolute consideration with the mentioned methodology. So, do we ever find human nature as it is in Socrates apart from his white complexion? We do when we find Socrates tanned.

With these types of distinctions in mind, there is the possibility that absolute consideration establishes only a conceptual distinction between items

---

31. The references can be found collected in Owens, *Elementary Christian Metaphysics*, 106n13.

that are also really distinct but for other reasons. Is this possibility true in respect to the substance/*esse* distinction used in the *De Ente* text?

Aquinas does assert that our ability to know what a man and a phoenix are and not know whether they have *esse* in reality establishes that *esse* is other (*aliud*) than essence. At this point, is this otherness a real otherness or a conceptual otherness? From the perspective of my interpretation of the *duplex operatio*, the answer is that at this point the otherness is just conceptual. Judgment does not tell us whether as composed with the thing the *esse* actuates the thing by remaining really distinct from it or by merging with it. Phenomenologically one can observe that as judgment retreats to the thing as real, judgment definitely gets to a point different from the point it began, but judgment cannot tell if the different point is marked by a real distinction from the other point. In the rebounding of our attention from the existence-neutral thing to its *esse*, we cannot tell if the *esse* actuates the thing by shading into it or by not doing so. Both are possibilities for the *esse* distinctly grasped in judgment. Somewhat similarly, as you look from your hand to your arm, can you tell exactly where your hand leaves off and where your arm begins? But you have no doubt that they are different. Because the thing is of itself existence-neutral, *esse* could actuate the thing in either of these ways. Both modes of actuation are possibilities as far as what is revealed to the judgmental eye of the intellect. In other words, the rebounding activity of judgment is too fast for us to discern accurately the nature of the *de facto* border between the thing and its *esse*.[32]

To appreciate what I am saying, it is crucial that one's attention stay on what is presented by the data. In other words, I am not speaking about the situation in which the mind goes on to form expressions of what it sees in the data. As I mentioned earlier when I cited *SCG* I.53, these expressions are more separate and discrete than the objects seen in the data. If the twofold operation is conducted on these intellectual expressions, then their separateness and discreteness could lead one to conclude too quickly to a real distinction.

---

32. In his "Aquinas's Real Distinction and Some Interpretations," *The New Scholasticism* 62, no. 1 (1988), Walter Patt understands the first stage's *intellectus essentiae* argument to establish a "real" (27) difference between essence and existence. In the context of *ens* existing outside and *ens* existing inside the mind, Patt describes the difference thus: "Perhaps one may put it this way: the thing insofar as it is in the content of its proper concept is a universal; the thing insofar as it has the perfection of existence is an actual singular being" (5). One can admit this real distinction but insist that the absolutely considered essence abstracts from every *esse*, even *esse in anima*. Also, Patt's real distinction is between real being and mental being. Aquinas is striving for a real distinction within real being.

Before going on, I want to try and to clarify this second possibility for *esse*: that when composed with the thing, the *esse* actuates the thing by merging with it. I want to emphasize that this possibility does not mean a retreat from the point that the absolute consideration of a thing shows the thing to be of itself existence-neutral. This point is not overcome even if the actuating *esse* is considered to be really merged with the thing. In other words, the thing and the *esse* remain different in the existent, even though the difference may not include a real distinction between the two. Other cases of difference without real distinction exist. Consider the distinction between rational and animal. What we mean by one and what we mean by the other is certainly different. Otherwise every animal would be rational. While holding on to this difference, we nevertheless assert their merging in the existing individual that is Tom. For we say, "Tom is rational" and "Tom is an animal." Hence, their difference does not mean that they are also really distinct. And not being really distinct does not mean that they are the same. In an existent you can have difference without real distinction, and without real distinction you can have difference.[33]

Finally, the phenomenological situation so far suffices to speak of the thing as a subject and the real existence as an attribute. The two do not appear like the two ends of a stick. There too we have difference without real distinction. But it is a difference of equals. With the thing and existence the difference is marked by an inequality. Somewhat similarly we have inequality in the mentioned visual difference between the hand and the arm.

So have we come to a logical dead end? It is worth our while to try to answer this question on our own. Obviously, Aquinas does not leave us in this situation of difference without real distinction. Somehow he goes further. Given what we know so far, can we see how he would do it?

---

33. In fact, Aquinas presents the distinction between a thing and its *esse*, as known by the two operations, just this way. There is an analogy between the way a thing is distinct from its *esse* and the way animal is distinct from rational: "An accident is here called that which is not of the meaning of something [*accidens dicitur hic quod non est de intellectu alicujus*], just as rational is said to happen to animal, and so [*esse*] happens to every created quiddity, because it is not of the meaning of some quiddity; for humanity is able to be understood, and nevertheless it is able to be doubted whether a man has being [*habeat esse*]." *In I Sent.*, d. 8, *expositio primae partis textus* (ed. Mandonnet, 1:209). Such a situation between the thing and its *esse* is what is being envisaged by the second alternative. Though the situation as revealed by the *duplex operatio* does not exclude in the existent that the thing and its *esse* are not only different but also really distinct, the situation does not reveal that to be the case.

Is not the openness of the material to further thought found in the stratification of the thing and its existence? As really different, they are not really equal. They are stratified respectively as subject and attribute. This situation is ripe for causal reasoning. An attribute is *ipso facto* dependent, at least upon its subject as material cause. But as a material cause, the subject lacks the actuality to account for the characterizing attribute. This insight shifts the full explanation of the attribute either to the subject in some other respect, or to another subject.

Of these two alternatives, only the second will fit *esse*. Subjects that account for their attributes are in some other respect already in act. For example, I can move myself locally because one leg is actually in a place while the other leg is moving to a place. The problem with applying this model to the subject and its *esse* is that we know that apart from the *esse* the subject is not at all actual. As the phenomenological analysis showed, judgment proceeded from the subject as existence-neutral. As existence-neutral, the subject possesses no resources to be in some other respect the cause of *esse*.

What then is the identity of this something else that completes the explanation of the attribute of *esse*? As I explained at the end of chapter 2, the something else must be a thing whose *esse* is intellectually included in it. Another thing like the first will not do. As the second thing of itself is existence-neutral, it cannot be the direct cause of *esse* in the first thing.

Also, accepting the fantasy that the second thing can be a cause of the *esse* of the first only generates an unacceptable infinite regress. In that regress each thing would be asking for a cause of its *esse* that no other thing in the regress would be able to be. One would be trying to explain the unexplained by more of the unexplained.

If this reasoning correctly brings out implications in the first stage, how does the reasoning reach the real distinction? If I am correct, then somehow that distinction must be a further implication lurking in the reasoning. So, does knowing that *esse* has its cause in something that is *esse* help us? Let us look at the two possibilities again but now in the light of subsistent *esse*.

In the light of the second intellectual operation, the first possibility was that *esse* actuates the thing by remaining really distinct from the thing. The second possibility was that *esse* actuates the thing by merging with the thing. Are both possibilities equally plausible in light of *esse* being caused by subsistent being? As it appears to me looking at the available data, the answer lies in *esse* as the proper effect of subsistent *esse*. True, *esse* is not subsistent *esse*'s only effect. For in causing *esse* subsistent *esse* causes also the thing to which the *esse* belongs. But *esse* is subsistent *esse*'s proper effect. To remain that proper effect, *esse* must also remain distinct from the thing that it actuates. In other words, before *esse* actuates the thing, the *esse* has to be subsistent *esse*'s real and proper effect. Hence, when it goes on to actuate the thing, *esse* will do so as really distinct from the thing. Coming to know the first cause of *esse* requires adjusting our understanding of the *esse* grasped by judgment. That cause needs its proper effect, and only by understanding *esse* as really distinct do we have a metaphysical viewpoint that provides that item. In other words, the point is that once one has subsistent *esse* in reality, the question becomes: how will *esse* be communicated? Having subsistent *esse* in reality leaves only two possibilities, namely, (1) *esse* as a nature or (2) *esse* as a really distinct act of a nature. The third possibility of *esse de facto* merged with a nature no longer applies.

Other Opinions

John Wippel and Scott MacDonald argue that Aquinas secured knowledge of the real distinction in the paragraph preceding the *De Ente* reasoning. Hence, the *De Ente* reasoning would be starting without any question about a real distinction. To remove any ambiguity and so to preserve the demonstrative character of the *De Ente* text, I am required to engage in a critical discussion of their arguments.

In his "Aquinas' Route to the Real Distinction: A Note on *De Ente et Essentia*," John Wippel sees Aquinas as establishing the real distinction in the paragraph preceding the argument for *esse subsistens*. Wippel refers to this paragraph as the "second stage." In other words, Aquinas immediately uses the distinction made by the *duplex operatio intellectus* to argue the real distinction. According to Wippel, in this earlier reasoning, Aquinas shows from a merely hypothetical consideration of a thing whose meaning includes its existence that in all other things essence and existence really differ.[34]

I find four problems with Wippel's interpretation. First, the interpre-

---

34. John Wippel, "Aquinas' Route to the Real Distinction," *The Thomist* 43, no. 2 (1979): 289. Kerr, *Aquinas's Way to God*, 28–29, follows Wippel's interpretation. Also, Edward Feser argues similarly for the real distinction between essence and existence, *Five Proofs of the Existence of God* (San Francisco, Calif.: Ignatius Press, 2017), 120.

tation does not satisfy Wippel's own first objection to it. Wippel asks why Aquinas goes on to argue for a thing whose essence is its existence, *esse tantum*, if it is not required to establish real otherness of essence and existence in all else? Wippel gives two replies.[35] First, Aquinas gives the argument for *esse tantum* for the sake of completeness. But Wippel must show that Aquinas is always so neat and tidy. The reasoning looks sufficiently complete without the argument for *esse tantum*. Perhaps sensing the weakness of his first reply, Wippel gives another: the proof for *esse tantum* shows that creatures receive their *esse* from God and so are known to be related to that *esse* as potency to act. But the judgmental grasp of *esse* suffices to know *esse* as act. Judgment composes the *esse* with what is understood as existence-neutral.

My second problem is that the second-stage reasoning is logically geared to prove only a conceptual, or intellectual, distinction. In other words, if a conceptual identity between essence and existence destroys a multiplicity of instances, then a conceptual distinction will save a multiplicity of instances.[36] In Wippel's favor, the conclusion of the second stage uses the same *aliud* terminology that Aquinas uses when he reaches a real distinction at the end of my *De Ente* text. But this observation is not decisive. Aquinas has already used the terminology in lines just preceding Wippel's second stage. There Aquinas famously remarks that we can know what a man or a phoenix is and not know if that exists. Wippel concedes that in those lines, called the *intellectus essentiae* argument, the terminology expresses only a conceptual distinction.[37]

My third problem is that in Aquinas's text, Wippel's second stage is introduced by the thought that essence and existence are distinct in everything unless there is a reality whose essence is its existence because this reality is unique and primary (*una et prima*). Wippel's second stage proves only that *esse subsistens* is unique. For the primacy of *esse subsistens* the reader must continue to the paragraph presenting the causal reasoning for *esse subsistens* as first cause (*prima causa*) of *esse*. The characterization of *esse tantum* as *both* unique and primary suggests that Aquinas's reasoning is not complete after

---

35. Wippel, "Aquinas' Route to the Real Distinction," 293–94.

36. In his "Aquinas' Distinction at *De ente et essentia* 4, 119–123," *Mediaeval Studies* 48 (1986): 282, Joseph Owens agrees that the purpose of the second stage reasoning is *to extend* the conceptual distinction to everything but one thing whose essence is its existence.

37. Ibid., 186n18.

Wippel's second stage. This appreciation of the full extent of the reasoning accords with my above interpretation that knowing the real distinction ties in with knowing that *esse* is the proper effect of *esse subsistens* and that *esse* would not be that proper effect if it were not really distinct from the essence that it actuates.

Fourth, as I will point out in chapter 10, in another early text Aquinas is content to argue immediately from the *intellectus essentiae* to a thing that is its *esse*.[38] Wippel's "second stage" is absent. In this stage Aquinas supposedly concluded to the real distinction from a hypothetical consideration of a thing intelligibly one with its *esse*. Evidently for Aquinas, the causal reasoning of the *De Ente* text does not require a real distinction between a thing and its *esse*.

Yet, in notes 26 and 35 Wippel gives another argument. It is a strong argument. Note 26 cites the first argument at *SCG* II.52 in which the topic is a composition of being (*esse*) and what is (*quod est*) in intellectual substances. The topic obviously is parallel to my *De Ente* selection. In his first argument Aquinas appears to present this conclusion right on the heels of the argument for the unicity of subsistent existence. Wippel would appear to be correct to view the second stage of the *De Ente* as reaching a real composition. Does that impression withstand scrutiny?

The argument begins by maintaining that nothing is added to existence in a subsistent configuration. Aquinas initiates his explanation of this claim by noting that to the *esse* with which we are familiar, something is added only indirectly insofar as the addition is united to the thing whose act is *esse*. Hence, without a thing or a subject, subsistent *esse* cannot undergo addition. Next Aquinas claims that if *esse* as *esse* (*esse inquantum est esse*) is to be diversified, it will be as the act of something. Hence, subsistent existence can only be one. Aquinas applies this to God, whom he earlier argued to be subsistent *esse*. Then, the first argument concludes with two propositions: "Hence, nothing beside Him can be its own being. Of necessity, therefore, in every substance beside Him the substance itself is other than its being" (*Nihil igitur aliud praeter ipsum potest esse suum esse. Oportet igitur in omni substantia quae est praeter ipsum, esse aliud ipsam substantiam et esse eius*).[39] The wording "Of

---

38. *In II Sent.*, d. 1, q. 1, a. 1.
39. *SCG* II.52, *Si enim* (trans. Anderson, 2:153).

necessity, therefore" of the last line suggests a distinction between "not being one's own being" in the first line and being "other than its being" in the second line. Could this be true? The second line is about the real composition in intellectual substances. Could, then, the first line be about just a distinction by the *duplex operatio*?

The argument's mention of how *esse* is diversified by something besides itself had been explained by Aquinas in *SCG* I.26. There the topic is whether God is the *esse formale* of all things. From the context a reader can understand that by *esse formale* Aquinas means an intelligible object, a commonality, spied within each particular *esse* of each particular thing. In the second argument, Aquinas speculates that *esse formale* could be diversified in two ways. The first way is through added differences. The second way is through *esse formale* itself which diversifies itself in light of the different natures to be actuated. Aquinas eliminates the first on the basis that being (*ens*) is not a genus to which differences are added. In the previous chapter, Aquinas noted that the differences added to a genus must be extrinsic to the genus under pain of placing the genus twice in the definition of the species. Aquinas insists, however, that nothing is outside of being. Hence, being cannot be a genus.

The appeal of *SCG* II.52 back to *SCG* I.25–26 is the obvious indication of a close connection between *esse* and *ens*. The basis for the connection lies in the role of *esse* if one is to have something that is more than existence-neutral, in short, more than nothing. In other words, there is nothing outside being because apart from *esse* there is nothing. Hence, *esse inquantum est esse*, or *esse commune*, will not be diversified by differences coming from the outside. Rather, it will diversify itself in light of the thing it will actuate.

What, then, is my point about how *esse qua esse* is diversified? As this common *esse* is spied within individual *esse*s known by judgment, and insofar as judgment provides what is at best an intellectual distinction between the thing and its *esse*, then a conceptual distinction suffices to understand Aquinas's explanation of how *esse* is diversified even if reality includes an instance of *esse* that is subsistent. Again, if an intellectual identity between a thing and its *esse* excludes diversity, then an intellectual distinction permits diversity.

In this light the first argument at *SCG* II.52 is explaining how diversification can or cannot occur in this case or in that. The explanation stays within the ambit of intellectual identity or distinction. If there is an intellectual distinction between things and their *esse*, then *SCG* I.26 explains how the nature of that *esse* can be diversified. If there is an intellectual identity between them, then *SCG* II.52 explains how diversification of *esse* in that configuration is impossible. Only if causal considerations are brought into this scene of diversification does it appear that anything more can be reached. What prompts causal considerations is the intellectual distinction between the thing and its *esse*. We now know that subsistent existence is not just unique but also a cause. As its proper effect, caused *esse* must be really distinct. So the first of the two concluding lines of *SCG* II.52 refers to a situation in which *esse* is intellectually distinct from the thing but perhaps really merged with it in all beings other than subsistent existence. The second of the concluding lines would refer to the real otherness of *esse* in these beings. The second line would be concluding to that real otherness by the causal implication in the intellectual distinction.[40]

So the first argument in *SCG* II.52 can be read in the same way that I have read my selection of *De Ente*, chap. 4. I would repeat this analysis for the second argument, for the second argument also appeals to Aquinas's explanation of how *esse* grasped in judgment and subsequently conceptualized as *esse commune* is diversified. This shows that Aquinas is entertaining simply intellectual distinctions or identifications. Only the introduction of causal considerations lets one jump beyond this context. The prompt for that move is the intellectual distinction. In fact that prompt is so proximate that Aquinas finishes the second argument asserting just the first of the two concluding remarks of the previous argument. Evidently Aquinas regards the reader as able to fill in the rest. This regard is not incongruous if one realizes that Aquinas did not intend *SCG* to be read alone, that is, without a teacher familiar with Aquinas's other writings.[41]

---

40. For Owens's remarks on this first *SCG* argument, see his "Aquinas' Distinction at *De Ente et Essentia*," 286n43.

41. See John F. X. Knasas, "Thomistic Existentialism and the Silence of the *Quinque Viae*," *The Modern Schoolman* 63, no. 3 (1986): 170n38. Aquinas's two arguments for *quod est* and *esse* differing *realiter* at *In de Hebdomadibus*, l. 2, can be read in the same way. The first argument begins from the simplicity of *ipsum esse*. Earlier Aquinas explained that unlike matter and substance, which participate in form and accident, *esse* is too abstract to be so regarded. Also, as most common *ipsum esse* cannot participate in something higher like Socrates participates in man and man in animal. Hence, *esse* itself is simple. From this thought Aquinas concludes that a composite is not its *esse*. He further concludes that the composite and *esse* are other because the *esse* is participated. The first conclusion can be understood as an intellectual distinction, for if intellectual identity between thing and *esse* means simplicity, then compositeness means intellectual distinction. The second conclusion is of the real distinction

In his "The *Esse/Essentia* Argument in Aquinas' *De ente et essentia*," Scott MacDonald, like Wippel, argues that the real distinction is known before the *De Ente* reasoning for subsistent *esse*. He disagrees on how the argument starts. Regarding the earlier lines in which Aquinas famously remarks that we can know what a man or phoenix is and not know if it exists (a paragraph Wippel calls the first stage), MacDonald argues that the logic of the text is not the *intellectus essentiae* argument. Consequently, MacDonald concludes that Aquinas's epistemology of the two operations is not the crucial context for the argument.

Why is the logic different? The answer lies in noting that Aquinas's opening assertion is not logically complete. That opening assertion is: whatever is not of the understanding of the essence comes from without and makes a composition with the essence. To be logically complete the assertion must be changed to (A) "whatever belongs to a thing" and is not part of its essence either comes from without and effects a composition with that essence or (B) "itself constitutes the entire essence."[42] First, (A) is necessary because otherwise you could say that squareness makes a composition with man because squareness is not part of man's essence.[43] There is the further possibility that what belongs to the thing and is not a part of its essence is the essence itself. So it is necessary to add (B) to the opening assertion. In fact, Aquinas later in stage two mentions (B) as a third way in which a subsistent instance of something could be multiplied. MacDonald thinks, however, that it is more tidy logically to include (B) in the opening remark of the first stage.[44]

Hence, the underlying logic of the *De Ente* reasoning as it runs through the first two stages is a process of elimination. The opening gambit is to list

---

consequent upon causal implications in the first conclusion. The second argument concludes to a composition in simples from their determination to a species, while *ipsum esse* does not, as mentioned, participate in something higher. Again the thinking is: if an intellectual identity between thing and *esse* means something not in a determinate species, then being in a determinate species seems to imply intellectual distinction. The reality of the distinction would be a further conclusion. Like Wippel and against Gilson, McInerny, *Praeambula Fidei*, 144–50, interprets this text to produce knowledge of the real distinction without any reference to subsistent *esse* as actual.

42. Scott MacDonald, "The *Esse/Essentia* Argument in Aquinas' *De ente et essentia*," *The Journal of the History of Philosophy* 22, no. 2 (1984): 157.

43. Ibid., 160.

44. "The logical structure of the argument is displayed most straightforwardly if the qualification [Aquinas says "unless perhaps there is something whose quiddity is its very *esse*"] is incorporated into the general principle rather than added to the conclusion" (ibid., 161).

all the possible ways how what is true of a thing, that is, a property, may relate to that thing. The possibilities are threefold: (1) the property is a part of the thing; (2) the property is outside the thing but composed with it; (3) the property is the thing itself. MacDonald admits that he can understand alternative (2) only as the real distinction. Consequently, MacDonald argues that the *intellectus essentiae* reasoning of the first stage eliminates alternative (1) and that the second stage reasoning for the unicity of subsistent being eliminates alternative (3).[45] Hence, we reach the real distinction at the end of stage two. As a second reason for his conclusion, MacDonald admits that he "can see no other way to read Aquinas's second stage conclusion that in everything other than subsistent being, *esse* is other than essence and so an intellectual substance is form and *esse*."[46]

In the remainder of the article and in response to Joseph Owens, MacDonald questions whether Aquinas's epistemology of the *duplex operatio intellectus* is relevant for interpreting the *De Ente* argument. First, MacDonald argues that the epistemological approach would have the argument starting with the concepts of essence and *esse*. By MacDonald's understanding of the underlying logic, however, Aquinas's opening assertion "assumes that some things exist, and so the entire E/E Argument from the first premiss on is concerned with *esse* in things."[47] Earlier MacDonald explained that Aquinas's talk of what belongs to a thing but is not part of its essence indicates that Aquinas is speaking about a property known empirically.[48] Second, because of its empirical starting point, the alternatives mentioned in the general proposition of the underlying logic can only be alternatives about "relations between the *esse* and essence in real things."[49] There is no place in the argument for a conceptual distinction only.

In light of my earlier interpretation, many remarks can be made upon MacDonald's thoughts. The first remark that comes to mind is his impoverished view of *esse*. Instead of keeping *esse* the act by which the thing is a

---

45. Ibid., 166.
46. Ibid., 167.
47. Ibid., 169–70. For Owens's comment, see his "Aquinas' Distinction at *De Ente et Essentia*," 277n28.
48. "If the argument assumes the knowledge that F belongs to x, and if the particular F in question is not an essential characteristic of the x in question, then the argument must assume some empirical knowledge." MacDonald, "The *Esse/Essentia* Argument," 165.
49. Ibid., 170.

fact, MacDonald repeatedly equates *esse* with the fact of the thing. He says, "Aquinas must assume the knowledge that *esse* in fact belongs to things; that is, that some things exist."[50] Also, "[Aquinas's] strategy assumes that we have knowledge of the fact that things exist, and a general principle tells us what the possibilities are."[51] MacDonald seems oblivious to contradicting his other descriptions of *esse* as a property and as "belonging" to a thing. Does a fact "belong" to a thing? In Aquinas's text the *actus* sense of *esse* appears to be assumed throughout. That is why Aquinas can seamlessly go on in my *De Ente* text to compare *esse* to the accidents of risibility in man and to light in the air. But if the technical *actus* sense of *esse* is involved in the *De Ente* reasoning should not the resources of the *secunda operatio* be involved as well? As far as I know, judgment is the only *ex professo* way admitted by Aquinas that the philosopher gains access to *esse*. In sum, MacDonald's allusions to the fact sense of *esse* show that he is reading the argument with an insensitivity to the refined nature of its terms.[52]

MacDonald is correct to stress that Aquinas's thinking begins from existing things. But he is wrong to think that such a starting point excludes the *duplex operatio* and conceptual distinctions. In fact in my phenomenological analysis, the beginning data is richer than really existing things. As noted, the data pool also includes those things cognitionally existing in a current act of sensation. The first datum is immediately known in sensation, the second is immediately known in a reflection upon current sensation. One could correctly refer to the data as facts. But Aquinas's talk of *esse* shows that these facts have already been run through the *duplex operatio*. Having spotted something the same in these facts, we appreciate each fact as a composite of (1) the something the same and (2) some peculiarity. In our appreciation, each fact goes from glossy to grainy, to borrow terminology from photography. Likewise, the hot and cold coffee are both facts. But if one begins speaking about the hot temperature as belonging to the coffee, then this way of speaking indicates an analysis of the facts in which the coffee has already been distinguished from the temperatures. Finally, as I also pointed out, the use of the

---

50. Ibid., 165.

51. Ibid., 170. Patt, "Aquinas's Real Distinction," 7n21, also seems to understand *esse* in terms of facticity: "As the example of the phoenix shows, this indifference of a definition with respect to facticity is also meant in the *De ente* passage."

52. Also see Owens, "Aquinas's Distinction," 275, on the need for the *duplex operatio*.

duplex operatio on the existential multiplicity does not automatically give one a real distinction between thing and *esse*. MacDonald's insistence that if the *De Ente* reasoning begins with reality and not concepts, then the distinctions that it entertains must be real distinctions does not automatically follow.

Also, if I am correct about the central presence of the *duplex operatio*, I think that I am also correct to say that it runs havoc with MacDonald's underlying logic of the *De Ente* reasoning. MacDonald's underlying logic presumes that one and the same thing can be considered in three possible relations to its *esse*: (A) a thing's *esse* is part of its essence; (B) a thing's *esse* comes to its essence and is composed with it; (C) a thing's *esse* is itself the thing's entire essence. Hence, if not A, then C, if not C, then B. But I would insist that once one has distinguished *esse* from the thing by the *intellectus essendi* argument, it simply makes no sense to speak of his alternative C, namely, the *same* thing as now identical with its *esse*. In fact, Aquinas's own text appears to bring up McDonald's alternative (C) as another and different thing than Aquinas has been considering in (A): "Nisi forte sit aliqua res cuius quiditas sit ipsum suum esse."[53] For MacDonald this would have to be translated as something like, "unless the being of the thing that we have been considering is its quiddity."

Finally, *contra* McDonald, there is another way to read Aquinas's second-stage conclusion that in everything other than subsistent *esse*, *esse* is other than essence and so an intellectual substance is form and *esse*. As I referenced Owens, the purpose of the second-stage reasoning is to extend the conceptual distinction to everything but one thing whose essence is its existence.[54]

Efficient Causality

Another issue relates to Aquinas's mention of efficient causality in the *De Ente* reasoning. Lawrence Dewan argues that Aquinas cannot assert it without also asserting a real distinction between the thing and its *esse*. John Cahalan argues that the reasoning presupposes efficient causality and does not conclude to it. Finally, some readers wonder how other Thomistic texts assert-

---

53. Aquinas, *Opera Omnia*, ed. Fratrum Praedicatorum (Rome: Editori di San Tommaso, 1976), 43:376.103–4.

54. For another Owens remark on MacDonald's inability to read in another way the conclusion to stage two, see Owens, "Aquinas's Distinction," 284.

ing a causality of *esse* by form are compatible with the first causal alternative mentioned in step (2) of my *De Ente* text. Again, my interpretation of the *De Ente* reasoning requires a response to these views.

In his article, "Saint Thomas, Joseph Owens, and the Real Distinction between Being and Essence," Lawrence Dewan has also ventured an interpretation of our text. For two reasons Dewan questions if the *intellectus essendi* reasoning (Wippel's mentioned first stage) is providing simply a conceptual distinction.[55] At the least it must be providing "a real distinction confusedly known."[56] Dewan's first reason is that a prior lack of a real distinction debilitates Aquinas's later causal reasoning for subsistent existence:

> The precise root of need for a cause, whether intrinsic or extrinsic, is the reality of the distinction between the factors. Only if one falls short of *per se* unity is a cause introducible.... "cause" in any real sense cannot enter the picture without a real lack of *per se* unity between a thing and its *esse*. Thus, it seems that a knowledge of real distinction must be at the starting-point of the causal reasoning.[57]

Dewan continues by noting that the thing is a potency and *esse* is its act, hence, they must be really other:

> If we have grounds, in things, for distinguishing between the existence of a thing (the existence of a caused thing does not belong to it "of itself") and the thing itself (the thing itself is an "itself," a domain of *per se* unity), then the thing has the ontological status of a potency, and this is to be "really other" than *esse*, in the only way "really other" can be said of items in the ontological analysis of one existent.

Dewan admits that our awareness of the thing as caused is the "solid background" for the *intellectus essentiae* argument. This solid background "involves the experience of generable and corruptible, and so caused, substances."[58]

In comment, as I have argued, the "solid background" for stage one is Aquinas's epistemology of the *duplex operatio*. In that context, the appearance of the thing as an absolute passive potency for *esse* is precisely the problem for asserting the real distinction. Such a status for the thing allows the *esse*

---

55. Lawrence Dewan, "Saint Thomas, Joseph Owens, and the Real Distinction between Being and Essence," *The Modern Schoolman* 61, no. 3 (1984): 147.
56. Ibid., 149.
57. Ibid., 151. Kerr, *Aquinas's Way to God*, 114, shares Dewan's misgivings.
58. Ibid., 153.

to actuate the thing either by merging with it or by remaining really distinct. The judgmental rebound is incapable of discerning the nature of the borderline between the two when the *esse* is actuating the thing. Unfortunately, not every potency with which the mind is acquainted means a real distinction.[59]

Also, it is doubtful that an acquaintance simply with the generable and the corruptible is the proto-introduction to the thing/*esse* distinction rather than simply to the matter/form distinction. In the latter context, the "existence of the thing" will be second-order talk for a matter/form composition.[60] This understanding of the thing's existence hardly makes an approach to what Aquinas's means by *esse*. What is true is that after judgment has acquainted us with the thing's existence in the *esse* sense, then we can mentally experiment with it and understand that changeable things, a multiplicity of things, and a gradation of things are all sure signs of the distinction. None of these facts themselves would need to be run through the intellect's two operations. But again, these experiments presuppose an acquaintance with *esse* through the *secunda operatio*.

Second, Dewan argues that not only does the causal reasoning of my *De*

---

59. For Owens's comment on objection one, see his "Being and Natures in Aquinas," *The Modern Schoolman* 48 (1986): 165.

60. For example, "The continued existence of Tibbles consists in there being this individualized life in a continuously changing parcel of matter." Peter Geach, *Three Philosophers* (Oxford: Basil Blackwell, 1961), 83. Also, "Similarly, there is no such thing as a thing's *just* going on existing; when we speak of this, we must always really be referring to some form or nature, X, such that for that thing to go on existing is for it to go on being X" (ibid., 91). Also Davies, "Aquinas, God, and Being," 511: "On Aquinas's account, the existence of Thor is reportable by saying what Thor is.... To exist is to be or to have form." Finally, "With respect to material things, existence means the actual composition of the components of the essence. 'Man exists' means that the substantial form and prime matter are actually composed. This actuality is not another essential principle; it is not a tertium quid composed of the principles. It is the actual composition of the essential principles, the actuality of that which is a man." Ralph M. McInerny, *Being and Predication* (Washington, D.C.: The Catholic University of America Press, 1986), 212. Also, "but for the act which is form actually to be in matter is an act other than the act the form is. This absolutely fundamental actuality is what Thomas means by *esse*." Ralph M. McInerny, *A History of Western Philosophy* (Notre Dame, Ind.: University of Notre Dame Press, 1970), 2:328. On *esse* as a *sui generis actus* in itself, see above chapter 2, note 6. My disagreement is not to say that form is not a principle of being, *principium essendi*. In *SCG* II.54 Aquinas explains that the form is such as the *complementum* of the substance whose act is *esse*. I take this to mean that form causes being in so much as it establishes the potency that will be made a being (*ens*) by *esse*. My reason is that Aquinas's words can be understood in the context of my phenomenology of the two intellectual operations. So my disagreement is to insist that *esse*-talk should be kept first-order talk. Hence, Aquinas can say, "The second operation has to do with a thing's being [*esse*], which results from the union of the principles of a thing in composite substances." Aquinas, *In de Trin.*, q. 5, a. 3, co. (trans. Maurer, 28).

Ente text presuppose the real distinction, the just previous reasoning for the unicity of a thing that is its *esse* also presupposes it.

My contention is that one can arrive at this conclusion only by premising a real distinction. One sees this need to premise real distinction when one considers the nature of *esse* as entering into the premises. *Esse* must be dealt with in the premises as something in itself common, and as requiring a certain situation of plurification. This does not mean that *esse* is being treated exactly like substantial form, since *esse*'s way of being common is not the same. However, the two are comparable. I suggest that to posit *esse* as somehow really common, one must distinguish it from its subject really.[61]

I understand Dewan's second argument to be the following. Aquinas's argument for the uniqueness of something that is *esse* uses a common conception of *esse*. This common conception could not be fruitful in the argument unless it was based upon a really distinct *actus* in the things. In other words, just as specific and generic common natures like rational and animal are based upon substantial form and matter respectively,[62] so the common nature of *esse* must be based upon another real aspect of things.

But the *esse* upon which the common notion of *esse* is based is judgmentally grasped. Judgment's grasp of *esse* is sufficiently distinct to present particular *esses* that will then serve as the data in which the common notion is reached. As noted, however, judgment does not reveal the nature of the borderline between *esse* and the thing. So having a common nature of *esse* is not a decisive indication of a real distinction between a thing and its *esse*.[63]

John Cahalan's remarks on the *De Ente* pertain to what I have numbered points (1) to (5) of my *De Ente* text. Cahalan's remarks have this focus because he is analyzing Joseph Owens's earlier argued thesis that the causal proposition is a demonstrated proposition.[64] According to Owens, Aquinas's *De*

61. Dewan, "Saint Thomas, Joseph Owens," 153.

62. "From this it is clear why genus, species, and difference are related proportionately [*se habent proportionaliter*] to matter, form, and composite in nature, though they are not identical [*non sint idem*] with them. A genus is not matter, but it is taken from matter as designating the whole; and a difference is not form, but it is taken from the form as designating the whole." Aquinas, *On Being and Essence* (trans. Maurer, 41).

63. For Owens, see "Being and Natures in Aquinas," 166–67.

64. Joseph Owens, "The Causal Proposition—Principle or Conclusion?," *The Modern Schoolman*, 32, nos. 3–4 (1955): 257–70 and 323–39. This reference is to the second and third installments of a much longer article.

Ente reasoning shows this to be the case. Cahalan's reflections are contained in two simultaneously published articles that bracket Owens's reply to Cahalan's first article.

Cahalan's central claim is that any attempt to prove efficient causality involves a preceding *per se* claim of efficiency. Otherwise, according to Cahalan, one is concluding to a type of causality not involved in the premises.[65] But if by "efficient causality" one means "the efficient causality of some other thing than the one about whose *esse* one is speaking," then I do not see a problem. In that sense, efficient causality is demonstrated from the absolute priority of *esse* to its subject. In light of that priority the subject is not actual in some other respect, and so there is no possibility of the subject giving a full account of its *esse*.[66]

But as I also noted, step (3) of my *De Ente* text opened with a more general claim about efficient causality. That claim is contained in Aquinas's words that "everything that belongs to another is caused" (*omne autem quod convenit alicui . . . est causatum*). Is this claim a *per se* claim? Again, I do not think so. As I explained, the claim is a conclusion from two previous claims, neither of which is a claim of efficiency. One claim is *per se*, about the dependence of accidents. An accident is a dependent item because of its need to exist in and of another, its subject. The second claim is about the neutral, or potential, character of the subject that the accident needs to be in and of. Neither of these claims is about efficient causality. As one considers them, however, one can see that the subject *qua* subject, though some explanation of the accident, cannot be the total explanation. A dependent act cannot be fully explained simply by reference to its subject as potency.[67]

So, in contrast to Cahalan, I find in step (3) of my *De Ente* text no claims about efficient causality that are not conclusions from other claims. Cahalan seems to concede that there is a proof for my claim that accidental *esse* is efficiently caused by something other than its subject. In support of this claim, Cahalan, agreeing with Owens, appeals to the priority of *esse* to its subject:

---

65. John C. Cahalan, "On the Proving of Causal Propositions," *The Modern Schoolman* 44, no. 2 (1967): 131; "Remarks on Father Owens's 'The Causal Proposition Revisited,'" *The Modern Schoolman* 44, no. 2 (1967): 156 and 159.
66. For Owens's reply, see his "The Causal Proposition Revisited," 147 and 150.
67. For Owens's reply, see ibid., 148–49. In sum, "In the demonstration of the causal proposition, on the contrary, dependence is positively proved through the accidentality of existence to the thing, and dependence on something else is proved through the priority of existence" (148).

Based on the priority of existence over essence, the arguments of Aquinas show that, if something were the cause of its own existence, it would be the cause of itself, an impossibility. And since Aquinas assumes that whatever a thing has in addition to its essence is caused efficiently, either by the thing itself or by some other thing, it follows that accidental existence is caused efficiently in a thing by something other than the thing itself.[68]

As is clear from these words, what Cahalan has difficulty conceding as demonstrated is my second claim that accidents are efficiently caused. What blocks Cahalan from agreeing with me is his belief that you cannot use one line of causality to prove another: "My argument was, and is, that if one and only one kind of causal relation is referred to in the premises, no other kind of causal relation can appear in the conclusion."[69] In other words, Cahalan fails to understand how after acknowledging the material dependence of an accident upon its subject, there is anything else left to conclude. My saying that the accident is also efficiently caused looks to be completely arbitrary.

In reply, from the perspective of my interpretation, I think Cahalan is myopic about Aquinas's reasoning. I agree that if "one and only one" kind of causal relation is referred to, then no other kind can appear. But in the relation of an accident to its subject is there only one kind of causal relation—a material one? I do not think so. An accident is a dependent *act*. As a form, an accident does something. An accident qualifies its subject. In sum, it is a formal cause. So in the data of the proof, one is not dealing only with one kind of causality. Hence, there is something about the accident that the simple reference to its subject cannot explain. One perceives an incongruity in referring a dependent act to a potential subject. There is more in the accident than can be accommodated by material causality simply. In sum, an appreciation of material causality combined with formal causality produces an appreciation of efficient causality.[70]

---

68. Cahalan, "Remarks on Father Owens' 'The Causal Proposition Revisited,'" 154–55. Cahalan also objects that by emphasizing the priority of *esse*, Owens fails to make clear why more standard accidents must be regarded as caused. See Cahalan, "On the Proving of Causal Propositions," 142n6. In my case, every accident is caused because of the potency of the subject *qua* subject. The priority of *esse* comes in as a decisive reason to exclude the cause from being the subject in some other respect.

69. Cahalan, "Remarks on Father Owens' 'The Causal Proposition Revisited,'" 159.

70. My reply to Cahalan's type of objection differs from that of Reichenbach, *The Cosmological Argument*, 63. Reichenbach identifies knowing the causal proposition with knowing that the attribute of existence is caused by something other than its subject: "Existence does not arise from the being

It is this general thinking that Aquinas applies to all accidents, even the *sui generis* accident of *esse*. Even though judgment has apprehended *esse* as an act over and beyond a form so that *esse* can be the act of all acts and the perfection of all perfections, *esse* qualifies its subject. *Esse* qualifies by making its subject more than a possible, more than existence-neutral. Just as my acquired ability to play the piano makes me a pianist, or my running makes me a runner, so too my *esse* makes me a being (*ens*), an existent (*existens*). *Esse* is the act in virtue of which I am a fact. The existence of the thing as grasped in judgment reveals the existence to be a suitable candidate for Aquinas's reasoning and so to a syllogistic introduction to an efficient cause for the existence. Aquinas is making no assumption that an accident needs an efficient cause. That idea is concluded to from the potency of the subject *qua* subject of the accidental act. The remaining issue is the identity of the efficient cause. Is the efficient cause the subject in some other respect than that of subject or is the efficient cause another subject? Aquinas answers this question for *esse* by appealing to the priority of *esse*. The priority of *esse* to its subject prevents the subject from anteceding the *esse* and possibly being its efficient cause from that respect. *Esse* is caused by another subject.

Essence as a Cause of *esse*

Some think that the priority of *esse* is contradicted by other texts that speak of *forma* as a cause of *esse*. For example, from the second chapter of *De Ente*: "Unde oportet ut essentia, qua res denominatur ens, non tantum sit forma nec tantum materia, sed utrumque: quamvis huiusmodi esse suo modo sola forma sit caussa." Also, in his commentary on Boethius's *De Trinitate* and in speaking about the *duplex operatio*, Aquinas says that in composites the *esse* looked at by the *secunda operatio* results from the congregation of the thing's principles: "resultat ex congregatione principiorum rei in compositis."[71] Aqui-

---

itself; the being is not the efficient cause of itself. If such were the case, the absurdity would result that something not in existence brought itself into existence; hence, it is dependent on something other than itself for its existence. Its existence is (logically) prior to itself or its essence. Consequently, the relation of dependence in the case of existence is not that of inherence ... but dependence on something else as cause of it." To prove that the attribute of existence is not efficiently caused by its subject, however, is to assume that the attribute of existence is efficiently caused. To establish the first is not to establish the second.

71. Aquinas, *In de Trin.*, q. 5, a. 3, co. (trans. Maurer, 28).

nas seems to intend the same when he says in the *Sentences* commentary that in things composed from matter and form, the *esse* of the thing consists in a certain composition of form to matter: "consistit in quadam compositione formae ad materiam."[72] Finally, in *SCG* II.54, while arguing that the substance/*esse* distinction is not identical to the matter/form distinction, Aquinas distinguishes form from *esse* by placing an order between them. He says: "because form is compared to being itself as light to illuminating, or whiteness to being white."

In sum, texts like the previous lead one to question the priority of *esse* because they create a confusion as to what causes what. On the one hand, if, as we have seen Aquinas to maintain, *esse* renders the substance an existent, an *ens*, then *esse* seems to be a *sui generis actus* of the substance. Unlike other attributes, *esse* must be *primus* or in a prior relation to its subject. In light of Aquinas's emphasized priority of *esse*, there is some question of how form as part of the substance made a being (*ens*) by *esse* can exercise any causality at all. On the other hand, if form is a principle of *esse*, it seems to have some priority to *esse*. Moreover, the comparisons of *esse* to illumination and to being white picture *esse* as something subsequent and posterior. For some readers, until this issue in point (5) of the *De Ente* reasoning is resolved, the reasoning cannot proceed.

These puzzles seems to drive one to think of *esse* as caused in the first of the two ways mentioned in the *De Ente* text at point (2). In that case, *esse* is a proper accident and has as its efficient cause the subject insofar as it is in act.[73] Even without Aquinas's understanding of *esse* as an accident prior to its subject, however, his previous analysis of essence as abstracting from every *esse* tells us that efficient causality is not the model for understanding how form is a cause or principle of *esse*. So absent efficient causality, how are we to understand the form's causality of *esse* in the above texts?

In the paragraph following the above text from *SCG* II.54, Aquinas not only repeats the claim that form is a cause of *esse* but briefly indicates how form is such. He remarks, "Per hoc enim in compositas ex material et forma dicitur forma esse principium essendi, quia est complementum substantiae cuius actus est ipsum esse." Aquinas repeats the point that *esse* is the act of the

---

72. Aquinas, *In I Sent.*, d. 38, q. 1, a. 3, co.
73. See above chapter 2, note 54.

material substance, hence reiterating the priority of *esse*, all the while claiming form to be the principle of the *esse*. In the following line Aquinas asserts that form causes the *esse* by completing the substance. By completing the substance, form sets up the proper subject whose act will be *esse* just as transparency sets up the air to be the proper subject of light: "Thus, transparency is in relation to the air the principle of illumination, in that it makes the air the proper subject of light [*proprium subiectum luminis*]."

But even though Aquinas has left the paradigm of efficient causality for something like material causality, the issue of priority returns. The analogy's comparison of *esse* to illumination made possible by transparency in the air seems to picture the *esse* as posterior to something prior. The air exists prior to its illumination. That Aquinas does not intend this part of the analogy to apply to substance is plain textually. In the last paragraph of the chapter, Aquinas asserts that the composition of form and matter gives a substance and that the composition of the substance and *esse* gives a being (*ens*), an existent. It is clear, then, that as form completes the substance whose act is *esse*, substance should not be understood as already existing.

What is Aquinas's philosophical reason for the idea that as the proper subject for *esse*, the substance is not an *ens*? As I noted from texts from the *Sentences* and *De Trinitate* commentaries, Aquinas makes the claim that *esse* results from the principles of the essence within the context of the *duplex operatio intellectus*. The answer to my question would lie in a reconsideration of that doctrine.

That doctrine originally presented *esse* as an act *of the thing*. *Esse* does not run around by itself and only incidentally actuates something. Rather, its entire metaphysical mission, its *raison d'être*, is to be the act *of something*. That observation of *esse* grasped in the *secunda operatio* enables one to understand that *esse* is in a sense dependent on the potency that it actuates. *Esse* will not be without an intrinsic orientation to actuating a thing. Hence, any conditions for that potency, for example, form as the structure of matter in bodies—what the text calls the *complementum*—become causes of the *esse*. So, matter which is of itself formless cannot have *esse*. Contradictions which are a profusion of incompatible forms also cannot have *esse* in reality. In sum, form causes *esse* by completing the potency that will be made an *ens*, or more than nothing, by the *esse*. In that way one understands my present section's first quotation from the *De Ente* that by essence a thing is denominated a being:

essentia, qua res denominatur ens. By relentlessly keeping one's focus on *esse* as an object of the *secunda operatio*, it becomes clear that in the comparison of *esse* to light and its conditions, the terms "act" and "potency" are used analogously. *Esse* is a basic and fundamental act, and essence, of which form is a part, is a total and complete potency.

Into these parameters of *SCG* II.54, I think it is helpful to place Aquinas's much later remark in *In IV Meta.*: "though a thing's existence is other [*aliud*] than its essence, it should not be understood to be something added to its essence after the manner of an accident [*superadditum ad modum accidentis*], but something established, as it were [*quasi constituitur*], by the principles of the essence."[74] What is interesting here is that Aquinas uses the thesis of constitution by the principles of the essence to distinguish *esse* from the other accidents that are added above the essence. At *SCG* II.54, every act, illumination as well as *esse*, in a sense resulted from the principles of the essence. It was form in the case of substance and *esse* and transparency in the case of air and illumination. Why the divergence?

There is more to be mined from the phenomenology of the *duplex operatio intellectus*. This *operatio* is truly the mental furnace in which Aquinas's hammers out his basic metaphysical ideas. Not all acts constituted by the principles of the essence are equal. As constituted by the principles of the essence in the way that I have explained, *esse* is an act of the substance that is basic and fundamental to the substance. In a sense, this positioning of *esse* places it inside substance while being outside substance. Recall that Aquinas characterized *esse* as *magis intimum*. Because the potency actuated by other acts of the thing is already actual in a respect, the potency determines the act to an extrinsic position. The text says that it is superadded. Hence, one makes sense of Aquinas insisting in the following lines that when one says, for example, "Socrates is a being," the term "being [*ens*]," which is taken from *esse*, is an essential predication. Predication on the basis of other acts, those superadded, is not essential. For example, one would not regard "The air is lit" as an essential predication even though the illumination is constituted by the principles of the thing.

In this part of the *Metaphysics* commentary, Aquinas takes pains to distinguish himself from Avicenna. Even though Aquinas agrees with Avicenna

---

74. *In IV Meta.*, l. 2, n. 558.

that the *esse rei* is other than the *essentia rei*, Aquinas disagrees with Avicenna that the *esse* is a superaddition. At no. 555, Aquinas repeats the Averroean critique of Avicenna: if a thing is a being by an addition, then the addition is a being by an addition, *ad infinitum*. Aquinas navigates between both Avicenna and Averroes in virtue of his existence-neutral understanding of essence in the essence/*esse* distinction. Where Averroes will conclude that a substance is through itself a being, Aquinas will distinguish the substance from its *esse*. While Avicenna will superadd the *esse* to the substance, Aquinas will have the esse constituted by the essence of the substance. Essence as abstracting *ad quodlibet esse* makes intelligible Aquinas's position against both Averroes and Avicenna.

Aquinas's position makes intelligible a further disagreement with Avicenna. At *De Pot.*, q. 5, a. 3, while discussing whether God can reduce a creature to nothing, Aquinas discusses the positions of Avicenna and Averroes on whether there is in things a real possibility not to be. Aquinas says that Averroes's position is more intelligible (*rationabiliter*). Averroes's position is that only terrestrial bodies have a real possibility not to be. This possibility is the possibility of their matter to lose its present form and to acquire another.

This thinking makes sense for Aquinas. Form renders a substance a suitable subject for actuation by *esse*. As mentioned, judgment originally presents *esse* as the act *of a thing*. Form, however, is a requirement for a thing. Hence, without matter subject to contrariety of form, a substance is simply a potency to *esse*. Such a substance has no real potency to nonbeing.

On the other hand, the Avicenna that Aquinas read in Latin translation did not construe essence as existence-neutral. Avicenna afforded to essence as such a proper existence, an *esse proprium*.[75] This *esse proprium* was an existence distinct from the existence that essence supposedly received from God. Avicenna's philosophical case for essence with a proper being seems to be grounded in his position about possibility. Things are possible in them-

---

75. "Et hoc est quod fortasse appellamus esse proprium; nec intendimus per illud nisi intentionem esse affirmative, quia verbum ens signat etiam multas intentiones, ex quibus est certitudo qua est unaquaeque res; et est sicut esse proprium rei." Avicenna, *Meta.* I, 6, fol. 72vl (C), in *Opera Omnia* (Venice, 1508). See also "ex hoc enim esse nec est genus nec species nec individuum nec unum nec multa. Sed ex hoc esse ist tantum animal et tantum homo, nec comitatur illud sine dubio esse unum vel multa." Ibid., V, 1, fol. 87rl (C). Cited in Joseph Owens, "Common Nature: A Point of Comparison between Thomistic and Scotistic Metaphysics," *Mediaeval Studies* 19 (1957): 4.

selves because otherwise they are impossible and then no cause could produce them.[76]

Avicenna's position on a real potency to nonbeing in all creatures follows his existence-positive view of essence. The *esse proprium* completes the essence's disposition, or potency, to existence such that the *esse* received from God has no potency to complete. It merely floats on the essence without any ties to the essence. In this way Avicenna can philosophically accommodate the Koranic verse: "All things go to destruction but thy face."[77] In Aquinas's metaphysics, however, essence is existence-neutral. Hence, Thomistic essence preserves its potency for the *esse* that it receives from God.

To some readers the previous may seem to be arcane points, but they are well worth pondering. Aquinas's doctrine that form is a *principium essendi* makes one realize that, as dense as it is, my *De Ente* text is a minimal form of theistic reasoning. With its emphasis on the priority of *esse*, the *De Ente* text leads straight to *esse tantum*. Aquinas even seems to mention the consideration of an infinite regress as an afterthought. If, however, one does not focus on the priority of *esse* but on form's causality of *esse*, then any conditions for the presence of form in matter become conditions for the *esse*. As Aristotle's reasoning in *Physics* VIII and *Metaphysics* XII shows, these conditions can stretch to great length. The conditions will involve univocal and equivocal

---

76. "Omne enim quod incipit esse antequam sit, necesse est ut sit possibile in se. Si enim fuerit non possibile in se, illud non erit ullo modo. Non est autem possibilitas sui esse, eo quod agens sit potens supra illud, quia agens non est potens super illud, cum ipsum non fuerit in se possibile." Avicenna, *Meta*. IV, 2 (Venice, 1508), fol. 85vl (H). "Nam possibilitas sui esse est ei propter se, non propter principium, sed est ei a principio necessitas sui esse." Ibid., IX, 4 (Venice, 1508), fol. 104v2 (B). See also Avicenna's argument that possible being is possible in itself from *Metaphysices Compendium* lib. I, pars II, tract. I, cap. II; ed. Nematallah Carame (Rome: Pontifical Institute of Mediaeval Studies, 1926), 68–69. The translation is in Gerard Smith, "Avicenna and the Possibles," *The New Scholasticism*, 17, no. 4 (1943), 341–42. Aquinas cites the argument at *De Pot.*, q. 3, a. 1, obj. 2, without mentioning Avicenna. Aquinas presents the argument as an objection to creation being *ex nihilo*. Finally, it is worth noting that Averroes thought that Avicenna's possibles had an existence of their own: "But the possible into which Avicenna divides existence is not an entity actually outside the soul, and his theory is wrong, as we have said before. For the existence which for its existence is in need of a cause can, as an entity by itself, only be understood as non-existence—that is to say, anything that exists through another thing must be non-existence by itself, unless its nature is the nature of the true possible." Averroes, *Tahāfut al Tahāfut*, dis. 3; trans. Simon Van den Bergh (London: Oxford University Press, 1954), 119. Francis A. Cunningham, however, maintains that Averroes never criticized Avicenna "for holding an independent order of possibles." "Averroes vs. Avicenna on Being," *The New Scholasticism* 48, no. 2 (1974): 197.

77. *Koran* 28:88.

causes, eternal self-movers, and immaterial beings as final causes. In this vein *esse tantum* will reappear as the immaterial final cause that can transfix the eternal self-movers. In short, acquaintance with *esse* will enable the philosopher to open up two causal paths from *esse*. The openness of the *De Ente* reasoning to this elaboration on its consideration of *esse* will be a crucial factor in seeing how it can handle a recurrent disjunction made by Aquinas in many of his *viae*. In that way, the *De Ente* reasoning will help to secure its status as a hermeneutical key for interpreting Aquinas's *viae* to God.

In conclusion, I have argued that many Thomistic problems with the *De Ente* reasoning stem from a failure to relocate its discussion of *essentia* and *esse* within the context of the *duplex operatio*. Others have also said as much, but I have attempted to provide a more experiential and personal appropriation, a "phenomenology" if you will, of the Thomistic texts that present these operations. The phenomenology reveals an ebb and flow of attention in our intellectual life. When this seesawing of attention is brought to bear upon individual things as both really and cognitively existing, Aquinas's key metaphysical notion of *ens* as *habens esse* takes its shape. If their perspective is assiduously maintained, then Aquinas's *De Ente* reasoning for a first cause of *esse* that is *esse tantum* appears as one of the most probing metaphysical reflections in the history of Western philosophy.

[4]

Actus essendi and Analytic Thomism

Recently a group of Thomists has emerged within the British analytic tradition of philosophy. On the basis of twentieth-century analytic discussion of "exists," they have offered interpretations of *esse* that either conflict with the Thomistic Existentialist interpretation or outright reject Aquinas's doctrine of *esse* as bad philosophy. In the first group are Peter Geach and Brian Davies. In the second is Anthony Kenny. My showcasing of Aquinas's *De Ente* reasoning requires that I critically analyze the reasons for their positions to defend the view of *esse* as a *sui generis actus* of its own.

Peter Geach: *Esse* as Double-talk for Form

In his *Three Philosophers*, Peter Geach concludes, "Aquinas's doctrine of *esse* really adds nothing over and above his doctrine of form."[1] To understand the reasons for Geach's interpretation one must note the counter-interpretation with which he is dealing. The counter-interpretation claims that by *esse* Aquinas means something to do with what is asserted by affirmative answers to the question "Does it exist [*An sit*]?" In other words, *esse* means what we mean when we assert "There is...." According to Geach, Aquinas at one time

---

1. Geach, *Three Philosophers*, 92.

held the counter-interpretation. But Geach finds three reasons for claiming that Aquinas eventually jettisoned the "there is . . ." interpretation. First, a privation like blindness is not a being and has no *esse*.[2] Nevertheless, we assert that blindness exists. For instance, we say "Blindness is in the eye." Hence, the existence asserted in this case is quite different from Aquinas's meaning of *esse*. Second, the counter-position would commit us to saying that asserting God to exist is the same as asserting what God is.[3] That is not only ridiculous but also disputed by the texts. Saying "God exists" has nothing to do with apprehending God's *esse*. It has to do with saying that the term "God" is affirmatively predicable. As a supplementary textual reason here, Geach says that only if "God" is not used as a proper name does it make sense to ask, as Aquinas does, if God is one or many.[4] Third, citing from Aquinas's *Quaestiones Quodlibetales*, Geach quotes an opponent's objection concluding to two *esses* in Christ.[5] The opponent's argument says that anything about which we can ask if it exists (*An sit?*) has an *esse*. But one can ask if human nature exists. Hence, in Christ there are two *esses*, one that belongs to him as human and another that belongs to him as divine. Apparently appealing to his above-cited first reason, Geach summarizes Aquinas's reply this way: "this 'there being,' he says, has nothing to do with the case, for in the same way we can speak of 'there being' blindness, where there is no *esse* at all."[6]

With these arguments presented, Geach confidently concludes that "Aquinas's conception of *esse* thus depends on there being a sense of the verb '*est*' or 'is' quite other than the 'there is' sense."[7] What is that other sense? As noted, Geach regards *esse* talk as just form talk. Hence, to talk about the continued existence of something is really just to talk about the continuous presence of a form in matter.[8] This obviously implies that talk about existence *simpliciter* is just talk about the presence of form in matter *simpliciter*.

---

2. Ibid., 88; also Peter Geach, *God and Soul* (London: Routledge and Kegan Paul, 1978), 57.
3. Geach, *Three Philosophers*, 89; Geach, *God and Soul*, 57.
4. Geach, *God and Soul*, 57.
5. *Quodl.* IX, q. 2, a. 3.
6. Geach, *Three Philosophers*, 90.
7. Ibid.
8. "The continued existence of Tibbles consists in there being this individualized life in a continuously changing parcel of matter." Geach, *Three Philosophers*, 83. Also, "Similarly, there is no such thing as a thing's *just* going on existing; when we speak of this, we must always really be referring to some form or nature, X, such that for that thing to go on existing is for it to go on being X" (ibid., 91).

Accordingly, Geach goes on to quote Aquinas saying that existence (*esse*) follows form and Aquinas saying that in living things their life, or *vivere*, is their *esse*.[9] But life proceeds from form, so again *esse* talk reduces to form talk.

Geach's interpretation certainly sucks the blood from the *esse* doctrine understood as an original contribution to philosophy. And there have been other Thomists who argue similarly.[10] In their cases, a Latin Averroist interpretation of Aquinas is provided without any excuse, though in the Middle Ages a Latin Averroist like Siger of Brabant at least acknowledged that by *esse* Aquinas was trying, though unsuccessfully, to call attention to something new.[11]

Before addressing Geach's three reasons, an Existential Thomist proponent of the view that *esse* stands for a distinctive *actus* of its own would agree qualifiedly with Geach's disassociation of the "there is . . ." sense of existence and Aquinas's sense of *esse*. For Geach they are not the same because *esse* means the form. For the Existential Thomist, they are not the same because *esse* stands for the act in virtue of which the thing, already understood as composed of form and matter, is a fact. In chapter 2 I cited many texts expressing this idea of existence. To recall just one text, in his commentary on Boethius's *De Hebdomadibus*, chap. 2, Aquinas makes the following analogy. Just as a man is called a runner by having the act of running, so too the man is called a being, or an existent, by having his act of being, or existing. The "there is . . ." does not express *esse* but rather the datum in which Aquinas metaphysically analyzes out what he means by *esse*. The philosophical burden for the Existential Thomist is to show how the mind is prompted by naturally ascertainable data to regard the fact of the thing as dependent upon a deeper *actus* than form. I attempted to shoulder that burden in my discussion of the *duplex operatio intellectus* in chapter 2. But the fact of the matter is that Geach nowhere discusses the Existential Thomist sense of *esse* as a distinctive *actus* of its own. For Geach the alternatives remain: the fact sense of existence and the reductive sense of existence to form. There is some excuse for this.

---

9. Geach, *God and the Soul*, 59–60.
10. See chapter 3, note 60.
11. "Sed dicere quod esse sit aliquid additum essentiae rei, ita quod non sit res ipsa neque pars essentiae, ut materia vel forma, et dicere quod non sit accidens, est ponere quartam naturam in entibus." Siger of Brabant from a portion of his *Questions on the Metaphysics of Aristotle*; ed. Armand Maurer, in "*Esse* and *Essentia* in the Metaphysics of Siger of Brabant," *Mediaeval Studies* 8 (1946): 71.

As I mentioned when discussing Gilson, Gilson hesitated to accept the man/phoenix argument of the *De Ente*. That I could know what they are and not know that they are might only be indicating a distinction between a thing and the fact of the thing. I also admitted this ambiguity when discussing Aquinas's doctrine of absolute consideration. But the texts for an act-view of *esse* are unavoidable. It is not to Geach's credit that the *actus* sense of *esse* is absent from his reflections. By targeting for criticism Gilson's Existential Thomist understanding of *esse*, Brian Davies will address this lacuna in Geach.

Nevertheless, what of Geach's three reasons? First, is it correct, as Geach's first reason claims, that blindness is not a being and does not have *esse*? Not in every sense. Geach cites *ST* I, q. 48, a. 2, ad 2, where Aquinas distinguishes between two senses of being (*ens*). Aquinas first says that anything that falls within the ten categories elaborated by Aristotle is a being. But Aquinas says that in a second sense being signifies the truth of a proposition. In this way, privations are called beings. Geach takes this to mean that anything about which we can talk truly is a being, though it lacks *esse*. But in my opinion, Geach misconstrues the focus of Aquinas's remarks. To see why we have to go back to some earlier texts.

Aquinas makes the same twofold distinction of being back at the very beginning of *De Ente*.[12] In a second sense, being (*ens*) signifies the "truth of propositions," and so "anything can be called a being if an affirmative proposition can be formed about it, even though it is nothing positive in reality." But in works written just after *De Ente*, Aquinas makes some remarks on truth that elucidate what this second meaning of being is and whether or not it involves *esse*. In his *De Ver.*, q. 1, a. 9, co., a famous text in Thomistic studies, Aquinas describes the existence of truth in the intellect. He says: "truth follows the operation of the intellect inasmuch as it belongs to the intellect to judge about a thing as it is." Aquinas discussed this doctrine back in q. 1, a. 3. Treating the question of whether truth is only in the composing and dividing intellect, he remarks: "The nature of truth is first found in the intellect when the intellect begins to possess something proper to itself [*aliquid proprium*], not possessed by the thing outside the soul [*res extra animam*],

---

12. In his *The Five Ways: St. Thomas Aquinas' Proofs of God's Existence* (London: Routledge and Kegan Paul, 1969), 83, Anthony Kenny makes the same point in order to dispute Geach's claim of a change of mind in Aquinas.

yet corresponding to it [*ei correspondens*], so that between the two—intellect and thing—an adequation [*adequatio*] may be found." Such a moment is the intellect's judgment: "when the intellect begins to judge about the thing it has apprehended, then its judgment [*iudicium*] is something proper to itself —not something found outside in the thing." But the intellect judges "at the moment when it says that something is or is not." In articles 3 and 9, Aquinas uses the words *iudicare* and *iudicium* to designate the intellect's formation of propositions. The second sense of being, *viz.*, the truth of propositions, seems to be talking about cognitional beings, things that exist only in the soul. A remark in *SCG* I.58 confirms this: "Furthermore, in the case of a proposition formed by a composing and dividing intellect, the composition itself exists in the intellect, not in the thing that is outside the soul [*in ipso intellectu existit, non in re quae est extra animam*]."

Does the intellectual presence of the proposition involve *esse*? Evidently. Back in the third chapter of the *De Ente*, which is devoted to the relation of essence to genus, species, and difference, Aquinas says that a nature like humanity has a twofold *esse*. One *esse* is in individual things, while the other is in the soul. Furthermore, accidents accompany the nature because of either *esse*. One of the accidents that follows *esse in anima* is predictability of the nature and "predication is something achieved by the intellect in its act of combining and dividing."[13] These points imply that Aquinas's second sense of *ens*, namely, the truth of the proposition, signifies a cognitional existent that has its own distinctive type of *esse*. Furthermore, insofar as privations can be talked about through propositions, then, through their presence in propositions, they too would be cognitional beings with their own distinctive type of *esse*. Accordingly, Geach is inaccurate to claim that privations have no *esse* and that the second sense of being has nothing to do with *esse*.

The above conclusion that privations have a type of *esse* is confirmed by a text from another early work, Aquinas's *Sentences* commentary. At *In II Sent.*, d. 37, q. 1, a. 2, ad 3,[14] and again within the context of a twofold sense of *ens*,

---

13. Aquinas, *On Being and Essence* (trans. Maurer, 49).

14. "Being [*Ens*] is said in two ways [*dupliciter*]. In one way what signifies the essence of the thing existing outside the soul, and in this way of speaking of the deformity of sin which is a certain privation, is not able to be a being, for privations do not have an essence in the nature of things. In another way insofar as [being] signifies the truth of a proposition, and so deformity is said to be, not on account of this that it has being [*esse*] in reality, but because the intellect composes a privation with a subject just as a

Aquinas admits that a privation does not have an *esse in re*. But insofar as being signifies the truth of a proposition, deformity is said to exist. Whence, Aquinas says that just as from the composition of form to subject or to matter there results a certain accidental or substantial *esse*, so too the intellect signifies the composition of a privation with a subject through a certain *esse* (*per quoddam esse*). This *esse* is only an *esse* of reason (*esse rationis*), because in the thing there is non-*esse*. Nevertheless, *esse rationis* is sufficiently *esse* to justify saying that insofar as the privation has an *esse* in reason, then the privation is from God who, according to the *responsio* of the article, is source of *esse*.

Aquinas definitely is not espousing Geach's thesis that privations have no *esse* at all. Privations have no *esse in re* but they possess an *esse in anima*. Hence, Geach's first reason against the counter-position disappears.[15] In review, Geach claimed that *esse* could not be associated with the object of affirmation because one makes affirmations about blindness and blindness has no *esse*. But one can now see that *esse* is an object of affirmation, even in the case of privations, because the object of an affirmation can be the *esse* had by the privation in the *ens rationis* that is the proposition. Geach's first reason works only by telescoping *esse* into real *esse*. Among Thomists the standard practice has the single term *esse* standing for real *esse*, *esse* possessed by things independent of cognition. But the standard practice should not fool a reader, as it has fooled Geach, into thinking that there is only real *esse*. *Esse* is a term with a multivalent meaning. *Esse* can also stand for cognitional *esse*, and cognitional *esse* can be as much an object of affirmation as real *esse*. I, however, will follow the standard practice unless otherwise noted.

---

certain form. Whence just as from the composition of form to a subject or to matter there follows a certain being [*esse*] substantial or accidental, so also the intellect signifies the composition of the privation with a subject through a certain being [*esse*]. But this being [*esse*] is not except a being of reason [*esse rationis*] since in reality it is more a non being [*non esse*], and according to this that in reason the privation has being [*esse*], it stands that it is from God." *II Sent.*, d. 38, a. 1, a. 2, ad 3 (ed. Mandonnet, 2:947).

15. It is doubtful that Aquinas ever claimed, as Geach seems to presuppose (see Kenny, *Five Ways*, 84), that every assertion expresses *esse*, or real (that is, non-mind-dependent) existence. For example, Maurer, "St. Thomas and Eternal Truths," 91–107, shows that the "is" in "eternal" truths corresponds to no *esse* proper to the truth itself. For Aquinas, just as essences considered in themselves abstract from every being, so too do truths when considered in themselves. Using terminology taken from John of St. Thomas, Maurer says (101) that at best these truths can be said to have a "negative" eternity in that in themselves they abstract from any subject in and through which they can come and go. As so entertained, the truth is not being envisaged with any existence at all. Nevertheless, the texts that Geach brings up require that I respond along the lines presented above.

This reply to Geach's first reason is applicable to Geach's third reason. As Geach summarizes Aquinas's reply to the objection in behalf of two *esses* in Christ, Geach has Aquinas claiming that to answer the question *"An sit?"* by some assertion "There is ..." does not involve *esse*. The reason is because we can assert "There is blindness" when there is no *esse* at all. In his own reply, however, Aquinas does not say that the question *"An sit?"* can be answered by an affirmation that has nothing to do with *esse*. Rather, Aquinas replies that the *"An sit?"* question can be answered by an *esse* that consists in an act of the soul. Hence, Aquinas says that we are able to ask concerning blindness if it exists: "This objection focuses on the *esse* that consists in the act of the soul, because 'Does it exist?' is also able to be asked concerning blindness." In his *responsio* Aquinas described this *esse* in already familiar terms: "Hence this *esse* is not something in the nature of things, but is only in the act of the soul composing and dividing. And so *esse* is attributed to everything about which a proposition is able to be formed, whether it is a being or a privation of being. For we do say that blindness exists."[16] Note that unlike Geach Aquinas does not deny that all questions about existence are questions about *esse*. Rather, Aquinas asserts it and then goes on to distinguish between types of *esse*. Hence, some questions are about something having real *esse* while others are about something having cognitional *esse*. In the case of the incarnation, the only creaturely *esse* in Christ's human nature about which it is appropriate to ask is the *esse* had by Christ's human nature in our soul when we think about it.[17]

Employing the above points, an Existential Thomist can finally address Geach's second reason. As the reader will recall, Geach, citing *ST* I, q. 3, a. 4, ad 3, maintains that the proposition "God exists" has nothing to do with talk about an *esse* that belongs to God but rather has everything to do with Fregean talk about something having the divine attributes. The transposition of "God exists" into "Something is God" is the issue that Aquinas is referring to when he states that we know God's *esse* in the truth of a proposition. Obvi-

---

16. Author's translation. The Latin is: "Unde hoc esse non est aliquid in rerum natura, sed tantum in actu animae componentis et dividentis. Et sic esse attribuitur omni ei de quo potest propositio formari, sive sit ens, sive privatio entis; dicimus enim caecitatem esse." *Quodl.* IX, q. 2, a. 3 (ed. Spiazzi, 180–81).

17. Aquinas sometimes gets at the *ens rationis* that is the proposition by talking about what answers the question *"An sit?"* See *ST* I, q. 48, a. 2, ad 2.

ously this still leaves unknown God's *esse* as it is in itself. Consequently, the objection that because in God *esse* and essence are the same, then knowing one is knowing the other is answered. As plausible as Geach's reading is, it is not the appropriate one. Aquinas is bringing up a second sense of *esse* that signifies the composition of the proposition which the soul makes joining a predicate to a subject. As we have seen, this composition involves an *esse* for the proposition. Hence, insofar as we can know the cognitional *esse* of the true proposition about God, then in a sense we can know God's *esse*. For Aquinas the proposition "God exists" is about God's *esse*. It is about the *esse* that God has in a true proposition about him. Obviously, this reading also leaves intact the other claim that God's *esse* as it is in itself is unknown. The virtue of my reading is that it is in line with the Thomistic texts cited in my earlier replies to Geach. So going on here is, in my opinion, no Fregean reinterpretation of "God exists" into "Something is God."

But what about Geach's noting that for Aquinas "God" is not a proper name but the name for a type of thing such that propositions that employ the term "God" in the subject position can be transposed into those the employ the term in the predicate position? Geach's reason is that at *ST* I, q. 11, a. 3, Aquinas asks whether God is one or many. Geach says that the question only makes sense if the term "God" is not being used as a proper name. In my opinion, Geach's observation philosophically amounts to a red herring. Granting him his reason, the substance of my interpretation of *ST* I, q. 3, a. 4, ad 2, still stands. For instead of talking about the *esse* that God has in the proposition about him, Aquinas will be speaking of the *esse* that the something that is God has in the proposition about it.[18] Geach has not successfully resolved the issue of *esse* understood as a distinctive *actus*.

What of Geach's citation of Thomistic thesis that *esse* follows form? As I explained in the previous chapter, in *SCG* II.54, a text that depicts *esse* as so much a distinctive *actus* that its composition with the material thing can be compared to the matter/form distinction within the thing, Aquinas explains how we are to understand *esse* following form: "form is said to be a principle of being for this reason: that it is the complement of the substance, whose act is being" (*dicitur forma esse principium essendi, quia est complementum*

---

18. Kenny, *Five Ways*, 84, however, correctly notes that at *ST* I, q. 2, a. 1, co., "Deus est" is "consistently treated as a subject-predicate one."

substantiae, cuius actus est ipsum esse). *Esse* follows form not because *esse* is just the fact of the thing but because as the very act of the thing it is in a strange sense dependent upon the thing and upon any principles of the thing, for example the thing's form. In this case in which the entire metaphysical mission of *actus essendi* is to realize the thing, *esse* is a cause in a sense dependent upon its effect, and so any causes in the constitution of the thing actuated by *esse* are also in a sense causes of the *esse*.

Finally, what of Geach's use of Aquinas's texts saying that in living things *esse* is *vivere*? Also, the texts make it clear that when Aquinas says *esse* is *vivere*, he is not identifying *esse* with vital operations. Rather, he is using the word *vivere* to stand for his metaphysical principle of *esse* when *esse* is found in living things. For example, "Et secundum hoc, vivere nihil aliud est quam esse in tali natura.... Quandoque tamen vita sumitur minus proprie pro operationibus vitae" (*ST* I, q. 18, a. 2, co.) and "vita dicitur dupliciter. Uno modo, ipsum esse viventis... Alio modo, dicitur vita ipsa operatio viventis" (*ST* I-II, q. 3, a. 2, ad 1).[19]

In conclusion, Geach's contention that in Aquinas *esse*-talk is just doubletalk for talk about form, and not talk about a further and distinctive *actus*, is textually unverified. Again, for Geach *esse simpliciter* just means the presence of form in matter. But as mentioned, at *SCG* II.54 and elsewhere,[20] the matter/form composition is so distinct from *esse* that it is compared to *esse* as the potency to which *esse* is the very act.

Brian Davies and Etienne Gilson's Existential Thomism

In his "Aquinas, God, and Being,"[21] formatted in medieval *disputatio* style, Davies provides three arguments against the view that "exists" is a first-level predicate. Even though Gilson is mentioned in passing, Davies's article is a

---

19. For other texts and commentary, see Joseph Owens, "The Accidental and Essential Character of Being in the Doctrine of St. Thomas Aquinas," in *St. Thomas Aquinas on the Existence of God* (ed. Catan), 243–44n22.

20. See above chapter 2, "Aquinas's Meaning of '*Esse*.'"

21. From *The Monist* 80, no. 4 (1997): 500–517. For an excellent discussion of whether Davies's Fregean view of existence is suitable for Aquinas's notion of *actus essendi*, see Brian J. Shanley, "Analytic Thomism," *The Thomist* 63, no. 1 (1999): 125–37.

sustained criticism of the Gilsonian view that for Aquinas existence is an attribute of its own. I will argue that, as with Geach, so too with Davies's arguments, a myopia exists regarding Aquinas's unique *actus essendi* conception.

Davies criticizes the view that existence is a property or attribute but leaves untouched the view that existence is a property or attribute basic and fundamental to its subject and fully actuates the subject from that stance. Hence, Davies concludes,

> On Aquinas's account, the existence of Thor is reportable by saying what Thor is.... To exist is to be or to have form. Hence, for instance, Aquinas can only make sense of statements like "Thor exists" (*Thor est*) on the understanding that they tell us what something is. *Thor est*, said of Thor the cat, means, for Aquinas, "Thor is a cat." Or, to change the example, according to Aquinas names like "Socrates" or "Plato" signify human nature as ascribable to certain individuals. *Hoc nomen "Socrates" vel "Plato" significat naturam humanam secundum quod est in hac mataeria*. On Aquinas's account, saying *Socrates est* or *Plato est* is not to inform people of a property of existence had by Socrates and Plato. It is to assert what Socrates and Plato are by nature, i.e., human.[22]

Davies's first argument for the above view is that if a Thomist considers existence to be a predicate, then positive existential statements are true of neces-

---

22. Davies, "Aquinas, God, and Being," 511–12. In his "The Action of God," in *Mind, Method, and Morality: Essays in Honour of Anthony Kenny*, ed. John Cottingham and Peter Hacker (Oxford: Oxford University Press, 2010), 174, and replying to Russell's claims that we cannot ascribe existence to individuals, Davies argues that we can. But this ascription is translatable and so to my mind "exists" is still a second-order predicate. For instance, "'Socrates does not exist, but Smokey [Davies's cat] does.' That, I claim, is both meaningful and true (at the time at which I write). Can I unpack it somewhat? Clearly I can. I can say 'Socrates is dead, but Smokey is alive.'" Turning to the existence of inanimate things like Davies's desk and to the World Trade Center, Davies glosses their existence: "Both came to exist when they were built. My desk sits solidly in my living room. Unlike the World Trade Center, it has not been destroyed. It could be destroyed and would then not exist, just like the World Trade Center" (175). I do not see this later presentation as making any significant advance over Davies's *Monist* article. In both pieces, Davies fails to consider the Existential Thomist view that "exists" is a first order predicate for a *sui generis* attribute of its own. It appears that Davies is content to regard the existence of the singular, at least partly, as just the fact of that singular: "This is partly (and here I stress 'partly') what Aquinas has in mind when he speaks of things having *esse*. His view is that something has *esse* if it actually exists, if it is there so that we can truly say what it actually is considered as the substance that it is" (ibid., 172). Yet how is that different from Davies's claim in *The Monist* article that "Thor (the cat) exits" really means "Thor is a cat"? Finally, for Davies's version of cosmological reasoning and for comment, see John F. X. Knasas, *Aquinas and the Cry of Rachel: Thomistic Reflections on the Problem of Evil* (Washington, D.C.: The Catholic University Press of America, 2014), 264–76.

sity and negative ones are of necessity false. Beginning with the latter, Davies argues:

> If "___ exist(s)" serves to tell us something significant about some object or individual, then denying that "___ exist(s)" is truly affirmable of some object or individual is denying that this something significant (expressed by "___ exists") is truly affirmed of some object or individual. But of what non-existent object or individual can "___ does not exist" be saying anything significant.... So, on the assumption that "___ exist(s)" can serve to tell us something about some object or individual, it looks as though denials of existence must always be false.[23]

In other words, if existence is a predicate, then it is ascribed to something even when it is being denied. Hence, "Fun-loving Welshmen do not exist" is really saying "The fun-loving Welshmen that exist do not exist." This last is a contradiction and, of course, is necessarily false. But this fate for negative existential propositions cannot be right. For example, "Sunny weather does not exist" is not necessarily false. A little imagination should reveal how positive existential statements become necessarily true. If existence is a predicate, then existence will be truly affirmed of some object or individual, thus rendering the proposition a tautology and so necessarily true.

Again, I cannot overemphasize Davies's presupposition that the attribute or predicate view of existence understands existence as an item subsequent and posterior to an already-there subject.[24] This conception of attribute seems tied to a view of the individual as *ipso facto* an existent. As noted in chapter 2, Aquinas does not share that point. To have an individual substance, a composition of matter and form, is not *ipso facto* to have an existent. It may suffice for Aristotle and Averroes, and for most of us in ordinary conversation, but Aquinas requires the addition of a further *actus* if the substance is to be an existent (*ens*). Hence, Davies is working with a presumption that fails to engage Aquinas. *Esse* is basic and fundamental to its subject that is of itself existence-neutral. Ascription of *esse* to its subject, then, does not presume that the subject is there or that it is not there. The existential neutrality of the subject is not an assertion that the subject is not there nor that it is

---

23. Davies, "Aquinas, God, and Being," 503.

24. Hence, there is some justification to Gilson's claim that in the contemporary signification of "predicate," Thomistically understood existence is not a predicate. For a discussion of the Gilsonian claim, see Quinn, *The Thomism of Etienne Gilson*, 60–62.

there. That is why it makes sense to wait for further information about the existence or nonexistence of our fun-loving, but existence-neutral, Welshmen. On Aquinas's account, "Existentially neutral fun-loving Welshmen do not exist" is not a contradiction and so not necessarily false.

Davies's second argument against existence as a predicate is that positive existential propositions can be morphed into propositions without "exists."

> The work done by "___ exist(s)" in sentences like "Fun-loving Welshmen exist" is the same work as that done by "some" in sentences like "Some Welshmen are fun-loving." Nobody, I presume would take "some" to ascribe any kind of property or characteristic to any object or individual. But if in such cases the work done by "___ exist(s)" is the same work as that done by "some," then "___ exist(s)" does not function so as to ascribe any kind of property to any object or individual.[25]

In some following tightly reasoned paragraphs, Davies underwrites the equivalency of "Fun loving Welshmen exist" and "Some Welsh men are fun-loving" by showing that the negation of the latter is equivalent to "Fun-loving Welshmen do not exist."[26]

In comment, Davies's second argument requires and presupposes the success of his first argument. For the second argument, "exists" functions only in propositions in which the subject is a description. That thesis is what allows translation of "___exist(s)" into assertions of the fact of individuals of a certain nature. Propositions like "I exist" are particularly resistant to this analysis and Davies denies that they "make sense."[27] Why? Ordinary conversation is full of assertions of the existence of individuals. The answer appears to be the controlling idea of Davies's first argument, namely, because individuals already exist, then "exists" as a predicate would render the proposition a tautology and so a necessary truth. But Aquinas regards individuals as not *ipso facto* existent but of themselves existence-neutral. Hence, it is appropriate to assert or to deny their existence. In sum, Aquinas could grant Davies's second argument. Yet Aquinas would go on to insist that when the subject is an individual, "exists" is a predicate signifying an attribute, albeit a *sui generis* one.

Davies's third argument against existence as a predicate or property is

---

25. Ibid., 503.
26. Ibid., 504–5.
27. Ibid., 507.

twofold.[28] First, he borrows from Frege the rejection that numbers are properties. On the one hand, the expression of number may mimic the expression of a property. I can speak of "four horses" just as I can speak of "thoroughbred horses." Nevertheless, I know that though each horse is a thoroughbred, each horse is not a four. Hence, the number four fails to designate a property of any individual horse. On the other hand, if numbers did designate properties of objects, of what object does "zero" designate the property in the statement "Venus has zero moons"? Rather, is it not the point of the statement that Venusian moons do not exist?

An affirmative answer here brings one to the second portion of Davies's argument. If "zero moons" means no moons exist, then asserting existence means asserting another number. Davies quotes Frege, "Affirmation of existence is in fact nothing but denial of the number nought." Here Davies also appeals to C. J. F. Williams to make the second portion of his argument. For Williams, statements of number are answers to "How many A's are there?" But "A's exist" is one legitimate answer to that question. Hence, "A's exist" is a statement of number. In sum, if existence statements are statements about number and number is not a property of objects or individuals, then existence is not a property or a predicate.

Davies's third argument cleverly makes the point that existence statements imply number statements. The trouble is that the reverse is untrue. To be numbered does not necessarily mean to be existent. I can be thinking of a Hawaiian vacation that I wish to take. My going on to make it a six-day vacation brings it no closer to existent. It can remain frustratingly unrealized. In Thomistic categories, number can be applied to what is existence-neutral without introducing any redundancy. Just as "Existence-neutral martyrs exist" is not redundant, so too "Six existence-neutral martyrs exist" makes good sense. That observation suffices to break Davies's equivalency between existence and number and to ruin his third argument. Existence still may not be a predicate, but that will be for other reasons. The only further arguments mentioned by Davies are his first two, and I have replied to these.

28. Ibid., 505–6.

Anthony Kenny: The Fatal Flaw of the Man/Phoenix Argument

At the start of the reasoning that leads to my *De Ente* text, Aquinas states that one can know what a man or a phoenix is and yet not know if they have being in reality (*ignorare an esse habeant in rerum natura*). I understood this remark as reiterating Aquinas's earlier doctrine of the absolute consideration of essence. That doctrine in turn could be understood as the *prima operatio* of the intellect. Hence, the *esse* that Aquinas mentions in the remark was the technical sense of *esse* grasped in the *secunda operatio*. Hence, Aquinas was furnished with the materials needed to advance the causal reasoning of our *De Ente* text. For Anthony Kenny "the *On Being and Essence* argument from phoenixes to the real distinction between essence and *esse*, can be seen to be fatally flawed."[29] Kenny's difficulty with the argument is not what rattles most Thomists, *viz.*, whether the argument establishes the real distinction between essence and existence. Kenny says that it does.[30] Rather the difficulty is that the argument's conclusion is at odds with the context of the chapter. The context is one of distinguishing separate immaterial substances, called intelligences, from God. Aquinas will argue that though these substances lack a matter/form composition, they do not rival the simplicity of God. In them is still found a composition of essence and existence. But far from supporting that way of distinguishing separate substances and God, the phoenix argument leaves the two still conflated, for God also can be thought not to be in the same manner as men or phoenixes. As Kenny says, "Atheists, after all, have a concept of God; otherwise they wouldn't know what it was they were denying when they deny that God exists."[31] Hence, both intelligences and God would have to be essence/existence composites.

---

29. Kenny, *Aquinas on Being*, 62. Given that the phoenix is a mythical bird, I understand our existential ignorance about it to consist in not knowing if it has cognitional existence in the mind of some imaginer. For a lengthy Thomist discussion of Kenny's *Aquinas on Being*, see Lawrence Dewan, "Discussion of Anthony Kenny's *Aquinas on Being*," *Nova et Vetera* (English Edition) 3, no. 2 (2005): 335–400. For a more focused critique, see Kerr, *Aquinas's Way to God*, 158.

30. Ibid., 36. But Kenny admits difficulty in formulating an understanding of the real distinction. His best attempt is "a picture of two entities of a similar kind with a metaphysical fissure separating them" (36). With that understanding in mind, he mentions that the question of a real distinction between essence and existence is as strange as asking if there is a real distinction between the threeness and the blindness in three blind mice. For another Kenny attempt to construe the real distinction, see note 35 below.

31. Ibid., 37.

Importantly, Kenny concludes that the best way to understand Aquinas's notion of God as pure being is to realize that being does not mean existence. What does it mean? It means that God is something and that God is this something alone, whether God exists or not.[32] In the end, the phoenix argument is embraced by Kenny not for Aquinas's purposes of distinguishing essence from existence but for purposes of de-existentializing God's nature. Kenny thinks that he has Aquinas on his side because outside of his early writings, Aquinas never employs the phoenix argument again.[33]

What would remain of the real distinction between essence and existence? In his earlier book on the *quinque viae*, Kenny is happy to help Thomists attain clarity.[34] Kenny translates statements of individual existence, for example, "Socrates exists," into statements of essence. The guiding idea is taken from Aquinas: "Everything has existence through form" (*Omnis res habet esse per formam*). Hence, "Socrates exists" is retranslated into "Socrates is a human being."[35] The real distinction in Socrates can, then, be understood as the distinction between form considered by itself or as had by something.[36] So, because what God is is what God is alone, then God would lack this sense

---

32. "Being enters into the quiddity of God as it does into the quiddity of phoenix, with this difference: that being is the only thing that enters into the quiddity of God, so that it can be said to be identical with it. But this being is something quite different from actual existence: it enters into the quiddity of God whether or not there is such a thing as God" (ibid., 62).

33. But it is certainly implied by Aquinas's first *ST* reasoning for the identity of essence and existence in God. See *ST* I, q. 3, a. 4. The first reasoning clearly reiterates the reasoning of the paragraphs following the phoenix argument in the *De Ente*. The phoenix argument is essential for the reasoning of those paragraphs.

34. Kenny, *The Five Ways*, 88–90.

35. But this guiding idea should be understood in the light of *SCG* II.54, in which form is a *principium essendi* insofar as it is the *complementum* of the substance whose actualization is through *esse*. This thinking leaves *esse* a distinctive act from form and ruling over form. Form is a part of a substance that is still not a being (*ens*) until composed with *esse*. For the idea that the *esse* of a form is the form's being had or possessed by a subject, Kenny cites *ST* III, q. 17, a. 2: "If any form or nature does not pertain [*pertineat*] to the personal *esse* of a subsistent individual, that *esse* is not called the *esse* of that person without qualification." It seems an interpretive stretch to take the antecedent of this conditional proposition as: "If any form is not had or possessed by a subsistent individual."

36. "Goodness and humanity, he says, are not signified in actuality save insofar as we signify that they *are*. Only if John *is* good, not just if he will be, or can be, or is thought to be good, will John's goodness be actual and not merely potential. So the *esse album* of Socrates appears to be not simply the form, Socrates' whiteness, but the actual having of the form; but of course that form will itself only have real existence, or *esse*, if Socrates has *esse album*. It is in this sense that Aquinas says that *esse* is the actuality of every form and nature." Kenny, *The Five Ways*, 88–89.

of real distinction. But at this point Kenny ceases any further collaboration with Thomistic metaphysicians. That God is understood to be some predicate alone, that is, a subsistent form, has problems avoiding issues with Plato's ontology. In particular, back in *Aquinas on Being*, the issue is that of a predicate without a subject.[37]

Is the phoenix argument in opposition to Aquinas's understanding of God as subsistent existence? At first glance, Kenny's claim that they are incompatible appears to be correct. If I can distinguish the phoenix from its existence because I can know what a phoenix is without knowing that it is, then I can do the same thing for God. So, whatever God is essentially, it is not existence. A quick and simple reply to Kenny might appear to be the following. Whatever has the essence/existence distinction is caused. But God is the first cause. Therefore, God lacks the distinction. As neat as this reply looks, it fails to acknowledge that Kenny has *already* tagged God with the distinction, and so the conclusion seems to be not that God lacks the distinction, but that God is caused. The more fundamental challenge for the Existential Thomist is to show that *from the beginning* of one's deliberations our existential ignorance of the phoenix is different from our existential ignorance of God. To meet that challenge I think that it is necessary to understand Aquinas's doctrine of formed intentions.

Aquinas succinctly presents the doctrine in his *SCG* I.53, where he describes how having been informed by the species of the thing, the intellect goes on to form an intention of the thing understood.

---

37. "But it is hard to see how the notion of pure form can be explained by reference to predication. Forms are forms of the entity which is the subject of predication: Socrates' wisdom is what corresponds to the predicate in the sentence 'Socrates is wise,' ... In the same way, a pure form would be something that corresponded to a predicate in a sentence that had no subject: but this seems close to an absurdity." Kenny, *Aquinas on Being*, 30. Kenny's complaint seems similar to Aquinas's observation that my way of signifying the existent is in composite fashion; see *ST* I, q. 13, a. 1, ad 2. Below in my text at notes 55 and 56, I attempt to explain how the "negation" capacity of the intellect's second operation can remove this mode of signifying for *esse subsistens*. In his "On Kenny on Aquinas on Being," *International Philosophical Quarterly*, 44, no. 4 (2004): 577–78, Gyula Klima defends the real distinction in another way. Using remarks of Geach, Klima uses the distinction between a creature and its vital activity to present the distinction. In God there is no such distinction, so God's essence is his existence. Klima is influenced by Geach's interpretation of Aquinas's use of Aristotle's remark (*De Anima* II.4, 415b13) that the life of living things is their being. But Joseph Owens shows that Aquinas identifies life with *esse*, not *esse* with life. *Esse* remains a distinct *actus* of its own and is not glossed in other terms. For the reference to Owens, see note 19 above.

Now, since this understood intention is, as it were, a terminus of intelligible operation, it is distinct from the intelligible species that actualizes the intellect, and that we must consider the principle of intellectual operation, though both are a likeness of the thing understood. For, by the fact that the intelligible species, which is the form of the intellect and the principle of understanding, is the likeness of the external thing, it follows that the intellect forms the intention like that thing, since such as a thing is, such are its works. And because the understood intention is like some thing, it follows that the intellect, by forming such an intention, knows that thing.[38]

This formed intention is distinct from the intelligible species that both actualizes the intellect and is the principle of intellectual operation. In the preceding paragraph Aquinas says that such a formed intention is necessary because the intellect, like the imagination, understands both a present and absent thing and also because the intellect "understands a thing as separated from material conditions, without which a thing does not exist in reality."[39]

This text suggests two contrasting views. One view is the more original. It follows the intellect's actualization by the species of the thing. With its talk of "an act of understanding," "the definition" that the notion signifies, and the comparison to the imagination, the preceding paragraph makes clear that Aquinas is referring to the first of the two operations of the intellect that Aquinas describes in his commentary on Lombard's *Sentences*. It is this first intellectual operation that Aquinas glosses in the *De Ente* as the "absolute consideration of essence." As I described in chapter 2, characteristic of absolute consideration is a penetrative movement of intellectual attention from some presented multiplicity of instances to the perception of a commonality, or essence.

Another view is subsequent and follows the intellect forming an intention of the essence. While absolutely considering the essence, we are aware that on the side of our considering we are fashioning a likeness of the essence. The latter results in a view of essence separated from material conditions of the instances in the mentioned multiplicity. Hence, the original view of essence should be a view of essence still immersed within the material data. And the second view should be of essence more independent from the data.

---

38. *SCG* I.53 (trans. Pegis, 1:188–89). See also Aquinas, *Quodl.* V, q. 5, a. 2, co.
39. *SCG* I.53 (trans. Pegis, 1:188).

The importance of this distinction of views will become evident as I go along. Suffice it to say now that the distinction is valuable for understanding a conundrum associated with Aquinas's claim in his *De Ver.* that there can be falsity in the first operation insofar as the first operation can produce wild combinations, for instance, understanding a non-sensing animal or understanding the definition of a circle of a triangle.[40] Such crazy views could not result from the absolute consideration of essence insofar as it is understood to be controlled by the data. In other words, intellecting animal in the data of Tom and Fido would mean always coming back to those instances. Inasmuch as Gibraltar is not among those original instances, then in that context animal would never be combined with it. One sees that for these exotically false combinations to be made the essence must be represented in a manner more independent of the data that first acquainted us with it. This more independent representation is what is achieved by what Aquinas calls in *SCG* I.53 the "intention formed within the intellect." As represented independently from the data set that originally acquainted us with the essence, the essence is free to be erroneously combined with other intentions.

So far the doctrine of formed intentions has been described in terms of the first operation of the intellect. But the doctrine continues into the second operation. As I attempted to explain it phenomenologically, the second operation is a rebound of intellectual attention from some commonality grasped in the first operation. The rebound brings the commonality back to the data in which it was spied. It also affords a distinct appreciation of the peculiarities of the data, for example, the differentiae of the species man and brute. Once the intellect knows the differentiae, then it can also form intentions of them that set the differentiae apart from the species in which they are found.

We now have a flurry of formed intentions of intelligible objects. They are found independent of the contexts in which the objects were originally delivered to intellectual awareness. As mentioned, this situation with formed intentions permits wild combinations that would be impossible if our attention stayed on what we were aware of before we formed the intentions.

---

40. "For it may happen that a definition will be applied to something to which it does not belong, as when the definition of a circle is assigned to a triangle. Sometimes, too the parts of a definition cannot be reconciled, as happens when one defines a thing as 'an animal entirely without the power of sensing.'" Aquinas, *De Ver.*, q. 1, a. 3, co. (trans. Mulligan, 1:13–14). See also *In I Sent.*, d. 19, q. 5, a. 2, ad 7.

Noteworthy is that the original contexts in which the commonalities and peculiarities are originally spied are different. One is the first operation, the other is the second operation. The first context is a penetrative movement of attention into a data set; the second is a reflexive movement of attention back to that data set. This is the original life of the intellect. Formed intentions are independent expressions of the results of these mental movements.

Now among the formed intentions of the second operation can be the *esse* of the thing, that is, the thing's existence understood as a distinctive *actus* had or possessed by the thing. As I mentioned in chapter 2, sometimes the commonalities that we know are individuals. Not only is a commonality like animal spread out in a multiplicity of its species, so too is Socrates spread out in a multiplicity of temperatures, complexions, postures, etc. In these cases it is the individual that is the commonality. But an individual also is found in an existential multiplicity. In light of Aquinas's immediate sense realism, the real individual also cognitively exists. This multiplicity allows the individual to be conceived as existence-neutral by the first intellectual operation and its real existence to be grasped by the second intellectual operation as an *actus* of its own.

The relation of this act to the substance with which it is composed also bears repetition. As I remarked in chapter 2, in respect to the substance rendered a being by composition with *esse*, *esse* is prior (*prius*), first (*primus*), most profound (*profundius*), and most intimate (*magis intimum*). *Esse* is the core around which the thing revolves. We are so accustomed to conceiving acts of a thing as items subsequent and posterior to the thing that the notion of an act basic and fundamental to its thing is strange. But if one is to correctly appreciate *esse* as provided by the intellect's second act, usual ways of thinking must be suspended.

Presented with the *esse* of something, the intellect is in a position to form an intention of this *esse*.[41] Like any formed intention, the formed intention of the thing's *esse* acquires a certain independence from the context in which it was first grasped. This means that the intellect possesses an intention of

---

41. That the intellect forms intentions of the objects of its second operation was a truth Gilson was forced to clarify by F.-M. Régis. This admission led Gilson to reserve *conceptus* for formed intentions of the first operation, and *conceptio* for formed intentions of the second operation. For the discussion between Régis and Gilson, see Gilson, *Being and Some Philosophers*, "Appendix." As I will explain, this distinction between formed intentions is crucial for addressing Kenny's challenge.

existence that does not present it, as does happen in its second operation. Consequently, I can think not only of a vacation in Hawaii, knowing that it does not exist, but I can think of an *existing* vacation in Hawaii knowing that it does not exist. In the latter case, to know that the vacation does not exist does not mean that we are not thinking of it as existing. Also, thinking of it as existing does not mean knowing that it exists.

It is this formed intention sense of *esse* that is involved in the Latin predicate *est*. Propositions, or enunciations, are also cases of formed intentions. In the commentary on Aristotle's *Peri Hermeneias*, Aquinas says that as employed in propositions "*est*" principally signifies "the actuality of every form commonly, whether substantial or accidental."[42] Two paragraphs earlier this actuality is the *esse* composed with the thing in what is meant by being, *ens*.[43] But because the *esse* is signified, it is clear that we are not dealing with *esse* as known in the second intellectual operation. That distinction is why it is always appropriate to ask whether a proposition is true or false. So, it is clear that the intellect goes on to form an intention that is a similitude of the *esse* of the thing that it grasps by the second operation. The formed intention is not so much a similitude that it presents the *esse* that it is a similitude of. Only when the formed intention of existence is spotlighting what is grasped by the second operation will the formed intention have implications for reality. Otherwise, the formed intention may express or mean existence, but it will not present existence, as happens in the second operation. In sum, the intellect is in possession of an existence-neutral sense of existence.

So far this material promises to answer Kenny. If this formed concept of *esse* is what is used in our thinking about God, then obviously it will still make sense to ask if God exists. To accommodate that question, it is not necessary, as Kenny thinks, to de-existentialize our conception of God. But two issues loom up. First, as expressing what is grasped in the second operation, the formed intention of *esse* is highly individual and particular. Just as your

42. *Aristotle: On Interpretation Commentary* (trans. Oesterle), Book I, l. 5, n. 22 (53).
43. "This is indeed most clearly seen in saying 'being' [*ens*], because *being* is nothing other than *that which is*. And thus we see that it signifies both a thing, when I say 'that which,' and existence [*esse*] when I say 'is' [*est*]" (ibid. [52]). In *Aquinas on Being*, 56, Kenny disputes the existential sense of *est* "since existential statements are only a tiny fraction of the number of sentences that we compose and employ." It is true that for Aquinas not every assertion expresses *esse*. Again, Maurer, "St. Thomas and Eternal Truths," 91–107, shows that the "is" in "eternal" truths corresponds to no *esse* proper to the truth itself. See above, note 15.

tan is yours and mine is mine, so too are our *esses*. An understanding of the nature of *esse*, of *ipsum esse*, remains to be presented, for God, according to Aquinas, is the nature of *esse*. Second, as expressing what is grasped in the second operation, the formed intention of *esse* expresses *esse* as the act *of a thing*. It is a portion of a composite situation. But in God *esse* is the thing; in God *esse* is not something possessed. In Thomistic terms there is a difference in the mode of signification. As Aquinas says, we think the simple as that by which something is and we think the composite as what exists. To think God as *esse* we have to somehow think the simple act of *esse* as an existent. As Kenny said, we have to Platonize and to think a predicate without a subject.[44] In sum, these two issues indicate that for all our efforts so far, the formed intention of *esse* has nothing to do with God.

Both issues require telling more of Aquinas's position on *esse*. So, to the first issue, Aquinas does not leave *esses* in disintegration. He reapplies the first intellectual operation to formed intentions of *esses*. Just as there is something the same in your tan and in mine, so too there is something the same in our *esses*. Aquinas variously refers to the sameness in *esses* as *esse formale*, *esse commune*, the *ratio essendi*, and *ipsum esse*.[45] But as a commonality, *esse* is unique.

---

44. Kenny, *Aquinas on Being*, 102, hits the mark when he says that "Aquinas's approach makes it look as if he is not opposed to Platonic Ideas in general or logical grounds, but merely has qualms about particular examples of such Ideas." Consider the following from Aquinas's proem to his commentary on the *Divine Names*: "The Platonists considered by an abstraction of this kind not only the ultimate species of natural things but also the most common species, which are the good, the one, and being [*bonum, unum et ens*]. They maintained one first thing that is the essence itself of goodness and of unity and of being [*ipsa essentia bonitatis et unitatis et esse*], which we call God and which [we say] all others are called good or one or beings through derivation from this first thing.... Hence, this position of the Platonists is not agreeable to the faith or truth insofar as it contains separate natural species, but in respect to what they say about the first principle of things, their opinion is most true and consonant with the faith of Christians." Of course, my present section is an attempt to show the logical grounds upon which Aquinas can hold this distinction.

45. *Esse commune* and *esse formale* are used interchangeably in *SCG* I.26. There a key point is that *esse formale* is not diversified in and through additions from the outside, as happens when a difference is added to a genus. At *De Pot.*, q. 7, a. 2, ad 9, Aquinas is again speaking of *esse commune* (see ad 6), and he repeats this key point. But he goes on to say that *esse* is not determined as potency by an act but as an act by a potency. Then at *ST* I, q. 4, a. 1, ad 3, Aquinas characterizes *ipsum esse* as received to receiver (*receptum ad recipiens*) rather than receiver to received (*recipiens ad receptum*). Finally, in the next article, God is characterized as *ipsum esse per se subsistens* and so has the entire *perfectio essendi* just as a subsistent heat would have heat *secundum perfectam rationem*. In these spots the thinking about *esse* is the same, though the terminology is modulating from *esse commune* to *esse formale*, *ipsum esse*, *perfectio essendi*, and *ratio essendi*. For further discussion, see Knasas, *Being and Some Twentieth-Century Thomists*, 208–10.

Even though it seems to be most general, it does not have a content in inverse relation to its extent. It is not, as Kenny claims, the "thinnest" predicate.[46] One can see this richness in Aquinas's description of the diversification of *esse formale* into individual *esse*s in his *SCG* I.26. In the second argument, Aquinas speculates that *esse formale* could be diversified in two ways.[47] The first way is through added differences. The second way is through *esse formale* itself which diversifies itself in light of the different natures to be actuated. Aquinas eliminates the first on the basis that being (*ens*) is not a genus to which differences are added. In the previous chapter, Aquinas noted that the differences added to a genus must be extrinsic to the genus under pain of placing the genus twice in the definition of the species. But, Aquinas insists, there is nothing outside of being. Hence, being cannot be a genus.

The appeal of *SCG* I.26 for a reading of I.25 is the obvious indication of a close connection between *esse* and *ens*. The basis for the connection lies in the role of *esse* if one is to have something that is more than existence-neutral, in short, more than nothing. Hence, *esse inquantum est esse* or *esse formale* will diversify itself in light of the thing it will actuate.

The formed intention of *esse formale*, then, is not pale and insipid but full and robust. And so, it is no surprise to see Aquinas transferring its richness to God as God is understood to be *ipsum esse subsistens*. For example, in *ST* I, q. 4, a. 2, Aquinas argues that because the perfections of all things pertain to the *perfectio essendi* and because God is *ipsum esse subsistens*, then God has the perfections of all things.[48] Elsewhere, Aquinas states that God is a thing that is the "essence of goodness, of unity, and of existence" (*ipsa essentia bonitatis et unitatis et esse*).[49]

---

46. Kenny, *The Five Ways*, 92.

47. "Furthermore, things are not distinguished from one another in having being, for in this they agree. If, then, things differ from one another, either their being must be specified through certain added differences, so that diverse things have a diverse being according to their species, or things must differ in that the being itself is appropriate to the natures that are diverse in species. The first of these alternatives is impossible, since, as we have said, no addition can be made to a being in the manner in which a difference is added to a genus" (trans. Pegis, 1:129).

48. "Since there God is subsisting being itself [*ipsum esse subsistens*], nothing of the perfection of being [*de perfectione essendi*] can be wanting to Him. Now all the perfections of all things pertain to the perfection of being; for things are perfect precisely so far as they have being after some fashion [*aliquo modo esse habent*]. It follows therefore that the perfection of no thing is wanting to God." Aquinas, *ST* I, q. 4, a. 2 (trans. Pegis, 1:39).

49. See above, note 44.

Now we are brought to the second issue. *Esse formale* is a portion of a larger picture. As mentioned, it expresses a commonality that is seen in individual *esses*, each of which is an act *of a thing*. As such, *esse formale* is connected with the nongeneric notion of being, the *ratio entis*. It will be understood to exist only as part of a being, just as running is understood to exist as part of a runner. Hence, Aquinas uses this observation about *esse formale* to deny adamantly the error of those who identify God and *esse formale*: "Their reason also failed because they did not observe that what is most simple in our understanding of things is not so much a complete thing as it is a part of a thing. But, simplicity is predicated of God as of some perfect subsisting thing."[50]

Aquinas is both using *esse formale* to think God and not using it. If this is not to be a contradiction, then Aquinas somehow is modifying *esse formale*, as originally apprehended, in order to make it appropriate for claims about God. From originally viewing it as a part, we come to view it as a subsistent. How can the mind look at *esse formale* so that it is less representative of a part of a being and more representative of a being itself? In short, how does Aquinas employ *esse formale* to think of God?

It should be noted that neither abstraction nor forming an intention has enabled *esse* to shed its status as a part. The abstraction of *esse formale* was formed from various *acts* of *esse* brought before the mind in its second operation. The relation of those acts to a subject is retained in the abstraction. That relation continues in the formed concept of *esse*, as, for example, it would continue in the formed concepts of differentiae. Is there another manner in which *esse* might be handled?

In the sixth question of his commentary on Boethius's *De Trinitate*, Aquinas says that our confused cognition of the divine quiddity and of the quiddity of separate substance is attained "by negations; for example by understanding that they are immaterial, incorporeal, without shapes, and so on."[51] Earlier negating is identified with separating: "Nevertheless, we reach a knowledge of [God and separate substances] . . . by way of negation (as when we separate from such beings whatever sense or imagination apprehends)."[52] Finally, separation is explained as another capacity of the intellect's second

---

50. *SCG* I.26. There are other issues: *esse formale* is open to addition, *esse subsistens* is not; *esse formale* is an abstraction existing only in the mind, *esse subsistens* is in reality.
51. Aquinas, *In de Trin.*, q. 6, a. 3 (trans. Maurer, 78).
52. Ibid., a. 2 (70).

act.[53] Not only can the second act compose in the reflective manner previously mentioned, but it can divide or separate in the sense of bringing negation to bear on some mental material.

Can negation be wielded on the formed intention of the *ratio entis* of which *esse formale* is a portion so that *esse formale* stands forth less as a portion and more as a reality? I believe so. By using negation to occlude, or to blot out, the non-*esse* portion of the *ratio entis*, called *essentia* by Aquinas,[54] he leaves *esse formale* standing less as a part and more as a whole unto itself. The unique nature of the negating permits this result. In this case negating is not and cannot be an erasure. *Esse formale* arises as a commonality in individual *esses* that are acts of various things. To erase the things would be to lose the *esses* and the commonality of *esse formale*. The things have to remain even while they are removed so that their *esses* can present *esse formale*. This handling of the subjects is made possible by negation in the sense of an occluding or blotting out. As the things are only covered over, their *esses* remain to present *esse formale*, but now as *ipsum esse subsistens*.[55]

---

53. "... and another [intellectual operation] by which it joins and divides, that is to say, by forming affirmative and negative statements." Ibid., q. 5, a. 3 (28).

54. "Essence must mean something common to all the natures through which different beings are placed in different genera and species, as for example humanity is the essence of man, and so with regard to other things." Aquinas, *On Being and Essence* (trans. Maurer, 30).

55. This understanding of negation as blotting out also solves the other two difficulties with using *esse formale* to think *esse subsistens*. By occluding the things, negation dumbs down the *esses* in which *esse formale* is a commonality. Hence, *esse formale* is presented less as an abstraction. Likewise, its capacity for addition by its diversification into individual *esses* is removed because the things in the light of which *esse formale* diversifies itself are removed. For other presentations of this play of negation to craft, for metaphysical purposes, a representation of *esse subsistens*, see Knasas, *Being and Some Twentieth-Century Thomists*, 236–44, and Knasas, *Aquinas and the Cry of Rachel*, 270–75. In his "The Universality of the Sensible in the Aristotelian Noetic," in *Aristotle: The Collected Papers of Joseph Owens*, ed. John R. Catan (Albany: State University of New York Press, 1981), 69–71, Joseph Owens uses negation to attain concepts for the hylomorphic components of matter and form. Unlike my wielding of negation, in Owens's usage negation does not render the remainder as subsistent but still as a part. To accommodate my present use of negation and Owens's mentioned use, I think that the "blotting out" character of the negation should be understood as able to be either heavy or light. Some coverings allow what is covered to still appear. Also, in "Aquinas: 'Darkness of Ignorance' in the Most Refined Notion of God," *The Southwestern Journal of Philosophy* 5 (1974): 107, Joseph Owens further employs negation to produce the *ignorantia* and *caligo* in which Aquinas says, at *In I Sent.*, d. 8, q. 1, a. 1, ad 4, that God is best known in this state of life. In my opinion, this point of application, which is still a natural state, is obviously outside of metaphysics. But those interested in seeing how I, in contrast to Owens, understand the application of negation at this point can see Knasas, *Being and Some Twentieth-Century Thomists*, 245n74.

Thus the original grasp of *esse* as the individual act of a thing does not preclude going on to form an intention of *esse* that expresses the conclusion of subsistent *esse*. But because we are speaking of God in terms of a formed intention of existence, then by the intention itself we do not know if God exists. These thoughts explain how Aquinas can say that "God exists" is in itself a self-evident proposition because God is his existence, but it is not self-evident to us.[56] You would think that not being evident to us would mean that we could not know that the proposition is self-evident in itself. The situation is clarified, however, by realizing that the terms of the proposition are what I have described as formed intentions of *esse*. Because God is his existence, the formed intention of the predicate *est* just repeats the formed intention of the subject *esse subsistens*. So, we can see that the proposition is *per se notum quoad se*. But because we are dealing with formed intentions here, the proposition is not *per se notum quoad nos*. In other words, it is perfectly appropriate to ask if "God exists" is true.

So what is my answer to Kenny's objection? Our ignorance about the existence of the phoenix and our ignorance about God do not have the same basis and so they do not lead to the same conclusion, namely, a distinction between thing and existence in both cases. The notion of the phoenix is existence-neutral because it is reflective of conceptual notes that have to be existence-neutral in order to be in existential multiplicities. Our notion of subsistent existence is not existence-neutral in this way, but it is composed of a formed intention of existence that gives it an independence from the context of the second operation in which it was formed. The first case leads to a situation involving a distinction between essence and existence. Knowledge of the existence of the phoenix adds something over and beyond the essence of the phoenix. In the second cause, knowledge of the existence of subsistent existence does not do that because existence is what the formed intention here is of. What knowledge of subsistent existence adds does not belong to it. It belongs to us. It adds our second operation knowledge of the *esse* of sensible things and our reasoning from that to subsistent existence.

---

56. *ST* I, q. 2, a. 1, co.

[5]

The *De Ente* Reasoning and Objections to Cosmological Reasoning

But if the *De Ente* reasoning can be explained to fellow Thomists, how would it fare with non-Thomists? Aquinas's reasoning does have some features that are hotly contested in debates on cosmological reasoning. This chapter isolates six such features and examines how they would fare in non-Thomist discussion.

First, at its very start the *De Ente* argument understands *esse* as a first-level predicate. As my chapter 4 discussions of Geach, Davies, and Kenny illustrated, *esse* designates an attribute of its own. The term should not be glossed as the fact of the thing or as the thing having a form. Moreover, *esse* designates an attribute that is unique in at least two respects. First, it is prior to its subject and so explains why the subject cannot be in any respect an efficient cause of its *esse*. These views on *esse* are prepared for by human consciousness presenting things in an existential multiplicity. Things both really and cognitionally exist. These data can be submitted to the intellect's twofold operation with significant metaphysical results. In sum, just as a complexion or temperature multiplicity would drive the mind to understand the thing of itself to be complexion- or temperature-neutral and to understand its complexion or temperature to be an attribute, the existential multiplicity drives the mind to understand the thing as existence-neutral, as ontologically hollow, and to understand its existence as an attribute basic and fundamental to the thing.

Second, as prior to the thing with its substantial and accidental determination, the *esse* of the thing reveals itself to be a nonformal act or attribute. Hence, without contradiction, Aquinas can call it the act of all acts and the perfection of all perfections. Finally, as mentioned in chapter 2, Aquinas regards *est* as a predicate that refers to *esse* in the previous senses. So, how does Aquinas's view of existence as an attribute of its own, and so able to ground a predicate about itself, fare in the secular discussion?

Existence as an Attribute, "Exists" as a Predicate

In chapter 1, I mentioned Kant's critique of the ontological argument. Kant's critique focuses on the proposition "The *ens realissimum* exists necessarily." Kant took the proposition to be logically necessary, and so he regarded "exists" as a predicate reiterating what was involved in the *ens realissimum*. Kant dispatched the ontological argument by explaining that "exists" is not a predicate. Predicates add some determination to their subjects. Existence cannot do that. His key remark to validate that claim is that if existence were a predicate adding some determination to its subject, then the actual would not be what was possible. I understand Kant's worry to be like, but not identical to, one's wanting coffee but the coffee always arriving with cream. The actual would always give us something that we did not quite want. So, to keep the actual the same as the possible, Kant asserted that existence simply posited the thing with all of its predicates. The positing did not itself add a predicate. Hence, there is no difference between one hundred possible thalers and one hundred actual thalers. Kant's thinking is one way to defend the "existence as fact" view.

If I have understood Aquinas correctly, he would say that Kant has made an understandable mistake. As distinctly known originally in judgment, *esse* is the act of all form without being a form. It does not manifest itself as something determinate and finite so that its addition to the existence-neutral thing would appear as like the addition of color to the complexion-neutral thing or temperature to the temperature-neutral thing. Without being a determinate act, it is nevertheless the act that makes all determination more than existence-neutral. Hence, its addition to the thing can be missed while one recognizes only the effect of that addition, namely, the fact of the thing. In sum, Kant has unwittingly understood all predicates as adding determination to their subjects. Aquinas can show how that is myopic.

More recently, A. J. Ayer, citing Kant, provided his own version of the thesis that the metaphysical view of a thing's existence as an attribute of the thing is nonsense. In his well-known *Language, Truth and Logic*, Ayer criticizes metaphysics for its making the existence or being of the thing an attribute of the thing. Ayer writes:

A simpler and clearer instance of the way in which a consideration of grammar leads to metaphysics is the case of the metaphysical concept of Being. The origin of our temptation to raise questions about Being, which no conceivable experience would enable us to answer, lies in the fact that, in our language, sentences which express existential propositions and sentences which express attributive propositions may be of the same grammatical form. For instance, the sentences "Martyrs exist," and "Martyrs suffer" both consist of a noun followed by an intransitive verb, and the fact that they have grammatically the same appearance leads one to assume that they are of the same logical type. It is seen that in the proposition "Martyrs suffer," the members of a certain species are credited with a certain attribute, and it is sometimes assumed that the same thing is true of such a proposition as "Martyrs exist." If this were actually the case, it would, indeed, be as legitimate to speculate about the Being of martyrs as it is to speculate about their suffering. But, as Kant pointed out, existence is not an attribute. For, when we ascribe an attribute to a thing, we covertly assert that it exists; so that if existence were itself an attribute, it would follow that all positive existential propositions were tautologies, and all negative existential propositions self-contradictory; and this is not the case. So that those who raise questions about Being which are based on the assumption that existence is an attribute are guilty of following grammar beyond the boundaries of sense.[1]

Ayer's argument against metaphysics is as follows. Metaphysicians who are engrossed with talking about the existence of a thing as if it were an attribute of the thing simply have had their thought misled by the way they speak. Metaphysicians have wrongly assumed that because we speak about the existence of the thing in the same grammatical fashion that we speak about genuine attributes of a thing, then the existence of the thing is also an attribute of the thing. But for two reasons, this thinking of the metaphysicians, understandable as it is, must be erroneous. When we are speaking of reality, both our ascription and the denial of an attribute to a subject presupposes the subject as there. For example, "Dr. Knasas studies Thomas Aquinas" attri-

---

1. Alfred Jules Ayer, *Language, Truth and Logic* (New York: Dover, 1952), 42–43.

butes studying Aquinas to an already existing Dr. Knasas. Hence, it really is saying "The existing Dr. Knasas studies Aquinas." And if we made the negative attributive statement, "Dr. Knasas does not study Hegel," we once more would be presupposing the fact of Dr. Knasas, as is indicated by the appropriateness of asking, "Well, what then is Dr. Knasas doing?" Hence, thought through, the metaphysical attempt to make something of the being of a thing by considering the being an attribute collapses. The attempt collapses because it renders perfectly good ways of speaking into bad ways of speaking. Whatever the logic of existential propositions is, the logic is not subject/attribute as maintained by the metaphysicians.

Ayer's refutation of metaphysics is just another way that a philosopher makes the case for the fact-view of existence. For Ayer, saying something exists is simply saying something is a fact. Would it be appropriate to include Aquinas in the metaphysicians of being ably refuted by Ayer? It seems not. For these metaphysicians, the being of the thing is not simply an attribute. More accurately speaking, they conceive existence as an attribute posterior and subsequent to the thing. What force would Ayer's argument have against the view that the existence that the thing possesses is an attribute basic and fundamental to the thing?

The judgmental grasp of the thing's real existence enables Aquinas to treat the logic of positive and negative existential propositions as subject/attribute without incurring any of the problems of which A. J. Ayer spoke. For Aquinas the existence of the thing means more than the fact of the thing. It is an act of the thing. But because the thing's existence is a prior and fundamental act, it is not just *an* act but *the* act of the thing. It is *the* act of the thing because without it we have the thing just as existence-neutral. Accordingly, for Aquinas "Martyrs exist" is subject/attribute but translates to "The existence-neutral martyrs exist." This is not a tautology. Also, "Martyrs do not exist" translates to "The existence-neutral martyrs do not exist." This is not a contradiction. Aquinas is not one of the metaphysicians of being whose thinking is lead astray by the way they speak. It is not the superficialities of grammar that have engendered Aquinas's metaphysics but the facts of reality manifested through the metaphysical exercise of the *duplex operatio intellectus*.

Ayer's argument works with a presupposition: the thing's existence considered as an attribute, as a predicate, can only be an item subsequent and posterior to a subject that is understood to be already there. Aquinas's thinking about *esse* escapes Ayer's mold. *Esse* is, if you will, an attribute or predicate, but one that the metaphysician observes is basic and fundamental to a subject that is understood to be of itself existence-neutral. As noted, this Thomistic conception renders Ayer's tautology and self-contradiction embarrassments nugatory.

Far from being outdated, Ayer's critique is echoed in Davies's cited critique of Etienne Gilson. Ayer's criticism that metaphysicians make all positive existential statements tautologies is expressed by Davies's claim that in the Gilsonian view of existence all such statements become necessarily true. Ayer's criticism that metaphysicians make all negative existential statements contradictions is expressed by Davies's claim that in the Gilsonian view all such statements become necessarily false.

Still more recently in his article, "Necessary Being," Alvin Plantinga provides two arguments that "God exists" cannot be analytic.[2] The second argument is of interest here. In the course of that second argument, Plantinga reasons that existence is not a property, or if so, then existence is so odd a property that it prevents existential statements from being analytic. Plantinga begins by explaining how any nonexistential subject predicate statement can be made analytic. One simply reads the predicate into the subject. Hence, "The shoes are brown" becomes the analytic "The brown shoes are brown." But existential statements cannot suffer this transition, that is, (A) "Existing turkeys exist" from (B) "Turkeys exist" is not analytic.

Plantinga provides two reasons. First, it is not at all clear that (A) says anything more than (B). But you can deny (B) without contradiction. So (A) would not be analytic. This first reason appears to take advantage of Kant's claim that existence is not a predicate because it cannot qualify in a determinate way. Hence, Plantinga says that the difference between a centaur and an existent centaur is far from clear.

His second reason concedes that "existing" could specify a property, for example, "nonimaginary." Made analytic (C) "Centaurs exist" would be (D) "Nonimaginary centaurs are nonimaginary." Would not the denial of (D) be

---

2. Alvin Plantinga, "Necessary Being," in *The Cosmological Arguments: A Spectrum of Opinion*, ed. Donald R. Burrill (Garden City, N.Y.: Anchor Books, 1967), 125–42.

a contradiction? Would it not be "Nonimaginary centaurs are not nonimaginary"? Plantinga denies that the denial of (D) must be contradictory. The denial can be simply the denial of centaurs. In other words, just as I can deny "Brown shoes are brown" not by claiming "Brown shoes are not brown" but by denying that there are any shoes, so too I can deny "Non-imaginary centaurs are non-imaginary" simply by denying that there are centaurs.

Plantinga's second reason could be considered as Plantinga again taking advantage of Kant, namely, Kant's view that existence is the positing of a thing with all of its predicates. On the other hand, not existing would be not positing the thing with all of its predicates, or as Plantinga says "denying that there are any centaurs at all." Hence, in sum, for these two reasons Plantinga's second argument concludes that unlike subject-predicate statements, existential statements cannot be made analytic and so existence is not a predicate or property.

I do not believe that these two reasons capture Aquinas's view of existence. "Exists" stands for *esse*, a nonformal property. As such it adds to the thing but does not add further determination. It adds the act that makes the thing and all of its determinations more than nothing, or more than existence-neutral. As explained earlier, the intellect's second operation is the philosophical access to this act. So, for Aquinas there can be no doubt that there is a difference between centaur and existing centaur. "Centaur" designates an existence-neutral object of the first operation. "Existing centaur" adds a formed intention of the *esse* grasped in the second operation. Consequently, by taking advantage of Plantinga's explanation of how subject predicate statements like "The shoes are brown" can be made analytic, the Thomist could translate "Centaurs exist" into the analytic "The centaurs that have *esse* have *esse*." The denial of that would be the contradiction "The centaurs that have *esse* do not have *esse*."

What about Plantinga's *total* denial move? First, without at all getting into Thomistic matters, one can say that the total denial move proves too much and so self-destructs. As noted above, the total denial move would allow one to deny without contradiction that the brown shoes are not brown. But here we are supposed to have a contradictory denial. What I am saying is that Plantinga's strategy would prevent *any* subject-predicate statement from becoming analytic. Second, Plantinga's second reason equivocates on the meaning of existence. His second reason concedes that existence is a property and then, as I observed, criticizes that view in light of an arbitrarily introduced Kantian nonproperty view of existence as just the positing of the thing. Aquinas has his philosophical reasons for his *sui generis* property view of existence. What are Plantinga's reasons for his view?

The answer seems to be a commitment to an interpretation of existential assertion in his first argument. Plantinga argues that no existential statement is analytic. My understanding of the argument is as follows. An analytic statement is one whose denial is self-contradictory, but a self-contradictory statement is one that entails two statements, one of which is the denial of the other. "Jones is a married bachelor" is self-contradictory because it entails "Jones is married" and "Jones is unmarried." Plantinga will show that no existential statement can be analytic because its denial will never produce a statement that entails two statements, one of which is the denial of the other. He begins by laying down what asserting existence means. To assert existence is to claim that there is at least one thing that satisfies a certain description.[3] The description may be complex. For example, ABCD. If it is complex, then denying existence asserts the statement "Nothing is ABCD." But that statement is translatable into "Each thing is either non-A, or non-B, or non-C, or non-D." So, let us go with the first disjunct "Each thing is non-A." Unlike "Jones is a married bachelor," the statement "Each thing is non-A" is a simple statement not able to be translated into two statements one of which is the denial of the other. So, no existential statement is analytic.

Does Plantinga's claim that to assert existence is to assert that a certain description applies capture Aquinas's thinking? In other words, does asserting that elephants exist mean that there are certain things to which the description of elephant applies square with what I have shown of Aquinas's thinking? I think that what gets in the way is what I called the priority of *esse*. The absolute consideration of some individual as existence-neutral insofar as the individual both really and cognitively exists is the condition for judgment's appreciation of the priority of *esse*. In this context one would never be fooled into thinking that *esse* is added to what is already there. Rather, it is clear that even though judgment is adding *esse* last, judgment is adding what we understand as really first. Consequently, "Elephants exist" means "Existence-neutral elephants have *esse*." "Having *esse*" could never be a description in Plantinga's

---

3. Ibid., 131.

sense because what it applies to is not something that is already there. As just noted, what the *esse* applies to is what the mind has good reasons to understand as existence-neutral. Yet Aquinas's approach still allows self-contradictory statements to entail two statements, one of which is the denial of the other. "Existing elephants do not exist" translates into "Existence-neutral elephants have *esse*" and "Existence-neutral elephants do not have *esse*."

Terence Penelhum argues that because it is demonstrable that "exists" is not a predicate, then "God exists" cannot be *per se notum* even *quoad se*, or in itself: "To say that although God's existence is self-evident in itself it is not to us is to say that it is self-evident in itself, and the error lies here. It is not our ignorance that is the obstacle to explaining God's existence by his nature, but the logical character of the concept of existence."[4] My thoughts in the present section dispute this claim. If "exists" stands for a *sui generis* attribute known in the intellect's second operation, "exists" can be a predicate. This opens the way to the possibility of an analytic existential proposition. My discussion of Plantinga shows that such a proposition need not concern God. Of course, Aquinas offers "God exists" as such a case. Just as "Bachelors are unmarried" is self-evident because what we mean by "bachelor" is "unmarried male," so too "God exists" is self-evident because what we mean by God is that God is intelligibly identical with its *esse*. "Exists" will just repeat the *esse* that has been placed in the subject.

None of this treads on ontological reasoning. The terms of the proposition "Subsistent existence exists" are formed intentions of *esse*. So though they may express *esse*, none of them present *esse*. Only judgment presents *esse* and that *esse* is the *esse* of sensible things. Consequently the proposition can be known as self-evident without being known as true. Likewise, *ipsum esse* can be the most proper name of God and still be to us only a nominal definition.

It might be helpful to conclude this section by illustrating the resiliency of Aquinas's *esse* conception in the analytic discussion of "exists." Much of that discussion is devoted to criticisms of the view that "exists" is a predicate of individuals with a distinctive, that is, unresolved, meaning of its own. My list of these criticisms is drawn from the second chapter of Barry Miller, *The Fullness of Being: A New Paradigm for Existence*.

---

4. Terence M. Penelhum, "Divine Necessity," in *The Cosmological Arguments* (ed. Burrill), 153.

A fundamental criticism is drawn from negative existential propositions, for example, "Socrates does not exist." The criticism goes as follows. If "exists" stands for a property, then "exists" is like "red" which also stands for a property. Furthermore, the behavior of the two predicates should be similar. Hence, just as the negative proposition "X is not red" translates into the positive "X is some other color," so too "Socrates does not exist" should translate into "Socrates does something other than existing." That result becomes problematic when one realizes that according to the similarity we should be talking about existing subjects in all the propositions. Hence, "Socrates does something other than existing" becomes "The existing Socrates does something other than existing." Ontologically speaking, that looks absurd: namely, an existent that does not exist. Logically speaking, the proposition is a blatant contradiction. Insofar as truth does not generate absurdity or contradiction, the thesis from which these embarrassments follow—*viz.*, "exists" stands for a property of its own—is not true.[5]

By my analysis the major premise in this criticism is that predicates that stand for properties in propositions about reality can be predicated only of what really exists. But for Aquinas the property for which the predicate "exists" stands is *esse* and *esse* is a *sui generis* property. Unlike the garden-variety property that is subsequent and posterior to its subject, *esse* is fundamental and basic. This thinking means that when "exists" is predicated, it is predicated of a subject that is not understood as already really existing. Rather, the subject stands for what had been grasped as of itself existence-neutral. Accordingly, "Socrates exists" translates into "Socrates, of himself existence-neutral, in fact exists." This radical basicness for *esse* ruins the similarity that drives the first criticism. In Aquinas's philosophy not only are positive existential propositions unlike positive attributive propositions, for example, "X is red," negative existential propositions do not mimic negative attribute propositions. Because "exists" stands for *esse*, the fundamental *actus* apart from which the subject is simply existence-neutral, then negative existential propositions are not talking about the subject doing something other than existing just as the "not red" object is being some other color. Only a property subsequent and posterior to its subject admits the possibility of replacement

---

5. C. J. F. Williams, *Being, Identity, and Truth* (Oxford: Clarendon, 1992), 5–6. A more classic formulation is A. J. Ayer's critique that I discussed above.

by another like property. For the Thomist the negative existential proposition is simply saying that in fact the subject, of itself existence-neutral, has no *esse*. Unlike a negative attributive proposition, a negative existential proposition cannot be predicating a nonexistential property. As basic and fundamental, *esse* does not allow another property to replace it as the property red allows replacement by the property blue. In other words, in Thomism negative existential propositions are resistant to translation into some positive proposition.[6] One can do it but only with care, for example, "Socrates, of himself existence-neutral, is in fact doing something other than existing." The predicate here actually refers to Socrates's staying existence-neutral.

As I mentioned when discussing Kenny, for Aquinas predication is a logical phenomenon that requires the subject of predication to cognitively exist in the formed intention, the *ens rationis*, about it. As so present the subject can undergo the predicative relation of identity with the meaning of the predicate. But this logical requirement makes no commitment to the real status of the subject itself. The subject that is cognitively existing in the concept about it can be some previously absolutely considered existence-neutral individual.

A second fundamental criticism is one that Miller attributes to Michael Dummett. If "exists" expresses a property, then we could speak of something losing and acquiring its existence. But actually such talk is nonsense. For example, when I lose my tan, I am around subsequent to losing it. But when my existence goes, I go also.[7] There are no properties *tout court*. Even beauty is a property only if regarded as something had at certain stage in one's life. In reply, I believe Aquinas would say that this objection pays insufficient attention to the way in which *esse* is apprehended by the second operation. The second operation adds *esse* to what can either really or cognitively exist because that thing is of itself existence-neutral. So *esse* comes across as an accident, just as the tan comes across as an accident with respect to an indi-

---

6. In *The Fullness of Being: A New Paradigm for Existence* (Notre Dame, Ind.: University of Notre Dame Press, 2002), Miller observes that this first problem results from confusing a name's reference with its bearer (32) and by thinking that nonexistence is more than a Cambridge property (33–37). Also in replying to a similar problem from Dummett, Miller renders talk about nonexistents to be noncontradictory in virtue of first and second order uses of "exists" (46).

7. Michael Dummett, *Frege, Philosophy of Language* (Cambridge, Mass.: Harvard University Press, 1981), 387.

vidual of itself complexion-neutral. But the respective status of the subjects here rebounds to the status of the respective accidents. As existence-neutral, the subject for *esse* entails that *esse* is a basic and fundamental accident. This scenario allows one to speak, as in fact we actually do, of something losing or acquiring its existence but not to take that talk as meaning that the thing exists before or after. Appreciated as a *sui generis* property, *esse* generates the appropriate qualifications in talk about it.

In the wake of these perceived problems, analytic philosophers try to formulate other phrasings of singular existential statements. Yet from a Thomistic point of view, none of these are required. Still drawing upon Miller's summary, I would like to show this superfluity. Following Frege, C. J. F. Williams understands a proposition like "Socrates exists" as referring, not to Socrates, but to the name "Socrates." Hence, the meaning here is that "Socrates" is a name used of some real individual.[8] But for Aquinas "Socrates" refers to an individual that is of itself existence-neutral. As I noted in chapter 2, Aquinas contrasts the individual essence from the universal essence. Both are existence-neutral. Aquinas does not assume that the individual is of itself an existent.[9] What prevents Aquinas from making that assumption is his analysis of the individual as both really and cognitively existing. For the individual to be doing both, the individual must not have proper to itself any existence. Rather, proper to the individual itself is existence neutrality. Hence, it is perfectly appropriate to formulate existential propositions that have singular things as their subjects and that express whether in fact the individual has existence or not.[10]

---

8. Williams, *Being, Identity, and Truth*, 34.

9. Pears and Thomson, *Is Existence a Predicate?*, 4, and Williams, *Being, Identity and Truth*, 6, think that some existential propositions can be so constructed that the subject alone referentially implies existence, e.g., "This room exists," and so these propositions are tautologies. The only way to avoid tautology, according to Pears, is to have the subject referring to an existence different from the existence asserted by *exists*. The existential interpreter of Aquinas could claim that the use of the demonstrative pronoun does not imply some kind of actual existence for the subject. The pronoun continues to qualify a room that is of itself existence-neutral. Hence, in terms of his epistemology, the full meaning of the proposition is "This of itself existence-neutral room exists." Aquinas could give the same treatment to "I exist." These treatments clear the way to regard *exists* as expressing the addition of the *sui generis* attribute of *actus essendi*.

10. Miller, *Fullness of Being*, 28, answers that "Socrates exists" can be understood as embedded in "Socrates no longer exists," and because the latter is not about the name but the person, then so too must be the former.

Another move concedes that "Socrates exists" is not about the name "Socrates" but about the instantiation of a property unique to Socrates.[11] Hence, "Socrates exists" translates into "There is an individual that has a unique property." This property could be "teacher of Plato," as Russell says, or it could be "socratizes," as Quine says. But again in Aquinas's view the individual is existence-neutral and this holds true even if one adds that the individual is unique. It may be true that an existent is unique. But for Aquinas the converse fails. The unique need not be the existent. The unique could be the existence-neutral. This thinking leaves the logical room for "exists" to add a distinctive property of its own.[12]

Consequently, Aquinas can go on to defuse the claim that "Socrates exists" means "Socrates has some other property." For instance, Jonathan Barnes attempts to translate "exists" into the copula plus the indefinite locative. Hence, "Socrates exists" translates into "Socrates is in some place."[13] But though it may well be that initially to exist involves being in a place, the converse again does not hold. To be spatial does not mean to be existent. The reason is that the individual that is of itself existence-neutral can be a spatial individual.[14] The same inability of conversion holds with any other property one may want to consider, for example, Socrates with a definite weight, complexion, or gait. Socrates may need to exist with one of these definites, but the point is that Socrates with one of these definites does not have to exist. Hence, Williams's claim that existence statements are statements about number also collapses.[15] Number can be added to what is existence-neutral without changing that status. For Aquinas, to be numbered does not necessarily mean to be existent.

Finally, some try to analyze "exists" to be an excluder.[16] Hence, just as "X

---

11. Williams, *Being, Identity, and Truth*, 34–35.

12. To handle this move, Miller, *Fullness of Being*, 41, cites Kripke on the idea that names are rigid designators and cannot be reduced to definite descriptions. Miller also makes a distinction (41–42) between "precise" individuals and "precisely" one individual. "Exactly one thing is the teacher of Plato" is about precisely one individual but not about the precise individual that is Socrates.

13. Jonathan Barnes, *The Ontological Argument* (London: St. Martin's Press, 1972), 62–65.

14. Miller, *Fullness of Being*, 49, replies instead that "all material entities are individual, but not all concrete individuals need be material." In my opinion, that is too much to claim at the beginning of metaphysics. At the start of metaphysics we are still ignorant of existing immaterial individuals.

15. Williams, *Being, Identity, and Truth*, 9–11.

16. For example, Roland Hall, as described by Miller, *Fullness of Being*, 50–53.

is a barbarian" means "X has no manners," that is, precisely lacks a property, so too "X exists" means "X is not nonexistent." This claim appears to be very similar to Kant's claim that existence adds nothing to the possible; it is simply the possible realized. Aquinas can do justice to these observations while still holding on to his unique conception of *esse*. As the act of the individual with all of its determinations, *esse* adds but without adding further determination. Revealed in the intellect's second operation as the act of forms, *esse* is the act of determination without itself being a determination. So for Aquinas the existent is the possible realized, but not just that. The realized possible involves the *actus* in virtue of which the possible is real. Because we do not notice any further determination, we can think that the actual involves no more than the possible and that "exists" functions as an excluder. But attention to the intellect's twofold operation clearly reveals actuality as involving the addition of *esse*.[17]

Admittedly, I have not covered all analytic criticisms of the thesis that "exists" stands for an attribute of its own. But even if the coverage had been exhaustive, the critique has long been a genie out of the bottle and will undoubtedly morph into other forms. I have tried only to say enough to show the reader that Aquinas's conception of *esse* as a unique *actus* of the thing has the "legs" to keep up with the ongoing discussion.[18]

Sense Realism

Cosmological reasoning presupposes cognitional access to a really existing world. In the literature, even in Kant's critique of the reasoning, that presupposition surprisingly rarely comes in for criticism. The critiques are directed elsewhere. But in Aquinas's *De Ente* reasoning, realism is more than a presupposition; it is an important basis for the argument. That the thing's *esse* is something "had" by the thing is a viewpoint attained in virtue of the fact that the real thing is also cognitionally existing and so is of itself not real. To be really existing the thing must *have* its existence. Somewhat similarly, for the hot coffee to be cold, the hot coffee cannot of itself be hot. It is hot only

---

17. Miller, *Fullness of Being*, 52, replies that "exists" cannot be an excluder because there is nothing for it to exclude.

18. For still further analytic treatments of existence, for example, indexical-possibilist, indexical-actualist, actualist, and for Existential Thomist comment, see Kerr, *Aquinas's Way to God*, 76–84.

by having that temperature as an attribute. Aquinas indicates this realism in the *De Ente*. In describing the absolute consideration of essence, he says that essence can have a twofold existence, *duplex esse*. One *esse* is *in re*, the other is *in anima*. As noted in chapter 2, however, this ascription can be made of some individual thing, an individual essence, and so Aquinas can be understood as asserting a cognitional existence in sensation for some real individual. Since the onset of modern philosophy, however, the presence of the real in sense cognition has been called into doubt. I would like to address some of the reasons offered for this doubt about sense realism.[19]

A list of the many objections to sense realism includes the following. There are the relativities in perception. For example, I see the straight stick bent in the water. If the real stick is straight and I am seeing something as bent, then I am not seeing the reality. Also, the colorblind person sees the poppy field as gray. If the field is red and the person is seeing gray, then the person is not seeing the reality. People in a particular position see a piece of rectangular paper as trapezoidal. They are not, then, seeing what is real. Also consider seeing the moon as the same size as the quarter held at arm's length. It follows that the visual moon is not the reality. Likewise, seeing the square tower through the mist or from a distance as round seems to vacate the real tower from our awareness. From Husserl, I always see the six-sided die as only three-sided. Again, I am not seeing the reality, and so my judgments of real existence are to be bracketed. Finally, consider seeing a star long ago extinguished, or feeling pain in a leg that has been amputated. Are not all of these cases of sensation presenting us with an unreal object? That was the conclusion the moderns came to and so the basis of philosophy shifted from sensation and away from a basically receptive account of cognition to a projective one.[20]

---

19. In his "The Leibnizian Cosmological Argument," 28, Alexander R. Pruss uses sense realism to defend the PSR: "Starting with the observation that once we admit that some contingent states of affairs have no explanations, a completely new skeptical scenario becomes possible: no demon is deceiving you, but your perceptual states are occurring for no reason at all, with no prior causes." I do not think that Aquinas would need this causal account to defend sense realism nor would Aquinas need the PSR to bring in causality. As my present section describes, my perceptual state presents reality. So, I do not have to reason to reality. Also, that my perception of reality needs a cause can be determined by the fact that the perception happens and every happening is a substrate/determination situation. In the case of perception, the substrate is the amplitude over matter of the sensor's form and the determination is the form of the real item. See references provided below at note 23. Aquinas can then reason to the real thing as cause by the *De Ente* principle, "What belongs to a thing is caused."

20. For Descartes's listing of relativity cases, see *Meditations on First Philosophy* VI. For John

There are also the famous dream and hallucination possibilities mentioned by Descartes in his *Meditations on First Philosophy* and still being employed in the twentieth century as grounds for bracketing our judgments of real existence in the phenomenology of Husserl.[21] In sum, have you not dreamed that you have been reading? So how do you know that you are not dreaming right now?

Finally, there are Immanuel Kant's arguments that space and time are not real characteristics of real things but *a priori* forms of our sensibility. In other words, because space stays the same whether it is populated with these things or with those things, then space is less a characteristic of the experienced and more a characteristic of the experiencer.

None of these three types of arguments, as well as some others that I will mention, are knockout blows to immediate sense realism.[22] First, there is always enough realism in the relativity examples to do philosophy. In other words, when I look into the water, I see something real, but I do not know if it is straight or bent. Maybe I will never know its precise shape, but I cannot gainsay that I know some shaped reality. Likewise, I may see the poppy field as red while the colorblind viewer sees it as gray. My point would be that both of us see real color, we just disagree on the precise shade of the real color that we both see. Likewise, I see the shape as rectangular, you see it as trapezoidal. What is important philosophically is that we both see real shapes, though we disagree on the exact configuration. The reader can go on to guess my replies to the moon, tower, and die examples.

I know what my objector will say to all of these replies. He will insist that if something is directly and immediately present, then it must be present ex-

---

Locke's, see *An Essay Concerning Human Understanding*, Book II, chap. VIII, pars. 14–21. Joseph Berkeley extends Locke's arguments for subjectivizing the secondary qualities to the primary ones; see his *A Treatise Concerning the Principles of Human Knowledge* I, 9–15. Finally, David Hume, *An Enquiry Concerning Human Understanding*, Section XII, repeats Berkeley's arguments. In the twentieth century, Edmund Husserl employed the perspectival character of sensation to argue that the physical object is not a real "constituent part of consciousness" but necessarily "transcendent to perception." See his *Ideas*, 120.

21. "Not only can a particular experienced thing suffer devaluation as an illusion of the senses; the whole unitarily surveyable nexus, experienced throughout a period of time, can prove to be an illusion, a coherent dream." Edmund Husserl, *Cartesian Meditations: An Introduction to Phenomenology*, trans. Dorion Cairns (The Hague: Martinus Nijhoff, 1964), 17.

22. For still other issues and a defense of sense realism, see Christopher A. Decaen, "The Viability of Aristotelian-Thomistic Color Realism," *The Thomist* 65, no. 2 (2001): 179–222.

actly as it is. For example, if I am present in this room, then I have to be here moustache and all. For example, if the real me is two-armed, then I am absent if a one-armed person is present. Hence, for my objector, you cannot have me directly present to you right now as I turn sideways and a one-armed man is in your cognition.

But the thinking of my objector seems to conflate direct physical presence with direct cognitional presence. Direct presence as physical is what brooks no inexactitude. As my replies to the relativities in perception indicated, realities can be directly present in cognition inexactly. My objector gives no arguments that cognitional direct presence should be thought of as just like physical direct presence. Until my objector does so, my objector has not given an integral objection.

The distinction between physical presence and cognitional presence enables one to answer the following questions. If sense realism is true, am I not in two places at once when someone senses me? Again, the objector assumes that cognition equals physical presence. Also, when my hand is in the oven I feel the heat; if the real me is in your sense awareness, why do I not feel your sensation? Again, as the reference to the oven indicates, the objector is assuming that cognitional presence is just like physical presence.

How sense cognition can directly, but inexactly, present a reality is a question worthy of pursuit. And at the end of the second book of his *De Anima*, Aristotle gives some enlightening remarks to explain how sense receives the form of the thing known without the matter.[23] But how-questions need not be answered to keep assertions *that* something is so. An aboriginal man from the jungles of New Guinea on the streets of a large city would know for certain that vehicles were going down the street but be perfectly ignorant of how they were doing it. Likewise, the realist has good reason to say that sense directly presents reality, albeit inexactly, even though the realist might be unable to explain how this can happen for cognitional presence but not for physical presence.

Finally, direct but inexact presence of reality in sense awareness is also useful to deal with other phenomena used by the skeptic. First, what about seeing the long-extinguished star and the amputee still feeling pain in an ab-

---

23. For an enlightening commentary, see Joseph Owens, "Aristotle: Cognition a Way of Being," in *Aristotle* (ed. Catan), 74–80. See also Owens, *Cognition*, chap. 2.

sent limb? These cases seem to indicate that sensation does not necessarily provide an existent. But just as the precise shade or shape of the real body may elude sensation, so too the precise time of the reality may not be given by sensation. Nevertheless, sensation still gives a reality even though sensation may be imprecise about whether it is giving the reality in the present moment or in a past moment. The important point is that I am seeing something real even though it may not be real right now. Likewise, like time, number may not be an original factor in vision. By pressing my pupil, I can double whatever I am seeing. Does this mean that I must doubt whether I am seeing one thing or many? Yes it does. But it does not follow that I have to doubt that it is real. Whether my object of sensation is one thing or a multiplicity, the object still comes across as real. The exact location of real color, namely, on distant bodies or on the pupil, may also be admitted to be an issue without loss of realism.

What of the dream and hallucination possibilities? Are they sufficient to destroy immediate sense realism? No. Dreaming involves a model of cognition that I can verify right now is not true for my sense awareness. In dreams we are aware of nonexistents because our dreaming takes advantage of ideas. What I am calling ideas are the formed intentions of Aquinas that I mentioned when replying to Kenny in chapter 4. Ideas are reflexively observable mental entities that possess an intentional charge. Because of this intentional charge, they can convey our awareness to something other than themselves, even to something that does not really exist. What I am calling ideas are also found in memory and imagination. So the dreamer never immediately relates to the dreamer's object. Between both is the idea that the dreamer is using to get the dreamer's attention to the object. So how do I know that I am not dreaming right now? Because right now I can sweep my current sense awareness with an act of reflection and see that it is an idea-free zone. In my awareness right now as I look this way, there is only me and some reality. I can see that my awareness is not employing an idea that might make me wonder if I am doing something like dreaming or hallucinating.

That my current awareness can be reflexively confirmed to be an idea-free zone also makes it impossible for an evil spirit—a *spiritus malignus*—or even for God, to bring my current awareness into an awareness of something that does not really exist. If sensation is a direct presence of the real, then a superior being cannot cause me to sense and not also cause the reality. Only if sensation employed ideas could some superior being cause me to have a false sensation. Finally, I want to note that if one studies the reprise of methodic doubt in *Meditation* VI, it is clear that Descartes's dream and hallucination possibilities all assume that sensation operates in and through ideas.

But what about the scenario presented in the 1999 film, *The Matrix*? In this case someone has his brain hooked up to a computer and by electrically stimulating his brain, the person is brought to experience an entire world that does not exist. Does not the possibility of the Matrix destroy confidence in sense realism? I do not think so. What is called a possibility here has really not been established. It is pure Hollywood. In experiments of electrical stimulation of the cortex, the noted neurophysiologist Wilfred Penfield could only give patients an experience of what they recognized to be a past event.[24] So, obviously, the electricity caused a stimulation of the patient's ideas of memory. A blow to the head causing one to see lights or a migraine doing the same could be handled along the same lines. What the experiments have failed to do is provide a person blind from birth an experience of color or a person deaf from birth the experience of sound. Those experiments would be a problem for the immediate sense realist. It is true that video technology has given us a case of going from pure electricity to color and sound. But that transition is to real color and sound, real color on the TV screen and real sound from the speakers. As Penfield showed, we are still lacking a transition from real electricity to color and sound in cognition. So the Matrix is pure fantasy.

Finally, what about Kant? Again, Kant noted that if space was an attribute of real things, then space should change with things, but space does not. Hence by process of elimination, Kant concludes that space is a characteristic of the sensor, not the sensed. But the sense realist could respond that the space about which Kant is speaking is an imaginative enlargement of the real extension of larger bodies against which smaller bodies profile themselves. For instance, I see the picture frame only against the wall, I see the tower only against the sky. Here the backgrounds that stay the same are real extensions. What the knower can do is take real extension and imagine that it is infinite

---

24. Wilfred Penfield, *The Mystery of the Mind: A Critical Study of Consciousness and the Human Brain* (Princeton, N.J.: Princeton University Press, 1978), 21–27.

so that there is one imaginary space against which anything can be profiled. Even though this space is imaginary, it is not *a priori*. The imagination builds up this space using real extension given immediately in sensation. This reply, or a type of it, can be used with Kant's other arguments for the apriority of space and for the apriority of time.

It is true that immediate sense realism establishes itself by conceding a form of minimalism. For example, I do not immediately perceive full-blooded bodily substances. Rather, my sensation only goes as far as the real accidents of those substances. That is why impersonation of one substance by another is possible. Also, the direct presence of those real accidents can be fraught with inexactitude. I see the real straight shape as bent, the red poppies as gray, the rectangle as trapezoidal, etc. Yet, in my opinion, which I have explained elsewhere, despite the minimalism, our sensations have enough purchase on reality to argue much further.[25] For example, a sufficiently clever philosopher will be able to argue to particular substances, to their matter/form composition, to their entitative composition with their act of existence, and to efficient causality behind these compositions. The immediate data, meager as they are, are also sufficiently varied to abstract an analogous notion of being that is recognized as the good. Against this notion of being, the data of sensation appear as goods but not as the good. This situation leaves us with a real freedom before any particular thing. Finally, our awareness of ourselves as intellectors of being reveals ourselves to be particularly intense instances of the good and so grounds a respect and solicitude owing to ourselves and others.[26]

The Scope of Explanation

In his "Divine Necessity" Terence Penelhum distinguishes between the existential and the qualitative cosmological arguments.[27] I noted a similar ambiguity in the texts of Leibniz's contingency arguments. Penelhum clearly affirms the fundamentality of the existential form. Though the existential argument may not fully explain the features which the qualitative argument

---

25. See Knasas, *Being and Some Twentieth-Century Thomists*, 9–17.
26. See John F. X. Knasas, *Thomism and Tolerance* (Scranton, Penn.: Scranton University Press, 2011), 14–23. In sum, if one is clever enough, one can produce what John Paul II in *Fides et Ratio*, par. 4, called "the implicit philosophy."
27. Terence Penelhum, "Divine Necessity," in *The Cosmological Arguments* (ed. Burrill), 143–64.

begins, "the Qualitative question presupposes the Existential. One cannot finally answer the question of why the world is as it is without explaining why it exists, for nothing can have features unless it exists."[28] But the existential cosmological argument quickly gets into trouble. Penelhum argues that the existential question "Why does anything exist?" is not a genuine question and so the principle of sufficient reason (PSR) is not just unproven, as William Rowe argued, but is demonstrably false.

Penelhum explains it this way. Both the existential question and the PSR aim for total explanation but total explanation is demonstrably impossible. If the whole is to be explained, then there are only so many possibilities for this explanation and they all come to nothing. To begin, we obviously cannot explain the whole by something outside the whole. Penelhum suggests that the most viable way of offering an explanation of the whole of reality is to say that one part of reality is self-explanatory and that the remainder of reality is explicable in reference to that part. Penelhum then focuses on showing the contradictory nature of a self-explanatory being. First, a self-explanatory being would be one whose existence follows upon its nature. His critique of the ontological argument has shown, however, that existence, because it is not a quality, cannot follow upon the nature of any being. Second, if one maintains that the relation between a self-explanatory being's nature and existence is a causal one, then one is forced to the absurdity of something causing its own existence. Penelhum concludes that the idea of universal explanation is bogus.

Recalling the opening line of the *De Ente* reasoning suffices to illustrate that Aquinas is not in Penelhum's aim. That line states: "Whatever belongs to a thing is caused." Aquinas is not making a universal claim about all existents. Only those existents that have *esse* require an explanation. Hence, to reach *esse tantum* would be to reach a being that does not provoke the need for explanation. Obviously, the *De Ente* reasoning goes on to explain that a thing that has *esse* cannot explain the *esse* that it has. So, Aquinas agrees with Penelhum that a self-caused being is impossible.

What about the possibility of a being whose existence follows its nature as in ontological reasoning? The parallel case to this is the way the sum of 180 degrees follows from the nature of the triangle. But in this case that nature

---

28. Ibid., 146. Penelhum reads Aquinas's *tertia via* in this existential way and considers the *tertia via* to be Aquinas's central proof (147).

of the triangle has, if not an ontological priority, at least a conceptual priority to the 180 degrees. In Aquinas's metaphysical thought, however, there is nothing conceptually prior to *esse*. That was the whole point about the second operation bottoming out in reality. No further act than *esse* is required for the thing to be a being. Hence, again, we can remember Aquinas's description of *esse* as the act of all acts and the perfection of all perfections. Without the thought of that further act, it is impossible to conceive a situation in which *esse* conceptually follows upon the thought of something else. The ideas of a self-explanatory being is a red herring as far as the metaphysics of Aquinas is concerned.

As a result of my replies to Penelhum, I think that a reader of Aquinas should very carefully, if at all, introduce the PSR into a hermeneutic of Aquinas. Applied to the divine existence, the PSR seems to entail a doctrine of divine aseity. If the existence of every being must have its sufficient reason, then in the case of God the sufficient reason can only be his nature. It is no surprise that Penelhum can see the ontological argument here. Any hint of divine aseity, however, is absent from the texts of Aquinas. William Norris Clarke puts it this way:

> In view of his radical reduction of essence to existence in the divine nature, St. Thomas carefully avoids the Anselmian way of speaking of the divine existence as though it were an attribute flowing necessarily from the divine essence, with its hint of a conceptual priority of essence. In fact, the term itself, *a se* (or aseitas), traditional though it be, is never actually used by Aquinas in speaking of God, possibly because of its faintly ambiguous suggestion of some causal relation between the divine essence and its existence.[29]

The divine existence is strictly identical with the divine nature. In no way can his nature and existence even be conceived separately. That conceptual identity was behind Aquinas's understanding of "God exists" as *per se notum*. The conceptual identity of essence and existence in God excludes any formal causality in which existence would flow from essence like certain predicates conceptually flow from certain subjects in mathematical propositions.

It is true that in the *De Ente* reasoning, Aquinas says: "Everything that is through another [*per aliud*] is reduced to that which is through itself [*omne*

---

29. William Norris Clarke, "Aseity (*Aseitas*)," *New Catholic Encyclopedia*, 1:946.

quod est per aliud reducitur ad id quod est per se]." This statement is undoubtedly close to "Whatever exists has a reason for its existence either in itself or in something else." Again, though, the subject of Aquinas's remark is less universal. Also, is Aquinas's something that exists *per se* the same as what has in itself a reason for its existence? The next line of the *De Ente* indicates otherwise: "so it is necessary that there is something, that is the cause of existing [*causa essendi*] to all things, because it is existence only [*esse tantum*]." Just as Aquinas tweaked "God exists" to be *per se notum* because the predicate was identical to the subject, so too Aquinas takes what exists *per se* as what is existence alone. In other words, in the first cause there is no basis for even a conceptual distinction between God's existence and a "reason" for God's existence.

Though the PSR takes ample note of *esse*'s disconnect with things in our experience, it seems to struggle to apply itself at the upper levels of reality. As mentioned in chapter 1, for Leibniz God carries the reason for his existence (selections A and C), and is a pure consequence of possible being (selection B). Yet Leibniz also says, like Aquinas, "there must exist some one being metaphysically necessary, or whose essence is existence" (selection D). Leibniz's confusion about how to understand the God of his contingency argument probably stems from earlier confusions about the existence of contingent things. Did Leibniz have to begin by claiming a universal applicability for the PSR? Would it not have sufficed to claim simply, "What belongs to a thing is caused"?[30]

Finally, the *De Ente* reasoning's lack of concern for universal explanation enables the reasoning to sidestep the fallacy of composition charge that is

---

30. For a discussion of Garrigou-Lagrange's multi-understanding of the PSR and its liaisons with my understanding of Aquinas's metaphysics of *esse*, see my *Aquinas and the Cry of Rachel*, 136–41. Worth noting is a remark by Barry Miller. Miller's work is extremely interesting from my point of view. He appeared to be developing a Thomistic Existentialism from within analytic philosophy. No other analytic philosopher, never mind no analytic Thomist of which I am familiar, undertook that project. In an early article entitled "The Contingency Argument," *The Monist* 54, no. 3 (1970): 359–73, Miller provides an argument that clearly echoes Aquinas's *De Ente* reasoning. Miller never cites Aquinas. Clearly, nevertheless, Miller's understanding that "exist" is a modifier of a subject that is an "existential zero" echoes Aquinas's understanding of *esse* as a *sui generis* attribute. Consequently, he insightfully remarks (368) that there is no need to introduce the PSR or any other extraneous principle. The independence of the *De Ente* reasoning from the PSR has been missed by Thomists and non-Thomists. Insistence on the PSR reflects a shallow and unnuanced understanding of the existence of the thing. One might even say that the use of the PSR in contingency reasoning and the lack of the

sometimes made in discussion of cosmological reasoning. A fallacy of composition falsely extends to the whole specific properties of the parts. For example, because each part of a whole weighs one pound, so the whole weighs one pound. For cosmological reasoning, the fallacy would lie in claiming that because each thing in the world is caused or contingent, then the world itself is caused or contingent. A popular formulation of this criticism was given by Bertrand Russell in his radio debate with Fredrick Copleston, SJ. Russell maintained that asking for a cause of the whole because each member had a cause was like asking for the mother of the human race because each human had a mother.[31] The cosmological proponent is confusing real with logical wholes. Edward Sillem seems to answer Russell decisively.[32] Sillem rejects the parity for the obvious reason that one is not moving from a real to a logical whole when one asks for a cause of the universe. The order of things that we call the universe exists while humanity as such does not. A question about the cause of this or that existent thing is of the same logical type as a question about the existent universe. Both are looking for the real causes of real effects.

In all of the selections given of Leibniz's contingency reasoning, Leibniz at a point looks for a cause of the world. In his *De Ente* Aquinas does not. Provided it has *esse*, any existent logically suffices for Aquinas to conclude to God as a presently acting creative cause. It is true that if Aquinas did discuss the world as composed of things whose *esse* belongs to them, then he would argue for a cause of the world. Subsistent existence would be behind each thing and so a cause of the group that is the world. But the *De Ente* reasoning has no need to do this. Using the *duplex operatio intellectus*, the reasoning can begin from an analysis of any individual existent and proceed immediately to God. As Maritain remarked: "Let us but grant to a bit of moss or the smallest ant its due nature as an ontological reality, and we can no longer escape the terrifying hand that made us."[33]

PSR in Aquinas's *De Ente* reasoning disqualifies Aquinas as a proponent of contingency reasoning and hence of classic cosmological reasoning. I prefer to keep Leibniz and Aquinas talking to each other, and so I regard the *De Ente* argument as the more profound version of contingency reasoning.

31. Bertrand Russell, *Why I Am Not a Christian and Other Essays on Religion and Related Subjects* (London: Simon and Schuster, 1957), 152.

32. Edward Sillem, *Ways of Thinking about God: Thomas Aquinas and the Modern Mind* (New York: Sheed and Ward, 1961), 162–63.

33. Jacques Maritain, *The Degrees of Knowledge*, trans. Gerald B. Phelan (New York: Charles Scribner's Sons, 1959), 110.

Infinite Regress

Toward the end of the *De Ente* reasoning, Aquinas dismisses an infinite regress of causes each with accidental *esse*. The thinking seems easy enough to grasp. If the cause of the *esse* with which we are beginning is a thing like the first, namely, a thing whose *esse* belongs to it, then before the second thing can cause the *esse* of the first, the second thing must have its *esse* caused by another. Moreover, as mentioned in my chapter 2, the priority of accidental *esse* requires that the causes be causing the *esse* presently, not in the past but no longer. If the third thing is like the first two, then clearly before it can cause the second thing, the third must have a present cause for its *esse*. Continuing in this vein, an infinite regress would consist of a series of things each asking for a cause in order to cause but never having that cause forthcoming in the series. Instead of an image of an infinite stack of books each being supported by the book under it, the better image would seem to be an infinite series of zeros whose sum is still zero.[34]

I would like to observe, however, that in the *De Ente* argument Aquinas's denial of an infinite regress appears to be an afterthought. In other words, Aquinas does not initially conclude to *esse tantum* after the denial of an infinite regress. He makes that conclusion after stating that everything which is *per aliud* is reduced to that which is *per se*. In fact, it could be argued that Aquinas uses the truth of this reduction to eliminate the infinite regress. The infinite regress cannot stand because it only includes the *per aliud*. But some may wonder how the reduction of the *per aliud* to the *per se* could be known as true without knowing that an infinite regress is impossible. Aquinas seems to be trapped in circular reasoning. Namely, a reduction of the *per aliud* to

---

34. Paul Edwards is the one who offers the infinite stack of books scenario to think the infinite regress possibility. Paul Edwards, "The Cosmological Argument," in *The Cosmological Arguments* (ed. Burrill), 111. It is clear that the scenario, as Edwards explains it, does not apply to what Aquinas is thinking. But it could be questioned whether Edwards correctly describes his own example. Edwards says: "If a book, Z, is to remain in its position, say 100 miles up in the air, there must be another object, say another book, Y, underneath it to serve as its support. If Y is to remain where it is, it will need another support, X, beneath it." When Edwards says "If Y is to remain where it is, it will need another support" he is admitting that Y's supporting Z *means* Y's remaining where it is. But Y's remaining where it is is said to need another. So, there is no Y's supporting Z until that other is furnished which, of course, is not possible if the regress is infinite. Correctly understood, Edward's image actually illustrates a problematic infinite regress.

the *per se* is necessary because otherwise an impossible infinite regress results, but an infinite regress is impossible because it is necessary to reduce the *per aliud* to the *per se*.

But Aquinas knows that the *per aliud* must be reduced to the *per se* for another reason. The reason can be articulated this way. Because of the previous lines of the *De Ente* argument, Aquinas already knows as true that a thing whose *esse* belongs to it is caused by something else, an *aliud*. One would contradict that already argued truth if the *aliud* were another thing whose *esse* belonged to it. In other words, if the other is the *per aliud*, then the original thing is not reduced to an other.

Though the *De Ente* reasoning can handle objections to the impossibility of an infinite regress, the reasoning is not logically required to do so. The reasoning actually gets to *esse tantum* immediately from its starting point of *esse* that is accidental to a thing. Leibniz also said as much. If the universe is composed of contingents, then it must be caused by a necessary being. From the universe itself one goes immediately to a necessary being. As I noted at the conclusion of the previous section, Aquinas makes the same immediate reduction from any one thing in the universe. The virtue of Aquinas's perspective is that he can sidestep debates about the fallacy of composition.

Evil

A fourth issue is evil. It comes up not so much as an objection to cosmological reasoning as to theistic reasoning. The objection goes: how can an all-good, all-powerful, and all-knowing God create a world with evil in it? You would think that such a God would have the motivation, ability, and awareness necessary to avoid evil. Though the question is a "how" question that admits both God and evil, since Hume the problem has been taken as a problem for theism itself. In fact, Aquinas brings up the problem in the very article that contains his *quinque viae*. The problem of evil is a voluminous one in philosophy and theology. Elsewhere I have tried to do some justice to the task of defending theism.[35] So without intending to be curt and trite, I would like to explain how Aquinas's *De Ente* reasoning can logically sidestep the morass of the debate regarding the problem of evil.

35. Knasas, *Aquinas and the Cry of Rachel*.

Besides *ST* I, q. 2, a. 3, obj. 1, Aquinas raises the evil problem as a philosophical challenge to theism in two other locations. The locations are: *De Ver.*, q. 10, a. 12, ad 10, of the second set and *SCG* III.71 (*Per haec autem*). It is my contention that in these other two texts, Aquinas philosophically solves the theism problem of evil so decisively that it understandably becomes a theodicy problem thereafter. What is striking about these texts is the Aquinas's claim that evil is never so great that all good is lost. In other words, if evil exists, God still exists. I begin with the *SCG* passage.

In *SCG* III.71, Aquinas is intent upon arguing that divine providence is compatible with evil in things. At the close of the chapter, he says, "With these considerations we dispose of the error of those who because they noticed that evils occur in the world, said that there is no God. Thus, Boethius introduces a certain philosopher who asks: 'If God exists, whence comes evil?'"[36] Instead of using the stated ideas of III.71, Aquinas answers the question by taking a new tack: "But it could be argued to the contrary: 'If evil exists, God exists.' For, there would be no evil if the order of good were taken away, since its privation is evil. But this order would not exist if there were not God." "If evil exists, God exists" is quite a dramatic reversal of the atheistic use of the evil problem. It is worth the effort to see if Aquinas can make good on this claim. A brief commentary on Aquinas's argument follows.

First, in sum, Aquinas is saying that because evil is a privation in the order of good and because this order would not exist without God, then, if evil exists, God exists. Second, back in III.6, Aquinas provides an elucidation of the privation concept of evil:

Now, evil is in a substance because something which it was originally to have, and which it ought to have, is lacking in it. Thus, if a man has no wings, that is not an evil for him, because he was not born to have them; even if a man does not have blond hair, that is not an evil, for though he may have such hair, it is not something that is necessarily due him. But it is an evil if he has no hands, for these he is born to, and should have—if he is to be perfect. Yet this defect is not an evil for a bird. Every privation, if taken properly and strictly, is of that which one is born to have, and should have so, in this strict meaning of privation, there is always the rational character of evil.[37]

---

36. *SCG* III.71 (trans. Bourke, 3.1:240–41).
37. Knasas, *Aquinas and the City of Rachel*, 44.

For Aquinas, evil is real. But the trick is to understand its manner of existing. Generally, evil is not real in itself but in something else; evil is real reductively. In that respect evil is like the accidents of a substance. For example, the accident of color is real but only as in and of something else, namely, a surface and ultimately a substance. The experiential basis for this conception is twofold. The color cannot be found apart from the surface, but the surface can be found apart from the color. Evidently the color and the surface are two really different items. But in its real difference from the surface the color *qualifies* the surface. In the ontological scale of things, the color "bumps up" the surface. To qualify, the color must be understood as existing in and of the surface. So an accident is something positive that makes an addition to the total situation in which it is derivatively present.

Evil is derivatively real but not in that positive manner. Evil is not derivatively real in the positive manner of an accident. Rather, an evil is derivatively real as a type of absence or lack; it is the actual nonpresence of something positive. That absences or lacks are actual follows from the determinateness of things. For example, because I am pale complexioned, I am really neither tan nor ruddy. The pale complexion as something determinate actually excludes the others and grounds the reality of their absence.

Furthermore, evil is not a simple absence; evil is an absence of a certain kind. In the above text, Aquinas specifies evil to be an absence of something that should be there. Hence, the absence of sight in a rock is not an evil for the rock, but the absence of sight in a man is an evil. For example, the cataract in the eye is something determinate that excludes the due perfection of sight. This technical sense of real absence is called a privation and is distinguished from a mere negation of a perfection. So for Aquinas, evil is defined as the absence of a due perfection in a thing which because of its determinateness excludes that perfection.

This meaning of "privation" to speak of evil is a different sense of the word when "privation" names one of the conditions of change. In his *De Principiis Naturae*, Aquinas speaks of three conditions for change: matter, form, and privation. Here privation expresses the exclusion of the form to be acquired insofar as matter is under another form: "for insofar as [matter] is under one form, it has a privation of another and conversely, just as in fire is the privation of air and in air is the privation of fire."³⁸ As is clear from the examples, privation here does not connote an imperfection in the thing subject to the privation; fire is not supposed to have the form of air, and so as lacking that form fire is not suffering an evil. In that respect fire is not evil, it is something else. It is a principle of change. One would be wrong to conclude that because any changeable thing includes privation, then any changeable thing is evil.³⁹

In *SCG* III.71, Aquinas says that the order of good in which there is real privation would not exist without God. From my above remarks one knows that "the order of good" is the existing determinate substance that can lack what it ought to have and so be suffering evil. What, then, is the reduction from these substances to God? Help is provided by some passages in the earlier second book of *SCG*. At II.54, Aquinas remarks that for something to exist is for it to be a being (*ens*) but to be a being is for a thing to be composed with its *esse*: "the whole substance [of matter and form] itself, however, is that which is. And being itself [*ipsum esse*] is that by which the substance is called a being [*ens*]."⁴⁰ The reader will recognize Aquinas's metaphysics of the act of existing that I summarized in chapter 2. *SCG* not only echoes that metaphysics of what it means to be a being, but also provides the causal reasoning that follows that metaphysical understanding. One argument for a cause of *esse* is found in *SCG* I.22:

> But whatever belongs to a thing and is yet not of its essence belongs to it through some cause; for if things that are not through themselves one are joined they must be joined through some cause. Being [*esse*], therefore, belongs to that quiddity through some cause. This is either through something that is part of the essence of that thing, or the essence itself, or through something else. If we adopt the first alternative, and it is a fact that the essence is through that being, it follows that something is the cause of its own being. This is impossible, because, in their notions, the existence of the cause is prior to that of the effect. If, then, something were its own cause of being, it would be understood to be before it had being—which is impossible.⁴¹

---

38. "Inquantum enim est sub una forma, habet privationem alterius et e converse, sicut in igne est privatio aeris et in aere privatio ignis." Thomas Aquinas, *De Principiis Naturae*, ed. John J. Pauson (Fribourg: Société Philosophique, 1950), 2:83.

39. Some object that Aquinas's notion of evil is insufficiently encompassing. Some say that though Aquinas's privation definition works for blindness and lameness as evils, it fails to fit the evils of pain and suffering. Others claim that the definition makes sense for evils like blindness or lameness, but it does not apply to the evil of corruption, an evil that involves the complete destruction of a being. For a discussion of these two objections, see Knasas, *Aquinas and the Cry of Rachel*, 126 and 131–32.

40. *SCG* II.54 (trans. Anderson, 2:54 and 157).

41. *SCG* I.22 (trans. Pegis, 1:22 and 119–20).

No act as an act, even the *sui generis* act that is *esse*, is found by itself. Rather, an act is found as in and of a subject. No chance exists, however, to explain *esse* completely by the substance that is its subject. Substances that are complete explainers of an act are in some respect already in act. As a potency for its existential act, substance cannot position itself to explain completely its *esse*. The need for complete explanation in the case of *esse* drives the mind to conclude to a further being in which *esse* is not found as an act but as the very substance that is the further cause. Aquinas calls this further cause *esse subsistens* (subsistent existence), *esse tantum* (existence alone), and *esse purum* (pure existence). He also refers to it as *Deus* (God). Aquinas's stated reason at end of I.22 is God's revelation to Moses in the Book of Exodus that God's name is *Ego sum qui sum*: I am who am.

Reaching a first cause of *esse* in which *esse* is not an act of the substance but the substance itself, Aquinas can argue further that the first cause of *esse* is all-good in the moral sense as well as all-powerful. Aquinas's understanding of God's morality is approachable from what we know of morality in ourselves, as some philosophers have insisted.[42] As I have argued elsewhere, one can say that in Aquinas's natural law ethics morality consists in a respect and solicitude for epiphanies of being, that is, for those analogates that present the analogon of being in a heightened way.[43] As an intellector of being, the human is one such epiphany. Furthermore, turning to subsistent *esse* reached by the *De Ente* reasoning, one can say further that subsistent *esse* is necessarily moral in all of its free acts because it acts in light of itself who is, as subsistent *esse*, an epiphany of being *par excellence*. As explained in my chapter 2, when *esse* is intelligibly merged with the thing, it is communized and so is realized as the nature of *esse*, the intelligible heart of the *ratio entis*. By conforming its free actions to itself, the creator fulfills the moral norm of a respect and solicitude for an epiphany of being.[44]

42. "I wish to conclude from this set of theses that in calling God good a theist is committed to saying that God's reasons for permitting evils must be reasons that are acceptable according to the believer's own set of moral standards." Terence Penelhum, "Divine Goodness and the Problem of Evil," in *The Problem of Evil*, ed. Marilyn McCord Adams and Robert Merrihew Adams (Oxford: Oxford University Press, 1990), 76.

43. Knasas, *Being and Some Twentieth-Century Thomists*, chap. 8; *Thomism and Tolerance*, chaps. 2 and 3; and *Aquinas and the Cry of Rachel*, chap. 2.

44. Bruce Reichenbach, *Evil and a Good God* (New York: Fordham University Press, 1982), 138, objects to the attribution of moral goodness to God. A person who does good without the possibility

Aquinas argues also that God can do all things except contradictions. Contradictions are precisely the denial of the thing required by *esse* other than the one and only subsistent *esse*. First, subsistent *esse* is infinite and unique. As realizing the intelligible heart of the *ratio entis*, *esse* in a subsistent configuration has the infinite perfection of the *ratio entis*. That infinity is a basis for knowing its unicity. Two all-perfect beings would require for their distinction that one have something the other lacks.[45] From these two conclusions follows a third. If *esse* is to be anywhere else, *esse* must be in a nonsubsistent configuration and so with something. But a contradiction is precisely the denial of a thing. For example, a square-circle means either square plus nonsquare or circle plus noncircle. In both cases, one sees that square-circle involves the denial of a thing that can have *esse*. Precisely because a contradiction is a denial of a thing, Aquinas insists that the more proper way to speak is to say that contradictions cannot be made rather than to say that God cannot make contradictions.[46]

In sum, if evil exists, God exists. As evil exists only because of existing substances and substances exist only because of subsisting *esse* which is identifiable with the God of Exodus as well as the all-good and omnipotent God of Christianity, then evil proves God's existence. This earlier reasoning explains how Aquinas can say in *SCG* III.71 that God is compatible with evil. If a problem of evil remains, it is the problem of *how* God and evil are compatible. Whether Aquinas succeeds philosophically in answering this how-question, we can be assured that God and evil are compatible. F. C. Copleston reiterates my point:

> [Aquinas] was convinced that the metaphysician can prove the existence of God independently of the problem of evil, and that we therefore know that there is a solution to the problem even though we cannot provide it. And this, of course, is one of

---

of doing evil is neither morally good nor praiseworthy. Reichenbach applies this conclusion to Aquinas's conception of God. In my opinion, Reichenbach misses the point. Aquinas can say that God is praiseworthy not because God does not do evil but just because God does not have to act, e.g., create anything. Is not the gratuity of God's necessarily good act a basis for praise? Even among us gratuitous acts of kindness are praiseworthy.

45. "For, if none of these perfect beings lacks some perfection, and does not have any admixture of imperfection, which is demanded for an absolutely perfect being, nothing will be given in which to distinguish the perfect beings from one another. It is impossible, therefore, that there be many gods." *SCG* I.42 (trans. Pegis, 1:158); see also *ST* I, q. 11, a. 3, co.

46. *ST* I, q. 25, a. 3, co.

the ways in which he differs from the modern agnostic who is inclined to start with the problem in mind rather than to regard evil as something which has to be reconciled, so far as this is possible, with an already established truth.[47]

Heidegger and Ontotheology

Anyone discussing cosmological reasoning and Leibniz necessarily confronts Heidegger's ontotheological description of metaphysics. In his initial presentation of ontotheology in *Identity and Difference* (1957), Heidegger mentions Leibniz as an example of causal reasoning that reaches a highest being understood as a *causa sui*.[48] Leibniz did seem to embrace something like a *causa sui*. As mentioned in chapter 1, Leibniz asserts that the sufficient reason for contingent being was a being "which is its cause, or which is necessary being" and that necessary being was infinite because necessary being was "a pure consequence of possible being." What is Heidegger's problem with metaphysics as ontotheology?

One problem is the God that metaphysics reaches. With echoes of Pascal, Heidegger complains: "man can neither pray nor sacrifice to this God. Before the *causa sui*, man can neither fall to his knees in awe nor can he play music and dance before this God."[49] The basic reason for these inabilities seems to be that the God of philosophy is too much a creation of the philosopher: "But assuming that philosophy, as thinking, is the free and spontaneous self-involvement with beings as such, then the deity can come into philosophy only insofar as philosophy, of its own accord and by its own nature, requires and determines that and how the deity enters into it."[50] To understand how God comes into philosophy is to understand why metaphysics is ontotheological. In my opinion, to understand the ontotheological character of metaphysics it is first necessary to understand an ambiguity in what Heidegger calls the ontological difference between Being and beings.

In *Identity and Difference*, Heidegger devotes most of the prose to elabo-

---

47. F. C. Copleston, *Aquinas* (Baltimore, Md.: Penguin, 1961), 149.
48. Martin Heidegger, *Identity and Difference*, trans. Joan Stambaugh (New York: Harper and Row, 1969), 70 and 72.
49. Ibid., 72.
50. Ibid., 56.

rating the difference in a traditional sense. Beings are first and Being expresses a true idea derived from beings. As such Being expresses the ground of beings. Also, between beings there are causal relations. These relations lead the metaphysician to a highest being that explains why Being is in beings. Heidegger says: "Metaphysics thinks of the Being of beings both in the ground-giving unity of what is most general, what is indifferently valid everywhere, and also in the unity of the all that accounts for the ground, that is, of the All-Highest."[51] In the first respect metaphysics is onto-logic; in the second respect it is theo-logic.

There is another earlier discussion of the ontological difference between Being and beings in which Being is less *a posteriori* and more *a priori*. In *Basic Problems of Phenomenology*, Heidegger understands Being as an *a priori* condition for the presencing of things.[52] Many texts to this effect exist. One of the most striking is worth quoting at length. In detailing with what he means by "being" in the ontological difference between being and beings, Heidegger says:

> We are able to grasp beings as such, as being, only if we understand something like *being*. If we did not understand, even though at first roughly and without conceptual comprehension, what actuality signifies, then the actual would remain hidden from us. If we did not understand what reality means, then the real would remain inaccessible.... We must understand being so that we may be able to be given over to a world that is, so that we can exist in it and be our own *Dasein* itself as a being. We must be able to understand actuality before all experience of actual beings. This understanding of actuality or of being in the widest sense as over against the experience of beings is in a certain sense earlier than the experience of beings. To say that the understanding of being precedes all factual experience of beings does not mean that we would first need to have an explicit concept of being in order to experience beings theoretically or practically. We must understand being—being, which may no longer itself be called a being, being, which does not occur as a being among other beings but which nevertheless must be given and in fact is given in the understanding of being.[53]

---

51. Ibid., 58.

52. Martin Heidegger, *The Basic Problems of Phenomenology*, trans. Albert Hofstadter (Bloomington: Indiana University Press, 1988). The book is the text of a course that Heidegger gave at the University of Marburg in the 1927 Summer Semester. It was published only in 1975. Its close philosophical relationship to *Being and Time* is explained by Hofstadter in his "Translator's Introduction."

53. Ibid., 10–11. Also, see *Being and Time*, trans. John Macquarie and Edward Robinson (New

What is the early Heidegger saying about Being? As I understand him, he is saying that Being is the expanse up and against which realities are seen as realities. The driving idea is that the individual is only known in the light of the universal. Undergirding this driving thought is Heidegger's description of what we experience. Does not saying that we experience beings mean that the beings are appreciated as instances of something larger, namely, Being? Similarly, to experience Fido as a dog means to experience Fido as an instance of dog. But unlike dog, Being is underived from the beings that we experience. How could it be derived? Being sets up experienced beings in the first place. Whenever we have beings, we already have being. Hence, in the previous quotation Heidegger says that being is "before" all experience of actual beings and that the understanding of being is "in a sense earlier than the experience of beings." Continuing this *a priori* construal of being, *Basic Problems* says that "the understanding of being has itself the mode of being of the human *Dasein*."

What Heidegger accomplishes in *Identity and Difference* is an explana-

---

York: Harper and Row, 1962): "Inquiry, as a kind of seeking, must be guided beforehand by what is sought. So the meaning of Being must already be available to us in some way" (25–26); "But as an investigation of Being, [phenomenological interpretation] brings to completion, autonomously and explicitly, that understanding of Being which belongs already to *Dasein* and which 'comes alive' in any of its dealings with entities" (96); "understanding of Being has already been taken for granted in projecting upon possibilities. In projection, Being is understood, though not ontologically conceived. An entity whose kind of Being is the essential projection of Being-in-the-world has understanding of Being, and has this as constitutive of its Being" (188–89); "If what the term 'idealism' says, amounts to the understanding that Being can never be explained by entities but is already that which is 'transcendental' for every entity, then idealism affords the only correct possibility for a philosophical problematic" (251); "At the bottom, however, the whole correlation necessarily gets thought of as somehow *being*, and must therefore be thought of with regard to some definite idea of Being" (252); "[Common sense] fails to recognize that entities can be experienced 'factually' only when Being is already understood, even if it has not been conceptualized" (363); "All ontical experience of entities—both circumspective calculation of the ready-to-hand, and positive scientific cognition of the present-at-hand—is based upon projections of the Being of the corresponding entities" (371); "[the paradigmatic character of mathematical natural science] consists rather in the fact that the entities which it takes as its theme are discovered in it in the only way in which entities can be discovered—by the prior projection of their state of Being" (414). In sum, John Caputo, *Heidegger and Aquinas: An Essay on Overcoming Metaphysics* (New York: Fordham University Press, 1982), 53, remarks: "[In *Being and Time*] Being is the meaning or horizon of understanding within which beings are manifest. Thus instead of being an abstract concept, a vacuous abstraction when separated from concrete beings, ... Being for Heidegger becomes the meaning-giving-horizon, the transcendental *a priori*, which precedes beings and renders them possible in their Being. It is not an abstraction drawn from beings, but an *a priori* which precedes them."

tion of the connection between these two senses of the ontological difference between Being and beings. His explanation is found in his description of a certain transition that Being undergoes and through which it comes to be present. In the transition Being does not go out to beings that are already there. Heidegger describes it as Being unconcealingly overwhelming what arrives. What arrives are beings with a certain concealment.[54] This sounds as if the Being that crosses over constitutes the beings that arrive, but Being is somewhat misunderstood because the arrival of beings masks or veils their origin in Being. As the origin of beings is concealed, we think that Being is a true idea derived from beings and so in that sense expresses the ground of beings. This understandable misapprehension of the ontological difference is what perdures, and within this perdurance is metaphysics in the sense of ontotheology.[55]

An image might be helpful. Think the transiting of Being as along a line at which things will be at a midpoint. The transition of Being moves from left to right. This image will show the two senses of the ontological difference. The first sense in which Being functions as a constitutive *a priori* for the presentation of beings is to the left of the midpoint. The second sense in which Being is understood as an *a posteriori* apprehended ground of beings is on the right. As Being moves from left to right, its first character is masked by the beings.

It should now be clear what the challenge of ontotheology is to Aquinas's *De Ente* reasoning. By proceeding from beings to a first cause, Aquinas

---

54. "Being shows itself as the unconcealing overwhelming. Beings as such appear in the manner of the arrival that keeps itself concealed in unconcealedness." *Identity and Difference*, 64–65.

55. Heidegger mentions "the Same, the differentiation" as what "holds apart the 'between,' in which the overwhelming and the arrival are held toward one another, are borne away from and toward each other. The difference of Being and beings, as the differentiation of overwhelming and arrival, is perdurance" (ibid., 65). Thinking "the Same, or differentiation," seems to be placed outside of metaphysics: "For what these words [Being and being in the metaphysical sense], what the manner of thinking that is guided by them represents, originate as that which differs by virtue of the difference. The origin of the difference can no longer be thought of within the scope of metaphysics" (ibid., 71). Earlier, Heidegger describes this more basic thinking as "a step back" in which the difference between Being and beings suffers an oblivion (50). Iain Thomson brings out the ambiguity of "Being." He says: "This notion of the 'same' is recognizable as one of Heidegger's names for 'Being as such' (that is, Being in its difference from the metaphysically conceived Being of beings)." "Ontotheology? Understanding Heidegger's *Destruktion* of Metaphysics," *International Journal of Philosophical Studies* 8, no. 3 (2000): 309.

is naïve about the initial presence of beings. Aquinas has not thought through the founding role human *Dasein* plays in the setting up of beings. In short, the ontotheology critique targets the immediate realism of Aquinas's estimate of sensation. Aquinas no longer has the thing doubly existing so as to be grasped as existence-neutral and then judged to be real by its *actus essendi*.

Earlier I mentioned that much discussion of cosmological reasoning takes place within the context of an admitted real world. Even Kant in his discussion of the reasoning does not use his transcendental philosophy to critique the reasoning's starting point in a real world. Heidegger does. Metaphysicians are naïve to think that they can begin with beings and then proceed to their causes. They fail to realize the role of *Dasein*'s projection of some sense of Being in the setting up of those things in consciousness. In *Identity and Difference* Heidegger is not quite clear on why we should regard Being as this masked and forgotten constitutive *a priori*. How does Heidegger make the case that Being is a constitutive *a priori*?

If we return to *Basic Problems* Heidegger seems to argue his case in two ways. First, Being is wide enough to include God.[56] Because God is not immediately known, then it seems that Being cannot come from our initial knowledge of things. For its source we must turn to ourselves. Elsewhere, I have discussed this first way of making Heidegger's case and how Aquinas would fare in the face of it.[57] Heidegger's second case is what interests me now. By analyzing *Dasein*'s productive comportment in chapter 2 of part 1 and *Dasein*'s basic determination of understanding/freedom in chapter 1 of part 2, Heidegger translates our experience of beings as being into an experience of things as handy and as equipment.[58] Because of the translation, Being becomes identified with the world, or significance, involved in our freely

---

56. "What can there be apart from nature, history, God, space, number? We say of each of these, even though in a different sense, that it *is*. We call it a being.... We are able to grasp beings as such, as beings, only if we understand something like being. If we did not understand, even though at first roughly and without conceptual comprehension, what actuality signifies, then the actual would remain hidden from us." Heidegger, *Basic Problems*, 10.

57. John F. X. Knasas, "A Heideggerian Critique of Aquinas and a Gilsonian Reply," *The Thomist* 58, no. 3 (1994): 415–39.

58. "Only when we have apprehended the more original temporalizing are we able to survey in what way the understanding of the being of beings—here either of the equipmental character and handiness of handy equipment or of the thing-hood of extant things and the at-handiness of the at-hand—is made possible by time and thus becomes transparent." Heidegger, *Basic Problems*, 294.

chosen projects.⁵⁹ The correctness of this analysis will rest on a defense of the universality of productive comportment. In other words, our relation to things is always mediated in and through our freely chosen projects.

Heidegger is aware that sometimes we experience things as non-handy. Such an experience would seem to belie the universality of productive comportment. In defense of his thesis Heidegger says that the experience of things as non-handy means to experience things as "unfamiliar." This latter in turn is reduced to some free projection of *Dasein*. In other words, the non-handy, or the unproduced as nonmaterial for production, is better described as the unfamiliar. This description can only happen thanks to the non-handy failing to fit into my presently chosen project.⁶⁰ Heidegger mentions the example of entering a shoemaker's shop. If you are a banker, you will not just experience things. You will experience unfamiliar things. That experience is understandable given that the contents of the shop do not mesh with the project of high finance. In sum, our experience of things occurs within a dichotomy of things as handy or not handy, and *Dasein*'s productive comportment is the basis for the dichotomy. So, productive comportment remains a universal mediating factor for our awareness of things. It is a level of *Dasein* more fundamental than Dasein's awareness of beings between which we place causal connections.

Does Heidegger's transcendental reduction succeed? It is true that we experience the non-handy as the unfamiliar, that is, as what does not fit into one's project. The description, however, should not end there. By presenting itself as the unfamiliar, as not fitting into one's project, something can give us pause, something can bring our projecting to a halt. The noteworthy point is that the temporary suspension of the projecting does not mean the non-presencing of the thing. The thing remains suspended before us without the mediation of some freely chosen project.

The presence of things as what-I-do-not-know-what-to-do-with is an open invitation to consider things in terms of what they are doing for themselves, namely, existing. Returning to Heidegger's example of the shoemaker's shop, it is true that someone entering the shop with the preoccupations of a banker

---

59. "Interpretation of the possibility of being-in-the-world on the basis of temporality is already intrinsically interpretation of the possibility of an understanding of being in which, with equal originality, we understand the being of Dasein, the being of fellow-Daseins or of the others, and the being of the extant and handy entities always encountered in a disclosed world" (ibid.).

60. Ibid., 304–5.

will experience the shop's contents as "unfamiliar." Is it that difficult to imagine the banker as dropping the project of banking and as letting things just present themselves?[61]

In sum, presencing outstrips productive comportment. Productive comportment has an ebb and flow that contrasts with the continued presence of things. The unfamiliar can stop the comporting in its tracks. Other factors can do the same. Exhaustion in the midst of a difficult task can lead us to place the projecting aside but without the loss of the presence of things. In his *Metaphysics* I.2, Aristotle noted that success in meeting practical needs and necessities meant a diminution of practical concern without a commensurate diminution in the presencing of things. In fact, philosophy took its rise from this continued presencing of things.

Hence, I fail to see productive comportment as subsuming the presencing of things. The phenomenology of sensation fails to lead in a transcendental direction. Real items stay basic and fundamental to sensation. By beginning with beings given in sensation, metaphysicians are not falling prey to the ontological error of missing the more profound dimension of *Dasein*'s setting

---

61. "Despite his apparent realization that the otherness of the *Seinde* is somehow a controlling factor in our encounter with things, Heidegger at no time squarely confronts the problem of the otherness of the thing as otherness, the lack seems even more acute when we have penetrated the fourfold erection of the thing to the source of all meaning, even in *Seinden* revealed in the past: it is only the projection of Dasein which can be the source of the 'other's' meaning—i.e., a source that is not other at all! ... Nowhere do we find any effort to delineate the contribution of the brute thing and the contribution of the exstatic horizon, nowhere a description of what it means to 'let the thing be as it is,' for nowhere is an effort made to search out indications of what things might be 'in themselves.' ... Had Heidegger directed his attention to circumscribing by careful analysis the *Seinden* precisely in their otherness, there is a strong possibility that he might have been led in the direction of conclusions that would have jarred seriously with the 'beyond metaphysics' stand of his interpretation." Thomas Langan, *The Meaning of Heidegger* (New York: Columbia University Press, 1966), 229. *Basic Problems* does contain some apparently realist assertions. First, Heidegger insists (49) that a window "does not receive existence from my perceiving, but just the reverse. I can perceive it only if it exists and because it exists.... Perception or absolute position is at most the mode of access to the existent." Second, he says that "perceivedness is not equated with extantness but is only a necessary though indeed not a sufficient condition of access to extantness" (67). But realism is not the sure interpretation here. To the first text, one could say that perceiving does not give the window existence because the projecting of being does that. As Heidegger says (52), "being is what makes a being what it is as a being." In the same vein one can read Heidegger's *Being and Time* remark: "Entities *are*, quite independently of the experience by which they are disclosed" (228). To the second text, one could say that the necessary further condition for perception is not only the extantness of the perceived but *Dasein*'s projection of being. In *Basic Problems* Heidegger does say "with respect to its possibility perceivedness is grounded in the understanding of extantness" (71).

up of beings in the first place. In Aquinas's case the sense realism is especially important insofar as it gives the real thing as also cognitionally existing. That double existence for the thing enables the *duplex operation intellectus* to work out the *actus essendi* understanding of the thing's real existence.[62]

Finally, what of Heidegger's complaint that the *causa sui* god of the metaphysicians is something before which one cannot feel awe or dance? Does that complaint hold of Aquinas's *De Ente* conclusion of subsistent *esse*? Earlier when discussing Kenny I argued that *esse commune* suitably modified by negative judgments provided us with some representation of subsistent *esse*. Accordingly, Aquinas can reason from what he knows of the *perfectio essendi* to what is true in subsistent *esse*. For example, at *ST* I, q. 4, a. 2, Aquinas argues from the perfection of the *perfectio essendi* to the perfection of God understood as subsistent *esse*. Such a case illustrates why Aquinas, in *SCG* I.5, agrees with Aristotle that the little we know of higher substances is loved and desired more than all the knowledge about less noble substances. Furthermore, this little and imperfect knowledge produces "intense joy" (*vehemens sit gaudium eius*) and brings the "greatest perfection to the soul" (*maximam perfectionem animae*). Later in *SCG* I.8, Aquinas expresses the matter in terms of intellectual vision and consideration, weak as they may be: "For to be able to see [*posse inspicere*] something of the loftiest realities, however thin and weak the sight may be [*parva et debili consideratione*] is, as our previous remarks indicate, a cause of greatest joy."[63]

What is behind these remarks is the phenomenon of analogical conceptualization. Understood as the grasping of sameness precisely within differences of beings, any analogical concept is an intrinsically fascinating item. For example, "charming city" said of Paris and Rome expresses a sameness in difference. How else than by describing its winding alleys, ruins, baroque, and gelato can one answer the question "Why is Rome a charming city like Paris?" Of course these things are just what Rome has and Paris lacks. The

---

62. Heidegger also uses Suarez to critique from within the metaphysical tradition Aquinas's essence/existence distinction. The critique is one that assumes that the distinction is of two *rei* and then points out: "The question would then arise how the two can be taken together in a single unity which itself is." *Basic Problems*, 95. That understanding of the distinction is a far cry from the distinction as it is known in the *duplex operatio intellectus*. The two can make a unity because of a strict potency/act understanding of the essence/*esse* distinction.

63. *SCG* I.8 (trans. Pegis, 1:76).

sameness is in the differences. Because the sameness is grasped in the differences, it is to an extent hidden by them and so is grasped imperfectly. Nevertheless, one's imperfect grasp of the sameness, or analogon, can be stunning enough to engender a lifelong love for travel. Before I ever saw Paris, I never realized a charming city could take that form. What other charming cities are on the map? The grasp of the analogon, dim as it may be, is what produces both the wonder and the excitement.

The *perfectio essendi* is another analogon. It is one way something can be communicated but not according to the same formality.[64] Modified by negative judgment to represent subsistent *esse*, the *perfectio essendi* presents the first cause as an unfathomable deep of perfection. Before it, one cannot but experience profound awe and joy. Aquinas's thinking is ontotheological in the best sense of the word.[65]

64. "But only according to some sort of analogy; as being itself is common to all: sed secundum aliqualem analogiam, sicut ipsum esse est commune omnibus." *ST* I, q. 4, a. 4, co. (trans. Pegis, 1:41). The philosophical case for *esse* being analogous is found in Aquinas's explanation of how *esse commune* is diversified into the *esse* of this thing and the *esse* of that thing. *Esse* is diversified not by something extrinsic but by itself in light of the thing it will actualize. See above, chapter 4, "Anthony Kenny: The Fatal Flaw in the Man/Phoenix Argument."

65. For another discussion of how Aquinas would defend himself against the charge of ontotheology, see Merold Westphal, "Aquinas and Onto-theology," *American Catholic Philosophical Quarterly* 80, no. 2 (2006): 173–93. Westphal (185) saves mystery in Aquinas's metaphysics by making metaphysics an *ancilla* for Aquinas's theology. I have attempted to keep the mystery more intrinsic to Aquinas's metaphysics.

PART 2

The *De Ente* Reasoning and Aquinas's Proofs for God

[6]

Aquinas's Metaphysics and Our Knowledge of God's Existence

In part 1, I argued that Aquinas's *De Ente* reasoning possesses sufficient logic to be a proof for a first cause of existence. As such, it has surprising resources to deal with problems in classic cosmological reasoning. In part 2 my concern is more historical. In short, I wish to argue that Aquinas's proofs for God are in fact the *De Ente* reasoning in different guises. Joseph Owens especially, but also others such as Frederick Copleston and Terence M. Penelhum, have made this claim.[1]

My argumentation is unique in two ways. First, I weigh heavily Aquinas's opinion about where and when the philosopher proves God's existence. I un-

---

1. See Joseph Owens, "Aquinas and the Five Ways," in *St. Thomas Aquinas on the Existence of God* (ed. Catan), 132–41. See also Copleston: "The third way of proving the existence of God appears to presuppose the real distinction between essence and existence in finite things"; "the fundamental proof [in the *quinque viae*] is really the third proof or way, that from contingency. In the first proof the argument from contingency is applied to the special fact of motion or change." Copleston, *A History of Philosophy*, 2.2:53 and 65. Terence M. Penelhum quotes E. L. Mascall to the same effect: "As I see it, the ultimate function of the Five Ways is to make it plain, by calling attention to outstanding features of finite being, what the fundamental characteristic of finite being is. And that fundamental characteristic is its radical inability to account for its own existence." "Divine Necessity," in *Cosmological Arguments* (ed. Burrill). Penelhum himself agrees but not to the exclusion of a qualitative inquiry: "Aquinas is surely concerned not only with the contingency of the being of finite things, but also with that of their manner of being" (147–48). Penelhum's observation is insightful and prefigures, I believe, the more robust version of the *De Ente* reasoning that I will present here.

derstand Aquinas's opinion to be that the metaphysician accomplishes the task of proving God's existence. As Aquinas seeks philosophically cogent *viae* for God (as indicated by his rejection of Anselmian reasoning),[2] then his *viae* should embody his opinion of metaphysics as the place in which the philosopher proves God's existence. I will show that the *De Ente* reasoning is what the metaphysician would have to use if the metaphysician is to reach God from the subject of metaphysics: *ens inquantum ens*.

Second, in chapter 7 I argue that the metaphysician uses a more robust version of the *De Ente* reasoning than has been seen so far. There are other points to make about *actus essendi* than are made in the *De Ente* reasoning. One of these points is Aquinas's understanding of how form is a principle of *esse*, *principium essendi*. With its emphasis on the priority or fundamentality of *esse* to the thing, the *De Ente* reasoning did not have occasion to mention this. Yet if one returns to the grasp of *esse* in judgment, *esse* is not just prior to what it actuates, *esse* is also the act *of what it actuates*. Judgmentally grasped *esse* does not run around by itself. It is in and of the potency it actuates and so in some measure is dependent upon it. Hence, any conditions for the thing that is a potency for *esse*, for example, the form of the thing, are conditions for *esse*. This thinking opens a second causal path to *esse subsistens* that is more lengthy and indirect than the one in the reasoning of the *De Ente*. It is a path that permits the metaphysician to borrow much material from natural philosophy, a borrowing that unfortunately can camouflage the metaphysical

---

2. Aquinas is not interested in a common sense approach or with what is simply apologetically useful. Throughout his career Aquinas rejected Anselmian reasoning for God. This consistency is telling. His basic objection to Anselm's type of reasoning is that "a thing and a definition [*ratio*] of a nature are posited in the same way." But it is not clear that the *ratio* of "greatest" includes anything more than a formed intention of existence. As mentioned in my chapter 4, formed intentions represent items of knowledge apart from the contexts in which they are known. The formed intention of existence represents *esse* outside of the context of the second operation of the intellect in which *esse* is originally known. Hence, the formed concept of existence may express existence but the concept fails to present it. You could say that it is an existence-neutral sense of existence. Hence, I can think an existent vacation in Hawaii and not be asserting it. I can even be thinking the greatest as necessarily existent and still not be asserting it. The only existence I am asserting is the formed intention of existence in my mind. Hence, Aquinas can say in *SCG* I.11, "Now, from the fact that that which is indicated by the name God is conceived by the mind, it does not follow that God exists save only in the intellect. Hence, that than which a greater cannot be thought will likewise not have to exist save only in the intellect." My point is this. It is the sophisticated level of this kind of philosophical critique used on Anselm that Aquinas obviously wants to avoid on himself. For himself Aquinas wants arguments that meet philosophical muster.

character of Aquinas's *viae*. The *De Ente* reasoning with this second causal consideration of *actus essendi* is what I call the more robust version of the *De Ente* reasoning. It is especially exemplified in the first two *viae* of the *SCG* I.13.

Metaphysics and God

Besides finding that Aquinas desires God arguments that resist philosophical critique, a reader would also find that Aquinas has a quite sophisticated understanding of philosophy. In his commentary on Boethius's *De Trinitate*, Aquinas describes much of it. In *In de Trin.*, q. 5, a. 1, we find the divisions of speculative and practical with the former subdivided into natural philosophy, mathematics, and metaphysics. Given Aquinas's interest in a philosophical approach to God, one can correctly assume that the approach will be conceived in terms of one of these divisions of philosophy. In other words, I think that it would be quite strange if Aquinas were to hold the opinion that the philosopher proves God's existence in division X of philosophy and would not carry that opinion over into the understanding of his actual God proofs, his *viae*. So, among these parts of philosophy, does Aquinas ever indicate to which part he assigns the philosopher's knowledge of God?

I believe that he does and that a good text with which to begin is *In de Trin.*, q. 5, a. 4, co. In a context of coming to know their existence, Aquinas says: "Philosophers, then, study these divine beings only insofar as [*nisi prout*] they are the principles of all things. Consequently, they are the object of the science that investigates what is common to all being, which has for its subject being as being. The philosophers call this divine science."[3] A few lines later Aquinas acknowledges that the divine science of the philosophers is also named metaphysics.[4] The point of the above quote is unambiguous: philosophers know both God and the angels only in metaphysics. Aquinas's use of *nisi prout* excludes from philosophy any nonmetaphysical study of the immaterial beings. I know of no other Thomistic text that is as unambiguous as this one. For example, as far as I know, Aquinas never said, "the philoso-

3. Trans. Maurer, 44.
4. "Accordingly, there are two kinds of theology. There is one that treats of divine things, not as the subject of the science but as the principles of the subject. This is the kind of theology pursued by the philosophers and that is also called metaphysics." Ibid.

pher proves God's existence in natural philosophy, or physics." The closest to such an assertion is Aquinas saying that the philosopher proves God's existence through motion. The problem, however, is that Aquinas admits a metaphysical consideration of motion: "The metaphysician deals with individual beings, too, not with regard to their special natures, in virtue of which they are special kinds of being, but insofar as they share the common character of being [*commune rationem entis*]. And in this way matter and motion [*materia et motus*] also fall under his consideration."[5] Aquinas's remark suffices to cancel the argument that because we prove God from motion, then we prove God in physics.

Despite the clarity of *In de Trin.*, q. 5, a. 4, co., some have claimed to find ambiguities. First, it is sometimes said that one can construe the above quote as saying that metaphysics studies *what* these beings are while another branch of philosophy, that is, natural philosophy, studies *that* these beings are. For three reasons, this interpretation of article 4 is highly unlikely. First, as is clear from the text, for the metaphysician to study these beings as causes of being as being is to come to know that they exist. Second, with its talk of reaching divine realities "by the light of natural reason only to the extent that their effects reveal them to us," this passage parallels earlier remarks from *In de Trin.*, q. 1, a. 2, and q. 2, a. 2. But in those earlier cases the issue is knowledge of God's existence. Third, to support his claim that by the light of natural reason philosophers came to these beings, Aquinas cites Romans 1:20: "The invisible things of God are clearly seen, being understood by the things that are made." But earlier in the commentary, at q. 1, a. 2, s.c., Aquinas quotes the same passage to introduce his position that the existence of God can be demonstrated.[6] One confidently assumes that the use of the *Romans* text in q. 5, a. 4, indicates again that Aquinas is speaking of a metaphysical knowledge of God's existence.

Another ambiguity regarding article 4 is created by Aquinas himself who, just two articles earlier (a. 2, ad 3) apparently gives natural philosophy a demonstration of immaterial being. Aquinas is replying to the objection that natural philosophy does treat what exists apart from matter and motion because it considers the first mover that is free from all matter (*immunis*

---

5. *In de Trin.*, q. 5, a. 4, ad 6 (trans. Maurer, 49).
6. See also *SCG* I.12.77 and *ST* I, q. 2, a. 2, s.c.

ab omni materia). In reply, Aquinas admits that natural philosophy treats the first mover that is "of a different nature from natural things." Natural philosophy does this as the terminus of its subject that is about material and changeable things. This remark seems to catch Aquinas giving natural philosophy proof of an immaterial being.

Not necessarily, however. The reader surely would wonder how Aquinas could contradict himself two articles later. For the above reasons, the interpretation of q. 5, a. 4 is secure, but arguably some ambiguity at q. 5, a. 2, ad 3 is escaping the reader's eye. Where is the ambiguity located? The reader should note that neither the objection nor the reply names the first mover, *primus motor*, as God. Moreover, the reader knows from *SCG* I.13 that Aquinas uses the similar phrase, *primus movens*, to refer to the outermost celestial sphere.[7] Could the third reply's *primus motor* be a celestial sphere? At first thought it seems not. The *primus motor* is "free from all matter," but a sphere is a body and so is material. Is this reasoning conclusive? Not completely. Earlier, at *In II Sent.*, d. 12, q. 1, a. 1, co., Aquinas asks if the matter of all bodies is the same. He says no. As ungenerable and incorruptible, the heavens lack the prime matter of terrestrial bodies. Considered in itself, the prime matter of terrestrial bodies is in potency to all natural forms, both inferior ones and superior ones. Hence, any terrestrial body is corruptible. The matter of the heavens, however, is in potency only to the form of the heaven. With that form, the matter is in potency to no other, and so the heaven is incorruptible. This distinction between terrestrial and celestial matters provides the interpretative possibility that the *primus motor* free from all matter is a celestial sphere free from all terrestrial prime matter. Because this reading of q. 5, a. 2, ad 3 removes the contradiction with q. 5, a. 4, I think it is fair to say that a reader is justified in making it.

Second, some remarks prior to the *viae* in *SCG* I.13 indicate the same metaphysical assignment. First, in I.4 Aquinas mentions that the naturally attainable truth about God is difficult to reach because it belongs to metaphysics, the last part of philosophy to be learned. But in I.3 Aquinas includes

---

7. *Primum agens* has the same equivocity: "Thus, we see that all things potentially existent in the matter of generable and corruptible entities can be actualized by the active power present in the heavenly body, which is the primary active force in nature [*primum activum in natura*]. Now, just as the heavenly body is the first agent [*primum agens*] in respect to lower bodies, so God is the first agent [*primum agens*] as regards the totality of created beings." *SCG* II.22, *Amplius* (trans. Anderson, 2:66).

God's existence in naturally attainable truth.[8] So, in a text with various parts of philosophy in mind, among which is natural philosophy, Aquinas appears to assign knowledge of God's existence to metaphysics. Second, this thesis would appear as the context to appreciate a remark in I.12. There Aquinas says that the order of the sciences shows that knowledge of God is demonstrable. Aquinas reasons that if there were only sensible things, then physics would be first philosophy. But "beyond physics" is the science of metaphysics. Therefore something beyond the sensible is demonstrated to exist. Which science makes this demonstration of the non-sensible? Again, with its reference to the order of the sciences, I.12 appears to be reiterating the metaphysical knowledge of God's existence in I.4.

Third, in I.3 Aquinas describes our natural reason's knowledge of the existence of God as our knowledge of the existence of the first principle (*primum principium*). But in I.1 Aquinas approvingly cites Aristotle's opinion that the truth of the "first principle whereby all things are" (*primum principium essendi omnibus*) is established in first philosophy (*primam philosophiam*). First philosophy is another name for metaphysics.

Later Texts

It might be said that the above remarks of Aquinas from the *De Trinitate* commentary and the *Summa contra Gentiles* are those of a young "Avicennian" Aquinas. In his mature years Aquinas changed his mind about where and when the philosopher proves God's existence. The possibility obviously makes it incumbent upon me to make some observations about later texts. I have four observations to make.

First, at *ST* I, q. 44, a. 2, co., Aquinas expressly says that reasoning based on matter/form principles takes the philosopher to a first body only: "These transmutations [of essential forms] they attributed to certain more universal causes, such as the oblique circle, according to Aristotle." The oblique circle is a reference to the celestial sphere that moves the sun. Importantly, the text says that if philosophers reason further it is not by continuing this line of

---

8. Later, Aquinas will remark, "For the science [*scientia*] to whose province it belongs to prove the existence of God [*pertinent probare Deum esse*] and many other such truths is the last of all to offer itself to human inquiry [*addiscenda proponitur*], since it presupposes many other sciences." *ST* II-II, q. 2, a. 4 (trans. Pegis, 2:1079).

reasoning from matter/form principles. Rather, philosophers reasoned further on the basis of *ens inquantum ens*. Aquinas says that this viewpoint involves a reference to the *esse* of sensible things.⁹ Even though Aquinas does not mention the names of physics and metaphysics, the sciences are clearly present. Matter/form are the intrinsic principles of *ens mobile*, the subject of Aristotelian physics, and *ens in quantum est ens* expresses the subject of metaphysics as we saw, for example, back in *In de Trin.*, q. 5, a. 4, co. Finally, Aquinas's claim that matter/form reasoning would get the philosopher only to a first body fits in well with my previous interpretation of *In de Trin.*, q. 5, a. 2, ad 3, in which I understood the *primum motor* free from all terrestrial matter to be a reference not to God but to the heavens.

That Aquinas is not allowing natural philosophy to transcend the material order is clear from another consideration. If one considers the arguments in *SCG* I.20 that God is not a body, the bulk of these arguments are taken from Aristotle. According to Aquinas, the arguments are based on the "supposition" that motion is eternal. The suppositional nature of the eternity of motion indicates that Aquinas does not regard the proofs for the eternity of motion in *Physics* VIII.1 as demonstrative. In fact Aquinas regards the eternity arguments as inconclusive, but for an interesting reason. In relation to the first argument from the need of a mobile, Aquinas appeals to a metaphysics already in place in which the first principle is a cause of *esse* to all existing things:

Moreover, this does not agree with Aristotle's intention. For he proves in *Metaphysics* II, that that which is most true and most being is the cause of being for all existing things [*causa essendi omnibus existentibus*]. Hence it follows that the very being [*ipsum esse*] in potency which primary matter has is derived from the first principle of being [*primo principio essendi*], which is the most being [*maxime ens*]. Therefore, it is not necessary to presuppose something for its action which has not been produced by it.[10]

9. "Then others advanced further and raised themselves to the consideration of being as being [*ens inquantum est ens*], and who assigned a cause to things ... according to all that belongs to their being [*esse*] in any way whatever" (trans. Pegis, 1:429). In passing I wish to note that my comment should not be confused with Gilson's comment which claims that in q. 44, a. 2, Aquinas says that Aristotle does not attain *ens inquantum ens*. I am not speaking of Aristotle but of natural philosophy reasoning based upon the defining notes of *ens mobile*: matter/form. Ashley, *The Way toward Wisdom*, 159, confuses me with Gilson and so misses my point.

10. Aquinas, *In VIII Phys.*, l. 2, n. 974; trans. R. J. Blackwell, *Commentary on Aristotle's Physics*

In other words, absent metaphysics, the first argument for motion's eternity is a strict demonstration. Hence, that *SCG* I.20 uses motion's eternity as a "supposition" suggests that the argument for God not being a body is not simply a natural philosophy proof. Again, only the metaphysician is in a position to see that motion could be caused either from eternity or in time. Hence, only the metaphysician would be in a position to "suppose" motion's eternity.[11]

At this point a reader might ask why Aquinas does not allow natural philosophy to demonstrate an immaterial substance. In other words, why does Aquinas maintain at *ST* I, q. 44, a. 2, that reasoning on matter/form principles attains only a body as the first efficient cause of generation and corruption? What could be causing the roadblock?

Some indication of Aquinas's mind might be found in recent Aristotelian scholarship. At one point in his lengthy argument for separate substance, Aristotle proceeds from the animating principle of a celestial sphere to a separate and so purely formal substance. The purely formal substance functions as a final cause, or point of attraction, for the sphere soul whose attention is transfixed upon it.[12] What remains problematic at this stage is the manner in which the sphere soul apprehends the separate substance. This apprehension is problematic because on Aristotle's own principles separate substance, pure form, cannot be an efficient cause. As an Aristotelian scholar explains:

(New Haven, Conn.: Yale University Press, 1963), 507. At *SCG* II.37, *Et hanc quidem* (trans. Anderson, 2:110), Aquinas assigns the philosopher's knowledge of creation to metaphysics: "And on this account it is the business not of the philosopher of nature [*Naturalem Philosophum*] to consider that origination, but of the metaphysician [*Philosophum Primum*], who considers universal being [*ens commune*] and things existing apart from motion."

11. In his *The Way toward Wisdom*, 95, Benedict Ashley admits that metaphysics establishes the supposition of motion's eternity but believes that natural philosophy can do the same. In that regard, Ashley has a confusing discussion of the eternity of the celestial spheres. He admits that at *In VI Meta.*, l. 1, n. 1164, Aquinas maintains on metaphysical grounds that the spheres have a cause both of their circular motion and of their being. But Ashley claims that Aquinas does the same at *In VIII Phys.*, l. 21, n. 1153: "Yet to this it must be said that if the first mover is not said to be self-moved, it is necessary that it should be moved immediately by what is entirely non-moving." The obvious problem is that while in the *Metaphysics* commentary Aquinas clearly states a cause for the being of the sphere, in his *Physics* text Aquinas is speaking of the first mover only for the motion of the sphere. There is no mention of the being of the sphere.

12. On separate substance as a final cause through its being apprehended, see Aristotle, *Metaphysics* XII.7, 1072a26–28.

For the actuality of an efficient cause as such is, according to the *Metaphysics*, in the patient not in the agent. The finitude of the Aristotelian perfect Beings must inevitably bring them under strict application of this norm. As long as the separate Entities are conceived essentially as finite and perfect forms, they cannot have any actuality outside themselves. They cannot be efficient causes. There is no room for efficient causality in the source of Being as conceived by the Stagirite.[13]

Here the difficulty of accommodating efficiency is brought up in respect to the separate substances of *Metaphysics* XII. But the same difficulty can be raised of the sphere souls of *Physics* VIII. As causing eternal motion, the souls would have infinite power and so not be in bodies. They would be subsisting forms. Hence, the above difficulty would apply to them as well as to the separate substances. The desire to avoid this conundrum may be behind Aquinas's noted insistence to read the proof from motion from the supposition of motion's eternity, namely, metaphysically. Aquinas can relieve Aristotelian subsisting forms of the impossible burden of trying to be both instances of pure act and efficient causes. In Aquinas's metaphysics *esse* is the act of all acts and so is a type of act distinct from formal act. As a locus of pure act, subsistent *esse* would not be something essentially finite. Hence, in a subsistent instance, *esse* should be pure actuality compatible with efficiency. On the other hand, in a subsisting form efficiency would not compromise its status as pure act because it is no longer pure act as it was in Aristotle.

Second, Aquinas's commentary on the *Physics* (1269–70, hereafter "*In Phys.*") appears to assign the consideration of a wholly unmoved mover to metaphysics. At *In II Phys.*, l. 11, n. 245, Aquinas says: "Natural philosophy does not consider every mover. For there are two kinds of moving principles, namely, the moved and the non-moved. Now a mover that is not moved is not natural because it does not have in itself a principle of motion. And such is the moving principle which is altogether immobile and the first of all movers, as will be shown in Book VIII." But a few paragraphs earlier in l. 11, Aquinas described the consideration of an immobile mover as a third philosophical study. It assigns the study to metaphysics: "Certain things are immobile, and around this is one study of philosophy. Another study of it is around those things that are mobile but incorruptible, as are celestial bodies. A third study

---

13. Joseph Owens, *The Doctrine of Being in the Aristotelian Metaphysics* (Toronto: Pontifical Institute of Mediaeval Studies, 1963), 467–68.

of it is around mobiles and corruptibles, just as are inferior bodies. And the first study pertains to metaphysics; the other two to natural science" (n. 243). Is not Aquinas assigning the consideration of a wholly unmoved mover to metaphysics? It seems so. I think most Thomists hesitate to accept this conclusion because they assume that the *Physics* is a book of natural philosophy and that means only natural philosophy. But Aquinas does not share that assumption. The book that is the *Physics* may contain the general science of nature but it is not identical to it. It contains other considerations like those of the metaphysician. Aquinas specifies Book VIII's treatment of a moving principle as altogether immobile as a case of those metaphysical considerations.

These remarks about the unmoved mover of Book VIII are valuable to interpret the last sentence of the commentary in which Aquinas says that Aristotle ends his common consideration of natural things "in a first principle of all of nature which is God above all things blessed forever" (*in primo principio totius naturae, qui est super Omnia Deus benedictus in saecula*). But the only preceding discussion of the *primum principium* is early in the commentary on the eighth book at n. 974. There the first principle is the *principium totius esse*, not of *forma substantiale*. This metaphysical assignment of the *primum principium* correlates with what I just mentioned from Book II. The remark at the end of the *Physics* commentary does not necessarily mean that natural philosophy reaches the *primum principium*.[14]

Third, a remark from Aquinas's commentary on the *De Anima* (1269–70, hereafter "*In de An.*") is also important. Aristotle's *De Anima* is often placed under the general science of nature presented in the *Physics*. The treatment of the soul presupposes certain categories established in physics. In his commentary Aquinas is adamant that physics has not established anything immaterial:

[Aristotle] puts a question about things that exist immaterially: whether, that is, our intellect, though conjoined with spatial magnitude (i.e., the body), can understand "anything separated," i.e., any substance separated from matter. He undertakes to pursue this enquiry later,—not at present, because it is not yet evident that any such substances exist nor, if they do, what sort of thing they are. It is a problem for metaphysics. In fact, we do not know Aristotle's solution of this problem, for we have not

---

14. For further discussion see John F. X. Knasas, "Materiality and Aquinas' Natural Philosophy: A Reply to Johnson," *The Modern Schoolman* 68, no. 3 (1991): 251–54.

the whole of his *Metaphysics*; either because it is not yet all translated, or possibly because he died before he could complete it.¹⁵

Aquinas's metaphysical assignment of the consideration of the existence of substances separated from matter is certainly congruent with his previously noted metaphysical character of *Physics* VIII.

Sensitive and Rational Souls

A comment on how natural philosophy deals and does not deal with the sensitive and rational soul is also appropriate here. Aquinas explains this in his commentary on Aristotle's *De Anima*. The natural philosophy treatment is very oblique because it is very physiological. For example, anger is treated as a certain movement of blood around the heart. On the other hand, the activities of sensation and intellection in themselves are understood as movements and alterations only improperly speaking: "et ideo iste motus [sentire] simpliciter est alter a motu physico."¹⁶ Aquinas goes on to extend this improper meaning of motion and passivity to the operations of intellect and will: "Et hujusmodi motus dicitur proprie operatio, ut sentire et intelligere et velle."¹⁷ They should not then be "physical" changes under *ens mobile*. The reason is that they involve reception of form without the destruction of previous form. One would suspect that the metaphysician is the philosopher that investigates these activities in their proper nature. Two remarks from the *De Trinitate* commentary cement that suspicion: "Spiritual creatures, moreover, are mutable only with regard to choice [*secundum electionem*]; and this sort of motion [*talis mutatio*] is not the concern of the natural philosopher [*ad naturalem*] but rather of the metaphysician [*diuinum*]."¹⁸ And what sort of motion is choice? "Motion with respect to choice [*secundum electionem*] is reducible to the sense in which the act of the intellect or will [*actus intellectus uel voluntatis*] is called motion; which is an improper sense of the term

---

15. *In III de An.*, l. 12, n. 785 (trans. Foster and Humphries, 233).
16. Aquinas, *In III de An.*, l. 12, n. 766; ed. Angeli Pirotta, in *In Aristotelis Librum de Anima* (Turin: Marietti, 1936), 251–52. At *ST* I, q. 78, a. 3, co., Aquinas calls sensation a spiritual change "immutatio spiritualis."
17. Aquinas, *In III de An.*, l. 12, n. 766.
18. *In de Trin.*, q. 5, a. 2, ad 7 (trans. Maurer, 25).

[*improprie dictum*], motion being understood as operation [*pro operatione sumpto*]."[19]

Texts to the Contrary?

Finally, earlier in discussing *In de Trin.*, q. 5, a. 4, co., I mentioned that I do not find Aquinas ever explicitly saying that the natural philosophy part of philosophy proves God's existence. Other students of Aquinas differ from me. They claim that Aquinas's commentary on the *Metaphysics* (1269–72) contains such assertions. For example, Aquinas says, "If there is no substance other than those which exist in the way that natural substances do, with which the philosophy of nature deals, the philosophy of nature will be the first science. But if there is some immobile substance, this will be prior to natural substance; and therefore the philosophy which considers this kind of substance will be first philosophy [*per consequens Philosophia considerans huiusmodi substantia erit Philosophia prima*]."[20]

We have seen this assertion before in *SCG* I.12. Then it mentioned the order of the sciences. I used that reference to trace the assertion back to

---

19. *In de Trin.*, q. 5, a. 4, ad 3 (trans. Maurer, 47). At *In II Phys.*, l. 4, n. 175, Aquinas assigns to metaphysics the rational soul as separate from matter. He says that the consideration of physics ends with forms in some way separate from matter but having existence in matter: "forms which indeed are in some way separate, but nevertheless they have being in matter" (formas quae quidem sunt aliquot modo separate, sed tamen esse habent in materia). How are these forms separate, what is the "aliquot modo"? Aquinas remarks, "insofar as the intellective power is not the act of some corporeal organ; inquantum intellective virtus non est actus alicuius organi corporalis." Who provides this explanation? Not the *naturalis*, or natural philosopher, but the metaphysician: "But how forms are totally separated from matter, and what they are, or even how this form, i.e., the rational soul, exists insofar as it is separable and capable of existence without a body, and what it is according to its separable essence are questions which pertain to first philosophy [*philosophum primum*]." The opening reference to forms totally separated from matter echoes *In de Trin.*, q. 5, a. 4, co., in which philosophical knowledge of these existents is exclusively reserved to the metaphysician. The *Physics* text goes on to include the rational soul as separable. The text fails to say that the natural philosopher attains the rational soul as separable. The text merely says that the natural philosopher attains it as the part of a generable thing. Aquinas repeats himself in the *Metaphysics* commentary: "But if any soul can exist separately from a body, then insofar as it is not the actuality of such a body, it does not fall within the scope of the philosophy of nature." *In VI Meta.*, l. 1, n. 1159 (trans. Rowan, 401).

20. *In VI Meta.*, l. 1, n. 1170 (trans. Rowan, 462). In his Dumb Ox republishing of the Rowan translation, Ralph McInerny changes the last line to "therefore the philosophy of nature, which considers this kind of substance, will be first philosophy." See also *In III Meta.*, l. 4, n. 398, and *In XI Meta.*, l. 7, n. 2267.

SCG I.4. Here and in its other occurrences in the commentary, the assertion stands alone. In itself does it say that natural philosophy proves God's existence or even gets to the immaterial substance? It might be doing so. By itself all the text claims is that if there is no substance higher than natural, then philosophy of nature becomes first philosophy. The text does not say that higher substance is reached by philosophy of nature. So, without less ambiguous texts, this remark from the *Metaphysics* commentary is indecisive. Of course, I think that Aquinas's writings do contain less ambiguous remarks, but these indicate metaphysics as the science that gives knowledge of immobile substance.

What would the present text be saying for me? I think that *ST* I, q. 44, a. 2, is important to answer that question. There the approach to a more universal cause at each of the three stages of philosophy is correlated with the philosopher discovering a more profound aspect of sensible things. So at the first stage the aspect is an accident of sensible substances. At the second stage it is the more profound substantial form of the sensible substance. The discovery of substantial form leads to a more universal cause than at stage one, though the more universal cause is still material in Aristotle's case. Finally at stage three the most profound aspect of sensible things is reached. This aspect is *esse*, and *esse* leads to the most universal cause. Hence, our present text would be saying that without a non-natural kind of substance, sensible reality would lack an aspect that would ground a scientific consideration other than physics. The science of physics would be the only science of the sensible.

In summary, in light of the previous points, I do not believe that someone could blame a reader for concluding that Aquinas's philosophical approach to God is an exclusively metaphysical affair. The points are as follows. First, at *In de Trin.*, q. 5, a. 4, co., Aquinas has the philosopher reaching both God and the separate substances only (*nisi prout*) in metaphysics. Second, at the beginning of his *Summa contra Gentiles*, Aquinas reserves knowledge of God's existence to the last part of philosophy—metaphysics. Third, at *ST* I, q. 44, a. 2, co., Aquinas understands matter/form reasoning as getting the philosopher to a celestial body only. The philosopher proceeds further, not by extending natural philosophy reasoning, but by grasping the *esse* of the sensible thing—*ens inquantum ens*. Fourth, at *SCG* I.20, the argument for the immateriality of the mover of the celestial spheres from the eternity of motion begins from the "supposition" of the eternity of motion. But in natural philosophy the eternity of motion is a strict conclusion. Aquinas's suppositional way of speaking indicates a metaphysics already in place. Fifth, *In II Phys.* Aquinas assigns the consideration of a wholly unmoved mover to metaphysics. A remark of Aquinas from the *De Anima* commentary, while he is speaking of "separate substances," repeats this assignment. Sixth, as far as I can tell, Aquinas never explicitly claims that the science of physics proves God's existence as he so claimed for metaphysics. Texts for the former claim are ambiguous and hence only apparent.

The Division of the Sciences

I would like to conclude with one final issue. Does the assignment of knowing God, the separate substances, and the sensitive and rational souls to metaphysics have metaphysics proving its subject matter? One of these items would have to be already known to know that *ens inquantum ens* has a separateness from matter both in being and in notion. In reply, as far as I know, Aquinas never says that we "begin" metaphysics by grasping the immateriality characteristic of the *ratio entis*. In various places—for example, *In de Trin.*, q. 5, a. 1, co., *ST* I, q. 85, a. 1, ad 2, and *In VI Meta.*, l. 1—Aquinas does argue that because of the immateriality of the intellect and of the necessity of science, the speculative sciences are "differentiated according to their degree of separation from matter and motion." But he does not say "*initially* differentiated" by different relations to matter. Rather, the argument seems to be that various degrees of separation from matter "somewhere" will differentiate the sciences. For example, in *In de Trin.* Aquinas notes any number of possibilities for a third speculative science whose object includes separation from matter. First the science could deal with something that never exists in matter, for instance, God and the angels. Second, it could deal with an object as able to be in matter and apart from it, that is, objects such as substance, quality, being, potency, act, and so on. Third, the science could deal with both of the previous. These manifold possibilities should cause one to hesitate to say just how metaphysics is separate from matter. In fact, in the listed text from the *Metaphysics* commentary, Aquinas has metaphysics satisfying this condition by dealing with God. Then as almost an afterthought, Aquinas mentions Avicenna's opinion that the common things metaphysics considers need not have existence in matter.[21] If Aquinas were intending to say that metaphysics is initially differentiated from the other speculative sciences by the immateriality of its subject matter, then it is strange to say the least that he would express this key point as an afterthought in a text that appears to sufficiently distinguish the immateriality of metaphysics by its consideration of God. Also, even here Aquinas does not say that these common things are those from which metaphysics begins. Finally, in the text from the *Summa Theologiae*, Aquinas indicates that the apprehension of these common things depends upon a knowledge of immaterial substances. He says: "But some things can be abstracted even from common intelligible matter, such as being [*ens*], unity, potency, act, and the like, all of which can exist without matter, as can be verified in the case of immaterial substances [*ut patet in substantis immaterilaibus*]."[22] As Aquinas is already on record assigning knowledge of the existence of immaterial substances to metaphysics, he cannot be initiating metaphysics with the immateriality of its subject matter.

Aquinas should then be initiating metaphysics with its subject matter understood in another way. What that initial understanding is is clear if one recalls the remarks on the sensitive soul. Human consciousness is never so sunk into its object that it loses all awareness of itself. Furthermore, because, as recently mentioned, sensation is not one of the instances of change under the subject matter of natural philosophy, then we have a multiplicity not covered by *ens mobile*. The multiplicity of the real and the cognitional is covered by a wider sense of *ens*. This wider sense is sufficiently distinct from *ens mobile*. Another object of science is offered. How separateness from matter is realized in a third way different from physics and mathematics should be left to the unfolding of the science. An initial requirement to rise to a third degree of abstraction is a red herring for understanding Aquinas's approach to metaphysics.

So, finally, the metaphysical interpretation of Aquinas's approach to God

21. "Unless perhaps [*Nisi forte*] we may say, as Avicenna does that common things of the kind which this science considers [*perscrutatur*] are said to be separate from matter in being, not because they are always without matter, but because they do not necessarily have being in matter, as objects of mathematics do." Aquinas, *In VI Meta.*, l. 1, n. 1165 (trans. Rowan, 402).
22. *ST* I, q. 85, a. 1, ad 2 (trans. Pegis, 1:815).

is as well-wrought as any other. As Aquinas remarked, the philosopher reaches both God and the separate substances only insofar (*nisi prout*) as they are the objects of that science whose subject is being as being and which is called by philosophers divine science and metaphysics. I know of no text comparably explicit that says otherwise. One would be foolish to approach Aquinas's *viae* from any other angle.

[7]

A More Robust Version of the *De Ente* Reasoning

―◇―

If the combination of *habens esse* is what the metaphysician first works out concerning the subject matter of the science, then the *De Ente* reasoning clearly explains how the metaphysician goes from his subject matter of *ens inquantum ens* to God. Elsewhere God is a cause of "omnia inquantum sunt entia" because God is an "agens per modum dantis esse."[1] Moreover, the metaphysician's conclusion of a *primum principium essendi* would clearly indicate the possibility of an immaterial substance between bodies and *esse subsistens*. The metaphysician would quickly, if not initially, establish the immateriality of the subject matter.[2]

As noted in *In de Trin.*, q. 5, a. 4, co., however, Aquinas has the metaphysician causally reaching separate substances as well. With God they are causes of the subject of metaphysical science. How do they play a role in causing *ens inquantum ens*? In his reply to the third objection, Aquinas tips his hand. He says that the metaphysician considers separate substances "from the same point of view as the First Cause or God." In light of what has just

---

1. Aquinas, *In VI Meta.*, l. 3, n. 1215. Aquinas also remarks, "Although the first cause, which is God, does not enter the essence of created things; nevertheless, *esse*, which is in created things, is not able to be understood unless as derived from the divine *esse*, just as no proper effect is able to be understood except as derived from a proper cause." Aquinas, *De Pot.*, q. 3, a. 5, ad 1.

2. See Aquinas's first argument at *Disputed Questions on Spiritual Creatures*, q. 1, a. 5, co.

been determined about how God causes *ens* by causing *esse*, then the separate substances, or angels, should do likewise. Aquinas goes on to say that they are "secondary principles of things at least through the movements of the spheres." The reader will recall from the second stage of *ST* I, q. 44, a. 2, co., that the spheres or heavens were the causes of the form in matter of generable and corruptible things. So, separate substances should be secondary causes of *esse* by causing form.

Borrowings from Natural Philosophy

In chapter 3 I explained how Aquinas regards form as a *principium essendi*. As grasped by judgment, *esse* is presented as the act *of the thing*. It has no other character and as such is in a strange way a cause dependent upon its effect. Hence, any conditions for the thing whose act is *esse* become conditions for the *esse*. One of these conditions is the form of the thing. It is the completion, the *complementum*, of the thing by way of its structuring the matter. Obviously presupposed here is natural philosophy's hylomorphic analysis of the generable and corruptible thing. The metaphysician would be taking over that analysis to elucidate the metaphysician's understanding of *esse*. The borrowing would not mean an intelligible shift into natural science. It is still metaphysics because the focus is on *esse*, a principle not known in natural science. As a caveat, I should mention that the reader is in danger of forgetting this point. The causal path that opens up from form as a cause of *esse* is a lengthy one with extensive borrowing from physics. But given that we are elucidating conditions for *esse*, then the causal path is correctly considered to be metaphysics. As much as I can, I want to enumerate the stages in this second causal path from *esse* and to provide the philosophical reasons for them. The resulting scheme will prove to be invaluable in understanding Aquinas's explicit God proofs.

That form in matter requires an explanation seems clear by reasoning analogous to the *De Ente* reasoning. Though there are obvious differences, the form is to the matter like an accident to its subject. As the act of the matter, form must exist in the matter.[3] Such a thought is behind much of the

---

3. "But forms and accidents and the like are called beings, not as if they themselves were, but because something is by them; as whiteness is called a being because its subject is white by it." *ST* I, q. 45, a. 4, co. (trans. Pegis, 1:438).

controversy of whether the human soul, a case of a substantial form, could also be the human's principle of intellection.[4] Hence, as the act of the matter, form is a dependent item and so needs the matter. Matter, however, cannot be the complete explanation of the form that the matter has. Precisely as subject of the form, matter lacks the form and so disqualifies itself as a complete explainer. The full explanation of the form must shift either to the matter in some other respect than subject or to another subject. But the matter is in no other respect than subject of the form, and so the full explanation of the form in matter is another subject.

I believe that a reader finds Aquinas making the above argument in the following:

> From what was said, therefore, it is clear that the principles of nature are three, namely, the matter, the form, and the privation. But these are not sufficient for generation. For what is in potency is not able to reduce itself to act, just as the brass which is in potency to the idol does not make itself an idol, but it requires an operator that extracts the form of the idol from potency to act. Form, however, is not able to extract itself from potency to act. I speak of the generated form which we call the term of generation. For form is not except in the thing made to exist. However, what is done is in the making while the thing is being made [*quod autem operator est in fieri, idest dum res fit*]. So, besides the matter and form there must be some principle which acts. This is said to be the efficient principle, or the mover, or agent, or whence is the principle of motion.[5]

The use of potency/act terminology here and its absence in the *De Ente* reasoning should not cause a reader to wonder if the reasonings are of the same type. One can be confident that these categories are in the *De Ente* text. Back at *In I Sent.*, d. 19, q. 5, a. 1, co., Aquinas describes judgmentally grasped *esse*, with which the *De Ente* is concerned, as that by which a thing is denominated a being. Just earlier at q. 2, a. 2, co., he stated that denomination by calling *esse* the *actus existentis inquantum ens*. So, even though the *De Ente* reasoning does not employ potency/act terminology, it easily could have. "What belongs" can be considered as not only *esse* but also *forma*.

---

4. "For from the fact that the intellectual substance is in matter it does not follow that it is a material form, because that soul is not present in matter in the sense of being embedded in it or wholly enveloped by it." *SCG* II.69, *Non autem* (trans. Anderson, 2:207).

5. Aquinas, *De Principiis Naturae*, ed. John J. Pauson (Louvain: Editions E. Nauwelaers, 1950), 87.

Like the *De Ente* reasoning, the *De Principiis* reasoning should be commencing causal considerations in virtue of the *per se* dependency of form. Like an accident, form is an act that exists as in and of a subject. But complete dependency upon its subject *qua* subject is impossible As the text says, form is in matter only in potency just as the statue is in the potency of the brass. Hence, something else is required. Aquinas calls it an operator.

Why does the *De Principiis* text go on to exclude the form as this operator? Has not the form been excluded by being understood as a dependent item? I believe that the reader has to remember the corresponding point in the *De Ente* reasoning. When Aquinas asked whether the form of the thing could efficiently cause the *esse*, he was speaking about the possibility of the thing in some other respect than subject of the *esse*. Hence, the *De Principiis* should be trying to speak about the matter in some other respect than subject of the form. But in that other respect the form remains only potentially in the matter. Hence, form cannot account for itself being in act. An operator outside the matter/form composite is necessary.

Can the philosopher determine the identity of the operator? Yes, but the story is long. The story begins with a renewed consideration of the matter/form relation. There are two possibilities to consider for this relation. The possibilities are detailed at *ST* I, q. 104, a. 1, co. On the one hand, a form can be in matter in such a way that it is preserved by the matter. Aquinas mentions the case of a house built of stone, cement, and wood which can receive and preserve the order that the builder places in them. In this case the operator, or agent, initiates the form in matter but does not conserve it. On the other hand, a form may be more superficially received. Aquinas mentions light received by the air. He describes the light as having no "root" in the air. In this case the agent must not only initiate the effect but also must maintain the effect.

What relation is found between the matter and form of a generated thing? As the matter of itself is formless, it possesses no form that would impede the received form from sinking roots into the matter. Hence, the agent responsible for the form in the matter would be necessary to initiate the form but not to maintain it. The agent would be, as Aquinas remarks, a cause of the becoming of its effect, but not directly of its being. Aquinas's thesis leads to the Scholastic division respectively of a *causa in fieri* and a *causa in esse*.

So, to the question about the identity of the cause of form in the generated thing, some answer is that it is a *causa in fieri*. A further point can be made. It suffices that the agent be of the same species as the effect. In other words, the agent belongs to the class of generated things. Why? As like its effect, the agent would have a form rooted in its matter. The agent is sufficiently in act to cause form in matter elsewhere. If the agent is an ungenerable body, then the agent must have a matter in potency to that form and to no other. Hence, from further consideration of the initial matter/form situation, one can conclude that it suffices that the operator must be not only a *causa in fieri* but also another generated thing like the first. Such an identity automatically reignites the *De Principiis* reasoning. Consequently, we have a second operator for the first operator. Little imagination is necessary to realize that we are assembling an infinite regress of operators into the past, an infinite horizontal or lateral regress if you will.

As necessary as this infinite regress is to strict matter/form reasoning in natural philosophy, Aquinas does not regard it as so. He regards it as a possibility and as a supposition for purposes of a most effective demonstration of God. As mentioned in chapter 6, those comments indicate an already-in-place metaphysics that has acquainted Aquinas with another way of coming into being than through generation. Here one should also remember that as deeply as Aquinas is borrowing material from natural philosophy, his focus was never just form but form as a *principium essendi*. That makes the consideration of form to be a metaphysical one.

So granting that a metaphysical consideration of matter/form reasoning expands to a possible infinite lateral regress of generated operators, does this infinite regress become the identity of the operator behind any generated thing? No, there is more to the story. Borrowing reasoning from *Physics* VIII.6, Aquinas explains that the infinite regress must take place within the continuous movement of an ungenerable body. In *SCG* I.13.25, Aquinas provides a summary of the reasoning.

It is further evident that, according to the position of Aristotle, some self-moved being must be everlasting. For if, as Aristotle supposes, motion is everlasting, the generation of self-moving beings (this means beings that are generable and corruptible) must be endless. But the cause of this endlessness cannot be one of the self-moving beings, since it does not always exist. Nor can the cause be all the self-moving beings together, both because they would be infinite and because they would not be simultaneous. There must therefore be some endlessly self-moving being, causing the endlessness of generation among these sublunary self-movers. Thus, the mover of the self-moving being is not moved, either through itself or by accident.[6]

From the infinite series of generated self-movers, Aquinas argues for an everlasting self-mover by a process of elimination. First, no one thing in the series could be the cause of all because no one thing always exists. In other words, any one thing might be called the cause of what comes after but certainly not called the cause of what came before. Second, the cause of the endless series of generations could not be all the things together. On the one hand, they are infinite. In other words, no one thing in the series gets a complete explanation from something else in the series. For example, before B explains A, B must be explained by C, etc.[7] On the other hand, the things in the series are not simultaneous. In other words, unlike in a simultaneous regress, we cannot argue to a first that explains the others in the regress. Hence, the philosopher probing the conditions for the matter/form relationship is forced to move vertically to a nongenerable body in whose continuous motion the eternal series of generations takes place.

Another way of seeing the necessity for moving one's consideration vertically is to go back to what *ST* I, q. 104, a. 1, called the "form as such" (*forma inquantum est talis forma*). Aquinas is no Platonist. Forms do not subsist; they exist only in things. Some idea of what Aquinas is speaking is available by contrast to the effect of the univocal cause—the form in this particular matter. The form as such should mean, then, the form throughout matter. This contrast makes the form as such similar to the infinite horizontal series of univocal generators, for example, your parents from their parents from their parents, etc. In fact the response mentions the heavenly bodies as the cause of the generation of inferior bodies.

---

6. *SCG* I.13, *Quod autem* (trans. Pegis, 1:93).

7. See Leibniz's claims back in selections (B), (C), and (D) quoted in chapter 1. This was the point of Copleston's reply to Russell's remark that the adequate explanation of the lit match is that one has struck it. Copleston just observed that the explanation is still inadequate theoretically. As effects of *causae in fieri*, the operators operate on their own, but they are not understood or explained on their own. They would not independently generate if they had not themselves been generated. So, a full understanding of their operating would involve an understanding of their history. Unfortunately an understanding of the history is made impossible if the regress is infinite.

This interpretation of the form as such is confirmed by an earlier parallel passage in *ST* I, q. 13, a. 5, ad 1. Instead of mentioning the form as such as the higher cause's effect, Aquinas describes the effect as "the whole species" and as "the generation of all men": "For the non-univocal agent is the universal cause of the whole species [*totius speciei*] as the sun is the cause of the generation of all men." In my opinion, by the "form as such" and "the whole species" Aquinas is speaking of the infinite series of generated self-movers mentioned in *SCG* I.13.25, and which is accounted for neither by each alone nor by all together. The need for a different kind of body than terrestrial bodies to account for the form as such is then clear. As causing form in some particular matter, no terrestrial body can cause form throughout all matter. The need to account for the form throughout the infinity of the past series can be a basis for concluding to a body that is a first physical cause of generated bodies and that is not itself generated.

This conclusion of a nongenerable body is logically derived from a sustained consideration of the matter/form relationship in generated things. But it is logically derived as only a possibility, not as a fact. The reason that it is limited to a possibility is that the eternity of the series of generated things is itself only a possibility. The status of the series as only possible derives from an already-in-place metaphysics that has acquainted the philosopher with another way of coming into existence than through generation, namely, creation. Hence, by turning to its fundamental act of *esse*, any generated thing in the series would have subsistent existence as its creative cause. Without this metaphysics, the matter/form reasoning would necessarily conclude to the eternity of the series. No medieval theologian would accept that. Given the common understanding of the opening verse of the Book of Genesis that God created the world in time, the assertion of the eternity of the series would be heretical.

Also, the conclusion of a possible first physical cause should be kept carefully distinct from any instantiation of it in terms of cosmology. Aquinas does in fact instantiate it. This nongenerable body appears to be the celestial body referred to by the "ecliptic" and called the "more universal cause" at *ST* I, q. 44, a. 2, co. The reason for the instantiation is found in the *De Caelo*. The reason is the long but limited past human observations of the constant and regular motions of the heavens. Obviously, this observation can provide only a probable motive to identify the conclusion of the first physical cause with some nonterrestrial body.⁸ The logical distinction between the conclusion and any empirical instantiation of it is crucial for realizing that the philosophizing is not brought down by any demise of the cosmology of concentric heavenly spheres. In fact, John Quinn argues that the conclusion of a first physical cause is so secure that one can admit that it may remain forever empirically unverified by science.⁹

Interlude

Vincent Smith and Benedict Ashley are proponents of a physical interpretation of the first way to God from motion. In their physical arguments, they proceed simply vertically. There is no consideration of the horizontal regress described above. I would like to say some words on each.

In "The Prime Mover: Physical and Metaphysical Considerations," Vincent Smith appears to be prejudiced by an understanding of the ordering of the sciences in which attaining metaphysics is dependent upon the fruits of natural science.¹⁰ In particular, physics proves a prime mover and so demonstrates a nonbody. This conclusion indicates that to be a being is not necessarily to be a body. But such an understanding of being marks the subject of metaphysics.

For the natural philosophy demonstration of the prime mover, Smith cites *Physics* VII.1. As he summarizes the argument, Smith explicitly says that he is setting aside the possibility that the prime mover is a self-mover.¹¹ This remark is revealing. It shows that Smith is incognizant of the possibility of a lateral regress. For by reaching a self-mover, the logical path to its generation by a prior one *ad infinitum* opens up. Smith shows no awareness of this un-

---

8. In the *Disputed Questions on Spiritual Substances*, q. 1, a. 5, co., Aquinas says that Aristotle, who Aquinas has presented as already sharing his metaphysics of *esse*, did misstep. From the human tradition of the observation of the heavens, Aristotle went from the possibility of eternal motion to asserting its fact.

9. John Quinn, "The Third Way to God: A New Approach," *The Thomist* 42, no. 1 (1978): 66–67. Quinn, however, understands the conclusion as true of an actual, not simply a possible. This is because he believes that there are Thomistic arguments for a first physical cause that need not involve an infinite series of generated self-movers. I argue that that these arguments misconstrue Aquinas; see my next section below.

10. Vincent Smith, "The Prime Mover: Physical and Metaphysical Considerations," *Proceedings of the American Catholic Philosophical Association* 28 (1954): 86.

11. Ibid., 82n9.

avoidable scenario and the need of the natural philosopher to address it as Aquinas does in the *secunda via* of *SCG* I.13. Consequently, Smith advances the claim that as a natural philosophy argument, the first way has no logical dependence on motion's eternity: "But as a scientist, [the Catholic] will still discover an authentically physical argument that has no intrinsic dependence on the belief in an eternal world."[12] As I have explained, this idea of the proof's independence from motion's eternity is open to easy rebuttal. Nevertheless, in this perspective, Smith interprets as a "dialectical aside" Aquinas's above mentioned use of metaphysics to counter Averroes's use of the eternity of motion proofs to deny creation. Of course, however, there is no textual evidence that in order to answer Averroes, Aquinas is relying upon a natural philosophy proof for a creator. As I said back in chapter 6, Ashley's cited interpretation of *In VIII Phys.* for a physical knowledge of a cause for the substance of the heavens is inaccurate.

Smith's blindness to motion's eternity as a necessary plateau in physical reasoning to a first mover continues in his monograph, *The General Science of Nature*. Again, he presents the reasoning of *Physics* VII.1. But in understanding the proof's first claim that what is moved is moved by another, Smith insists that the proof will stay with motion and not shift to substantial change: "Even if there is no substantial change in the world, motion in the strict sense would furnish evidence of a Prime Mover."[13] But, then, why not account for the motion of the rock by the motion of the stick by the motion of the arm by the soul of the man? Is it not clear that if we go on, it is because the human self-mover is regarded as generated? That lateral detour to an infinite series of generators must be dealt with.

Smith's consideration of the possibility of an eternal world is also instructive in a surprising way. For Smith the possibility is simply a metaphysical one. In the context of a metaphysics reached through natural philosophy, Smith says: "From the side of things made, there is no reason why any one creature should have been the first and why some other creature could not have been created before it, and why still another creature could not have preceded, and so on and on."[14] But before we supposedly get to metaphysics and

---

12. Ibid., 85.
13. Vincent Smith, *The General Science of Nature* (Milwaukee, Wis.: Bruce Publishing, 1958), 368.
14. Ibid., 378.

the idea that something can be caused without a preexisting subject, natural philosophy has already claimed something from the side of things made. The first argument for the eternity of motion shows that any supposed first motion follows the generation of the mobile.[15] In other words, from the side of things made and without a metaphysics not yet on the scene, the natural philosopher grasps motion's eternity. Moreover, the natural philosopher grasps it not just as a possibility but as a fact. Smith conveniently ignores these physical arguments for motion's eternity until he believes that he possesses a metaphysics that can neutralize them.

I now turn to Ashley. The pivot might seem strange in the light of my previous reference to him. In his *The Way toward Wisdom*, Ashley trumpets *Physics* VIII. Yet when it comes time to formalize the argument for a prime mover, the argument itself appears to be indistinguishable from *Physics* VII. For example, in his fourth step Ashley clearly presents the thesis of the impossibility of an infinite series of simultaneous movers: "The number of movers that, like C, act to move others only when they are themselves moved, cannot be infinite, since in an infinite series of such moved movers there would be no prime mover Z, and hence none of the intermediate agents would be in act but only in potency to act, and hence not actually causing motion."[16] Ashley, then, rushes to conclude to a prime mover Z that "cannot be a material mover, since no material thing either moves itself or is in motion without being moved by another." Yet a reader could ask, if the argument is simply physical, why could not Z be the moving part of a bodily self-mover itself generated in the past by another self-mover *ad infinitum*? On the next page Ashley acknowledges the possibility of natural bodies with their motions having been produced by other bodies. He remarks: "But when bodies are produced by other bodies, they receive their properties along with their substantial nature or essence. This causal chain of production again requires an immaterial prime mover, because changeable beings do not exist necessarily but are produced and perish."[17] It is far from clear that Ashley is speaking of Aquinas's already discussed infinite regress into the past mentioned in *SCG* I.13.25. Rather, it seems that at any point of production, past or pres-

---

15. See my chapter 8, "The '*Suppositio*' of Motion's Eternity."
16. Ashley, *The Way Toward Wisdom*, 97.
17. Ibid., 98.

ent, we can ascend to the immaterial prime mover. Again, need the ascent be such? Why not to a self-mover itself in a temporal series of self-movers? Just as there is a generational series of humans behind the cultivation of the vineyard, so that it produces year after year, so too the cause of the generation of natural bodies is not an immaterial prime mover but a temporal series of generated self-movers. Where is the further need to go vertical? Are we not stuck on a plateau? Aquinas has an answer to these questions, but it is consists in taking the lateral regress seriously.

Another interesting attempt to avoid the horizontal regress in natural philosophy reasoning is John Quinn's argument for a first physical cause in his interpretation of the *tertia via* of the *Summa Theologiae*.[18] Quinn believes that such a cause is the necessary *per aliud* apart from which there is "nihil in rebus," as stated in the first part of the *via*. This article is interesting for many reasons, not least of which is Quinn's claim that the conclusion of a first physical cause is still solid today despite the demise of the cosmology of celestial spheres in terms of which the conclusion was instantiated. What I want to consider is Quinn's listing of four arguments from texts of Aquinas for this first physical cause. The arguments conclude to a nonterrestrial body without any mention of the eternity of motion and the infinite past series of generations that that eternity implies. The arguments and my comments follow.

The first argument is from *ST* I, q. 104, a. 1. In sum, though a univocal cause can account for the form being in this particular matter, no univocal cause can account for the form as such. As under the form, the cause would also be the cause of itself. Hence, the cause of the form itself is an equivocal cause, a cause having a different type of form. Note that there is no mention of a horizontal regress of generators. To go vertical it suffices to see the contradiction in making a univocal generator the cause of the form as such.

In comment, I have already explained that Aquinas's talk at q. 104, a. 1 of the form as such is best understood as the infinite series of generated self-movers mentioned in *SCG* I.13.25 and which is accounted for neither by each alone nor by all together. In truth, Aquinas's first reasoning is not reasoning for the existence of a higher cause but reasoning for the equivocal nature of that higher cause. The reasoning for the existence of a higher cause

---

18. John Quinn, "The Third Way to God," 50–68.

remains that of I.13.25 which as mentioned should have the eternity of motion as a necessary element if we are proceeding only by natural philosophy.

The second argument is from *In IV Sent.*, d. 12, q. 1, a. 2. Quinn notes that no univocal agent exercises its causality immediately in virtue of its substantial form but in virtue of its active qualities which are accidents. Hence, no unassisted univocal agent should produce a substantial change. That univocal agents do produce substantial changes indicates the presence of a higher equivocal cause. In comment, in the cited text Aquinas does not make Quinn's argument. Aquinas makes the opposite argument. As the powers act in virtue of the substantial form, alteration leads to generation, or substantial change.[19] Aquinas's text neither includes nor implies any transiting to a higher cause.

The third argument is again an early one from *In II Sent.*, d. 13, q. 1, a. 3, ad 9. Here the universal physical cause is necessary in order that univocal causes can overcome contrary qualities in the patient. Univocal causes need a cause that alters without being altered. In comment, in the text Aquinas nowhere argues for a first physical cause. The only point that Aquinas draws from contrary qualities in the patient is that alteration of the patient is not simultaneous but successive.[20]

The fourth argument is from *In XII Meta.*, l. 6, nn. 2510–11. Quinn argues that the endurance of a species, in fact the quasi-perpetuity of some, is only accounted for by a cause that outlasts the flux of the individual members. In comment, this is in fact the reasoning of *SCG* I.13.25. But instead of speaking of the eternity of the species, as Quinn should do as a mere natural philosopher, Quinn speaks of the "quasi-perpetuity" of a species. In n. 2510 Aquinas himself admits that the conclusion of eternal heavens follows granting generation as the only way things pass from potency to act.

Therefore, granted [*Supposito igitur*] there is no other motion by which things that pass from potentiality to actuality have always been the same except that which proceeds according to the cycle of generation [*secundum circuitum generationis*], he con-

---

19. "Et ideo qualitates non solum agunt in virtute propria, sed etiam in virtute formae substantialis. Unde actio earum non solum terminatur ad formam accidentalem; et propter hoc generatio est terminus alterationis." Ed. M. Moos (Paris: P. Lethielleux, 1947), 4:509.

20. "Quod successio quae est in alteratione aliarum qualitatum contingit ex hoc quod in patiente est qualitas contraria, quae resistit actioni alterantis, quam oportet successive expelli" (ed. Mandonnet, 2:336).

cludes from what has been shown in the philosophy of nature [*in scientia naturali*] that, if something remains the same through the cycle of generation, something must also remain numerically the same, which will act in same way so as to cause the eternal motion of things.[21]

Only a metaphysician, however, would grant that supposition; not knowing of creation, a simple natural philosopher would endorse it necessarily. That point was seen in Aquinas's *Physics* VIII reply to Averroes's criticism of creation.

In conclusion, a deeper investigation of Quinn's four arguments shows that only the first and fourth arguments treat a higher cause. Moreover, if the arguments are simply physical arguments, they must involve a consideration of the eternity of motion and the implied horizontal regress.

The Second Metaphysical Path Continued

So far the reasoning from the matter/form composition has gone from an assumed eternal series of generated substances to an overarching continuous motion to a nongenerable body as the subject of that continuous motion. Is that the end of the reasoning? The second stage of *ST* I, q. 44, a. 2, in fact concluded at this point. In the third stage of a. 2, philosophers go to the most universal cause. The basis for the progress is the recognition of *esse*. This recognition grounds the consideration of the third stage as *ens inquantum ens*. A shift to metaphysics has occurred. The nature of the shift would consist in applying the *De Ente* reasoning to the *esse* of the first physical cause. Here the metaphysician would return to an emphasis on the priority of the *esse* to the substance and conclude to *esse subsistens*.

Though Aquinas appears to proceed in that manner from the conclusion of stage two to the conclusion of stage three, another metaphysical approach seems to be indicated by the text. This approach is metaphysical but does not consider *actus essendi* either as prior or as the act *of the thing*. It is metaphysical because it considers the previously mentioned *sui generis* alteration of cognition and willing. In this approach *esse subsistens* emerges as the final cause that transfixes a finite intelligence. The finite intelligence then moves the first physical cause, the nongenerable body whose accident is the eternal,

21. Trans. Rowan, 798.

continuous motion. The finite intelligence is the angels, or intelligences, that are secondary causes of *ens qua ens* by moving the spheres, as mentioned at *In de Trin.*, q. 5, a. 4, ad 3.

The initial reasoning for *esse subsistens* as a final cause can be found in *SCG* III.23. There Aquinas argues that the mover of the first physical cause must be an intellect. Aquinas's reasoning is basically a process of elimination. The nongenerable body cannot be moving by nature like heavy bodies move down and light bodies move up. Aquinas gives a number of arguments for this claim. One argument is that these natural motions as natural are for some definite end. Consequently, motion for its own sake is impossible. As the act of the potential as it is still potential, motion lacks form and so lacks definiteness. Hence, every natural motion comes to rest in something definite. Because the first physical cause moves eternally, the first physical cause cannot be moving by a natural form.[22] Also, because the first physical cause is ungenerated, it cannot be understood as informed by a nutritive or by a sensitive soul.[23] That leaves an intellect as the remaining mover. Aquinas admits that this intellect could be God himself or a conjoined intellect, namely a soul, or a finite separate substance.[24] Later in *ST* I, q. 70, a. 3, co., he understands the conjoined intellect as indistinguishable from a finite separate substance.[25] Hence, the possibilities are two: God or a separate substance.

This disjunction is interesting. Aquinas is not reaching God as a cause of the *esse* of the first physical cause as he seemed to do at q. 44, a. 2. Rather, God is a possible cause for the eternal *motion* of the first physical cause. Its motion can be considered either as caused by God or by a finite intelligence. We have seen a similar disjunction before. Because the *esse* of things could be considered either in light of its priority to the thing or in light of its status as the act *of the thing*, then the metaphysician could reason either to *esse*

---

22. *SCG* III.23, *Adhuc. Natura*. Other listed reasons for the same conclusion are: things moved by nature are generated but the heavens are not; things moved by nature have a natural place but the heavens do not.

23. *SCG* III.23, *Adhuc. Omne*.

24. "Nor does it make any difference, as far as our present purpose is concerned, whether a heavenly body is moved by a conjoined intellectual substance which is its soul, or by a separate substance; nor whether each celestial body is moved immediately by God, or whether none is so moved." *SCG* III.23, *Non differt* (trans. Bourke, 3.1:93).

25. "From what has been said, then, it is clear that the heavenly bodies are not living beings in the same sense as plants and animals, but only equivocally [*equivoce*]" (trans. Pegis, 1:660).

subsistens or to the generator responsible for the form, the *principium essendi*, in the matter. The current disjunction suggests a similar view on the eternal continuous motion. It too will have an *esse* that is both prior to the motion and that is the act *of the motion*. Hence, the philosopher can reason to God as the mover insofar as God causes the *esse* of the motion. As mentioned in chapter 6, Aquinas asserts a consideration of motion by the metaphysician. On the other hand, the philosopher can reason to a finite separate substance as a cause of the *esse* by causing the motion.

In other words, the *De Ente* reasoning would apply not only to the *esse* of substances but to an *esse* for their motions. Supporting this idea is the contention that there is an *esse* for the accidents of substances. I do not want to pursue this idea of an *esse* for accidents now. Rather, I prefer to continue with the possibility of a finite intellectual substance as a cause for the eternal motion of the first physical cause. Later I will take up the idea of an *esse* for accidents, especially for motion. Only then will we be able to determine the robust version of the *De Ente* reasoning.

So, assuming a finite intellectual substance, how does a philosopher proceed further? Again, Aquinas could apply the *De Ente* reasoning to the *esse* of that substance. A case of Aquinas making that application could be the *tertia via* at *ST* I, q. 2, a. 3, when he argues for the necessary *per se* as the cause of the necessary *per aliud*. But another approach is from the intellectual mechanics necessary for the separate substance to be the cause of eternal motion. An intellectual substance acts through will. So the question becomes how we must understand the intellectual substance so that it has an unwavering will to move the first physical cause.

In discussing angels in the *Summa Theologiae*, Aquinas treats their will and how their will can be confirmed in good by the vision of God. His argument is that just as the will is determined by the "common nature of goodness" (*commune rationem boni*), so too is the will of the angel determined by God in the vision of him.[26] The reason is that God is the "very essence of goodness" (*ipsa essentia bonitatis*). Moreover, just as we will anything only in the light of the good, so too the blessed angels will will anything only in the light of the divine good. Hence, because God cannot sin, these angels are confirmed in good. It might be said that because moving the spheres seems to

---

26. On this point, see my *Aquinas and the Cry of Rachel*, 18–24.

be an act neither good nor bad in itself, then this consideration of the inability of angels to sin is beside the point. That would be myopic. Aquinas's argument could be modified this way. Because God is simple, God's command to move the spheres is one with his goodness. But that goodness is necessarily willed by the angel, and hence so too is the divine command necessarily willed by the angel.[27]

But how does the reasoning conclude to God not as *bonum subsistens* but as *esse subsistens*? That is how the *De Ente* reasoning reached God. If the second path leading out from judgmentally grasped *esse* is to contribute to a more robust version of the *De Ente* reasoning, then it must involve knowing that the subsistent good is also subsistent existence. How do we know that? The question directs one to what we know of goodness according to Aquinas.

At *ST* I, q. 5, a. 1, ad 1, Aquinas says, "goodness expresses perfection, which is something desirable, and hence it expresses something final" (*sed bonum dicit rationem perfecti, quod est appetibile, et per consequens dicit ratione ultimi*). In this case, the good is a final cause, or attractive, because of its perfection. How is a reader to take *bonum*? Given the use of *ratio* to qualify the terms "perfection" and "end," one would think that Aquinas is speaking of the *ratio boni*. That general sense of the good is in fact in play in the topic of the article. But how is the notion of the good attractive? As a *ratio* the good is a generality and so seems to be too formal, too much of an empty frame, to be itself attractive. The solution lies back in the *responsio*. There Aquinas reduces perfection to actuality. Hence, "a thing is perfect so far as it is a being [*ens*]; for being [*esse*] is the actuality of everything, as is clear from the foregoing." Here the *esse* portion of the *ratio entis* is spotlighted as the concrescence of perfection.

The backward reference is to the third response to q. 4, a. 1. Aquinas is dealing with the complaint that God as *esse subsistens* cannot be perfect because *esse* is most universal and receptive. In reply Aquinas insists on the opposite. He states that *esse* is more accurately compared to something received

---

27. This seems to be the reasoning at *SCG* III.23, to answer an objection: "That the motion of the heavens is voluntary according to its active principle is not repugnant to the unity and uniformity of celestial motion because of the fact that the will is open to a plurality of actions and is not determined to one of them. In fact, just as a nature is determined to one objective by its power, so is the will determined to one objective by its wisdom, whereby the will is infallibly directed to one end" (trans. Bourke, 3.1:92).

than to a receiver. What Aquinas is getting at is explained in a number of places. One is *SCG* I.20. I have referred to this text when discussing Kenny's critique of Aquinas on being. Aquinas is distinguishing God from *esse formale*. *Esse formale* designates a conceptual fix on individual *esse*s known by respective judgments. In one argument Aquinas explains how the general notion of *esse formale* is diversified into judgmental instances of *esse*. The diversification does not take place by reception from without. Rather, *esse formale* diversifies itself in light of the things it will actuate. This thinking reveals each judgmentally grasped *esse* as packed with the perfection of the thing that it will actuate. It is that perfection that should be read back into what each *esse* diversifies, namely, *esse formale*.

So far from being most universal and receptive, the *ratio essendi* is the intelligible seed ground for everything else. Hence, in the third reply Aquinas says, "Being itself [*ipsum esse*] is the most perfect of all things, for it is compared to all as act. For nothing has actuality, except insofar as it is; hence being itself [*ipsum esse*] is the actuality of all things." In Aquinas the luster of the *ratio entis* reduces to the luster of the *ratio essendi*. That luster makes being attractive and so able to be called the good. If there existed a being that instantiated the *ratio essendi*, it would command automatic obedience from the will. The fact that the angelic movers of the first physical cause do so unfailingly indicates that such a being exists as the object of their wills. That is how the second pathway out of judgmentally grasped *esse* leads like the first to subsistent *esse*.

Esse accidentale

There is still more to the web of reflections that form around the metaphysician's consideration of judgmentally grasped existence. Recently, I noted that Aquinas has either God or a finite intelligence moving the first physical cause. As far as God is the mover, I pointed out that this scenario implied that like substances, motion in particular and accidents generally have their own *esse* for which God is also the cause. In *In de Trin.*, q. 5, a. 4, ad 6, Aquinas admitted that there was both a metaphysical and a physical consideration of motion, properly defined. I want to argue that characteristic of the metaphysical consideration of motion is a consideration of motion in the light of its *esse*. That is how motion would fall under *ens in quantum est ens*, the *ratio entis*.

Do accidents have an *esse*? There are texts to the affirmative but with a qualification on the kind of *esse*. In *SCG* I.22, Aquinas says, "This being [*esse*] is divided into the being [*esse*] of substance and the being [*esse*] of accident." Also, earlier in the sixth chapter of the *De Ente*, Aquinas makes the same distinction in *esse*:

> But that to which an accident is added is a complete being [*ens*] in itself, subsisting in its own being [*esse*]; and this being [*esse*] is by nature prior to the supervening accident. That is why the supervening accident, by its union with the subject to which it comes, does not cause that being [*esse*] in which the reality subsists, and through which the reality is a being in itself [*ens per se*]. Rather, it causes a secondary being [*esse secundum*], without which we can conceive the subsistent reality to exists, as what is primary can be understood without what is secondary. So the accident and its subject do not produce something essentially, but accidentally, one. This explains why their union does not result in an essence, like the conjunction of form and matter. It also explains why an accident neither has the nature of a complete essence nor is part of a complete essence. As it is a being in a qualified sense [*ens secundum quid*], so it has an essence in a qualified sense.[28]

This text echoes what the reader observed at *SCG* II.54. An *ens* without qualification is a composition of an essence, for example, a composite of form and matter, and *esse*. This sense of *ens* is extended with qualification to an existing accident, but the existing accident is an *ens* in the sense of being an essence composed with its own *esse*.

To the above two texts other texts attributing an *esse* to accidents could be added.[29] Nevertheless, texts apparently denying an *esse* to accidents could be also cited. Two examples are as follows.[30] The first is *ST* I, q. 45, a. 4, co.:

> To be created is a kind of coming to be, as was shown above. Now, to be made is directed to the being of a thing [*esse rei*]. Hence *to be made* and *to be created* properly belong to whatever *being* belongs. Now being belongs properly to subsisting things, whether they be simple, as in the case of separate substances, or composite, as in the

---

28. Trans. Maurer, 67.

29. The texts are too lengthy to cite here, but a list of the references is as follows: *In I Sent.*, d. 17, q. 1, a. 1, co.; *In III Sent.*, d. 1, a. 1, co.; *Quodl.* IX, q. 2, a. 2, co.; *SCG* IV.14, *Quamvis autem*; *De Pot.*, q. 7, a. 7, co., and q. 8, a. 1, ad 4; *ST* I, q. 28, a. 2, co. For still other texts, see Dominic Banez, *The Primacy of Existence in Thomas Aquinas* (Chicago: Henry Regnery, 1966), 99.

30. There are others, but again they are too lengthy to cite. The list includes: *De Ver.*, q. 27, a. 1, ad 8; *De Pot.*, q. 3, a. 8, co.; *In XII Meta.*, l. 1, n. 2419.

case of material substances. For being belongs to that which has being—that is, to what subsists in its own being. But forms and accidents and the like are called beings [*entia*], not as if they themselves were, but because something is by them; as whiteness is called a being [*ens*] because its subject is white by it. Hence, according to the Philosopher, an accident is more properly said to be *of a being*, than *a being*.[31]

The second is *ST* I, q. 90, a. 2, co.:

The rational soul can be made only by creation, which, however, is not true of other forms. The reason is that, since to be made is the way to being [*via ad esse*], a thing must be made in such a way as is suitable to its mode of being [*sicut ei competit esse*]. Now that properly exists which itself has being [*habet esse*], as it were, subsisting in its own being. Therefore, only substances are properly and truly called beings [*entia*], whereas an accident has not being, but something is by it, and so far is it called a being: for instance, whiteness is called a being because by it something is white. Hence it is said in *Metaph*. vii. that an accident should be described as *of something rather than as something* [*magis entis quam ens*].[32]

So, it seems that you can marshal texts on both sides of this question of whether accidents have *esse*. Thomists are divided on the question. In his article, "The *Esse* of Accidents according to St. Thomas," J. S. Albertson lists the proponents for the affirmative and for the negative.[33] To the affirmative side one could add Joseph Owens, Barry Brown, and Albert Krapiec.[34]

Albertson finds texts for the negative to be decisive. Consequently he goes on to interpret texts for the affirmative side in this light. Aquinas's talk about an *esse* for accidents is simply talk about the fact that the accident is in another. The problem with this interpretation is that it would seem to entail textually the denial of a distinct *esse* for the substance. I say this because in many of the texts in which Aquinas speaks of an *esse* for accidents, Aquinas compares this *esse* to the *esse* of the substance. Reconsider *SCG* II.54 and *De Ente*, chap. 6, cited above. If Aquinas is not going to be equivocating on *esse* in this short space, then interpreting accidental *esse* to mean the fact of the accident in the

31. Trans. Pegis, 1:438.
32. Ibid., 1:866.
33. *The Modern Schoolman* 30, no. 4 (1953): 271n14 and 273n16 (respectively).
34. Joseph Owens, "Actuality in the *Prima Via*," in *Aquinas on the Existence of God*, 194–96; Barry Brown, *Accidental Being: A Study in the Metaphysics of St. Thomas Aquinas* (Lanham, Md.: University Press of America, 1986); Mieczyslaw Albert Krapiec, *Metaphysics: An Outline of the History of Being*, trans. Theresa Sandok (New York: Peter Lang, 1991), 382 and 452.

substance should entail that the substantial *esse* means just the fact of the substance. Albertson admits this result: "We can consider the being as existing determined by its primary distinction from mere potency—its essence; and, considering it in that light, we attribute to the being an *esse substantiale*. If on the other hand, we consider the being as existing in a manner further determined by its accidents, we attribute to it an *esse accidentale*."[35]

This cannot be right. By the *esse* of the substance, Aquinas means not the fact of the substance, the substance as existing, but a distinct act of the substance by which the substance is a fact. In *SCG* II.54, *esse* is so distinct from the substance that it comprises one composition that can be compared to the matter/form composition. Albertson's position on *ens* is an Averroistic reduction of Aquinas in which a substance is of itself a being.[36]

Given this problem with Albertson's handling of the conflicting Thomistic texts on an *esse* for accidents, I would like to consider the possibility of a reverse strategy, namely, that the texts that deny an *esse* of accidents are compatible with texts that ascribe an *esse* to them. As representative texts for the denial, I want to study the reasoning of *ST* I, q. 45, a. 4, co. and q. 90, a. 2, co. I am going to claim that there is no outright denial of some kind of *esse* for accidents in these texts, and so Aquinas can admit such *esse* if constrained by other philosophical reasons.

The central concern of these *Summa* texts is to answer correctly the question, "What is created?" My summary breaks down Aquinas's answer into nine steps.

1. In both texts Aquinas begins his reply by noting that creation is a kind of making.
2. Aquinas says that making is directed to the being of the thing (*esse rei*).
3. Hence, properly speaking, what is made is that to which *esse* properly belongs.
4. Now, what is that? The text replies that *esse* properly belongs to what subsists in its own *esse*. What does that mean?

---

35. Albertson, "The Esse of Accidents," 274.

36. In summary of this criticism of Albertson, one could quote Owens, *Elementary Christian Metaphysics*, 160n5: "To interpret this text [*SCG* IV.14] and similar ones in any other sense than a real distinction can hardly avoid implying the denial of a real distinction between finite substance and its being."

5. In the context of q. 45, a. 4, this means what itself is. In the context of q. 90, a. 2, this means a mode of existence in which what is is itself a subject for existence. A check of De Ferrari under *subsistentia* and *subsisto* confirms that it is Aquinas's teaching elsewhere. For example, Aquinas remarks in *In I Sent.*, d. 23, q. 1, a. 1, co.: "Subsistere autem dicit determinatum modum exsistendi, prout scilicet aliquid est ens per se non in alio, sicut accidens" (To subsist however says a determinate mode of existing, namely as something is a being *per se*, not in another as is an accident).
6. Hence, I conclude what properly has *esse* is a substance or subsistent.
7. So what is created are substances.
8. Forms and accidents do not have *esse* in a mode in which what is is itself a subject for existence. By their natures, forms and accidents exist in and of something else. It would be correct to ascribe to them a mode of existence in which what is is not itself a subject for existence.
9. Therefore, forms and accidents are called "concreated" rather than created.

Now am I wrong to see this reasoning as simply saying that forms and accidents do not have *esse* properly or in a mode in which what is is itself a subject for existence? That assertion certainly suffices for the purpose of the argument that only substances are created. If I am correct, then it remains an open question whether forms and accidents have *esse* improperly or according to another kind of mode. Aquinas's conclusion that forms and accidents exist in and of something else does not necessarily mean that they do not have an *esse*. Again, for the above reasoning not to mention any *esse* for forms and accidents does not mean that they do not have an *esse*. The reasoning simply requires pointing out that as existing in and of something else, forms and accidents do not have an *esse* in which they subsist. As we have seen, Aquinas does characterize the *esse* of the accident as an *inesse*. That point suffices for answering the question about what is created.

Whether they have their own *esse*-in-which-they-do-not-subsist remains an open question. From the other cited texts, we know that Aquinas answers the question affirmatively for accidents. What philosophical reasons lie behind Aquinas's claim that accidents have an *esse* that is an *inesse*? The basic answer seems to be this. Once one acknowledges a real distinction between substance and accident, one notes that that the accident is situated in the twofold multiplicity of really and cognitively existing about which I spoke in chapter 2 on the *De Ente* reasoning. In fact, sense realism places the real accident in sense cognition more immediately than the substance.[37] When the two intellectual operations are applied to this multiplicity, the first operation grasps the accident itself as existence-neutral and the second operation grasps its real existence as a distinct act basic to the accident.

The *De Ente* Reasoning and the *inesse* of Accidents

Does this revelation of an *esse* for accidents mean that the *De Ente* reasoning from what-belongs-to-a-thing can be applied to the *esse* of accidents? It appears so. As long as one remembers that the *esse* is not the proper *esse* of a subsistent, then the *esse* of an accident could be argued to be dependent upon *esse subsistens* just as the *esse* of the substance was so argued to be. What would the application look like?

Let us first review the general framework into which Aquinas placed the substantial *esse* in the *De Ente* reasoning. The focus of the framework is what belongs to a thing. From the context Aquinas is clearly referring to an accident. The reference is indicated by the examples of the illumination of the air and the ability to laugh in humans. Understood as an accident it is obvious that what belongs to a thing is a dependent item. It is at least dependent upon its subject to be in and of. Next is the point that no subject precisely as subject fully or totally accounts for what belongs to it. What gets in the way of the subject being the total explainer is its intrinsic accident neutrality. For example, of itself the air is not the subject either of darkness or of illumination. Of

---

37. "The sense-objects which actuate sensitive activities—the visible, the audible, etc.—exist outside the soul; the reason being that actual sensation attains to the individual things which exist externally." *In II de An.*, l. 12, n. 375 (trans. Foster and Humphries, 249). "For what is seen is color which exists in an exterior body." *In III de An.*, l. 8, n. 718 (trans. Foster and Humphries, 419). Also, "Senses and imagination know only the exterior accidents." Aquinas, *De Ver.*, q. 1, a. 12, co. (trans. Mulligan, 50). "And because it is innate in us to judge of things by external appearances, since our knowledge takes its rise from sense, which principally and essentially [*primo et per se*] deals with external accidents." *ST* I, q. 17, a. 1, co. (trans. Pegis, 1:181). "Our intellect, which knows the essence of a thing as its proper object, derives knowledge from sense, of which the proper objects are external accidents." *ST* I, q. 18, a. 2, co. (trans. Pegis, 1:189).

itself it is neutral to both and therefore can be either. Hence, an accident is also caused by something other than the subject *qua* subject. This something else is the efficient cause that the subject as material cause needs in order to have the accident in and of it. The identity of this efficient cause is either the subject in some other respect than subject or another subject.

The application of this framework to an accident's *esse* is more straightforward than was the application to the substance's *esse*. Though prior to the accident, the accident's *esse* is not prior to the substance. Hence, like a garden-variety accident, the *inesse* is obviously dependent upon the substance to be in and of. But the *inesse* cannot be completely dependent upon the substance even in some other respect than as subject of the *inesse*. What gets in the way is the *per se* existence-neutrality of the substance. This neutrality can be regarded as previously worked out through the *duplex operatio intellectus* applied to the substance as both really and cognitionally existing. So from the viewpoint of an accident's *esse* as prior to the accident, an accident cannot be caused by the substance to which it belongs. It is true that a substance is already in act. Hence, Aquinas says at *SCG* I.22:

> Unless we understand that something is the cause of its own being in an accidental order, which is being in an accidental way [*causa essendi secundum esse accidentale, quod esse est secundum quid*]. This not impossible. It is possible that there be an accidental being [*aliquod ens accidentale*] that is caused by the principles of its subject before the substantial being of its subject is understood as given [*ante quod esse intelligitur esse substantiale subiecti*].[38]

From the side of its nature the substance can have the principles to account for the accident which then accounts for the *esse* of the accident understood as the act *of the accident*. This thinking takes advantage of having followed previously the second causal path out of *esse*, in this case the *esse* of an accident. But only if the substance were in act in respect to *esse* could it in some respect be the cause of its accident's *esse* considered as prior to the accident. Likewise, only if it were hot could it heat; only if it were lit could it illuminate. The substance is actual but the substance is not of itself existence. Another subject that is *esse* looms on the intellectual horizon as the other subject responsible for the accident's *esse* considered as prior to the accident.

---

38. Trans. Pegis, 1:120.

The above looks at the *inesse* in the way the *De Ente* reasoning looks at the *esse substantiale*. In both cases we are considering *esse* as prior to some nature. But just as the *esse substantiale* as act of the substance can be dependent in some measure on the substance, so too the *inesse* as act of the accident is in some measure dependent upon the accident. Hence, any causes of the accident are also causes of the *inesse*. As the general framework of the *De Ente* reasoning notes, these further causes could include the substance in some other respect than as subject of the accident. Here the existence-neutral character of the substance is not a problem. The substance can be in act in some other respect and so from that angle be a cause of the accidental nature and a further cause of the *inesse* of the accident. Aquinas's example of the ability to laugh in a man would be an example of this situation.

So just as there is a twofold metaphysical path out of the *esse substantiale*, so too there is a twofold metaphysical path leading out of the *inesse* of an accident. Also, just as the paths out of *esse substantiale* met in *esse subsistens*, the paths out of the accident's *inesse* do the same. The first path from the priority of the *inesse* to the accident easily concludes to *esse subsistens* as the only adequate cause for *esse* in a nonsubsistent configuration. The second path from the dependency of *inesse* on the accident of which it is the act leads either to its substance which through the priority of the *esse substantiale* is quickly reduced to *esse subsistens* or inserts that substance into the web of generation that the natural philosopher has worked out. In the latter case, the reasoning would continue to *esse subsistens* as the only transfixing object for the separate substance that possibly eternally moves the first physical cause. An appreciation of these multiple metaphysical treks will be important for understanding the many disjunctions that appear in Aquinas's proofs for God. They will also be important to understand how Aquinas can use the terminology and thinking of the natural philosopher within his own metaphysics, a move that unfortunately can camouflage the metaphysical nature of his thinking.

To conclude this section I want to cite a text that appears to catch Aquinas speaking of the *esse* of an accident in its relation to God:

Attending to the essence itself of the act, others have said that the action of sinning is from God, which is necessary by a twofold argument. First, by a common argument, because since God is a being through his essence, because his essence is his being [*esse*], it is necessary that what in whatever way exists, is derived from him, for nothing other exists which is its being. But all things are called beings through a certain participation. Yet everything that is called such by participation is derived from that which exists through its essence, just as all ignited things are derived from that which is fire through its essence. It is clear, however, that the action of sinning is a certain kind of being [*quoddam ens*], and it posited in a category of being. Hence, it is necessary to say that it is from God.[39]

Only God has *esse* essentially. Every other being, then, has *esse* by participation and from God. Among such beings that participate *esse* is an action. Hence, all actions *qua* actions, even sinful actions, are from God. The context of participation presupposes a metaphysics in which God has been reached as the one and only subsistent *esse*. Hence, it can be concluded *a priori* that every being other than God is a being only by having *esse* other than itself and so is dependent upon God. This metaphysical understanding of an existing action as a composition of itself and its *esse* can also be reached more directly by submitting it to the twofold operation of the intellect—conceptualization and judgment. Just as Tom exists both really and cognitively when I perceive him, so too do the accidents of Tom. The two operations would commence from that data.

Application of Aquinas's Metaphysics to Motion

A final topic that unrolls naturally from the previous is the metaphysician's consideration of motion that Aquinas mentioned in *In de Trin.*, q. 5, a. 4, ad 6. It should now be clear how *motus* participates in the common *ratio entis* and so belongs to the consideration of the metaphysician also and not just to that of the natural philosopher. Reflection upon experience seems to categorize motion as an accident of substances. Just as a substance can acquire and lose a color or an extension or a relation and so have these marked as accidents, so too the substance can acquire and lose a motion. After being still, a man can be running; while ill, he can be undergoing a rising temperature.

---

39. Aquinas, *Quaestiones Disputatae de Malo*, q. 3, a. 2, co.; in *Quaestiones Disputatae*, ed. P. Bazzi and Paulus M. Pession (Rome: Marietti, 1965), 2:498. Also see *In II Sent.*, d. 37, q. 2, a. 2, co. For a discussion of Aquinas's avoidance of determinism and divine culpability see Knasas, *Aquinas and the Cry of Rachel*, 214–44.

Both of these changes behave just like the other accidents of the man. In fact, Aquinas lists motion as an accident. At *In de Trin.*, q. 5, a. 3, co., he says: "But accidents [*accidentiae*] befall substance in a definite order. Quantity comes to it first, then quality, after that passivities [*passiones*] and motion [*motus*]." Then back in the *De Ente*, he remarks: "In cases like these the aptitude is an inseparable accident, whereas the completion that comes from a source external to the essence of the thing, or that does not enter into its constitution, will be separable from it like movement [*moveri*] and other accidents of this kind."[40] As an accident, motion should fall under *ens* and therefore be composed with its own *esse*, secondary as that *esse* is. This view should characterize the metaphysician's consideration of motion.[41] That is what it means for motion to be considered *sub ratione entis*.

It has been asked, if motion is an accident, then why do we not have a separate category of motion among the categories of accidents? Is Aquinas going beyond Aristotle in categorizing motion as an accident?[42] The resolution of the issue of how motion can be regarded as an accident yet not be mentioned as a separate category is expressed by Joseph Owens: "Regarded merely in itself, the motion or change is specified by its term and is placed reductively in the category to which it belongs (substance, quantity, quality, place), or is looked upon as a postpredicament."[43] There is not a separate category of accident for motion because motion is not an accident. Motion is an accident but it does not have a separate category because it is placed reductively into the accidental category of its term. Aquinas says as much in the following:

This is his meaning in saying that motion is not something apart from things themselves; for everything which is being changed is being changed according to the categories of being. And just as the ten categories have nothing in common as their genus, in a similar way there is no genus common to all the kinds of motion. Hence

---

40. Trans. Maurer, 69–70.

41. The metaphysician's consideration of matter *sub ratione entis* is in light of the *esse* that actuates the bodily substance of which matter is a principle. On matter as "pertaining" (*pertinent*) to this *esse*, see *ST* I, q. 44, a. 2, co. and ad 3.

42. Besides those texts already mentioned, we have the following: "Ideo dicit quod [accidentiae] non dicuntur simpliciter entia, sed entis entia, sicut qualitas et motus." *In XII Meta.*, l. 1, n. 2419. See also "Alia sunt inseparabilia, scilicet accidentia quia passions et motus et huiusmodi accidentia non possunt esse sine substantiis." *In XII Meta.*, l. 4, n. 2475.

43. Owens, *Elementary Christian Metaphysics*, 203.

motion is not a category distinct from the others but is a natural concomitant of the other categories.[44]

In conclusion, if, as I have argued, Aquinas wants philosophically resistant proofs for God and in his understanding of philosophy reserves knowledge of God's existence to the metaphysician, then one should study Aquinas's metaphysics and its demonstration of God for purposes of understanding his actual God proofs. Could Aquinas be so schizophrenic as to claim metaphysics for philosophical knowledge of God's existence and not follow that claim through in his God proofs? To the end of integrating his metaphysics into his God proofs, I have taken pains to understand the complexities of the metaphysician's approach to God from *esse*. This understanding provides a much more robust version of the *De Ente* reasoning. The robust version will provide the intelligible topography on which to locate the individual *viae*.

44. Aquinas, *In XI Meta.*, l. 9, n. 2291 (trans. Rowan, 739–40).

[8]

Viae for God

Summa contra Gentiles

The robust version of the *De Ente* reasoning portrays the wide field from which the metaphysician can select starting points to wend a way to God understood as subsistent existence. Every starting point involves the *esse* of some nature, either substantial or accidental. But depending upon the consideration of judgmentally grasped existence, different paths open up. If the priority of *esse* to the nature is focused upon, then the shortest path opens. This path is basically the original *De Ente* reasoning. If the focus is *esse*'s character as the act of some nature, then a much longer path through the metaphysically appropriated reflections of the natural philosopher opens. At each point of the second path, however, the priority of some *esse* is waiting to be focused upon. Hence, the metaphysician need not walk the entire length of the second path to its conclusion of *esse subsistens* as the transfixing final cause of the separate intellectual substance that moves the first physical cause. A consideration of the *inesse* of accidents reveals the same fork of paths. The priority of the *inesse* to the accident and the existence-neutral substance of the accident permits immediate reduction of the *inesse* to subsistent existence. Yet the *inesse*'s status as the act *of the accidental nature* opens reasoning to other natures possibly responsible for the accident and consequently responsible for the *inesse* which is in some measure dependent upon the accident.

Here too the priority of the *esse* will always be present. Hence, the motion of any self-mover, even a generable and corruptible one—for example, a human—can be immediately reduced to subsistent existence.

The resulting interpretative challenge will not consist in knowing whether Aquinas's *viae* can be read according to his metaphysics. A sufficiently nuanced understanding of the complexity of the *De Ente* reasoning will assure the reader that the interpretive challenge can be met. The true challenge will consist in discerning which path and/or which combination of paths is being mapped out in any particular *via*. In respect to that challenge, one can already anticipate signposts that will indicate which path a *via* is following. For example, when Aquinas mentions the eternity of motion, celestial spheres, finite separate intelligences, and final causality, one can suspect the second path. An absence of these or a conclusion to a first efficient cause will indicate the first path or a later switch to it. These possible references will provide some interpretive control.

But there will be no turning back from my earlier conclusion that Aquinas would be schizophrenic to write *viae* intended to be philosophically cogent apart from the textually verifiable thesis that the philosopher proves God's existence in metaphysics. Moreover, doing otherwise would make the *viae* purely arguments of natural philosophy. That approach would commit Aquinas to the heretical position of proving the eternity of the world and of motion, and it would confine the reasoning to the material universe as Aquinas admits at *ST* I, q. 44, a. 2.

In this chapter and the next, I wish to give a reading of Aquinas's explicit God proofs from the perspective of the robust *De Ente* reasoning. I understand those proofs to be the ones found at *SCG* I.13, *ST* I, q. 2, a. 3, and *Comp. Theol.* I.3. In a later chapter and from the same metaphysical perspective, I will consider other apparent proofs for God that occur in the process of arguing from something other than God's existence, for example, for God's unicity or eternity.[1]

---

1. For a comprehensive listing of Aquinas's God proofs in both of the mentioned roles, see Jules A. Baisnée, "St. Thomas Aquinas's Proofs of the Existence of God Presented in Their Chronological Order," in *Philosophical Studies in Honor of the Very Reverend Ignatius Smith, O.P.*, ed. John K. Ryan (Westminster, Md.: Newman Press, 1952), 29–64.

The *prima via* of *SCG* I.13

I would remind the reader that indications of a metaphysical approach to God's existence are found within the preceding chapters of the *Summa contra Gentiles*. In I.3 Aquinas includes the existence of God in the naturally knowable truth about God, and in I.4 Aquinas reserves that naturally knowable truth about God to the last part of philosophy to be learned—metaphysics. That assignment of our natural knowledge of God's existence to metaphysics is one of my warrants for launching into a metaphysical reading of the *viae*. Any further reasons intrinsic to Aquinas's *viae* will be noted as I comment on the *viae*. The *prima via* is as follows:

> Everything that is moved is moved by another. That some things are in motion—for example, the sun—is evident from sense. Therefore, it is moved by something else that moves it. This mover is itself either moved or not moved. If it is not, we have reached our conclusion—namely, that we must posit some unmoved mover. This we call God. If it is moved, it is moved by another mover. We must, consequently, either proceed to infinity, or we must arrive at some unmoved mover. Now, it is not possible to proceed to infinity. Hence, we must posit some prime unmoved mover.[2]

The *via* could be outlined as follows:

1. Some things are in motion—for example, the sun.
2. What is moved is moved by another.
3. This mover is either (a) unmoved or (b) moved.
4. If (a), then we have our conclusion.
5. If (b), then by (2), the mover is moved by another.
6. The series of movers either (c) goes to infinity or (d) does not.
7. But (c) is impossible.
8. Hence, an unmoved mover exists.

SCG I.13.4–16 is devoted to (2) and (7). Aquinas provides three proofs for (2):

9. The motion of the divisible depends upon the motion of its parts (pars. 5–6).

---

2. Trans. Pegis, 1:86. My cited paragraph numbers from I.13 are drawn from this Pegis translation.

10. An inductive proof (par. 8).
11. An act/potency proof (par. 9).

Aquinas then provides three proofs for (7):

12. From the impossibility of an infinite motion in a finite time (pars. 12–13).
13. From the denial of a first mover (par. 14).
14. From the nature of an instrumental cause (par. 15).

The starting point with some existing motion reaffirms Aquinas's sense realism. The type of error in Aquinas's claim that the sun is moving is one with which we are familiar. While daydreaming at a train window before departing, I can think that the truck on the platform is moving. In truth my train has begun slowly to leave the station. Though this phenomenon might cast doubt on knowing the precise subject of motion, it leaves unassailable the knowledge that something is moving. That is sufficient sense realism to begin the argument.[3]

Aquinas's previously described use of the *duplex operatio intellectus* on the existing motion could be responsible for a metaphysical consideration of the motion, a consideration *sub ratione entis*. Another approach is also a possibility. Once we are aware of the distinction between the thing and its *esse*, we can go on to fantasize about a thing not intellectually distinct from its *esse*. Aquinas himself did this mental experimenting in the fourth chapter of *De Ente*. Recall how Aquinas argued that such a thing would have to be a one and only. There are other implications of this mental experiment:

---

3. In his "Aristotelian Mover-Causality and the Principle of Inertia," *International Philosophical Quarterly* 38, no. 2 (1998): 144, Thomas J. McLaughlin argues that "in a purely inertial motion there is motion *per accidens* without a concurrent motion *per se*." That scenario is beyond my abilities to envisage. As a reason for his claim, McLaughlin provides (140) the example of two space ships both moving at a constant speed in a straight line with respect to each other. He concludes that "abstracted from all such forces, however, the motion of A and B would be merely an extrinsic change in spatial relations, that is, a relative change of distance and direction between the bodies. In such a case there would [be] no way to determine whether A were moving and B at rest, B were moving and A at rest, or both A and B were moving. One might equally well regard A as moving and B as resting, A as resting and B as moving, or both A and B as moving." As the reader can see from McLaughlin's description, real motion is admitted throughout the example; the problem is not to affirm real motion but to identify the precise subject of the real motion. The metaphysician, in my opinion, can leave that problem of the subject of motion unresolved and continue just with the assertion that something is in motion.

a thing not distinct from its *esse* would not be able to be separated from its *esse* and so could not not exist. Also, because the thing is at least common to itself both really and cognitionally existing, then *esse* merged with the thing is *esse* communized. But common *esse* is the intelligible heart of the *ratio entis* and so has the infinite perfection of that transcendental. In sum, a thing not distinct from its *esse* is infinite in perfection. No conceivable perfection or degree thereof would be lacking to it.

With these implications in mind, we can more quickly grasp *esse*. There would be no need to set the thing in an existence multiplicity and run the multiplicity through the two intellectual operations. If the things are multiple, if they are changeable, if they are finite, then it must be the case the *esse* is there as distinct from these things. Aristotle defined motion as the act of the potential insofar as it is potential. Like a ruddy or pale complexion, motion is an act of a substance. But unlike these two, motion is not an act fully actualized. It has some of its act outside of itself. As such it collides with the infinite situation of *esse* merged with a nature. Existing motion must be a situation of a nature distinct from its *esse*.

The disjunction mentioned at (3) in the numbered list above indicates the previously mentioned two paths from *esse*. On the one hand, the *via* can reach a prime mover identifiable with God immediately. This conclusion makes sense if we are considering the *esse* of the motion as fundamental to it. Because of the priority of motion's *esse*, the *esse* does not depend upon the motion, but rather the motion depends upon it.[4] Does the *esse* of the motion depend upon the thing that is the subject of the motion? The existential neutrality of the thing prohibits that. Upon what does the *actus* of *esse* depend? Clearly a thing that is *esse*. Such a thing has *esse* as its proper effect. It is also uncaused and identifiable with the God of Christian belief who revealed his name to Moses as "I am who am."[5]

---

4. In his *The Five Ways*, 11n1, Kenny objects to the metaphysical analysis of motion. Kenny takes the "existential act (*esse*)" of a motion to mean the actual occurrence of a motion. That equation leads to "the nonsensical view that when you have explained a particular motion at a particular time you have to explain also the occurrence of that motion." Kenny is confusing the fact, or occurrence, of motion with the *esse*, or act, of the motion. Just as you would never confuse the running that makes a man a runner with the fact of the runner, so too you should not confuse the *esse* that makes the motion a fact with the fact of the motion. The fact is a given, the *esse* is a product of metaphysical analysis. The act is in the fact and the metaphysician pulls it out of the fact.

5. Kenny also argues (ibid., 21–22) that we can never be sure of the identity of a cause. His basis

On the other hand, the *esse* of the motion as the act *of the motion* is in some sense dependent upon it. If this measure of dependency is stressed, then it is not immediately clear that one must go further. Is it obvious that the motion needs to be caused by another? It certainly is not obvious to the metaphysician who is considering the motion only *sub ratione entis*. As Aquinas remarks, "Just as metaphysics, which considers all things insofar as they are beings [*omnia inquantum sunt entia*], not descending to a proper cognition of morals or of natural things. For the notion of being [*ratio entis*], although it is diversified in diverse things, is not sufficient for a special knowledge of things."[6]

The natural philosopher, however, has thought long and hard about motion and has many things to say about motion. Hence, brought to confront motion in virtue of its *esse*'s dependence upon it, the metaphysician can enlist the reflections of the natural philosopher. These reflections consist of Aquinas's three listed proofs that what is moved is moved by another and the three proofs that an infinite regress of simultaneous moved movers is not possible. As a reader can see, there is no mention of the eternity of motion, a first physical cause, or an intellectual substance as its mover. Also, there is no mention of final causality. For all intents and purposes, the causality of the unmoved mover appears to be an efficient cause. At least that seems to be the character of the movers in the three proofs against an infinite regress at steps (12)–(14). In other words, the second path from *esse* in the *prima via* is a much truncated version of the path sketch in my chapter 7. To arrive at a first mover in any series, a self-mover like the man who moves the stick that moves the rock in the *prima via* of the *Summa Theologiae* would suffice. That mover would then be reduced to a mover that is *esse subsistens* either through its substantial *esse* as explained in *De Ente* reasoning or through the inability of its existential neutrality to account for the *esse* of its motion.

The absence of the eternity of motion is, in my opinion, especially signif-

---

is the often observed disjunction between the nature of the effect and the nature of the cause; e.g., heat as the effect of the rubbing of the hands. But Kenny's observation causes problems only where something can be the incidental effect of a proper line of causality. So, in the proper line of causality, the effect is the hands moving to a place and the cause is the stationary shoulders. The heat is thrown off as an incidental effect of this line of causality. Aquinas can be sure that the *esse* of a thing is not an incidental effect. *Esse* is absolutely basic and fundamental. *Esse* cannot presuppose something else and so cannot be construed as an incidental effect of a more basic line of causality.

6. *In I Sent.*, prol., q. 1, a. 2, co.

icant. As I explained in chapter 7, pure natural philosophy reasoning cannot avoid the conclusion of the eternity of motion. The eternity of motion is the basis to ascend further and to reach a first physical cause whose nature is different from changeable things.

I would like to go through each of the six arguments for steps (2) and (7). Aquinas gives three arguments culled from *Physics* VII–VIII for motion's being caused by another. A presupposition in these arguments is the natural philosopher's understanding of motion as "accidental." This is involved in the definition of motion as "the act of the potential insofar as it is potential." Motion is an imperfect act but as an act motion implies some subject. In reference to that subject, motion is accidental. So we already know that motion is dependent.[7] It is dependent at least on the subject of which it is an imperfect act. The remaining issue is whether motion's dependency involves something else. It is in that respect that the natural philosopher offers many reflections.

The first reflection is Aquinas's first argument that a body cannot be the primary cause of its motion because the motion of the body is dependent upon the motion of the body's parts. Aquinas's strategy is taken from Aristotle's *Physics* VII.1. The strategy is to prove that what is moved is moved by another by showing the falsity of its contrary. The contrary is that what is moved is moved by itself primarily.

It is important to clearly understand the contrary. The contrary position is something that has within itself the principle of its own motion. Otherwise it is obviously moved by another. Also, this interior principle is not a part of it but the thing itself. Again, otherwise the thing is moved by another, namely, its part. To distinguish the primarily moved, Aquinas gives the contrary example of an animal being moved by the motion of its foot. Finally, Aquinas says that the thing moving itself primarily is divisible, for it must be partly at the term of the motion and partly not.

Aquinas next proceeds to show the falsity of the contrary. If a part of the primarily moved is at rest, then the whole that is held to be in motion primarily must be at rest. Why? The reason is that otherwise the whole would be moved not primarily but by reason of the other part. But what is at rest

---

7. The point is important for answering Kenny's objection (*Five Ways*, 18–19) that the *omne quod movetur ab alio movetur* proposition assumes that what is moved is moved. Kenny asks, "Why cannot it just be in motion, without being moved by anything, whether by itself or by anything else?" Kenny is missing the underlying characterization of the motion as an accident.

because of the rest of another is moved by another. Hence, what moves itself is not moved primarily but by a part. Hence, what moves itself is moved by another.[8] I add that the argument only works on bodies because only bodies have the mentioned divisibility. Also, the argument indicates that the mover must be a nondivisible. This would be the soul of a self-mover.

Aquinas goes on to raise an objection to the proof's opening assertion. The objection is that the opening assertion is asking us to entertain a part being at rest in a whole that is primarily moved. This is like thinking man to be an elephant. In other words, the objection is that the start of the proof is at odds with what the proof is about.

Borrowing from Averroes, Aquinas gives an interesting reply. We can assume two things. We can assume either that a part of the primarily moved is at rest or that if such a part is at rest, then the whole is at rest. Aquinas says that the first alternative cannot be true and concedes to the objection that it should not be assumed. But the second alternative is true and can be assumed. Aristotle's argument commences with the second alternative and so can proceed.

Aquinas next (*SCG* I.13.8) uses an induction to confirm that what is moved is moved by another. In my opinion, in all the cases investigated, Aquinas assumes that motion is caused. Any reasoning is for the otherness of the mover from moved. The basis for the assumption is, as just mentioned above, that motion is an accident. As an act, although imperfect, motion exists as in and of another and so is a dependent item.

The first case is something in violent motion. Because violent motion is against the nature of the thing, or *contra naturam*, then obviously the thing cannot explain the motion. Something else must do it.

The second case is something in motion by accident. To understand why this motion is also accounted for by something else, it suffices to consider

---

8. Kenny (ibid., 19) thinks that Aquinas's argument fails to prove both that the motion of the body is causally dependent upon the motion of its parts and that the motion of the part is a causally sufficient condition for the motion of the body. All that the argument shows is that the motion of the body is logically dependent on the motion of its parts and that the motion of the parts is a causally necessary condition. Aquinas could grant Kenny's comments, for what the argument proves is that no body is in motion primarily and *per se*. The body at least depends upon the motion of its parts. Aquinas is not trying to causally explain motion in any sufficient fashion by the motion of the bodily parts. The argument, however, does indicate where a full explanation of the body's motion lies: something indivisible and simple, namely, the body's substantial form.

the two ways in which something is in motion *per accidens*. First, something is a part attached to a whole that is in motion. An example is the pen in my pocket as I walk about the room. Second, something is a whole, one of whose parts is in motion. For example, I move by the motion of my legs, or I wave by the motion of my hand. In both cases, the motion of something is explained by something else—the pen's motion by me, my motion by that of my legs.[9]

The third case is self-movers. Aquinas says that they are evidently moved by a part, their souls, and so in that way moved by another. Aquinas's passing remark repeats the conclusion of a lengthy analysis that he will summarize in *SCG* I.13.22. I will consider it. The key to the analysis is Aquinas's third argument for *omne quod movetur ab alio movetur* at step (11), above.

The fourth and final case is the most difficult. It involves things in natural motion but which are not self-movers. Examples include the motion of the elements. Fire spontaneously rises, earth likewise descends. In *In VIII Phys.*, l. 7, nn. 1026–28, Aquinas summarizes the four reasons for knowing that these things are not self-movers, which I will not dwell upon here. I wish to pass on to Aquinas's point that we know that these things are moved by another because we know that they have a cause of their generation. Aquinas leaves the claim unelaborated, but I think that my previous commentary on *De Principiis Naturae* is a fair construal of the reason. The form of the element needs an explanation because in respect to the matter, the form is like an accident in respect to its subject. In order to exist both the form and the accident require a material cause to be in and of. The matter of the element, however, cannot fully explain the presence of the form in it. The matter fails to fully explain because by its nature the matter is a potency to form. Hence,

---

9. Kenny (ibid., 14) argues that the examples of things in motion *per accidens* cause Aquinas's entire project to self-destruct. Kenny gives two reasons. First, my being in motion *per accidens* because of the motion of my fingers at the computer could never be construed as me being in motion by my fingers. Hence, my *per accidens* motion here is a counterexample to the principle that what is moved is moved by another. Second, if we waive the first problem, then it will be true that I move my fingers and my fingers move me and this motion situation is self-contained. In other words, we find no asymmetry of moved to mover by which to begin a regress to an unmoved mover. In my opinion, Aquinas can reply to these criticisms. To the first, Kenny's reluctance to admit that I am moved by the motion of my fingers seems to stem from the thought that they do not move me like I move them. This is correct; I moved them directly, they move me indirectly. But to be in motion indirectly is something real. I go from not typing to typing. Given this real effect, why not regard the fingers as a real cause and so that by which a motion occurs? To the second criticism, the asymmetry is not lost. I move the fingers *per se*, they move me *per accidens*. I still am the only principal cause.

any hylomorphic composite contains the intelligible seeds necessary to conclude to a cause of the composite, in a word, a generator.[10]

The third way (*SCG* I.13.9) in which Aquinas defends the truth of the proposition, "What is moved is moved by another," is by appeal to the ideas of potency and act. He uses these to characterize both mover and moved. What is moved is in potency, or lacks, that toward which it is moving. For example, the water being heated to the boiling point is in potency to that temperature. What moves is already in act in respect to that toward which the motion is going. For example, the flame is already at the temperature. Hence, to say that something in motion precisely insofar as it is in motion moves itself is to produce a contradiction, for it is to say that something is both in act and potency at the same time and in the same respect. So what is moved, or in motion, precisely insofar as it is so is moved by another.

Continuing along the second causal path from existing motion as it participates in the *ratio entis*, Aquinas next offers three proofs (*SCG* I.13.12–14) from natural philosophy that the other, the *aliud*, required by the moved cannot be a regress, even infinite, of moved movers. The regress must top off with an unmoved mover and in this conclusion Aquinas sees the visage of the God of his religious belief. Before we consider the proofs *contra* infinite regress, one caveat. The infinite regress envisaged is of simultaneous moved movers.

---

10. Kenny (ibid., 15–18) presents an interesting series of reflections on Aquinas's third and fourth cases. Kenny mentions that in a living thing the soul is the moving part (15). Kenny admits that this point would enable Aquinas to get asymmetry back in the typing example (14); for my soul moves my fingers but they do not move my soul. But now the presently existing mover is only the soul, not God. Likewise, Kenny admits (16) that Aristotle's theory on the motion of projectiles (they are moved by the air adjacent to them) comes up with a present mover for things in unnatural motion. Yet again, the present mover, the air, is not God. Kenny also deals with natural motions of nonliving things (17). Kenny recounts Aquinas's explanation that their motion is accounted for by their generator. That explanation is not to a present mover and so admits an exception to the *omne quod movetur* principle. In sum, either the first way comes to a present mover that is well short of God or it reduces that mover to its generator by changing the rules of the game and also opens up a regress of generators that Aquinas admits could be infinite. This fix in which Kenny places Aquinas is, in my opinion, an extremely instructive one. I will speak more about it later. Now I would note that in the vein of simply natural philosophy, the only way that Aquinas can escape is to introduce the reasoning of par. 25 in which an infinite regress of generators leads upwards to an encompassing self-mover. But par. 25 is not a part of the first motion proof. So it appears that the natural philosopher cannot make sense of the first way if he stays just with the order of the text. On the other hand, the metaphysical interpretation that I am following would reduce any presently existing mover less than God to God through its *esse*, as I will explain at the end of my commentary on the first way.

For example, the rock as moved by the stick, the stick as moved by the hand, the hand as moved by the man. That a simultaneous regress is what is being considered is plain from the first proof to which we now turn.

In the steps of the first proof Aquinas understands (A) that the regress consists of an infinite number of contiguous bodies: the stone pushed by the stick, the stick pushed by the arm, the arm pushed by the man, the man pushed by the another man, etc. (B) Understood as contiguous, all the bodies can be seen as comprising one infinite mobile body. Next, (C) Aquinas surmises that because the bodies are contiguous, it is also true that when any part of the infinite mobile body moves, then the whole does also. Hence, (D) if the part moves in a finite time, then the whole does also. But (E) that an infinite body moves in a finite time is the impossibility that proves the falsity of the assumption of an infinite regress. A finite time will always elapse with more of the infinite bodily mobile to move.

This argument is tricky because it appears that (D) contradicts (E). Is not (D) showing us how to think an infinite body moving in a finite time? So, (E)'s insistence that such is impossible looks like special pleading. I think that this impression can be removed by realizing that we are unwittingly conceiving (D) as a very large body but not an infinite one. If the body is very large but only large, then there is a finite time in which it can be entirely moved. For each portion of the finite time, one can coordinate some portion of the body, and so over the time one moves the entire body. But if the body is infinitely large, then one should readily see that in a finite time only some part of it will be moved.

Aquinas's second and third arguments against an infinite regress of moved movers are simpler but have their own problem. The problem is that they sound identical. So, why two arguments and not just one? At *In VIII Phys.*, nn. 1040–41, Aquinas explains the difference. The principle of distinction is the starting points. The second proof begins from the simply moved and ascends to movers. The third proof begins with a mover, in this case an instrumental cause, and descends. Otherwise the proofs are identical, just as the road from Athens to Thebes is the same as the road from Thebes to Athens. So, Aquinas argues in the second proof (*SCG* I.13.14) that in a series of movers, if the first mover is removed, the other movers are removed. But an infinite series removes the first mover. So an infinite series destroys all movers and all motion.[11] The third proof (*SCG* I.13.15) comes to the same conclusion but starts from instrumental movers. Instrumental movers are moved movers and so move by a principle. But a principle is what an infinite series of instrumental movers eliminates. Hence, motion is destroyed.

From these proofs the metaphysician's reasoning from *esse* that is the act *of some motion* terminates in some unmoved mover. According to the second causal path along which the metaphysician is proceeding, the character of this unmoved mover will not be *esse tantum*. The reflections employed here are from natural philosophy, and natural philosophy knows nothing of *esse*. From the perspective of natural philosophy, the unmoved mover may well be some generated self-mover, for example, the man whose arm moves the stick that moves the rock. At that point the natural philosopher can proceed only laterally to the generator of the man which in turn may be itself generated. Here the natural philosopher is inexorably brought to confront the possibility that at the top of his regress is a temporal series of generated generators infinitely back into the past. Aquinas confronts this possibility but in his second way from motion. In the first way the regress of the second path straight away reaches God as the unmoved mover. This makes sense if the first way is read according to Aquinas's metaphysics. For the metaphysician, the endpoint of the proofs against an infinite regress can admittedly reach some mover less than God. If so, it will be some unmoved nature that has *esse* as an *actus* belonging to it. At that stage the metaphysician can advert to the priority of *esse* to that nature in order to conclude to *esse tantum*. That is what the concluding words of the first way would mean: "Now, it is not possible to proceed to infinity. Hence, we must posit some prime unmoved mover." In that fashion the second path of the first *via* joins with the conclusion of the first path.

Again, in the metaphysical interpretation of the *prima via*, no logical necessity exists at any point to detour into a regress of generated self-movers that extends infinitely back into the past. Rather, by virtue of its *esse*, any reached point is open to immediate reduction to God. For example, from the man

---

11. Kenny argues (ibid., 26–27) that the second argument *contra* an infinite regress begs the question of a first mover. Aquinas begins by saying that in an ordered series when the first mover is removed, no other mover will move. Aquinas's talk of a "first" seems to assume what needs to be proved. But in fact Aquinas is carrying over what he knows from proving that what is moved is moved by another. The mover must be of a different nature than the moved; it must be in act. His second argument proceeds by showing than an infinite regress removes that different thing.

moving his arm that moves the stick that moves the rock, the metaphysician goes to the cause of the *esse* of the man. In this case, a cause of the *esse* of the substance that is a mover is not only a creator but a mover also. Both causal paths are regresses of presently existing things that top off with subsistent *esse*.

The *secunda via ex motu* of *SCG* I.13

The starting point of the second way is to determine whether the proposition "every mover is moved" is true. This assertion is about the same type of infinite regress mentioned in the first way. This starting point situates the second way amidst the regress of moved movers delineated in the first way's second path. In other words, the second way does not begin with a consideration of the priority of motion's *esse*. Rather, it begins from a point well along in the consideration of the causes of motion of which *esse* is the act and so upon which *esse* is in some measure dependent. Other signposts indicate that the second way follows the second path in all of its complexity. The *via* refers to the eternity of motion, an ungenerable self-mover as cause of the endlessness of generation, and a reference to the final causality of a separate mover for the causality of the ungenerable self-mover. Understandably, Aquinas's second *via* is quite lengthy, spanning pars. 17–28 of *SCG* I.13. I divide the argument into two main sections. The first section runs to the disjunction mentioned in par. 21. A summary that highlights the sense of the texts according to the robust *De Ente* reasoning is as follows.

"Every mover is moved," if true, is true either by accident or by itself. But the proposition cannot be true either way; therefore, it is false. First, the proposition cannot be true by accident (par. 17). If the proposition were so, it would be possible that nothing is moved, for what is accidentally the case could be otherwise. Motion, however, is necessarily eternal. Hence, the proposition cannot be true accidently.

Aquinas references Aristotle for the impossibility that there can be no motion. This reference clearly has in mind Aristotle's arguments in *Physics* VIII.1 for the eternity of motion. At the end of the second way of the *Summa contra Gentiles*, Aquinas comments on how and why motion's eternity is present in the second way. Because the precise role played by the eternity of motion in the second way will be, as we will see, another key to its metaphysical interpretation, we will soon study Aristotle's arguments for motion's eternity.

Next, Aquinas argues that the proposition "Every mover is moved" cannot be true by itself (I.13.19). That view would have the mover moving and being moved in the same respect and at the same time. If every mover is moved, then no mover can be explained by the series in which it is. A moved mover will have to explain itself. In other words, it will both have and not have something at the same time. In order to move, the mover has it; in order to be moved, the mover lacks it. For example, one would have a teacher teaching geometry while the teacher is still learning it, a pan of water heating another pan of water at the boiling point while it is still being heated to the boiling point, etc.

Two possible attempts to explain how the proposition is true by itself fail. First, say that the mover moves by one type of motion but is moved by another type. Aquinas points out that this first scenario would still encounter an unmoved mover because the types of motion are finite in number.[12]

---

12. In his *The Metaphysics of Theism: Aquinas's Natural Theology in Summa contra gentiles I* (Oxford: Clarendon Press, 1997), Norman Kretzmann disputes Aquinas's claim that the species of motion are finite. First (71), considering teaching as a species of motion, Kretzmann asks us to think of how many truths can be taught. Second (71), Kretzmann asks what is absurd about being past educated about something and then educating someone of it now. Kretzmann believes that Aquinas claims that scenario to be absurd when Aquinas says that something is "moved in accordance with the same species, albeit not directly, but indirectly." Finally (72), Kretzmann wonders if prior to the terminating motion only other species of motion are recycled. He writes: "And suppose that Z is moving whatever it moves locally and that it is the lonely local mover in the series, and that Z is moved by Y, which is moving Z by alteration and is moved by X, which is moving Y by increase and is moved by W, which is moving X by alteration and moved by V, which is moving W by increase . . . , and so on *ad infinitum*." Kretzmann concludes of this portion of the second way: "it can't be saved." I would like to reply to these criticisms. To the first, Aquinas does have a reason for claiming that the species of motion are finite. The species of motion are reduced to the species of the natures of bodies: "motus differunt genere et specie secundum differentias rerum in quibus sunt motus: genera autem rerum et species non sunt infinitae, ut alibi probavit; et sic neque genera aut species motus." *In VIII Phys.*, l. 9, n. 1046. The species of bodily natures are finite because if they were infinite than the quantity of the universe would be infinite which is impossible: "sed multitudo quae sequitur divisionem formalem rerum, non multiplicatur in infinitum; sunt enim determinatae species rerum, sicut et determinata quantitas universi." *In III Phys.*, l. 12, n. 394. For arguments against an actual infinite magnitude, see *ST* I, q. 7, a. 3, and *In de Caelo* I, ll. 13–15. To Kretzmann's second criticism, he takes Aquinas's mention of something "moved in accordance with the same species, albeit not directly, but indirectly" to refer to a regress of causes *in fieri*. But there can be indirectness in the relation of an effect to its *causa in esse*. To his third criticism, Aquinas would simply run his argument in the recycling portion of the regress. So, the problem would be in Y being moved by W. *The Metaphysics of Theism* is notable for its studied avoidance of Thomistic scholarship from Toronto.

Second, another possibility is to say that though the types of motion are finite, they cycle to infinity. For example, what alters is moved to do so by a local mover and what moves locally is moved to do so by an increaser, etc. But ultimately, this scenario returns us to the first difficulty if the proposition were true by itself. That first difficulty was that the mover is moving and being moved in the same respect and at the same time. As the series is infinite, the original mover must be conceived as moving itself in light of one of the prior types of motion. But one of those prior types is the very motion by which it is said to move. So the original difficulty remains. The only difference is that we now arrive at it mediately instead of immediately.

Shown to be true in no way, "Every mover is moved" must be false. Hence, not every mover is moved by something else. At this point Aquinas says (I.13.21) that either this mover is the unmoved mover that he is seeking or it is a self-mover. *Sub ratione entis* this disjunction makes sense. For the metaphysician, the last motion to which the latter portion of the second way's first part regresses (I.13.19) has an *esse*. If the priority of that motion's *esse* is focused upon, we immediately go to *esse tantum*. This is the absolutely unmoved mover. On the other hand, if the dependency of motion's *esse* on the motion is adverted to, then the cause of the motion could be a self-mover.

From par. 22 until the end of the second way Aquinas gives an interesting series of arguments that reveal how complicated the second path out of the *ratio entis* can be. First, a self-mover moves in virtue of an immobile part, its soul (I.13.22).[13] Second, in light of the everlastingness of motion, there must be some endlessly self-moving being (I.13.24–25). The argumentation at this point is particularly interesting. It shows that the self-mover that has been reached could quite well be a generated one. For example, it could be the man who moves the stick that moves the rock. But if motion is eternal, then the generation of self-movers can be extended endlessly into the past. At this point one would no longer be proceeding in a vertical series but in a

---

13. Kretzmann, *Metaphysics of Theism*, 74, argues that a self-mover is "incoherent theoretically." He says, "If 'Everything that is moved is moved by something *else*,' then, strictly speaking '*nothing* moves itself.'" Kretzmann misses the possible different considerations of the subject. If one can consider the subject in some respect other than subject of the motion, then from that respect the subject could cause motion in itself considered precisely as subject of the motion. Because the Aristotelian elements cannot be considered in that twofold way, then the movers of their motions are their generators. That would enable the self-mover to satisfy the *omne quod moveatur ab alio moveatur* proposition.

lateral one. So, the above man is generated by his parents, they by their parents, and so on. Aquinas cannot accept this eventuality to which the natural philosopher's reflections bring him. Somehow he must get back on track to an unmoved mover. Aquinas's intent will not be to terminate the endless regress of generations. That idea would repeat the absurdity of an absolute beginning for motion. Rather, his intent is to reach an overarching continuous motion in which the series can take place. This overarching continuous motion in turn will require as a subject an eternal self-mover.

In par. 25 Aquinas argues for such a cause by a process of elimination. First, no one thing in the series could be the cause of all, as no one thing always exists. In other words, any one thing might be called the cause of what comes after but certainly not called the cause of what came before. Second, the cause of the endless series of generations could not be all the things together. On the one hand, they are infinite. In other words, no one thing in the series gets a complete explanation from something else in the series. For example, before B explains A, B must be explained by C, etc. On the other hand, the things in the series are not simultaneous. In other words, we cannot argue, as in a simultaneous regress, to a first that explains the others in the regress. Hence, the thinking of the natural philosopher is prompted to move vertically to a nongenerable body in whose continuous motion the eternal series of generations takes place. This nongenerable body appears to be the celestial body referred to by the "ecliptic" and called the "more universal cause" at *ST* I, q. 44, a. 2, co.

The soul of this cosmic self-mover would be unmoved both in itself and *per accidens*. Having reached celestial soul as the unmoved mover, the second way, interestingly, does not proceed by finding an efficient cause for the substantial *esse* of the incorruptible self-mover. Rather, shifting from the *Physics* to the *Metaphysics*, the argument finds a final cause of sufficient excellence to transfix the cognition of the self-mover and guarantee the eternity of motion. The implicit use of Aquinas's metaphysics of *esse* becomes apparent when one realizes that Aquinas is speaking of something like the beatific vision. As subsistent *esse*, God is universally perfect and has the entire perfection of being, and so no motive for preferring something other than God is present.[14] In a concluding caveat, Aquinas mentions that though Aristotle's rea-

---

14. *SCG* III.62 and *ST* I-II, q. 5, a. 4.

soning is speaking about besouled celestial spheres, a Christian could still allow the reasoning by substituting for a sphere soul, a separate intellectual substance.[15]

The *suppositio* of Motion's Eternity

In *SCG* I.13.29–32 Aquinas mentions two possible criticisms of the second way. The first is the argument's positing of besouled celestial spheres. I have already mentioned this issue and Aquinas's resolution of it. The second criticism is the second way's use of the eternity of motion in pars. 17 and 25. In the Middle Ages the eternity of motion was widely regarded as contradicting the account of creation in the Bible. But Aquinas explains that in the second way the eternity of motion is just a supposition made for purposes of the most effective God proof. Aquinas's thinking is that an argument for a cause of an eternal thing is surely a stronger argument than an argument for a cause of a thing that begins to exist.

The question that I want to pursue in this section is this: if the motion proofs are just arguments of the natural philosopher, can the eternity of motion be just a *suppositio*? I know that I have argued from texts external to I.13 that Aquinas's proofs of God's existence are metaphysical. I am not now going back on that. The current issue is whether the suppositional presence of the eternity of motion in the second way is an indication internal to I.13 for the metaphysical interpretation. To begin, I want to review the arguments for the eternity of motion.

In his commentary on *Physics* VIII, Aquinas explains Aristotle's two proofs for motion's eternity.[16] The first proof assumes from the earlier books that motion as an act requires a subject, or a mobile (n. 972). The first proof goes on to argue (n. 976) that if motion has a beginning, or is to be made possible, then the mobile is either generated or not. If generated, then since the generation of one thing is the corruption of another, there is a mobile before the first mobile in union with its mover. So we have motion already going on before the first motion. In other words, to say motion began with

---

15. For the caveat, see pars. 31–32. For Aquinas's options for a mover of the celestial spheres, see *SCG* III.23.

16. See *In VIII Phys.*, l. 2 (paragraphing is from trans. Blackwell).

the generation of the mobile is to admit that the mover was in union with the corruptible and so motion existed before it supposedly began. If the first mobile is not generated, then a mobile with the mover should mean either that we already have motion or there is the previous motion of uniting mover and mobile. In the second case, we would be engendering an infinite regress of unitings of movers and mobiles.

Aquinas says (n. 985) that this thinking can be modified to conclude that motion has no end. If motion is to end absolutely, we need to separate the mover and mobile or to corrupt the mobile. Aquinas leaves the first alterative unelaborated and deals with the second alternative. Because the corruption of one thing is the generation of another, a second mobile is produced from the corruption of the first. Now the second mobile must be corrupted which in turn generates a third and the process goes on continuously into the future. In other words, we cannot end motion by separating the mobile from the mover by corrupting the mobile. Because the corruption of the mobile is the generation of another mobile, the mover will always be in contact with a mobile to cause motion. Something to be moved will always be there.

The second argument for motion's eternity is from time (n. 984). Earlier (n. 979) Aquinas says that the argument has two presuppositions. First, that there is no before and after without time; second, that there is no time without motion. Aquinas concludes (n. 980) that if time is eternal, then motion is. The argument for the eternity of time is as follows. Time is not actual without the now. Let us assume that some now is the beginning of time. Because "a beginning of time" implies a *before* in which there is no time and because there is no before without time, then any absolute beginning of time is impossible. Likewise, let us assume an end of time. Because "an end of time" implies an *after* in which there is no time and because there is no after without time, then any absolute ending of time is impossible.

Of course, Aquinas cannot regard these two arguments as demonstrative. So it is extremely enlightening to see the metaphysical basis for his critique of them. In the course of dealing with Averroes's use of the first proof to deny the Christian belief in creation, Aquinas criticizes the need for a mobile that is the crux of the first proof of motion's eternity. Not every coming-to-be is a motion that requires a mobile. How does Aquinas know that? He appeals to his previously developed metaphysics in which the first principle is a cause of the whole of being:

Moreover, this does not agree with Aristotle's intention. For he proves in *Metaphysics*, II, that that which is most true and most being is the cause of being for all existing things [*causa essendi omnibus existentibus*]. Hence it follows that the very being [*ipsum esse*] in potency which primary matter has is derived from the first principle of being [*primo principio essendi*], which is the most being [*maxime ens*]. Therefore, it is not necessary to presuppose something for its action which has not been produced by it.[17]

In other words, absent this metaphysics, the first argument for motion's eternity is a strict demonstration. Hence, that the second way of *SCG* uses motion's eternity as a "supposition" suggests that the second way is not simply a natural philosophy proof. Again, only the metaphysician is in a position to see that motion could be caused either from eternity or in time. Hence, only the metaphysician would be in a position to "suppose" motion's eternity.

Concerning the second argument from time, Aquinas explains (n. 990) that the before and after mentioned for a beginning and end of motion are only imaginary and not real. Again, the force of this remark that the "time" is not in reality but only in our imagination presupposes a metaphysics in which the first cause is a cause of universal being. Again, without metaphysics, it appears that the philosopher would have to concede the demonstrative status of the arguments for the eternity of motion. The philosopher would be in no position to "suppose" the eternity of motion.

So, is the supposition of motion's eternity in the second way an internal indication that the second way is not an argument of natural philosophy? Perhaps, but perhaps not. There is another possibility to consider. In this possibility, the natural philosopher has already reached an unmoved mover without the premise of the eternity of motion. Moreover, such a conclusion has allowed the science of metaphysics to blossom and so the unmoved mover has assumed the guise of a creator. That metaphysical knowledge tells the philosopher that the proofs for motion's eternity are not demonstrative. Generation is not the only way something can be brought into being. So, it could be that kind of natural philosopher who assumes motion's eternity for making another but more effective proof of God.

17. Aquinas, *In VIII Phys.*, l. 2, n. 974 (trans. Blackwell, 507). In *SCG* II.37, *Et hanc quidem* (trans. Pegis, 2:110), Aquinas assigns the philosopher's knowledge of creation to metaphysics: "And on this account it is the business not of the philosopher of nature [*Naturalem Philosophum*] to consider that origination, but of the metaphysician [*Philosophum Primum*], who considers universal being [*ens commune*] and things existing apart from motion."

Again, my chapter 6 argumentation from texts extrinsic to *SCG* I.13 eliminates this possibility for Aquinas. I am interested, however, in seeing if the possibility can be eliminated with the resources found within I.13. I believe that in his *Aquinas and the Five Ways*, Anthony Kenny makes an observation that leads to that elimination.

Kenny is critiquing the premise of the first way that what is moved is moved by another. Kenny begins his critique with the accidentally moved. He remarks that my being in motion *per accidens* because of the motion of my fingers at the typewriter could never be construed as me being in motion *by* my fingers.[18] Hence, my *per accidens* motion here is a counterexample to the principle that what is being moved is being moved by another. Even if we waive this problem, there is still another. If I move my fingers and my fingers move me, then the motion situation is self-contained. In other words, we find no asymmetrical relation of moved to mover by which to begin a regress to an unmoved mover. Kenny goes on to admit that Aquinas could get asymmetry back into the typing example by saying that in a living thing the soul is the moving part. My soul moves my fingers but they do not move my soul. Now the problem is that the presently existing mover is my soul and not God.[19] Kenny affirms a similar lack of identity for the mover of natural bodies. Their mover is their generator. Besides changing the mover from a present one to a past one, the generator of the natural body clearly is not God, for example, fire as the generator of air from water.

In my opinion, Kenny's critique can be used to understand the eternity of motion as unavoidable in the natural philosopher's study of motion and its causes. For not only are natural bodies generated but so too are self-movers like humans. The generators of humans, however, are not God, but fellow humans. Hence, the asymmetrical reduction of motion to a self-mover would not continue vertically but detour to the past generator of the self-mover. Aquinas admits that the lateral regress can be infinite.[20] In fact, in the course

---

18. Kenny, *The Five Ways*, 14.
19. Ibid., 15.
20. *ST* I, q. 46, a. 2, ad 7. The crucial idea is that in an accidental series, no cause causes as caused: "and it is likewise accidental to this particular man as generator to be generated by another man; for he generates as a man, and not as the son of another man." In his *Thomas Aquinas and Radical Aristotelianism* (Washington, D.C.: The Catholic University of America Press, 1980), 24–25, Fernand Van Steenberghen defends Bonaventure's position that human reason can demonstrate the impossibility of an eternal world. Van Steenberghen thinks that the following is Bonaventure's best argument. If

of the second way at I.13.25, Aquinas says, "for if, as Aristotle supposes, motion is everlasting, the generation of self-moving beings ... must be endless."

My point is that any physical vertical causal regress is open to a lateral detour of generators without end back into the past. Instead of reaching an unmoved mover, our vertical regress would only reach the latest in a string of generated self-movers. Aquinas has natural philosophy argumentation to curtail this dogleg. That argumentation is what I.13.25 presents. It enables the reasoning to rejoin the vertical regress to an unmoved mover. The fact remains that just within the context of the science of physics, the eternity of motion is not a supposition but an inevitable possibility that must be confronted and dealt with. There is no way a physicist can consider motion and not also consider the eternity of motion. The eternity of motion is not something that the physicist is free to suppose. Without considering it, his analysis of motion and its causes ceases to ascend to higher causes and veers left into an unending series of past generations.

Hence, the previously mentioned possibility of the natural philosopher proving the unmoved mover without facing the eternity of motion is false. The eternity of motion should appear in any physical proof of an unmoved mover. Hence, its presence as a supposition in Aquinas's second way is an internal indication that the second way is not the argument of the natural philosopher. The natural philosopher cannot be the one making the supposition for the most effective proof of God, as if the natural philosopher has the choice of making a proof without the eternity of motion. Every proof the natural philosopher makes will include the eternity of motion. But there is another implication. If what I have argued is correct, then the absence of the eternity of motion in the first way of I.13 is an internal indication that the first way is not an argument of the natural philosopher.[21]

---

the past is infinite, then something is infinitely distant from the present, then the present should never be reached. Consider what follows the first. If this second is not infinitely distant also, then neither is the first because the first is gotten by adding to the finite. Hence, all past events are as infinitely distant as the first and so the present should not be reached. Aquinas's reply to this argument is that traversal is always from one point to another. Van Steenberghen calls Aquinas's reply "totally unsatisfactory," as Bonaventure is speaking about something infinitely distant. Van Steenberghen is missing Aquinas's refusal to follow the reasoning that if the past is infinite, then something is infinitely distant in the past. What is possibly true of the past, is not true of things; there is an equivocation on the subject of infinite.

21. For some current natural philosophy attempts to argue simply vertically, see chapter 7, "Interlude."

Scott MacDonald

In a probing article, "Aquinas's Parasitic Cosmological Argument," Scott MacDonald analyzes the *SCG* arguments *ex motu* and comes to a conclusion similar but not identical to my own. I want to situate my analysis in respect to MacDonald's.

MacDonald argues that the *prima via* of *SCG* I.13 is incomplete and that Aquinas's reasoning in the *secunda via* indicates that Aquinas recognized this incompleteness. The *prima via* is incomplete because it reaches only a "mundane primary mover." Such a mover is unmoved in respect to the motion that it cause but there is no guarantee that it is unmoved in all respects. In other words, a mundane primary mover is unmoved but it may not be unmovable. MacDonald lists fire, animals, and human beings as examples of mundane primary movers.[22]

MacDonald argues that a reader can catch Aquinas trying to eliminate this gap between the unmoved and the unmovable in four arguments from the *secunda via* of I.13. Aquinas is at the point in the proof where he is arguing against a corruptible self-mover (par. 24). MacDonald says that in pars. 24–28, Aquinas provides four arguments to reason beyond a mundane primary mover. MacDonald lists the first three arguments: first (par. 24) Aquinas "argues that mundane primary movers are corruptible (or contingent), and so must be explained by appeal to something incorruptible." Third (par. 25), "there must be some eternal (beginningless) mover, since motion is eternal, but no mundane primary mover can be an eternal mover (each mundane primary mover's moving begins)." MacDonald does not explicitly list the second argument but it appears to be a variation of the listed third argument. Referring to par. 26, MacDonald says that mundane movers cannot be eternal movers because they are moved *per accidens*: "Animals that are primary movers with respect to some local motion, for instance, are moved *per accidens* in that they depend on nutritive processes such as digestion and breathing in

---

22. Scott MacDonald, "Aquinas's Parasitic Cosmological Argument," *Medieval Philosophy and Theology* 1 (1991): 147. "So in order to count as a primary mover ... P must be unmoved (because it is in actuality) in the relevant respect. But it does not follow from this that P must be unmoved (and hence in actuality) in all respects. If P were in actuality in all respects, P would be absolutely unmoved and unmovable, but the fact that P is unmoved with respect to some state S does not entail that P is unmovable" (ibid.). As I did, so too MacDonald (ibid., 147n49) acknowledges Kenny for this objection.

order to initiate local motion." In summary of these first three arguments, MacDonald says:

> I want only to point out that they are themselves cosmological proofs essentially different from the proof from motion. Their starting points are the existence of corruptible beings of a certain sort of the beginninglessness of motion, not the fact that some particular thing—the sun in the sky or the log on the fire—is moved.... If these arguments from contingency are the only bridges Aquinas has from mundane primary movers to an unmovable primary mover, then the proof from motion must contain another cosmological argument—perhaps the third way [of *ST*]—as an integral part. These other cosmological arguments might stand on their own, but the proof from motion is invalid without one of them. Of course, this is not to say that the proof from motion fails; it is just to say that it is parasitic on another version of the cosmological argument.[23]

MacDonald says that at I.13.28 Aquinas offers a fourth argument that mundane movers require an unmovable. There is the need of a final cause to explain the appetite of the mundane mover, for example, a farmer who plants his crops. MacDonald places little faith in this argument alone, as the final cause need be only the farmer's conception of happiness and need not even exist.[24] However, "appetible objects are good to some degree, and so they constitute a starting point for the fourth way [of *ST*]."[25] Again, however, the motion proof is parasitic on another kind of proof.

As a textual basis for his thesis that the *prima via* of *SCG* is logically incomplete and that Aquinas knows this, MacDonald turns to the *quinque viae* of *ST*. He notes that in the *Summa Theologiae*, Aquinas is more circumspect in characterizing the conclusion of the *prima via*. The *via* reaches only an unmoved, not an unmovable. Moreover, in the reply to the article's second objection, Aquinas admits that the gap can be closed by using the *tertia via*. The objection argues that the nature of the human intellect and will can deal with all features of the world. These seem to be instances of MacDonald's primary mundane movers. In reply, Aquinas says that "all things that are changeable and susceptible to corruption must be traced back to some primary principle that is unmovable and of itself necessary as has been shown. MacDonald

---

23. Ibid., 148–49.
24. Ibid., 151.
25. Ibid.

says, "the striking feature of this part of Aquinas's reply is his conjoining the starting points and conclusion of two of the five ways, the proof from motion and the proof from contingency... Aquinas has run together the first and the third ways, and it is here—with the first and third ways simultaneously called to mind—that he first claims that the primary mover must be unmovable."[26]

An admitted last problem for MacDonald is to explain why if the motion argument is parasitic on the third, then why does not Aquinas just present the third? MacDonald replies that the motion argument, incomplete as it is, is more in line with Aquinas's strategy of beginning from what is most given in sensation. "Ordinary processes of change are ready to hand, immediately obvious to the senses, in a way that the contingency of things, their degrees of nobility, and their being related in a providential world order are not." This advantage outweighs the difficulty presented by the parasitical nature of the motion proof. "After all, the proof is not seriously flawed, only incomplete. Aquinas intended his readers to find the completion of the proof in the immediately succeeding paragraphs of *ST*."[27]

What can I say to this amazing narrative? To make any useful correlations, one has to correlate my terminology with MacDonald's. I believe that it is correct to observe that where I speak of metaphysics and natural philosophy, or physics, MacDonald speaks of cosmological, or contingent, and the motion argument. I discuss the motion proof in terms of Aquinas's categories of the sciences; MacDonald adopts categories used in current discussion of cosmological reasoning. Hence, my comments are as follows.

MacDonald's narrative is cued by the claim that the *prima via* of *SCG* is incomplete in the way described. Insofar as I took a metaphysical approach from the start, I do not think that the *prima via* is incomplete because it fails to arrive at the unmovable. In that way I would transcend MacDonald's problematic and his solution. But is not my metaphysical approach substantially the same as MacDonald's? He says that the *via* is parasitic on later cosmological reasoning; I would be saying that it is parasitic on a metaphysical interpretation. My problem is the use of the word "parasitic." A parasitic relation is generally regarded as a inappropriate; it usually is to the detriment of the host. But metaphysics is not taking on something alien when it considers

---

26. Ibid., 154.
27. Ibid., 155.

motion. Like any other finite nature, motion is a potency for an *esse*. It naturally falls under the consideration of *ens inquantum est ens*. A metaphysical consideration of motion should not be regarded as an intrusion upon a topic that is the exclusive reserve of the natural philosopher. For MacDonald, however, motion seems to be something alien to cosmological reasoning. That is why in his interpretation there is a clear break between the *prima* and *secunda viae* of *SCG* and the *prima* and *tertia viae* of *ST*. Moreover, *pace* MacDonald's last remarks, the distinction is such that the way from motion can be sacrificed. At its best the motion argument is an appendage for cosmological reasoning, like an antechamber for a dwelling. In sum, if for Aquinas motion can be genuinely studied either by the natural philosopher or by the metaphysician, then there is no reason why the motion argument cannot be metaphysical from the start and so arrive at a mover than is unmovable.

I do agree with MacDonald that insofar as motion is considered simply in terms of natural philosophy, then the motion proof does have problems transcending the material order. We differ, though, on where the endpoint is. For MacDonald motion analysis terminates in any mundane mover. For me natural philosophy analysis would continue by placing the mundane mover into a lateral regress of generated generators, a *per accidens* series of movers. In that respect I believe that MacDonald falsely separates pars. 24 and 25 of *SCG* I.13 into two arguments. In my reading, par. 25 explains why par. 24 claims that corruptible self-moving beings must be reduced to some first self-moving being that is everlasting. As noted above, MacDonald also arbitrarily glosses "corruptible" as "contingent." Without a metaphysics already in place, it is impossible to do that. Outside the context of Aquinas's metaphysics, an analysis of the corruptible gives you the distinction between matter and form only. Also, from the perspective of natural philosophy, it is perfectly appropriate to go from motion to an analysis of the causes of motion, for example, in the case of corruptible self-movers. Motion is an accident of a substance. Hence, any conditions for the substance are conditions for the motion. Finally, without an already in place metaphysics, the eternity of motion would be an unavoidable consideration of the natural philosopher, or in MacDonald's terminology, for the argument from motion. So, the consideration of the eternity of generated things in par. 25 does not signal, as MacDonald claimed, that a cosmological consideration has begun. So, as I see it, I.13.24–26 just continues the natural philosopher's analysis of motion. The conclusion there of an everlasting self-mover, what I elsewhere called a first physical cause, marks the limit of natural philosophy reasoning. Again, however, I want to recall that in fact this is not the reasoning of a natural philosopher but that of a metaphysician appropriately borrowing points from natural philosophy. That is why Aquinas later says that he is just supposing the eternity of motion.

What about MacDonald's textual basis in *ST* I, q. 2, a. 3? I have yet to speak of the *prima via* of the *Summa Theologiae*. A reader can well imagine, however, that I will read it metaphysically just as I did the *prima via* of *SCG*. So, I do not think that Aquinas's concluding the *prima via* with the unmoved rather than the unmovable is significant. Moreover, Aquinas's unequivocal remark at the end of each of the *quinque viae* that this is what all understand to be God, presumably also the Christian that is Aquinas himself, makes MacDonald's opinion difficult. If Aquinas has not reached God in the *prima via*, why does he say that he has? If MacDonald is correct, then should not Aquinas have said something to the effect that this is not what all call God but that further reasoning will get us there?

Finally, I read Aquinas's reply to the second objection differently than MacDonald. When Aquinas says "for all things that are changeable and capable of defect must be traced back to an immovable and self-necessary first principle, as has been shown" (*oportet autem omnia mobilia et deficere possibilia reduci in aliquod primum principium immobile et per se necessarium, sicut ostensum est*), I understand the last "et" to refer to the conclusions of the *prima* and *tertia viae*, not to the conclusion only of the *tertia via*. In other words, the *prima via* provides the first immobile and the *tertia via* provides the necessary *per se*. My textual reason is that the *tertia via* mentions as its conclusion only the necessary *per se*, not a *primum principium immobile*. Moreover, is the conclusion of the *prima via*, namely, "a first mover which is moved by no one" (*Primum movens quod a nullo movetur*) distinguishable from *primum principium immobile*?

The Other *viae* in *SCG* I.13

The remaining three of the five *viae* are briefer than the first two. The third uses an argument for Aristotle in *Metaphysics* II.2, 994a1, against an infinite ordered regress of efficient causes. Aristotle's argument is meant to defend the thesis that first philosophy considers first causes. As Aquinas gives Aristotle's argument, the first efficient causes are movers. However, earlier in his commentary, Aquinas is insistent that the first causes that the first philosopher reaches account not only for the motion of the heavens but for their being also.[28] I take this to mean that at least for Aquinas the argument against infinite regress applies not only against efficient causes of motion but also against efficient causes of *esse substantiale*.

So how are we to interpret the third *via*? Because the first way had already argued against an infinite regress of moved movers, the third *via* would be repetitious if its focus was a first efficient cause of motion. Hence, it should be dealing with an efficient cause of *esse substantiale*. This fact plus the facts that the text does not include remarks about the eternity of motion, a first self-mover, and a first final cause, indicate that the argument is taking the short path from *esse substantiale* to *esse subsistens*. According to this path, the priority of the *esse* to the nature is what is emphasized. In short, the third *via* would basically be the causal reasoning of the *De Ente*, discussed above. The third *via*, however, would not be that causal reasoning in its entirety. The third *via* presupposes that we know that there is efficient causality of *esse* and that the efficient cause is other than the thing that has the *esse*.

The third *via* would pick up at that point and argue that the efficient cause of *esse* cannot consist in an infinite regress of things each with an *esse*. Aquinas's argument is as follows: "When you suppress a cause, you suppress its effect. Therefore, if you suppress the first cause, the intermediate cause cannot be a cause. Now, if there were an infinite regress among efficient causes, no cause would be first. Therefore, all the other causes, which are intermediate, will be suppressed. But this is manifestly false."[29] As I explained earlier, Aquinas's mention of a first cause in the course of the argument is not question-begging. By a "first cause" Aquinas means an "actual cause" that the effect is already understood to require. That *esse substantiale* requires an actual cause other than the thing that it actuates has already been argued. In that context, an infinite regress of things each with *esse substantiale* is an infinite regress of things all asking for an actual cause that no other thing in the regress can be. Each thing in the regress would be waiting to be caused in order to cause. So, granting that there is efficient causality of *esse substantiale*,

28. See below, note 32.
29. Trans. Pegis, 1:95.

then there must be some actual efficient cause whose nature is *esse subsistens*. Aquinas regards this conclusion to be identifiable with the God of his belief. Presumably, the *Ego sum qui sum* revelation of Exodus 3:14 is involved here.

The text of the *quarta via* is brief and is as follows:

> Another argument may also be gathered from the words of Aristotle. In *Metaphysics* II he shows that what is most true is also most a being. But in *Metaphysics* IV he shows the existence of something true from the observed fact that of two false things one is more false than the other, which means that one is more true than the other. The comparison is based on the nearness to that which is absolutely and supremely true. From these Aristotelian texts we may further infer that there is something that is supremely being. This we call God.[30]

The *via* begins from a gradation of true things. Aquinas argues that this implies something maximally true. Further, because a thing most true is a thing most a being, then a maximum being exists. Hence, God exists. At first the argument sounds more epistemological than metaphysical. The use of Aristotle's *Metaphysics* IV with its talk of propositions being more or less true helps to cement that impression. Yet Aquinas admits many understandings of truth besides the formal sense of an adequation of the intellect's propositions to things. For example, the true is said of things insofar as things are able to cause the intellect to be true. Things are able to be perfective in this respect from the side of their natures or essences.

The true and the good must therefore add to the concept of being a relationship of that which perfects. But in any being there are two aspects to be considered, the formal character of its species and the act of being by which it subsists in that species. And so a being can be perfective in two ways. (1) It can be so just according to its specific character. In this way the intellect is perfected by a being, for it perceives the formal character of the being.[31]

Aquinas's explanation clearly echoes the *De Ente*'s absolute consideration of essence in which essence abstracts from every *esse* and so can have both an *esse in re* and an *esse in anima*.

These texts allow a reader to understand the identity of the gradation of things in truth. The gradation is the gradation of essences in perfection. The

---

30. Ibid., 1:95–96.
31. Aquinas, *De Ver.*, q. 21, a. 1, co. (trans. Schmidt, 3:6).

more perfect the essence the more perfect the truth. Also, a reader can now understand how Aquinas can say that the most true is the most being. As I have mentioned, once one is aware of the distinction between the thing and its *esse*, one can fantasize a situation in which the thing is intelligibly one with its *esse*. In such a situation, the thinker can grasp that *esse subsistens* would be, for example, one, infinite, and eternal. In other words, the most perfect essence is an essence in which the *esse* is the essence. Subsistent existence would be the meaning of *maxime ens*.

Of course, this realization is not the knowledge that the most true thing, subsistent existence, exists. Yet it does provide a means to argue that conclusion. If the most true is *esse* in a subsistent configuration, then where you know that you have a gradation of true things, you know that you have *esse* in an accidental configuration. The situation is now ripe for the application of the *De Ente* reasoning. In this way, the gradation of truth in things implies more than what may only be an ideal still unrealized. The gradation implies a reality.

How does the *quarta via* fit the topography of the metaphysician's reasoning to *esse subsistens*? The answer depends on where one finds a gradation of essences. In his commentary on the fourth way's reference to *Metaphysics* II, Aquinas says that the most true things, God and the separate substances, are the cause of generable things and the eternal heavens.[32] That focus would have the fourth way beginning from data available in the second causal path out of judgmentally grasped existence of sensible things. The gradation of truth would be the second path's discovery of a gradation of bodies, namely, corruptible and incorruptible. One can wonder if this focus is necessary. Is there not a gradation of essences and of truth just among corruptible bodies? Among corruptible bodies we find the inanimate, the living, the sentient,

---

32. "From this [Aristotle] again concludes that the principles of things which always exist, i.e., the celestial bodies, must be most true. He does this for two reasons. First, they are not 'sometimes true and sometimes not true,' and therefore surpass the truth of things subject to generation and corruption, which sometimes exist and sometimes do not. Second, these principles have no cause but are the cause of the being of other things. And for this reason they surpass the celestial bodies in truth and in being; and even though the latter are incorruptible, they have a cause not only of their motion, as some men thought, but also of their being, as the Philosopher clearly states in this place." *In II Meta.*, l. 2, n. 294 (trans. Rowan, 112). For a discussion of Aquinas's use of the plural in speaking about the first principle of *esse*, see my "Aquinas' Ascriptions of Creation to Aristotle," *Angelicum* 73, no. 4 (1998): 487–506.

and the rational. That gradation also seems to suffice to run the fourth way.

The fifth way is also succinct. It goes as follows:

Damascene proposes another argument for the same conclusion taken from the government of the world. Averroes likewise hints at it. The argument runs thus. Contrary and discordant things cannot, always or for the most part, be parts of one order except under someone's government, which enables all and each to tend to a definite end. But in the world we find that things of diverse natures come together under one order, and this not rarely or by chance, but always or for the most part. There must therefore be some being by whose providence the world is governed. This we call God.[33]

Even though Aquinas says that the starting point is the government of the world, governance is actually a conclusion from the regular occurrence of a certain proportion between contrary things. Moreover, the need to explain this regular occurrence follows from a presupposed application of the major premise of Aquinas's *De Ente* reasoning: what belongs to a thing is caused. To make these points explicit, one can consider the following case.

Anyone who has tried to bake a cake knows that it is not sufficient simply to have the ingredients. The ingredients, for example milk and flour, have to be in a definite proportion. That proportion is the attribute the ingredients must have in order to bake the cake. The attributive status of the proportion is indicated by finding the milk and flour without it. The situation is now ripe for the application of the *De Ente* reasoning. As an attribute, the proportion is a dependent item and obviously dependent upon the ingredients. The dependency cannot be complete, however, if the ingredients are considered precisely as subjects of the proportion. The reason is that precisely as subjects of the proportion, the ingredients are proportion-neutral and do not have the wherewithal to completely explain the attribute within them. Hence, something other than the ingredients precisely as subjects is required to explain the dependency of the proportion as attribute. What is that? For example, it cannot be the flour in some other respect than subject because then the proportion would be in the flour more often than it is. In other words, the proportion cannot be understood as an attribute that is a property. It is not like the attribute of risibility that follows human nature mentioned in the *De Ente* text.

33. Trans. Pegis, 1:96.

Nevertheless, in the case of this bakery that I pass every morning, the proportion is found regularly in the flour because cakes are regularly seen in the window. So, something other than the flour is causing that proportion. Moreover, because the proportion occurs regularly, then that cause is intending the proportion. In other words, the causing of the proportion is a property of something just as risibility is a property of human nature. This is how the regular occurrence of a certain proportion or order among contrary things (flour is dry, milk is wet) logically implies the idea of intention or governance. These thoughts are a necessary introduction to get to the starting point of the *via*.

So what is the governor or intender? If the governor is a machine, then the governor does not fully account for its intending the proportion in the ingredients. The reason is that the intending is rooted in the design of the machine and the materials of the machine do not fully account for the design. The only thing that can itself intend an end is a thing whose design is itself. This would be a purely formal power or a purely formal being. From what we know of knowledge in ourselves, this purely formal cause would be an intellect.

Perhaps this is to move too fast. What of the possibility that the machine is an effect of chance? Because the machine is not a regular occurrence like the cakes, its occurrence could be construed as unintended. But even if the machine is by chance, it remains something caused. On the level of natural philosophy, the identity of that cause would be the series of occurrences extending infinitely back into the past. That identity is sufficiently like the infinite series of past generations that Aquinas referred to a first physical cause at *SCG* I.13.25. Because of the infinity of the series, no one thing in the series is ever fully explained and so the series does not fully explain itself. A reference to an external eternal thing is necessary.

So if one of the things in the series is a governor like the machine, then it also is not fully accounted for within the series. Chance is some explanation of the intender, but chance is not the entire explanation. But the switch to causality in a vertical line cannot be a switch to chance again. Explanations by chance can extend to infinity, a vertical causal regress cannot. Hence, the reasoning of my above next to the last paragraph holds.

I have been speaking about the regular occurrence of cakes. What is the analogate to this in the world of nature? An example would be snow at certain times of the year. For the snow there must be a certain proportion of moisture and cold. That proportion is not intrinsic to the water or air temperature, nor is its regular occurrence accounted for by either. Something else is intending it. Ultimately, as mentioned, it is an intellect. Obviously, this reasoning does not produce the knowledge that this intellect is God. So how is the *quinta via* read metaphysically?

The starting point would be the *esse* of the mentioned proportion between contrary items. So we would be beginning not from the *esse* of a substance but from the *esse* of an accident of the substance. If one focuses on the *esse* of the proportion as the act *of the proportion*, then we are beginning the second causal path out of *esse*. Any causes of the proportion become causes of the *esse*. Furthermore, if the regularity of the proportion is noticed, then the cause of the proportion becomes a governor or intender. A full explanation of this governor could go the entire length of the second path so that the conclusion is subsistent existence as the transfixing final cause for other intellects.

The *quinta via* itself is some prompt for reading the *via* according to the full length of the second path out of *esse*. The *via* speaks of the government of the *world*. Moreover, in *De Ver.*, q. 5, a. 3, co., Aquinas speaks of the same ordering of contraries but identifies them as the corruptible and incorruptible parts of the universe.[34] Yet that big picture may not be necessary. The latter lines of the *via* seem to say that finding in the world any situation of diverse things in a regular order suffices to get to a divine governor. Hence, one could read the *via* in other ways. First, the *via* could reach a nondivine intellect, for example the human engineer who produced the machine in the bakery. The reduction of the nondivine intellect to *esse subsistens* as intellectual would continue through a consideration of the priority of its *esse*. Second, if the priority of the *esse* of the regular proportion of diverse things is the focus, then there is an immediate reduction to an intellect that is *esse subsistens*.

---

34. "Consequently, whenever we find a group whose members are ordered to each other, that group must necessarily be ordered to some external principle. Now, the corruptible and incorruptible parts of the universe are related to each other essentially, not accidentally. For we see that corruptible bodies benefit from the celestial bodies, and always, or at least ordinarily, in the same manner. Consequently, all things, corruptible and incorruptible, must be in an order under the providence of an external principle outside the universe" (trans. Mulligan, 1:214).

[9]

The *viae* of the *Summa Theologiae* and the *Compendium Theologiae*

The two other texts in which Aquinas professedly sets out to demonstrate God's existence are *ST* I, q. 2, a. 3, and *Comp. Theol.* I, c. 3.

Introduction to the *via* of the *Summa*

I mentioned that in chapters prior to *SCG* I.13 one can find remarks in which Aquinas indicated a metaphysical context for I.13. Nothing comparable is found in the articles before the *quinque viae*. Nevertheless, there is a topical similarity between the two *Summae*. Both speak of the two kinds of truth found in divine revelation; both critique the self-evidency of God to us; and both present demonstration as a way to God's existence. So, we can say that as in *SCG*, so too in the *Summa Theologiae* Aquinas is interested in a philosophically astute approach to God. Unfortunately, no metaphysical terminology appears in *ST* to indicate that metaphysics will constitute the philosophical approach. One could argue indirectly, however, from the stated intention of the work.

The *Summa Theologiae* was intended to be taught. The latter was not a work to be tackled by the student alone. Rather, a study of the text was to be undertaken under the tutelage of a *magister*. In the prologue Aquinas writes:

Students in this science have not seldom been hampered by what they found written by other authors, partly on account of the multiplicity of useless questions, articles, and arguments; partly also because the things they need to know are not taught according to the order of learning [*secundum ordinem discipliae*], but according as the plan of the book might require or the occasion of disputing [*disputandi*] might offer; partly, too, because frequent repetition brought weariness and confusion to the minds of listening students. Anxious, therefore, to overcome these and other obstacles, we will try, confident of divine help, to present those things pertaining to sacred doctrine briefly and clearly insofar as the matter will permit.¹

In his *The Setting of the Summa Theologiae of Saint Thomas*, Leonard Boyle remarks:

Yet although the subject of this part of the prologue is "ea quae scripta sunt a diversis" and not, if it were teaching, "ea quae traduntur," there is a possible ambiguity in the passage, as though Thomas were speaking on two levels at once. For his complaint against the longueurs and disorder in the writings on theology in question ends with a seeming reference to classrooms and teaching ("eorumdem frequens repetitio et fastidium et confusionem generabat in animis auditorum") rather than, as one would expect, to reading and studying.²

Another indication that the *Summa* was to be a classroom text is furnished by James Weisheipl. In his *Friar Thomas D'Aquino*, Weisheipl indicates that Aquinas took up the writing of the *Summa* as a result of unsuccessfully teaching his commentary on Lombard's *Sentences*.³ It seems Aquinas wished to replace one classroom text with another more suitable.

But if Aquinas intended his *Summa* to be taught, there is also indication that he intended it to be taught by a *magister* familiar with his previous writings. The previous theological texts with which Aquinas was dissatisfied obviously included his own previous writings. Otherwise Aquinas would have taught them and not have begun the *Summa*. These previous works include

---

1. As translated by James A. Weisheipl, *Friar Thomas D'Aquino His Life, Thought and Work* (New York: Doubleday, 1974), 218. In *Basic Writings* (trans. Pegis), the translation of *in animis auditorum* is "in the minds of the readers."

2. Leonard Boyle, *The Setting of the Summa Theologiae of Saint Thomas* (Toronto: Pontifical Institute of Mediaeval Studies, 1982), 18.

3. Weisheipl, *Friar Thomas D'Aquino*, 197 and 217–18.

his *Commentary on the Sentences* (1252–56), *De Ente et Essentia* (1252–56), *De Principiis Naturae* (1252–56), *In De Hebdomadibus* (1256–59), *De Quodlibetales* (1256–59), *De Veritate* (1256–57), *De Trinitate* (1258–59), *Summa contra Gentiles* (1259–64), *De Potentia* (1265–66), and *De Malo* (1266–67). Also, all of these works fail to be systematic, brief, and clear expositions of sacred doctrine for the instruction of beginners in theology. While *SCG* is a possible exception, the welter of arguments contained in its chapters appears to make it an undesirable text.

No indication exists that Aquinas considered the seminal ideas of these works to be philosophically and theologically inadequate. Rather, the inadequacy was in the arrangement of the material. The arrangement was not *secundum ordinem disciplinae*.

How familiar with Aquinas's previous writings would the *magister* be? It is important to realize that the *magister* is one of Aquinas's own time. The *magister* would lack the benefit of Bergamo's fifteenth-century *Tabula Aurea*, or Deferrari's and Schutz's twentieth-century lexicons, and twenty-first-century computer search programs. He would also lack the precious listings of parallel passages that appear in subsequent editions of Aquinas's *Opera Omnia*. Also, he probably would not have read every line that Aquinas wrote. Yet, one can assume that the *magister* knew of the previously cited pre-*Summa* works and at least was familiar with their contents as these would be expressed in the titles of the various question and articles. With this kind of *magister* in mind, it is important that subsequent discussion confine itself to more obvious texts. Moreover, these texts ought to be those to which a *magister* of the *quinque viae* would be naturally led.

The silence about metaphysics in the *quinque viae* must be taken up in this context. If the *Summa* was intended to be presented to students through the medium of a *magister* familiar in the above way with Aquinas's other works, then it is no surprise that its texts can be elliptical and enigmatic, especially to a novice. The texts were not meant to stand alone. They were to be accompanied by the exposition of the teacher. The exposition would appropriately draw upon the wealth of insight and argumentation contained in Aquinas's more elaborate discussions. As I explained in chapter 6, those more elaborate discussions indicate a metaphysical context for any proof for God's existence. In this way, Aquinas's stated intention for the *Summa* could be considered intrinsic evidence for a metaphysical understanding of the *quinque viae*.

The *prima via*

The first and more manifest way is the argument from motion. It is certain, and evident to our senses, that in the world some things are in motion. Now whatever is moved is moved by another, for nothing can be moved except it is in potentiality to that towards which it is moved; whereas a thing moves inasmuch as it is in act. For motion is nothing else than the reduction of something from potentiality to actuality. But nothing can be reduced from potentiality to actuality, except by something in a state of actuality. Thus that which is actually hot, as fire, makes wood, which is potentially hot, to be actually hot, and thereby moves and changes it. Now it is not possible that the same thing should be at once in actuality and potentiality in the same respect, but only in different respects. For what is actually hot cannot simultaneously be potentially hot, but it is simultaneously potentially cold. It is therefore impossible that in the same respect and in the same way a thing should be both mover and moved, i.e., that it should move itself. Therefore, whatever is moved must be moved by another. If that by which it is moved be itself moved, then this also must needs be moved by another, and that by another again. But this cannot go on to infinity, because then there would be no first mover, and, consequently, no other mover, seeing that subsequent movers move only inasmuch as they are moved by the first mover; as the staff moves only because it is moved by the hand. Therefore it is necessary to arrive at a first mover, moved by no other; and this everyone understands to be God.[4]

One can divide the *prima via* into three stages: first, its starting point, the existence of motion; second, the proof that what is in motion is moved by another; third, the denial of the possibility of an infinite regress. Through these steps, the *prima via* concludes to a first unmoved mover. Aquinas remarks that such a mover everyone understands to be God. "Everyone" presumably includes the Christian believer who is Aquinas himself. Each stage will be discussed in detail.

Like the first way of *SCG* I.13, the *prima via* makes no mention of the eternity of motion. This fact already is an indication that the *prima via* is not proceeding simply on a physical plane. Insofar as the *via* is zeroing in on the actuality of motion rather than its eternity, one can spy a concern to make the existence of the motion accidental to the motion. We have already discussed

---

4. Trans. Pegis, 1:22. The citation of the other four *viae* will continue to come from this Pegis edition.

the fact that Aquinas assigns an *esse* both to substances and accidents and that Aquinas numbers motion among the accidents.

There are at least two ways this focusing on the *esse* of motion would be occurring. First, once the real difference between the actual motion and the substance that is its subject is recognized, the actual motion can be juxtaposed to itself as cognitively existing. Brought to bear upon this multiplicity, the intellect's first act grasps the motion as existence-neutral. When the intellect's second act recomposes this object with the really existing motion, it offers a distinct grasp of the motion's *esse*.

Second, once we are aware of the distinction between the thing and its *esse*, we can go on to intellectually fantasize about a thing not intelligibly distinct from its *esse*. Aquinas himself did this mental experimenting in the fourth chapter of *De Ente*. Recall how he noted that such a thing would have to be a one and only. But there are other implications of the same. A thing not distinct from its *esse* would not be able to be separated from its *esse* and so could not not exist. Also, because the thing is at least common to itself both really and cognitively existing, *esse* merged with the thing is *esse* communized. But common *esse* is the intelligible heart of the *ratio entis* and so has the infinity of perfection of that transcendental. In sum, a thing not distinct from its *esse* is infinite in perfection. No conceivable perfection or degree thereof would be lacking to it.

With these implications in mind, we can more quickly distinguish *esse*. There would be no need to set the thing in an existence multiplicity and run the multiplicity through the two intellectual operations. If the things are multiple, if they are changeable, if they are finite, then it must be the case the *esse* is there as distinct from these things. This second approach may also be what is involved in the first stage of the *prima via*. Aristotle defined motion as the act of the potential insofar as it is potential. Like a ruddy or pale complexion, motion is an act of a substance. But unlike these two, motion is not an act fully actualized. It has some of its act outside of itself. As such it collides with the infinite situation of *esse* merged with a nature. Existing motion must be a situation of a nature distinct from its *esse*.

The key proposition in stage two is "Whatever is moved is moved by another." This proposition is not presented as self-evident but as the conclusion of an argument. The argument appears to be a *propter quid* argument because it is based upon insights into the natures of the mover and moved. The argument is as follows. To deny this proposition is to affirm a contradiction; hence the proposition must be correct. Why is the denial a contradiction? First, consider what it is to be moved, or in motion. To be such is to be in potentiality, or to lack, that toward which you are moving. Second, consider what it is to be a mover. To be such is to be in act, or to possess, what is being realized in the thing in motion. So for a thing in motion precisely as in motion to move itself demands that it be in act and potency at the same time and in the same respect—a contradiction. So, what is in motion is moved by another.

How is this second stage understood metaphysically? The answer depends upon realizing that because existing motion is a situation of a nature distinct from its *esse*, what is moved is in a twofold potency. The moved is not only in a potency to receive the imperfect act that is the motion; it is also in potency to receive the *esse* of the motion. Approaching motion metaphysically, a reader of the *prima via* would be interested in the potency of the moved to the *esse* of the motion. That potency indicates that the subject of motion precisely as subject cannot fully account for the *esse* of the motion. What then does? Could the subject in some other respect than subject account for the *esse* of the motion? When I discussed the application of the *De Ente* reasoning to the *esse* of accidents, I noted that the existence-neutrality of the thing blocks the thing in some other respect than subject from explaining the *esse* of the motion. Only another thing, a thing that includes *esse*, could do the explaining.

So, if the priority of that *esse* to the motion is focused upon, it is difficult to think of the mover as a thing other than existence itself. Something that is the act of existence will explain existence, just as something hot will explain something that is hot. In this alternative, subsistent existence is a mover by causing the *esse* of some motion. On the other hand, if *esse*'s character as the act *of the motion* is focused upon, then a measure of dependency of the *esse* on the motion is acknowledged. This conclusion leads to considering conditions for the motion as conditions for the *esse*.

The third stage is introduced by the words "if that by which it is moved be itself moved." The disjunction of the first way of *SCG* seems to be implicit here. In other words, Aquinas would not have said "if" if the only conclusion from stage two was subsistent existence. Hence, Aquinas's concern in stage three to eliminate an infinite regress should be placed within the context of the second causal path that opens from the metaphysician's study of existing motion. This situating of the *prima via* renders it a scaled-down version of the first way in *SCG*. Aquinas's example in the *prima via* also indicates this coordination. The example is of the arm moving the cane. The envisaged infinite regress is one of efficient causality occurring in the present moment. Moreover, the example indicates that Aquinas wants to top off the regress with a self-mover, the man whose arm moves the cane. All of these data indicate that Aquinas is not interested in following this path to the eternal self-mover(s) which are responsible for generated ones and which, as intellectors, require the final causality of *esse subsistens*. We are not switching onto the second way of *SCG* as it includes all of these points. Rather, the *prima via* is content to follow the second path from a present motion to a present self-mover that is reduced to subsistent *esse* in virtue of the priority of its substantial *esse*. In this alternative, subsistent existence is a creator and a mover. It is a creator by causing the *esse* of the substance; it is a mover by causing the *esse* of a substance that is a condition for motion.[5]

Another interpretation of this final moment in the *prima via* is that instead of appealing to the priority of the substantial *esse* of the first finite mover to conclude to *esse subsistens*, Aquinas is appealing to the priority of *esse* of the motion of the first finite mover. As I have explained, whether the metaphysician focuses on accidental *esse* or on substantial *esse*, the metaphysician can go quickly to *esse subsistens* if the priority of *esse* is emphasized.

A reader might ask about the logical necessity for the disjunction in stage three. In other words, if the first causal path that emphasizes the priority of *esse* attains a mover that is subsistent *esse*, hence God, why take up the second path in *ST*, and for that matter in *SCG*? Is not the second path superfluous? I do not think so. Aquinas's thinking could be this. He may want to deal with possible metaphysicians of *esse* who conclude that second path with a being other than God and so present two first causes of *esse*. Hence, to counter this irreducibility of causes, Aquinas explains that though metaphysically there are two causal paths out of accidental *esse*, God as subsistent *esse* is at the end of both paths.[6]

---

5. Such seems to be the reduction of motion to God in *In VIII Phys.*, l. 2, no. 974. Aquinas says that God can cause motion because God can create mover and moved in a state of union from which motion follows.

6. In *Metaphysical Thought of Thomas Aquinas*, 457, Wippel interprets the *prima via* to develop through two stages: a physical stage and a metaphysical stage. He says: "Hence my view is that the first way as it appears in *S.T.* I, q. 2, a. 3 starts from a physical fact, but that if it is to reach the absolutely

Could the first finite mover be in an inertial motion? Yes, but that is not a problem for a metaphysical reduction to God. The metaphysician can leave Thomistic physics, or natural philosophy, to ponder how inertial motion is being actualized seemingly apart from a mover. My point is that the *esse* of the subject in inertial motion as well as the *esse* of this strange accident of inertial motion itself remain present for metaphysical analysis and reduction to *esse subsistens*.[7]

John Wippel raises another issue.[8] The problem is that the *prima via* does not seem to secure the unicity of the unmoved mover. This lacuna would make a Christian hesitant to identify the unmoved mover with the necessarily unique Christian God. Wippel's reason for his claim is that only later at q. 11, a. 3 does Aquinas argue for God's unicity. Some comments are the following. First, in Aquinas's exclamation at the end of each *viae* that the conclusion is what all call God, "all" would presumably include the Christian Aquinas. So, Aquinas does not think that there is any ambiguity about the five conclusions. There should be no need to prolong the *viae* either for Christians or for non-Christians. The current metaphysical interpretation can explain why this need does not exist. For non-Christians, the unicity for subsistent existence can be known before subsistent existence is concluded to. The

---

unmoved mover or God, it must pass beyond this and beyond a limited and physical application of the principle of motion to a wider application that will apply to any reduction of a being from not acting to acting. In other words, the argument becomes metaphysical in its justification and application of the motion principle, and only then can it succeed in arriving at God." I take Wippel to mean that the two stages correspond to physical science and metaphysical science respectively. In my interpretation both stages are metaphysical because both consider the *esse* of motion. Depending upon how that *esse* is considered, that is, either as prior to the motion or as in some manner dependent upon it, the metaphysician can go immediately to God as subsistent existence or more circuitously to God using reflections from natural philosophy on conditions for the thing that is the subject of the motion. This second alternative is not pure natural philosophy but the metaphysician using natural philosophy to understand his object of consideration, namely, *esse*. If the physical stage is taken as pure natural philosophy without any knowledge of metaphysics, then it is difficult to see how Aquinas could avoid strictly concluding to the heretical eternity of motion. Without considering this difficulty, Wippel claims that a total metaphysical interpretation "would no longer be Thomas's first way as this appears in the text of *S.T.* I, q. 2, a. 3." In reply I have two comments. Hopefully, my explanation of how the metaphysical consideration of *esse* can enlist the reflections of natural philosophy will qualm concerns of "appearance." Second, appearances notwithstanding, can one really believe that Aquinas position on where and when the philosopher proves God is not operative when Aquinas writes his *viae*?

7. For more on the Thomist discussion of inertia, see Wippel, *Metaphysical Thought of Thomas Aquinas*, 454–56.
8. Ibid., 458.

De Ente reasoning, it will be recalled, illustrated this point. For a Christian like Aquinas, *esse subsistens* has been divinely revealed as God's proper name [*proprium nomen*]. At the end of *SCG* I.22, Aquinas confesses this "most sublime truth." It is briefly reiterated in the *sed contra* of the *quinque viae* article. Hence, there should be no worry for Christians that in metaphysically reaching *esse subsistens* they are reaching *Deus*. For the fellow believers for whom Aquinas is writing the *Summa*, there is no need to bring in philosophical reasoning for God's unicity. Hence, for them it can be appropriately brought in later without redundancy or an admission of incompleteness in the *viae*.

The *secunda via*

The second way is from the nature of efficient cause. In the world of sensible things we find there is an order of efficient causes. There is no case known (neither is it, indeed, possible) in which a thing is found to be the efficient cause of itself; for so it would be prior to itself, which is impossible. Now in efficient causes it is not possible to go on to infinity, because in all efficient causes following an order, the first is the cause of the intermediate cause, and the intermediate is the cause of the ultimate cause, whether the intermediate cause be several, or one only. Now to take away the cause is to take away the effect. Therefore, if there be no first cause among efficient causes, there will be no ultimate, nor any intermediate, cause. But if in efficient causes it is possible to go on to infinity, there will be no first efficient cause, neither will there be an ultimate effect, nor any intermediate efficient causes; all of which is plainly false. Therefore it is necessary to admit a first efficient cause, to which everyone gives the name of God.

The *secunda via* has three stages: first, the starting point, an order of efficient causes in the world; second, the argument that no efficient cause can be the efficient cause of itself; third, the proof that ordered efficient causes cannot regress infinitely. Hence, a first efficient cause identifiable as God to the Christian is reached.

There are two points that I would like to make about stage one. First, in my opinion, the "order of efficient causes" about which Aquinas speaks is not yet the "ordered" regress of efficient causes that he will mention in stage two. I say that because if they were the same, then there would be no need to mention that no efficient cause is the cause of itself. That idea would already be implied by an "ordered" order of efficient causes. How then should a reader take the phrase "order of efficient causes"? Here "order" should be understood in terms of a level of reality such that on this level are found things that are efficient causes.

Second, how do we know that this level of efficient causes exists? Here it is important to think with eyes at the back of our heads. I mean by this expression that we should be aware of what we have already said as we confront new questions. So, I do not think that we know this level immediately, as we knew the starting point of motion that marked the *prima via*. But as the *prima via* indicated, the knowledge of an efficient cause is in and through the *propter quid* argument for the proposition: "Omne quod movetur ab alio movetur." As we saw, understood in terms of the new existence brought to the moved thing, motion need not immediately be reduced to *esse subsistens*. As the act of the motion, the *esse* has a measure of dependency upon the motion. The natural philosopher has investigated motion and its conditions extensively. The metaphysician can enlist those reflections to understand what is proper to his consideration, *viz.*, *esse*. One of those conditions is an efficient cause less than subsistent *esse*.

So, the starting point of the *secunda via* is a point further back in the *prima via*.[9] In terms of my commentary, that point is precisely in its third stage where the *prima via*, following the second path, posits a corruptible self-mover. For instance, it is the man whose arm moves the stick, etc. Because of the priority of its *esse* to itself, that self-mover is quickly reduced to *esse subsistens*. That claim is explained in stage two of the *secunda via*.

The second stage argues that no efficient cause is the cause of itself, for the thing would be prior to itself, which is impossible. The reasoning does not mention *esse*, but we have seen it before. Can anyone fail to recognize the *De Ente* reasoning for *esse tantum*? In the *De Ente* Aquinas argued that the *esse* of a thing belongs to the thing, the *esse* must be efficiently caused. Moreover, the thing about whose *esse* we are speaking cannot be the efficient cause of

---

9. Wippel insists that the starting point is "immediately given to us in sense experience" (ibid., 460). His reason seems to be that the *secunda via* says: "Invenimus enim in istis sensibilibus esse ordinem causarum efficientium." But *invenire* can be used for something found through some mediation. For example, the discovery (*inventio*) of the debtor by the man who decides to go to the market. See *SCG* III.74, *Adhuc*. Likewise, Aquinas can say that we find (*invenire*) certain forms by their various operations. See *SCG* II.68, *Invenimus enim*. Hence, there is no reason to distinguish the *secunda via* and the *De Ente* reasoning as Wippel (ibid., 462) goes on to do.

the *esse*. In the *De Ente*, Aquinas gives just "impossibility" as the reason. But in the parallel text for the *De Ente* reasoning, the impossibility is glossed in terms of the thing being prior to its existence, as in the *secunda via*. At *SCG* I.22, Aquinas remarks: "This is impossible, because, in their notions, the existence of the cause is prior to that of the effect. If, then, something were its own cause of being, it would be understood to be before it had being, which is impossible" (*si ergo aliquid sibi ipsi esset causa essendi, intelligeretur esse antequam haberet esse, quod est impossibile*).[10] The connection of the *secunda via* with the *De Ente* reasoning locks in a metaphysical interpretation of the *via*, even though the *via* makes no mention of *esse*. This implicitness of *esse* in a *via* should serve as a lesson to bear in mind when trying to understand other *viae*. It also shows that Aquinas can begin a *via* on the second path out of judgmentally grasped existence and quickly flip over to the first path.

The third stage of the *secunda via* considers the possibility of an ordered infinite regress of efficient causes, each of which is caused by another in the regress. Here Aquinas is again considering a regress of simultaneous things. This is not the infinite regress of generable things back into the past that comes up in the second motion proof of *SCG*. In his reply to the seventh objection in *ST* I, q. 46, a. 2, Aquinas distinguishes which series of efficient causes excludes an infinite regress and which does not. Efficient causes ordered *per se* exclude infinite regress. In a *per se* ordered series, the causality of subsequent causes presently depends upon the causality of the previous. The given example is not on the level of substantial *esse* but accidental *esse*: the stone being moved by the stick, the stick by the hand, the hand by the arm. Efficient causes are also ordered *per accidens*. In this case the causality of the subsequent causes is independent of the previous causes. The given example is a man, apart from his generator, generating another man. Hence, the *secunda via* is speaking of a *per se* ordered series of efficient causes, though on the level of substantial *esse*.

The third stage excludes the infinite regress. As the reader may recall, this point also is reflected in the *De Ente* reasoning. Hence, I consider the regress of the *secunda via* to be the fanciful one of the *De Ente*. Here we are supposed to entertain a subject of itself existence-neutral being the direct cause of *esse*. As in the first way from motion in *SCG*, the given reason is that the infini-

---

10. *SCG* I.22, *Amplius* (trans. Pegis, 1:119).

ty of the regress removes the first efficient cause needed by the middle cause which is needed by the ultimate effect. If his reasoning is not to be seen as question-begging, as claimed by Anthony Kenny, it is important to realize that the need for a first has already been argued for in the demonstration of the "Omne quod movetur ab alio movetur" proposition, which is a variation of the opening assertion of the *De Ente* reasoning that "omne quod convenit alicui ... est causatum." Hence, Aquinas's reason consists in pointing out that an infinite regress denies the cause that we already know is required by the caused.

Also, it is important to recall that the consideration of this infinite regress is not a logically necessary component of the *De Ente* reasoning, nor of the *secunda via* if it is interpreted in light of the *De Ente*. In the *De Ente* Aquinas first concludes to *esse tantum* and only afterward takes up the infinite regress possibility. This placement is understandable because the initial reasoning focuses upon the priority of *esse* to the subject. The priority of *esse* also explains Aquinas's repeated disjunction in the God proofs so far considered. In the first disjunct the proof concludes to God immediately. In natural philosophy reasoning one cannot immediately reach the unmoved mover. One has to regress first to an unending horizontal series of generations and then to the eternal motion of an eternal body and then to immaterial substance as an unwavering point of compelling attraction. One cannot immediately reach immaterial substance.

In conclusion, the *secunda via* is very much the *De Ente* reasoning for *esse subsistens*. There is no use of the robust form of the *De Ente* reasoning. Its second stage reasoning that no thing is an efficient cause of itself has *De Ente* pedigree. Also, the absence of the standard disjunction, reflective of the two pathways out from judgmentally grasped existence, indicates that the priority of *esse* to the nature that it actuates is the focus throughout the *secunda via*. Such a focus is also characteristic of the *De Ente* proof.

The *tertia via*

The third way is taken from possibility and necessity, and runs thus. We find in nature things that are possible to be and not to be [*possibilia esse et non esse*], since they are found to be generated, and to be corrupted, and consequently, it is possible for them to be and not to be. But it is impossible for all things that exist to be possible,[11] for that which can non-be at some time is not [*quandoque non est*]. Therefore, if everything can non-be, then at one time there was nothing in existence [*nihil in rebus*]. Now if this were true, even now there would be nothing in existence, because that which does not exist begins to exist only through something already existing. Therefore, if at one time nothing was in existence, it would have been impossible for anything to have begun to exist; and thus even now nothing would be in existence—which is absurd. Therefore, not all beings are merely possible, but there must exist something the existence of which is necessary. But every necessary thing either has its necessity caused by another, or not. Now it is impossible to go on to infinity in necessary things which have their necessity caused by another, as has been already proved in regard to efficient causes. Therefore we cannot but admit the existence of some being having of itself its own necessity, and not receiving it from another, but rather causing in others their necessity. This all men speak of as God.

The *tertia via* can be divided into four stages: first, its starting point, generable and corruptible things that are characterized as possible to be and not to be; second, all that exists cannot be possibles; third, there should, then, be something necessary either *per se* or *per aliud*; fourth, necessary being cannot be simply being necessary *per aliud*. Hence there exists something necessary *per se*.

The starting point of the *via* is in generable and corruptible things that are called *possibile esse et non esse*. I want to make two remarks about the starting point. First, in *SCG* I.15, *Amplius*, the phrase *possibile esse et non esse* has a metaphysical sense. Aquinas remarks: "We find in the world, furthermore, certain beings, those namely that are subject to generation and corruption, which can be and not be [*possibilia esse et non esse*]. But what can be has a cause because, since it is equally related to two contraries, namely being and non-being [*esse et non esse*], it must be owing to some cause that being accrues to it." This text shows that Aquinas can take the *esse* in the phrase *possibile esse et non esse* and understand it as more than just an infinitive. *Esse* can designate Aquinas's ultimate metaphysical principle. Because I have argued that

---

11. This translation omits *semper esse*, which is found in some manuscripts. The paleographical evidence undoubtedly favors the deletion. In the Vaticanus manuscript, which was officially authorized by the University of Paris, the *semper* occurs in the margin and the hand indicates that it is from the fourteenth century. For a list of those Thomists who delete the *semper* and those who do not, see Toshiyuki Miyakawa, "The Value and the Meaning of the *Tertia Via* of St. Thomas Aquinas," *Aquinas* 6, no. 2 (1963): 258n35. For a list of the manuscripts that do not include it, see Thomas C. O'Brien, *Metaphysics and the Existence of God* (Washington, D.C.: Thomist Press, 1960), 226–27n83.

Aquinas's philosophical approach to God is metaphysical, the metaphysical interpretation of *possibile esse et non esse* should be operative also in the *tertia via*. In the categories of the *De Ente*, the phrase designates that thing as absolutely considered. Elsewhere Aquinas calls it the absolutely possible.[12]

It is true that the phrase *possibile esse et non esse* is Aristotelian.[13] Aristotle used it to designate generable and corruptible things understood as matter/form composites. The composite can be and not be because the matter can have or not have the form. As *SCG* I.15 shows, Aquinas broadens this physical understanding of the possible. Metaphysically speaking, what can be and not be are not only generables and corruptibles but the universe and separate substances. On the other hand, Aquinas can accommodate Aristotle's limited physical sense of the possible. As I have emphasized, Aquinas does not understand the priority of *esse* to the detriment of other causal factors. Hence, form is called a *principium essendi*. This division makes the possible ambiguous between the physically and metaphysically possible and allows the philosopher to characterize something as both physically and metaphysically possible. Such is, in my opinion, the starting point of the *tertia via*. It also produces a similar ambiguity for the necessary. The drama of the *tertia via* will consist in how Aquinas will identify the physically necessary, that is, the ungenerable and incorruptible, with the metaphysically possible.

My second remark is that the *tertia via* need not be employing the intellect's two operations to establish the accidentality of *esse*. Rather, the generable and corruptible character of the sensible existent reveals this accidentality. This fact allows one to know that their *esse* is accidental. Yet far from usurping the role of the intellect's two acts, the approach from generable and corruptible things must be considered as presuming it. The reason for the presumption is that many philosophers have studied generation and corruption and have seen only the acquisition and loss of substantial form. For them talk of generable and corruptible things acquiring and losing existence is imprecise, or second-order talk, that is logically reducible to more accurate first-order talk of the matter acquiring or losing substantial form. Aquinas

---

12. For the texts and a discussion of the absolutely possible, see above, chapter 2, "Absolute Consideration and Modality," and also John F. X. Knasas, "Making Sense of the *Tertia Via*," *The New Scholasticism* 54, no. 4 (1980): 492–95.

13. For the phrase's Aristotelian lineage, see Dermot O'Donaghue, "An Analysis of the *Tertia Via* of St. Thomas Aquinas," *The Irish Theological Quarterly* 20 (1953): 131–40.

understands both generation and corruption to involve not only the first order *actus* of *forma* but also the first order *actus* of *esse*. What saves Aquinas's view from arbitrariness?

Before considering generation and corruption, Aquinas is already familiar with the *esse* of things. The intellect's two acts exercised on the multiplicity of real and cognitional existents acquaints Aquinas with the *esse* of a thing. Once aware of *esse*, however, one can surmise that if *esse* belonged to the nature of a thing, that is, *esse* was not intellectually accidental to but intellectually merged with the thing, then what that thing is would be what *esse* is. What is the nature of *esse*? When Aquinas performed this intellectual exercise in the fourth chapter of *De Ente*, he concluded that a thing hypothetically assumed to be intellectually merged with its *esse* is unique, a one and only. But elsewhere other implications are drawn. As I noted when discussing Kenny in chapter 4, Aquinas calls the nature of *esse* the "perfectio essendi" and "esse commune." He then remarks: "all the perfections of all things pertain to the perfection of being [*de perfectio essendi*]; for things are perfect precisely so far as they have being [*esse*] after some fashion."[14] Aquinas rightfully concludes that as subsistent existence, God contains the perfections of all things. For present purposes, it is necessary to catch only the connection between an infinite being and a being whose *esse* is not accidental. Such being is also immutable, because it can acquire and lose something only by ceasing to be infinite.[15]

In the wake of these reflections comes the realization that any changeable being must have accidental *esse*. No need exists to run the changeable existent through the intellect's two acts. Simply to know that the existent is changeable is to know that the existent is a thing with accidental *esse*. Generability and corruptibility are surefire signs of the accidentality of *esse*. The *tertia via* appears to take the contingency approach to accidental *esse*.

The thesis of the second stage is that the sum total of reality cannot be possibles. Because at some time the possible is not, total possibility would mean that at some time nothing was in reality. This entails the absurdity that nothing would be now. This portion of the *via* has proved a stumbling block to most commentators. Some wonder whether what can cease to exist must

---

14. *ST* I, q. 4, a. 2, co. (trans. Pegis, 1:39).
15. See the third proof at *ST* I, q. 9, a. 1, co.

cease. Others wonder if the *via* commits the fallacy of composition in asserting that the time each possible is not must be the same for all. Still others wonder if "nihil in rebus" is the inevitable outcome because the corruption of one thing is the generation of another.[16]

A metaphysical interpretation in which the priority of the possible's *esse* is focused upon makes the second stage more intelligible. *Esse* so considered is manifestly dependent upon something other than the generable and corruptible thing. Without that other thing, the possible would not exist. The "at some time is not" phrase would simply be referring to the absence of a cause without which the possible would not exist. The "at some time is not" is when the cause is not present. *Quandoque* need not be taken temporally. The use of *quando* to specify conditions or requirements is not foreign to the works of Aquinas. For instance, Aquinas says that the faith of the believer is directed to the true presence of the body of Christ under the appearances of sensible bread "quando recte fuerit consecratum."[17] In another text Aquinas says that fraternal correction is not good "quando est impeditive finis, scilicet emendations fratris."[18] In both instances, *quando* is specifying conditions under which Aquinas wants his assertion to have sense. It is this use of *quando* that is in the *tertia via*. The time at which the possible does not exist is when it does not have a cause of its *esse*. Obviously, if all things were possible in this sense, there would be nothing in reality. No fallacy of composition is involved.

So, if the priority of *esse* is made the focus of the reasoning, then *esse* needs a cause without which the possible is existence-neutral. This reflection is essentially the *De Ente* reasoning that we studied earlier. Hence, the *tertia via* would quickly reach a necessary being in the sense of subsistent *esse*. Yet another metaphysician might argue that as the act *of the possible*, the *esse* is in a way dependent upon the possible. This remark is opening up the second pathway to subsistent *esse* from the *ratio entis*. As it enlists natural philosophy reflections on the generable and corruptible thing, this pathway encounters beings that are not generable and corruptible. As we saw in the second way

16. For a survey of opinions on these three issues, see Knasas, "Making Sense," 476–90.
17. *ST* II-II, q. 1, a. 3, ad 4.
18. *ST* II-II, q. 33, a. 6, ad 3. For other instances, see references (2) (b) under *quando* in *A Lexicon of St. Thomas Aquinas*, compiled by R. J. Deferrari et al. (Washington, D.C.: The Catholic University of America Press, 1948), 924.

of *SCG*, this second pathway leads to an ungenerable body as the subject for the continuous motion required to explain the unending series of terrestrial generations. It also includes movers of the celestial spheres that are possibly separate substances. Such necessary beings are obviously not God. To show that philosophers who reason in this second way do not reach a cause of *esse* unreduced to subsistent *esse*, Aquinas includes a fourth stage to his *tertia via*. Needless to say, if this second approach to *esse* is taken, the first half of the *via* would be rewritten. Gone would be the metaphysical talk of "quandoque non est" and "nihil in rebus." This talk was possible because the focus was on the priority of *esse* to generable and corruptible substances.

The fourth stage of the *tertia via* is, then, demonstrating why a hypothesis of only possibles and necessary beings that are not subsistent *esse* is not metaphysically feasible. The fourth stage references the *secunda via* for the impossibility of an infinite regress of efficient causes. With this concern for efficient causes goes the reasoning of the *De Ente* with its emphasis on the priority of *esse*. Hence, the envisaged regress is the fantastic one in which some existence-neutral nature is understood to be a direct cause of another's *esse*. Any necessary being short of subsistent *esse* will by its prior *esse* be immediately reduced to subsistent *esse*. As in the *De Ente*, only the briefest reflection indicates the futility of accounting for a thing's *esse* by another thing, even an infinity of them, with *esse* accidental and prior. Again, Aquinas can begin the second path and at any time opt out of it by referring to the priority of the *esse* to the thing about which he is speaking.

Yet the crucial issue at the fourth stage of the *tertia via* is the intelligible cue for applying the *De Ente* reasoning to the ungenerable and incorruptible beings encountered in the second causal path out of accidental *esse*. I explained that at stage one the cue was generability and corruptibility. Obviously that fails to characterize the celestial spheres and their movers reached in the second path. These beings would be necessary being not yet called *per aliud*. How does the accidentality of their *esse* become manifest to the philosopher? Two possible ways occur to me. First, if one returns to *De Ente*, chap. 4, one will recall Aquinas's argument that a thing intelligibly one with its *esse* is necessarily singular, a one and only. The plurality of the spheres and their movers would, then, be an indication that they are not intelligibly one with their *esse*. In this way things physically necessary would be understood as metaphysically possible and so targets for the *De Ente* reasoning. Second, if subsistent *esse* is (as mentioned) infinite, then the finitude of these physically necessary beings would again indicate the accidental status of their *esse*. Hence, in either of these ways, Aquinas can reduce necessary beings to the metaphysically necessary *per se* understood as subsistent *esse*.[19]

Finally, it might be noted that that the *tertia via* mentions the necessary *per aliud* without any mention of the eternity of motion. Does this mean that for Aquinas the eternity of motion is not a required stage in the argument for a necessary being? In other words, does the *tertia via* lend credence to the positions of Smith, Ashley, and Quinn? Not necessarily. The supposition of the eternity of motion could be implicit in the mention of the necessary *per aliud*. Because the *via* begins from corruptible things, the answer to these questions has to be reduced to what is implied by that starting point when considered by the natural philosopher. I have argued that there is no way the natural philosopher can consider the conditions for *ens mobile* without concluding to the eternity of motion. When those considerations are taken up by the metaphysician, the conclusion of motion's eternity becomes a supposition for further considerations.

So my conclusion is that though, unlike the *secunda via* of *SCG*, the *tertia via* does not explicitly mention the horizontal regress of generated things that is reduced to an eternal first physical cause and then to an intellectual mover, the regress is implied in the *tertia via*. The equivocal cause of the species itself is an implication of the eternity of the species. Aquinas would be granting this implication to show that it does not derail reasoning for the necessary *per se* in the sense of subsistent *esse*.

---

19. As metaphysically necessary, subsistent *esse* would be understood as a logically necessary being. On logically necessary being in Aquinas's metaphysics, see above, chapter 4, "Anthony Kenny: the Fatal Flaw in the Man/Phoenix Argument." Interestingly, even though Bruce Reichenbach employs Aquinas's *De Ente* reasoning for a first cause, Reichenbach avoids characterizing the first cause as logically necessary: "Thus, the necessity involved in the cosmological argument is not logical necessity, but what we have called conditional necessity." Reichenbach, *The Cosmological Argument*, 116. There is no accommodation of Aquinas's claim that "God exists" is a self-evident proposition in itself.

The *quarta via*

The fourth way is taken from the gradation to be found in things [*ex gradibus qui in rebus inveniuntur*]. Among beings there are some more and some less good, true, noble, and the like. But more and less are predicated of different things according as they resemble in their different ways something which is the maximum [*ad aliquid quod maxime est*], as a thing is said to be hotter according as it more nearly resembles that which is hottest; so that there is something which is truest, something best, something noblest, and consequently, something which is most being, for those things that are greatest in truth are greatest in being, as it is written in *Metaph.* ii. Now the maximum in any genus is the cause of all in that genus, as fire, which is the maximum of heat, is the cause of all hot things, as is said in the same book. Therefore there must also be something which is to all beings the cause of their being, goodness, and every other perfection [*causa esse et bonitatis et cuiuslibet perfectionis*]; and this we call God.

The *quarta via* moves quickly from things graded according to goodness, truth, and nobility (*nobile*), or perfection, to a greatest being (*maxime ens*).[20] I divide the *via* into two stages. The first stage compares graded things to a maximum. The second stage affirms that the maximum is the cause of graded things.

The starting point of the first stage is wide open to Aquinas's metaphysics. As mentioned in the gloss of the *prima* and *tertia viae*, the metaphysician can fantasize that if judgmentally grasped *esse* were not *praeter essentiam*, it would render the essence both infinite and immobile. Hence, in the *tertia via*, generation and corruption are obvious and sure indications of accidental *esse*. The *quarta via* is reaching accidental *esse* in virtue of the infinite character of non-accidental *esse*. When that thought is compared to beings graded in perfection, it reveals graded beings to be things with *esse*. Just as accidental *esse* allows things able to be and not to be, so too it allows finite beings. In their turn, finite beings allow a gradation of beings. Hence, gradation and the finitude that accompanies gradation are surefire signs of accidental *esse*.

The second stage takes off from this view of graded things with their *esse*. Because accidental *esse* must be reduced to pure, or subsistent, *esse*, the max-

---

20. In *ST* I, q. 4, a. 2, co., *nobilitas* is used for *perfectio*: "Dicendum quod in Deo sunt perfections omnium rerum. Unde et dicitur universaliter perfectus, quia 'non deest ei aliqua nobilitas quae inveniatur in aliquot genere,' ut dicit Commentator."

imum entertained in thought in the first stage is concluded to be a reality in the second stage. Here, the reasoning of the *De Ente*, chap. 4, from the priority of *esse* is presumed. So if the maximum being is pure *esse*, is there any wonder why Aquinas says that "we" call it God?

This interpretation obviates the standard problem with the *quarta via*. The standard problem is how gradation implies not just an ideal but something real. All would admit that from gradation, our minds can go on to form the thought of an ideal. For example, the idea of the best car, musical performance, human life. But these ideas can be frustratingly unrealized. So how can Aquinas claim that the more and less imply a real maximum? In my opinion, the objection is reading the *quarta via* backwards. The ideal of truth and goodness and nobility is the thought of subsistent *esse* and that implies that things graded in these respects have *esse* rather than are it. But as accidental, the *esse* is reduced to subsistent *esse* as to its proper cause. Another way of stating my reply is this. The first stage does not assert the existence of the maximum.[21] It is asserting the *praeter essentiam* status of the *esse* of the graded. One's thought of subsistent *esse* as infinite allows that. Only in the second stage is the reality of the maximum asserted. The basis for the assertion is the argument from accidental *esse* as efficiently caused.[22]

Also, as moving from the top down in its first stage, the *via* is not necessarily Platonic. As I mentioned, the ideal of subsistent *esse* in the first stage is something that the metaphysician fantasizes based upon the judgmentally grasped individual *esse*s of sensible things. The ideal here is built up *a posteriori* and so is unlike a Platonic innate and *a priori* form.

---

21. Wippel, *Metaphysical Thought of Thomas Aquinas*, 472, disagrees: "The first stage of the argument concludes to the existence of something which is truest and best and noblest and hence being in the maximum degree." Is it necessary to take Aquinas's words "ad aliquid quod maxime est" as referring to a real existent? It does not seem necessary to me. The words could refer to the thought of something intelligibly one with its *esse*. As mentioned, Aquinas entertains such a thought in the *De Ente* to conclude that subsistent *esse* is unique and so is intelligibly distinct from the thing in everything else. Here in the *quarta via* Aquinas would be entertaining the thought of subsistent *esse* as infinite and concluding that in a graded thing *esse* is at least intelligibly distinct from the thing.

22. For example, the *De Ente* reasoning described on pp. 59–63.

The *quinta via*

The fifth way is taken from the governance of the world. We see that things which lack knowledge, such as natural bodies, act for an end, and this is evident from their acting always, or nearly always, in the same way, so as to obtain the best result. Hence it is plain that they achieve their end, not fortuitously, but designedly. Now whatever lacks knowledge cannot move towards an end, unless it be directed by some being endowed with knowledge and intelligence; as the arrow is directed by the archer. Therefore some intelligent being exists by whom all natural things are directed to their end; and this being we call God.

The *quinta via* has four stages: first, the starting point, directed motion in things lacking knowledge; second, the evidence for the starting point; third, the proposition that things lacking knowledge act for an end only in virtue of something possessing knowledge of the end; fourth, an intelligence causing the directed motion in all natural things. In usual fashion, Aquinas says that we all call this intelligence God.

The starting point of the *quinta via* is a more particular appreciation of the starting point of the *prima via*. Both begin from existing motion, but the *quinta via* deals with the existing motion *as directed, as for a goal or end*. Metaphysically speaking, the starting points of both *viae* contain accidental *esse*. Yet, the focus of the *quinta via* is the accidental *esse* of motion considered as ordered or directed in nonknowing things. This relation between the broader focus of the *prima via* and the narrower focus of the *quinta via* should still enable us to use the previous gloss of the *prima via* as the hermeneutical, or interpretative, context for the *quinta via*. My subsequent remarks will do that.

The starting point of the *quinta via* of the *Summa* is often contrasted with the starting point of the *quinta via* of *SCG*. The difference is that the latter begins from design while the former begins from directed motion. But as I noted, to begin from design, for example the proportion in the flour, is to be led to motion for that end. Moreover, though the starting point of the *quinta via* in the *Summa* is directed motion, what is cognitively prior, as Aquinas says, is the regular occurrence of a determination. Hence, the only difference I see is that in *SCG* Aquinas spends more time on this cue for directed motion.

Directed motion in nonknowers is not obvious. As noted in the *prima via*, motion itself may be immediately obvious. Its directedness requires discernment. I recall for the reader the steps that I mentioned in the *SCG* version. First is some determination in a subject. It could be a particular place to which fish or birds go. Second, as an attribute, or accident, the determination is dependent. Third, the determination is not completely dependent upon its subject *qua* subject. As determination-neutral, the subject *qua* subject cannot be a complete explainer of the determination. Hence, fourth, the determination also depends upon something else. A causality exists for the presence of the determination. The causality will be the directed motion if the determination is observed to be regular. The cause of the directed motion could be our original subject in some other respect than subject. For example, the cause could be the fish and birds as they swim and fly to their migratory home. On the other hand, that cause of the directed motion could be another thing as it was in the case of the proportion in the flour.

In stage three Aquinas identifies the ultimate cause of directed motion to be an intellectual subject. He says that "whatever lacks knowledge cannot move towards an end, unless it be directed by some being endowed with knowledge and intelligence." Though stated just by itself, the proposition is not intended to be self-evident.[23] First, the proposition can be the conclusion of a lengthy demonstration. That demonstration is an application of the second causal path from the *esse* of an accident. The nature for which the directed motion is a property would be reduced to the first physical cause that could have a subsisting form as its mover. Because of its immateriality, the subsisting form would be known to be an intelligence.[24] Subsistent existence, reached either as an efficient or as a final cause of that intelligence, would be known as an intelligence for the same reasoning.

A simpler demonstration would be from the priority of the *esse* of the directed motion. As I explained in chapter 7 when working out the first causal path from the *esse* of an accident, subsistent existence would quickly emerge as the logical conclusion for that *esse*.

23. As Anthony Kenny observes, for Aquinas intellectual agents act for ends but their behavior is irregular; see his *The Five Ways*, 110 and 119. Given the basis for the starting point of the *quinta via* in something regular, a first intellect appears problematic. In comment, I would remark that Aquinas's thesis about intellectual behavior would not prohibit an intelligence to cause other things to act regularly.

24. For immateriality as the condition for intellection, see *ST* I, q. 14, a. 1, co.

In stage four, Aquinas returns to directed motion in natural things. In virtue of stage three, he concludes that an intelligent being directs all natural things to their end and that this intelligent being is God. Noteworthy here is that Aquinas does not mention a disjunction. In the *prima via* he did. Hence, one can assume that Aquinas has been thinking in terms of the priority of the *esse* of directed motion to the directed motion itself. That priority would allow immediate access to the conclusion that God exists. To understand how the metaphysical interpretation would allow the *quinta via* to reach not only God but to reach God as intelligent the above second approach to stage three should be recalled. Understood in a metaphysical vein, the *quinta via* easily reaches an intelligence that all men, including the Christian Aquinas, call God.

I would like to conclude with some remarks on Kenny's analysis of the *quinta via*. Kenny studies five arguments in Aquinas for the thesis that every agent acts for an end. Right from the start this is confusing to a reader because the *quinta via* does not use this proposition as a premise. It occurs in the *via* but as the conclusion. Kenny is beginning at the wrong end of things, and this error will have consequences.

Of the five arguments the fifth is the one most relevant for critiquing my above interpretation of the *quinta via*. Aquinas reasons that in nature we find what is best happening always or for the most part. Hence, the occurrence of the best cannot be by chance but by intention. Kenny raises two objections. First, Aquinas obviously wants to fatten up his observation of a regular occurrence by claiming that the occurrence is not just regular but for the best. Kenny wonders what Aquinas could mean. Is it the best for the individual thing or best for the whole in which the individual exists? He thinks the most probable reading is that the regular occurrence is best for the individual.[25] The probable reading, however, would produce an intelligence for each regular occurrence and so contradict the conclusion of the *via* that there is a single intelligence.[26]

In comment, Kenny's quantifier shift criticism has some basis if Aquinas is following the second path from the *esse* of some determination. The second

---

25. This interpretative claim seems right. At *SCG* III.3, *Adhuc. Quod*, Aquinas mentions the examples of fruit having the determination of being under the leaves and so protected and the softer organs of the animal being interior and so protected.
26. Kenny, *The Five Ways*, 96.

path includes a stage at which a multiplicity of ungenerable celestial movers are themselves moved by separate intelligences. Aquinas reduces this multiplicity to one by presenting the necessarily unique subsistent existence as the only final cause capable of transfixing these intelligences. On the other hand, if Aquinas focuses on the priority of the *esse* of the regular and beneficial determination, then he can go immediately to subsistent existence which, as the *De Ente* reasoning illustrated, can be known as unique even while still a possibility.

Secondly, Kenny argues at length against identifying a natural inclination with intention or teleology. This claim seems to be the heart of his critique of the *quinta via*. Aquinas's *quinta via* fails because Aquinas is working with a dichotomy. In fact the logic is a trichotomy.[27] The options for what is behind the regular occurrence of the best are not just chance or teleology. Another option is that the cause is something acting from a natural tendency.

For the Thomist, the obvious question is why Kenny opposes teleological action and action of natural tendency. To answer that question a reader must turn to earlier comments by Kenny. These are found in his critique of Aquinas's first of the five arguments that every agent acts for an end. In this first argument Aquinas appeals to the observation that every natural agent appears to act for something definite. For example, fire heats and ice cools.

Kenny's opening comment is that there is no deep ontology to the fire and ice examples. They are linguistic phenomena relying on connecting an adjective with a verb. They are really saying that what is cool (ice) cools and that what is hot (fire) heats.[28] Kenny admits that a Thomist may want to change the example to cooled water turning to ice and not to coal. Kenny objects that it is odd to use this new example to illustrate action for a goal or teleology. Water is not aiming at freezing.

In comment, I do not think that a Thomist would want to use this new example at all. Of course, the water is not aiming at freezing because in this case the water is a patient not an agent. The water is freezing into ice or snow because of a definite proportion in it and in the atmosphere. As determinations, these proportions need an explanation. The explanation is not in the water *qua* subject of the proportion nor in the water in some other respect.

27. Ibid., 103.
28. Ibid., 100.

The explainer is something else and is the agent. If the proportion is regular, for example, at certain times of every year, then the determination is attributed to intention and not to chance. Kenny shows no awareness of the thing/accident framework of our *De Ente* text. If the determination is regular, then the determination as dependent upon the agent is correctly characterized as the aimed for goal and so enables Aquinas to conclude to intentionality or teleology even among natural things. Kenny misses this because he is beginning with natural agents and not concluding to them from some effect.

Kenny then moves to cases in which the supposed end is not an action but a product.[29] For example, to open a door is to bring it about that the door is opened. Does this consideration of actions lead back to teleology? Kenny says it would lead back if we knew how to distinguish between saying: "Some things have a natural tendency to perform actions specified by certain ends" versus "Some things have a tendency to perform actions for the sake of certain ends." The second has teleology, the first does not. So, if something, even a regular occurrence, results from a natural tendency, or a concatenation of natural tendencies, we cannot claim teleology. It could just be mechanism. This use of mechanism to denote the above first description is, in my opinion, odd. I would have thought that mechanism involved bodies without natural tendencies. But must we remain in the dark about whether a natural tendency is for an end?

Not if we follow Aquinas's procedure in the *quinta via*. Aquinas does not begin with agents. Kenny has the argument backwards. The possibility of natural tendency comes up in relation to a definite product, for example, a certain proportion in the ingredients of the cake or in ingredients of the snow. As an accident, the proportion needs something else other than its subject *qua* subject. If the proportion is noted to be regular, we have the basis for claiming that the something causing it is intending it. So, if, as Kenny claims, an agent's action is teleological only if the agent's action has a definite effect, then teleological action is what we have in the *quinta via*. We have that kind of action because it is what we need to account for the definite effect of some regularity. The important thing is not to start with agents and their actions, as Kenny does, but with something that will be understood as an effect of them.

29. Ibid., 101.

The *via* of *Compendium Theologiae* I.3

Regarding the unity of the divine essence, we must first believe that God exists. This is a truth clearly known by reason. We observe that all things that move are moved by other things, the lower by the higher. The elements are moved by heavenly bodies; and among the elements themselves, the stronger moves the weaker; and even among the heavenly bodies, the lower are set in motion by the higher. This process cannot be traced back into infinity. For everything that is moved by another is a sort of instrument of the first mover. Therefore, if a first mover is lacking, all things that move will be instruments. But if the series of movers and things moved is infinite, there can be no first mover. In such a case, these infinitely many movers and things moved will all be instruments. But even the unlearned perceive how ridiculous it is to suppose that instruments are moved, unless they are set in motion by some principal agent. This would be like fancying that, when a chest or a bed is being built, the saw or the hatchet performs its functions without the carpenter. Accordingly there must be a first mover that is above all the rest; and this being we call God.[30]

Aquinas prefaces the issue of God's existence by declaring it to be conspicuous by reason. This is not much of an admission. It is not clear that Aquinas intends "reason" to be the science of metaphysics or of physics or even philosophy. If the reader of the first book of the *Compendium* is patient, however, the reader will eventually encounter chap. 36, wherein Aquinas describes the truths about God that he has been considering as truths that have been subtly discussed by a number of pagan philosophers, though they made some errors about them and came to these truths about God only after a long time and with great effort. Aquinas then goes on to mention another part of the content of Christian revelation. This part contains truths above the ability of philosophers to know. In the context of this second kind of revealed truth, Aquinas locates the doctrine of the Trinity. In my opinion, no reader can fail to notice in these points from chap. 36 the framework of the opening chapters of *SCG* I. As I noted above in chapters 6 and 8, these opening chapters also indicate that Aquinas holds that the philosopher can demonstrate the first kind of truth about God in metaphysics. Hence, a reader of the *Compendium* will sooner or later understand that Aquinas is proceeding metaphysically in chap. 3.

With the *viae* from motion in *SCG* in mind, the reader of the *Compendi-*

---

30. Aquinas, *Compendium of Theology*, trans. Cyril Vollert (St. Louis, Mo.: Herder, 1947), 9.

um will notice an uncanny resemblance to what I called the second path from *esse* followed in the second *via* of *SCG*. The resemblances include the reference to the generable and corruptible elements and the higher substances that are the heavenly bodies. Nevertheless, the *Compendium* fails to mention the eternity of motion that was necessary to conclude that the heavenly bodies were ungenerable and incorruptible. Evidently the second path is not being followed to that length. Another indication of a mitigated trip on the second path is the *Compendium* reaches the first mover, not as a final cause, but as an agent, or efficient cause.

In the *Compendium*, then, Aquinas seems to bring in the heavens as present movers of some motions among the elements. For example, the moon produces the tides and the sun heats the air. As such movers, the heavens are similar to the man who moves the stick that moves the rock, the fire that alters the wood, or the carpenter that moves the tools. This interpretation would locate the *via* of the *Compendium* as an independent presentation of the second disjunction followed in the *prima via* of *SCG* and *ST*.

Hence, the interpretation of the *Compendium* would be as follows. As the act of some motion, the *esse* of the motion would in some measure depend upon it and upon any conditions for the motion. As an accident, motion would have conditions. At the least the motion requires a subject. But the requirement cannot be total. The potential character of the subject *qua* subject indicates to the philosopher that the imperfect act of motion cannot be totally dependent upon the subject *qua* subject. A further requirement, then, is either the subject in some other respect or another subject. This disjunction expresses the *aliud* in the proposition, "Omne quod moveatur ab alio movetur." This disjunctive requirement expresses the actuality that motion requires and which is used to deny the possibility of an infinite regress of movers. An infinite regress contains no *aliud* that is actual.

Furthermore, we know in a particular case that the identity of the *aliud* is some other subject by experiencing the first subject as not always in motion. Finally, the status of the other subject as a *causa in esse*, that is, as a sustainer of the first subject's accident of motion, would be indicated by its temporal conjunction with the first subject as moving. Hence, we arrive at a different subject that satisfies the *aliud* requirement in the first way. In other words, in some way it causes its own motion.

By borrowing from the reflections of natural philosophy, the elaboration of the second path from the *esse* of motion is still short of God. As Kenny observed, we could be at the man who moves the stick that moves the rock. Likewise, our consideration could be at the moon that moves the tides or the sun that heats the air. Aquinas would reduce all these movers to God by bringing in a consideration of the priority of their substantial *esse*. This actualizer of these finite movers is certainly a condition for the motion and so allows subsistent existence to be called a mover.

Another possible interpretation of this final moment in the *Compendium* argument is that the metaphysician focuses upon the priority of the *esse* of the motion that the nature of the finite mover in some way causes. In other words, the first path in the *prima via* of *SCG* and *ST* may be initiated at that point. This interpretation would have in the *Compendium* both paths from the *esse* of some sensible motion, but it would have them in reverse order. Such a reversal would explain the *Compendium*'s lack of the disjunctive approach followed in both *Summae*.

[10]

Other Possible *viae*

The titular "other possible *viae*" of this chapter refer to proofs for God's existence that are a portion of a larger proof for something else. As mentioned, in his reckoning Gilson avoided counting these subproofs as proofs for God's existence. Gilson considered as genuine *viae* only those arguments specifically designed to answer the question "Does God exist?" I pointed out that perhaps Gilson's reluctance to count the *De Ente* reasoning as a God proof was his inability to present Aquinas's admittedly philosophical thesis of *esse* in a philosophical way. This inability of Gilson concerned how to interpret the mind's second operation so that it presented the existence of the essence as more than the fact, or realization, of the essence. Others, however, are more confident about doing that, and so see no need to avoid the *De Ente* reasoning when it is brought up as an argument for other purposes.

My thesis here is that Aquinas's explicitly professed metaphysical approach to God is reflected in these other *viae*. This reflection is illustrated by the other *viae* being variations of the *De Ente* reasoning. These other *viae* do not constitute exceptions to the approach to God from accidental *esse* to subsistent *esse*. My reader should especially note, however, that by the "*De Ente* reasoning" I do not mean the simplified version found in that text. In this chapter I mean what I elaborated as the robust version of Aquinas's reflections from judgmentally grasped existence. Those reflections break out into two paths from *esse* depending upon whether one emphasizes the priority of *esse*, from which one can go immediately to God, or whether one emphasizes some dependency of the *esse* upon the nature that it actuates, from which one goes more circuitously to God.

In I Sent. III, *divisio primae partis textus*

Here Aquinas is commenting on four arguments for God's unicity given by Peter Lombard. Aquinas glosses them as versions of the three arguments by which Dionysius comes to God from creatures. Dionysius's three ways are (1) from causality, (2) from removal of imperfection, and (3) from eminence. Aquinas gives two versions of Dionysius's third way, and so a total of four arguments are presented. Importantly, right away Aquinas situates the arguments within his metaphysics by saying that the reason that we come to God from creatures is that the *esse* of creatures is from another: *ratio hujus est, quia esse creaturae est ab altero*.

The first way from causality states that everything that has its *esse ex nihilo* has its *esse* from another. Such a situation is true of every creature. The given reason is that every creature is imperfect and potential. Hence, this *aliud* from which creatures have *esse* is both one and God.[1]

I take the reference to having *esse ex nihilo* as a reference to the *esse* that a thing is judged to have after the thing's absolute consideration reveals that the thing "abstrahit a quolibet esse."[2] In the case of this first argument, however, the status of the thing as totally existence-neutral is not attained by the first intellectual operation. Aquinas's given reason for the *ex nihilo* talk is that all creatures are imperfect and potential. This approach indicates a previous use of the metaphysical application of the *duplex operatio*. That previous use provides the notions of thing and *esse* with which the philosopher can fantasize a merging of the two notions. The merge reveals something not only necessarily unique but something that is necessarily infinite and immutable.

---

1. "It is necessary that everything that has existence from nothing [*habet esse ex nihilo*] is from another from which its existence will flow. But all creatures have existence from nothing which is manifested from their imperfection and potentiality [*ex earum imperfectione et potentialitate*]. Therefore it is necessary that they are from some one first thing and this is God."

2. In his comments on the text, Wippel (*Metaphysical Thought of Aquinas*, 401–2) does not acknowledge my absolute consideration reading of *nihilo*. Hence, according to Wippel, *ex nihilo* has either a temporal sense, "after nothing," or a creation sense, "from no preexisting subject." In his opinion, both readings have problems.

Hence, wherever we find finitude and mutability, we have a surefire sign that the item is at least intelligibly distinct from its existence. This line of thinking is what Aquinas seems to follow here.[3]

If I am correct, then the first *via* is deep into the *De Ente* reasoning. Aquinas seems to call upon the previously discussed conclusion of the *De Ente* that a thing whose *esse* is intelligibly merged with it is necessarily one. Hence, in everything else they are distinct. This reasoning seems to underwrite Aquinas's stark division of God and creatures in the second *via*.

The second *via* is characterized as the way from the removal of imperfection. Its major premise is that beyond the imperfect there is the perfect. The *via* goes on to instantiate the imperfect firstly in a body, as a body is finite in dimensions and is mobile, and secondly in a soul and angel, as they are mutable also. The *Item* in the text indicates a possible disjunction such that from a finite body we go immediately to a perfect incorporeal that is God, or we can proceed mediately through mobile incorporeals.[4]

In my opinion the reference to souls and angels indicates that the body below them is the first physical cause that Aquinas thought might be identified with the celestial sphere cosmology of the time. As will be recalled in my presentation of the robust version of the *De Ente* reasoning, Aquinas admitted that the intellectual principle necessary to be the condition for the eternal motion of the first physical cause could be either an intellectual soul or a separate intelligence. Hence, in this portion the second *via* would be dealing with the *esse* of the supposed eternal motion of the heavenly body. It would be progressing in virtue of metaphysical reflections on intellectual psychology and the conditions necessary to transfix the will of a created intelligence. I described these conditions in chapter 7. In this way that portion of the *via* would reach a perfect incorporeal that is subsistent *esse* and so be identifiable with Aquinas's Christian God.

---

3. Wippel suggests something similar to explain Aquinas's claim that imperfect and mutable things have their being from another (ibid., 402n7). Because Aquinas himself does not mention this approach in the text, however, Wippel uses the omission to call the argument "neither a finished nor a fully satisfying proof" (402).

4. "Beyond every imperfect thing there is necessary to exist some perfect thing to which no imperfection is admitted. But body is imperfect because it is terminated and finite by its dimensions and is mobile. Therefore beyond body there is necessary to exist something that is not a body. Also [*Item*], every incorporeal is mutable of its nature and imperfect. Therefore, beyond every mutable species, as souls and angels are, is some incorporeal thing both immobile and wholly perfect, and this is God."

As I mentioned, the second *via* may contain a disjunction. The corporeal with which it begins is itself described as *imperfectum*. If I am correct that Aquinas is speaking of the first physical cause, then "imperfect" cannot mean deficient or lacking what it should have. The sense should mean finite, or not possessing all perfections. This understanding of "imperfect" should cue the reader to remember that the finitude of a thing is a clear sign of the accidentality of *esse*. By emphasizing the priority of the substantial *esse* of the heavenly body, Aquinas could go immediately to subsistent *esse* understood as a perfect incorporeal.

The third way of Dionysius is through eminence. After noting in the second way that there are various grades of imperfection in things, in the third way Aquinas will note various grades of goodness in things so that some things are more eminent than others. In his presentation of Dionysius, Aquinas divides the third way into two. There is eminence in *esse* and in cognition. As will be clear from the third argument, *esse* appears to have the first sense of *esse* mentioned at *In I Sent.*, d. 33, q. 1, a. 1 ad 1—the nature or essense.

In his first version Aquinas argues that we say good and better in relation to an optimum. But among substances we find bodies to be good and spirits to be better. Hence, there exists an optimum by which both are good.[5] As with the second way, the references to body and spirit indicate that Aquinas is dealing with conclusions reached along the second path out of judgmentally grasped existence. Also, once again "body" could stand for a celestial sphere insofar as the sphere is proximate to spirit. Hence, as I explained with the *quarta via*, if the optimum is understood as a hypothetical subsistent *esse*, then things graded in goodness have *esse* as an accident. This status enables both body and spirit to be reduced to an actual cause that is subsistent *esse*.

In the second version, Aquinas interestingly calls attention to another gradation in eminence.[6] In our cognition we find a gradation among the

---

5. "Good and better are said through comparison to best. But in substances we find body good and created spirit better in which nevertheless goodness is not from the thing itself [*bonitas non est a seipso*]. Hence, there is necessary to be some best by which goodness is in both."

6. "In whatever things one is to find more and less of beauty [*magis et minus speciousum*], one is to find some principle of beauty through whose proximity another is called more perfect than another. But we find bodies to be more beautiful by sensible species, and spirits to be more beautiful by intelligible species. Therefore, there is necessary to be something by which both are beautiful, to which the created spirit approaches more."

species of things. By "species" Aquinas seems to be referring to the likeness that our intellect forms subsequent to knowing intelligibles. I mentioned this Thomistic doctrine of formed intentions in chapter 4. In the second version Aquinas finds a gradation of beauty (*speciositas*) among species. The species of spirits are more beautiful than those of bodies. For Aquinas beauty basically consists in a certain radiance or splendor of form that is analogically common both to bodily form and spiritual form.[7] Because *esse* is that act of all form, a hypothetical thing that is *esse* because it is its *esse* should be the principle of beauty (*principium speciositatis*). A gradation of things in eminence should indicate the accidentality of their *esse* and open the way for the application of the *De Ente* reasoning.[8]

In II Sent., d. 1, q. 1, a. 1

In this text, Aquinas gives three arguments that the first principle must be one. The first argument is from the order of the universe and a reader can gloss it using my previous material on the *quinta via* of *SCG* and *ST*. The third argument is from God's immateriality and employs content from the second path from *esse*. It begins the path at the power not in matter that moves the heavens. If this power is envisaged as a diversity, then it must be graded according to being more complete and more in act. Aquinas says, however, that it is necessary to reduce this situation of diversity to complete perfection and to pure act which will be one only.[9]

Aquinas's mention of gradation indicates that he is appealing to the type of reasoning that I discussed in my remarks on the *quarta via* in *SCG* and *ST*. Where complete perfection is understood in terms of subsistent *esse*, even as

---

7. See Armand A. Maurer, *About Beauty: A Thomistic Interpretation* (Houston, Tex.: Center for Thomistic Studies, 1983), 10.

8. What I find intriguing here is the apparent incompatibility between our possessing this gradation in beautiful cognitive species and Aquinas's insistence that we can know that God and the separate substances exist but not know what they are. That our ignorance of the essence of God and separate substances is not so black as to prevent the negative formation of analogical species of their essence, see my above comments on Kenny in chapter 4.

9. "For it is necessary that the cause moving the heaven to be a power not in matter, as it is proved in Phys. 8. In those things which are without matter, there is not able to be diversity except insofar as the nature of one is more complete and existing in act than the nature of the other. Hence, it is necessary that that which comes to the perfection of completion and to the purity of act is one only, by which all that which is mixed of potency is established [*proficiscatur*]."

hypothesized, then graded things indicate accidental *esse*. The *De Ente* reasoning can begin from that point. So in his third argument, Aquinas would not be following the second path to subsistent existence as transfixing final cause of the finite intelligences moving the heavens. By switching to a consideration of the priority of the accidental *esse* of the intelligences, Aquinas would at that point be switching to the first path from *esse*.

What I find especially valuable from q. 1, a. 1 is Aquinas's second argument. Aquinas distinguishes the *esse* of things from their natures on the basis of the *intellectus essentiae* argument that I noted in the *De Ente*. He then uses the distinction to say that things that have *esse* must be from another. Next, under pain of an infinite regress, Aquinas concludes to something whose nature is its *esse*. This first cause must be one because its effect is one. The effect is the nature of entity (*natura entitatis*). The nature of entity is one in all things by analogy.[10]

My comments are as follows. First, the mention of analogy indicates that by the nature of entity Aquinas is speaking of the *ratio entis*. In the *Sentences* commentary, Aquinas describes the *ratio entis* as a commonality in things according to analogy.[11] Also in the commentary, Aquinas affirms that a thing is a being (*ens*) based upon having *esse*.[12] Understandably, the second argument then turns to *esse*. Second, the lines on *esse* do not have to be glossed in terms of the *De Ente*. In their mention of the *intellectus essentiae* argument, the consequent causality of *esse*, the denial of infinite regress, and the affirmation of something that is its *esse*, the lines strikingly repeat the *De Ente* text. Third,

---

10. "For the nature of being [*natura entitatis*] is found in all things, in some more noble [*nobilis*] and in some less. So nevertheless that the natures of things themselves are not this being [*esse*] that they have. Otherwise being would be of the intellection [*de intellectu*] of each quiddity which is false since the quiddity of each thing is able to be intellected not understanding about it whether it is. Therefore it is necessary that from something they have being, and it is necessary to come to something the nature of which is itself its being. Otherwise, one would proceed to infinity. This is what gives being to all. It is not able to be except one, since the nature of entity is of one notion [*unius rationis*] in all according to analogy [*secundum analogiam*]. For unity in the caused requires unity in the *per se* cause."

11. "Such a community [of analogy] is able to be twofold. Either from this that some things participate something one [*aliquid unum*] according to a priority and a posteriority, just as potency and act participate the notion of being [*rationem entis*], and similarly substance and accident." *In I Sent.*, prol., q. 1, a. 2, ad 2.

12. "Just as motion [*motus*] is the act of the mobile insomuch as it is mobile; so too being [*esse*] is the act of the existing thing [*actus existentis*], insomuch as it is a being [*ens*]." *In I Sent.*, d. 19, q. 2, a. 2, co.

the repetition is especially significant for the previously described chapter 2 discussion of how to understand Aquinas's thinking at *De Ente*, chap. 4. The repetition of that thinking here in the commentary on the *Sentences* catches Aquinas going through the *De Ente* reasoning without including its second stage on the unicity of a hypothesized thing whose essence includes its *esse*. The unicity of subsistent *esse* comes up in the present second argument only as a conclusion. The second argument indicates that one can go immediately from the *intellectus essentiae* argument to the argument for subsistent *esse*. In other words, a conceptual distinction suffices for causal reasoning.

De Potentia, q. 3, a. 5, co.

Aquinas devotes the article to the topic of whether there can be something not created by God. Along with *ST* I, q. 44, a. 2, and *SCG* II.37, Aquinas's response is another presentation of his threefold breakdown of the history of philosophy in which the philosophers have come to know the truth little by little and step by step. At the third stage of this history, Plato, Aristotle, and others following came to a consideration of *esse universalis*. *Esse universalis* appears to be the *esse commune* and *esse formale* that I described earlier in my chapter 4 critique of Kenny's assessment of Aquinas on being. As noted, in *SCG* Aquinas understands *esse commune* not as an *a priori* idea but as an *a posteriori* abstraction. It appears to be an intelligible fix on judgmentally grasped instances of *esse*. In the *De Potentia*, Aquinas says that this consideration enabled the third-stage philosophers alone to know a universal cause by which all others come forth in being: "aliquam univeralem causam rerum a qua omnia alia in esse prodirent." To illustrate the thinking at the third stage, Aquinas presents three arguments.

Aquinas characterizes the first argument as from Plato, who posited before all multiplicity something one not only in number but in reality (*in rerum natura*). The major premise of the first argument is that something common in many is caused in the many by some one cause. Aquinas gives a reason for this major premise. Something common to two things cannot belong to them from themselves (*ex seipso*). Each of the two in itself is distinguished from the other. In other words, what is common to many cannot belong to the many *ex se*. For *ex se* each is particular. Aquinas then remarks that *esse* is common (*commune*) to all things which are distinct from one another. Accordingly, things do not have *esse* from themselves (*ex seipsis*) but from some one cause.

How does this first argument reflect the *De Ente* reasoning? First of all, it is not clear that the reasoning proves a cause for *esse* so much as it proves the unicity of this cause. Remember, *esse universalis* is not first for Aquinas. It is not first because like all commonalities it is formed on the basis of data. In the case of *esse universalis* the data are judgmentally grasped existences. Moreover, it was from that data that the *De Ente* reasoning reached a first cause of *esse*. Hence, the first *De Potentia* argument seems to focus on something further in that data—a commonness. The commonness in judgmentally grasped existences also cannot be accounted for by the data *qua* data. Hence, in my opinion, the *De Ente* reasoning is not the logic of the first argument but is presupposed by the first argument as it proceeds to its conclusion of the unicity of the first cause of *esse*. In that respect the strategy of the first argument is similar to the above second argument at *In II Sent.*, d. 1, q. 1, a. 1: "This is what gives *esse* to all things; it is not able to be except one, since the nature of entity [*natura entitatis*] is one notion in all things according to analogy; for unity of the caused requires unity in the *per se* cause."[13]

The second argument comes from Aristotle. As is so often the case, Aquinas begins by stating a general framework. Something found participated according to more and less is from that in which it is found most perfectly. His given reason is that if things from themselves (*ex seipso*) had what is participated, then the participated would be perfectly in all and not according to more or less.

So far Aquinas seems to be speaking only of what is the case in our thought about the more or less. For only next does Aquinas claim that there exists one being which is a most perfect and most true being. Interestingly, Aquinas gives as the reason for his claim the proof that there is some mov-

---

13. Supporting the second *Sentences* commentary argument is the point that natures as such, assumed to be eternal, require a nonunivocal agent. I described that requirement in chapter 7, "Borrowings from Natural Philosophy." Consequently, Aquinas is open to multiplying separate substances beyond the number necessary to move the celestial spheres. At *ST* I, q. 110, a. 1, ad 3, Aquinas argues with past doctors that the species of things—for example, animals, trees, and plants—are governed by angels. In the second argument from the *Sentences* commentary, however, there would be no need to assume the eternity of the world. The transcendental character of the *natura entitatis* would suffice to conclude to the nonunivocal nature of its cause.

er wholly immobile and most perfect. Aquinas says that this is the proof of Aristotle and the reference provided directs the reader to Aristotle's proof at *Metaphysics* II.2, 994a7–10, for a first final cause.

This is an interesting twist because one would think that Aquinas could easily slip into the *De Ente* reasoning for a first efficient cause from the accidentality and priority of *esse* insofar as he can identify the perfect with subsistent *esse* and so identify the imperfect and graded with *esse* in a nonsubsistent, or accidental, configuration. I understood him to do that in my interpretations of the *quarta via* in *SCG* and *ST*. Instead Aquinas turns to the second path out of the *esse* of motion and to its conclusion of God as a wholly immobile and most perfect mover in the vein of a final cause. It is this final cause that then assumes the identity of the most perfect thing from which things receive their *esse* by efficient causality of others.

So, as in the various versions of the *quarta via*, this argument has two stages. The first stage shows how we can use the thought of the most perfect, understood as subsistent *esse*, to judge things as imperfect. The second stage argues for the real existence of that thing thought to be the most perfect. But unlike in the previous versions of the *quarta via*, Aquinas does not fulfill the second stage by arguing from the imperfect's accidentality and priority of existence. That is where the *De Ente* reasoning would come in. In the *De Potentia*, he reaches a most perfect being from the *esse* of some motion as the act *of some motion*. This opens the second path from judgmentally grasped existence. Rigorously pursued, the path comes to subsistent *esse* as the final cause that transfixes the finite intelligences that might be unfailingly moving the first physical cause. So it is the *De Ente* reasoning in its robust form that would be present in the second stage of this second argument.

Aquinas's third argument begins by saying that what is through another is caused by that which is *per se*. He then argues that there is a being that is its *esse*. The proof consists in showing the necessity of a first being that is pure act and in which there is no composition. This necessity follows from things which are not their *esse*. Hence, all other things have *esse* as a participation in this thing that is its *esse*.

That we have something through another, and that the other is the *per se*, follows from things that are not their *esse*. These words clearly call to mind the *De Ente* reasoning in which the *esse* that belongs to a thing cannot be caused by the thing. It must be caused by a thing that is *esse tantum*. In this third argument Aquinas concludes with the notion of participation. Here the participation talk is subsequent to talk about things not being their *esse*. It is only after the nature of *esse* has been established to be real that the *esse* of all other things can be characterized as a participation of the first being. So, the third argument is not the *De Ente* reasoning but the third argument employs it as a logically fundamental portion.

Prologue to the Commentary on the Gospel of John

Aquinas presents four arguments by which the ancient philosophers came to a knowledge of God. The first is from the motion of natural things for an end. This requires a reference to a higher being that is intelligent and directs the natural thing to the end. Again, I have discussed this reasoning extensively in my analysis of the *quinta viae* of *SCG* and *ST*. These arguments can be read according to the simple form of the *De Ente* reasoning or according to the more robust form so that the intelligence to which they conclude is understood as subsistent *esse*. Hence, Aquinas can say at the end of this first argument: *Hic est Deus*.

Aquinas calls the second way "from the eternity of God." The second way begins by noting that a gradation of nobility among mobile things. The heavens which are mobile only in respect to place are more noble than lower bodies which are also mobile in their substance. From this gradation Aquinas concludes to a supreme first principle of all things that is immobile and eternal.[14]

The references to the heavens and the lower bodies place Aquinas's second way into the context of the second metaphysical path out of judgmentally grasped existence. Aquinas's grading these bodies according to nobility calls to mind the *quarta via* of the *Summa Theologiae*. Read in this fashion, the

---

14. "For we see that whatever is in things, is mutable. Insomuch as something is more noble in the grades of things, it has only less of mutability. For example, inferior bodies are mutable according to substance and according to place. Heavenly bodies which are more noble are immutable according to substance; they are moved only according to place. According to this, therefore, it is able to be drawn [*colligi*] that a first principle of all things, supreme and more noble, is immobile and eternal."

second way would not be following the second path all the way to subsistent *esse* as transfixing cause of the finite mover of the heavens which significantly is unmentioned. Instead of reasoning in that fashion, the second way would be using gradation in nobility to manifest the accidentality of *esse* among mobile things. In other words, if a thing is its *esse*, it is infinite and so completely immobile. Mutability would then be a sure sign that *esse* is other than the nature. This thinking would enable Aquinas to immediately leave the second path for subsistent *esse* without going on to the intelligences as movers of the heavens.

Aquinas labels his third of these four ways "from the dignity of God" and states that it is made by the Platonists. The argument claims that what is through participation is reduced to what is that through its essence: "illud quod est per participationem, reducitur ad aliquid quod sit illud per suam essentiam." He then says that because all things which exist participate *esse* (*participant esse*) and are beings (*entia*) by participation, then necessarily there is something at the summit of all things which is its *esse* through its essence and from which all thing which exist participate *esse*.[15]

It is important to note that when Aquinas first says that things participate *esse*, he does not mean that things participate *esse* from the thing that is its *esse* and that is at the summit of things. The *esse* in which things are first said to participate is *esse commune*. This item is the analogous commonality formed from individual *esses* intellectually grasped in various acts of judgment. As I have mentioned, in *SCG* I.26 Aquinas argues that *esse commune* diversifies itself in light of the various things that will be actuated by it.[16] My point is that because the formation of the notion of *esse commune* presupposes the *secunda operatio intellectus*, then a reader of this third argument already knows that *esse* is uniquely accidental to things and so must be caused and caused by something else. Hence, Aquinas can say that because things participate *esse*, they must be reduced to something at the summit of things that is its *esse*.

---

15. "That which is through participation is reduced to something which is that through its essence, just as to the first and to the highest; just as all ignited things through participation are reduced to fire which is such through its essence. Hence, since all things which are participate being [*esse*] and are through participation beings [*entia*], there is necessary to be something at the summit of all things which is being itself [*ipsum esse*] through its essence, that is its essence is its being and this is God."

16. See above, chapter 4, "Anthony Kenny: the Fatal Flaw in the Man/Phoenix Argument."

The fourth argument is from the incomprehensibility of truth (*incomprehensibilitas veritatis*). In sum, Aquinas begins by claiming that every truth that our intellect is able to capture (*capere*) is finite. Aquinas takes the reason for this claim from Augustine: everything which is known is made finite by the comprehension of the knower. Hence, there is a first truth that surpasses every intellect. Aquinas characterizes it as incomprehensible and infinite.[17]

To begin to understand this argument it is important, in my opinion, to distinguish it from the *quarta via* of *SCG*. As I read that *quarta via*, the *via* was concerned with graded essences in reality. The fourth argument from the *Commentary*, however, deals with what happens to things when they are known. The focus is on cognition.

Hence, it is useful to recall Aquinas's above-mentioned argument from the beauty of species in *In I Sent*. I argued that the argument worked from the *esse in anima* of the species understood as a formed intention. In other words, it is not only an *ens reale* that has an *esse* but also an *ens rationis*. This ambiguity of *esse* allows the *De Ente* reasoning to be applied to two kinds of beings.

Furthermore, the formed intentions of bodies and spirits are able to be taken up into formed intentions that are propositions. A proposition is also an *ens rationis*. Elsewhere Aquinas describes the proposition as having an *esse* that is caused by God. Accordingly, in the fourth argument Aquinas is not disparaging our ability to know something of the truth of God. What is made finite is the propositional formed intention by which some knowledge of the infinite is conveyed.[18]

Summa contra Gentiles I.15

Aquinas argues that generable and corruptible things are "possibile esse et non esse." As equally (*aequaliter*) disposed to *esse* and *non esse*, they must have their *esse* from another. Because a regress to infinity is not possible here, this cause is either something necessary *per se* (*per seipsum necessarium*) or has a cause of its necessity from another (*causa suae necessitates aliunde*). Again,

---

17. "For every truth which our intellect is able to capture is finite, because, according to Augustine, all that is known is made finite by the comprehension of the knower. If it is made finite, it is made determinate and particularized [*determinatum et particularizatum*]. So it is necessary to be a first and highest truth, which is above every intellect, incomprehensible and infinite, and this is God."

18. For propositions as having an *esse*, see above comments on Geach in chapter 4.

an infinite regress, now of things whose necessity is caused, is not possible. Hence, there is a first necessary being and this being is God.[19]

As I have already glossed the *tertia via* of *ST* with this metaphysical sense of the possible, I will refer the reader to my reading of the *tertia via* to understand this argument from *SCG*. What I wish to emphasize here is that though Aquinas describes the possible as having itself equally to existence and to nonexistence, Aquinas's argument has only a superficial similarity to Leibniz's "V" model of cosmological reasoning (described in chapter 1, above). Just as matter may have this shape or that or this motion or that, a thing may have existence or nonexistence. That matter or the thing has one rather than the other is immediately indicative of a cause.

When Aquinas says that the possible is equally disposed to *esse* and *non esse*, however, he is speaking of the absolute consideration of the thing from whose perspective the *esse* is accidental. At this point Aquinas knows that the *esse* cannot be totally dependent upon the possible precisely as subject of the *esse*. *Esse* is then dependent either on the possible in some other respect or on another. The priority of the *esse* does not allow the thing in some other respect to complete the explanation for the *esse*. The fact that the *SCG* argument goes immediately to another shows that the priority of *esse* is presupposed.

So Aquinas's "V" model remark immediately establishes only the accidentality of existence and that the existence cannot be dependent simply upon the subject *qua* subject. Aquinas's remark does not indicate a wholesale acceptance of Leibniz's manner of cosmological reasoning. Whether the existence is dependent upon the subject in some other respect or upon another subject requires more reasoning. Aquinas can know with certitude that *esse* must be dependent upon another subject because of its priority to the subject of which it is an accident.[20]

---

19. "We find in the world, furthermore, certain beings, those namely that are subject to generation and corruption, which can be and not-be. But what can be has a cause because, since it is equally related to two contraries, namely, being and non-being, it must be owing to some cause that being accrues to it. Now, as we have proved by the reasoning of Aristotle, one cannot proceed to infinity among causes. We must therefore posit something that is a necessary being. Every necessary being, however, either has the cause of its necessity in an outside source or, if it does not, it is necessary through itself. But one cannot proceed to infinity among necessary beings the cause of whose necessity lies in an outside source. We must therefore posit a first necessary being, which is necessary through itself. This is God." *SCG* I.15, *Amplius* (trans. Pegis, 1:98–99).

20. In the case of standard accidents like motion or shape, the dependency on something else

Consequently, Aquinas's reasoning in *SCG* I.15 has none of the liabilities of Leibniz's "V" model of cosmological reasoning. For example, contrary to Kant's insistence that existence is not a predicate, Aquinas possesses the resources of judgment to access existence as a distinct nonformal perfection. Nor does Aquinas know dependency in and through the principle of sufficient reason's protest against simply *de facto* togetherness. Judgment also reveals *esse* as accidental to its subject and so as *ipso facto* dependent. Aquinas's major premise is not "Everything has a reason for its existence either in itself or in something else" but "What belongs to a thing is caused." Aquinas insists upon stratification. Moreover, he insists upon a unique stratification between the thing and its *esse*. The *esse* is prior and fundamental in respect to the subject. This insistence is not special pleading because Aquinas again uses the resources of judgment to reveal the stratification. Judgment adds *esse* to what is totally existence-neutral. Finally, Aquinas can again appeal to the accidentality of *esse* to know that the prior *esse* is not the end of philosophical reflection, because prior *esse* remains an accident: that is, prior *esse* remains *ipso facto* dependent and in need of further investigation.

---

seems to be a matter of experience. For example, I know that the motion of the billiard ball is also dependent upon something else that is not the ball precisely as subject of the motion only because I do not observe the ball to be moving unless it is struck by another ball. In other words, I can be philosophically certain that the motion is an accident and so is dependent. Also, I can be philosophically certain that the motion is not completely dependent upon the subject *qua* subject. Hence, I can be completely certain that the motion is also dependent upon something else. But that conclusion is ambiguous. The something else need not be another thing but the original thing in some other respect than subject. If the accident is a "garden variety" accident posterior to its subject, then it seems that we must now navigate the ambiguity simply on the basis of experience and with a loss of complete philosophical certainty.

[11]

Questions and Replies

———◇———

I have argued that according to Aquinas's mind, the philosopher is able to demonstrate the existence of the God of Aquinas's religious belief, and the philosopher accomplishes this demonstration in metaphysics. Moreover, we can know enough of Aquinas's understanding of the philosophical branch of metaphysics to understand how the metaphysician goes from the subject matter of the science to God. The movement is in virtue of the *actus essendi* component of the metaphysician's understanding of what it means to be a being. A rudimentary presentation of the reasoning can be found in the fourth chapter of Aquinas's *De Ente*. Finally, the *actus essendi* component is accessed through the second operation of the intellect exercised on an existence-neutral understanding of a thing that had been previously presented as both really and cognitionally existing.

It is my further contention that the reader is perfectly within bounds to use Aquinas's thesis of the philosopher's metaphysical approach to God as a hermeneutic for understanding Aquinas's actual proofs for God. My idea is the following. One can observe Aquinas to be serious about providing arguments for God that withstand philosophical scrutiny. His rejection of Anselmian reasoning illustrates this seriousness. The Anselmian notion of the greatest involves only a formed intention of existence. Also, Aquinas's insistence upon following the Aristotelian canons of logic for a *demonstratio quia* indicate his intended fidelity to the requirements of philosophy. In these lights, is it at all plausible to think that in his actual God proofs Aquinas sets aside his opinion of where and when the philosopher proves God's existence? I do not think that one can blame someone for thinking that it is implausible.

Admittedly, questions remain. For example, if the *De Ente* reasoning is the basic metaphysical reasoning found in all of Aquinas's *viae*, why did not Aquinas just present that reasoning? Why did Aquinas present this metaphysical reasoning in camouflage? Also, if the hermeneutic for the *viae* is the *De Ente* reasoning, often in its robust form, then the conclusions of the *viae* should be God understood as subsistent *esse*. Aquinas, nevertheless, goes on to ask if essence and existence are identical in God as if this is still an open question. Finally, does not the metaphysical interpretation make the *viae* accessible only to the learned? On the other hand, Aquinas often makes remarks that indicate that his *viae* are really less complicated and accessible to ordinary people. How could Aquinas hold both opinions?

Before I address these questions it is important to remember just where and when they are arising. They are arising after the establishment of the metaphysical character of the *viae* and evidence that the very words of the *viae* can be read metaphysically. In other words, to admit the present questions does not mean that one has to surrender what one already knows: namely, that the *viae* are metaphysical arguments. Many times one knows *that* something is so without knowing *how* it is so. For instance, I know that I can access the internet, but I do not know how that happens. Similarly, I can know *that* something is so without knowing *why* it is so. For instance, I know that I am suffering, but I really do not know for what purpose. The admitted ignorances of the how and why do not at all mean that I am ignorant of facts, that is, accessing the internet and my suffering. Likewise, the reader may never know why Aquinas always presented the *De Ente* reasoning in camouflage whenever he gave a *viae* for God. But that ignorance does not mean that one is not sure that Aquinas did make that presentation.

Joseph Owens ventures onto the deep waters of the first two questions.[1] As far as I can discern, Owens does not approach them from my angle. In his discussions, mainly of the way from motion, Owens makes no attempt to

---

1. See Joseph Owens, "The Starting Point of the *Prima Via*," in *Aquinas on the Existence of God*, 186–91, as well as (in the same volume), "Aquinas and the Five Ways," 132–41; "Actuality and the *Prima Via*," 196–202; and "Immobility and Existence for Aquinas," 218–26.

determine Aquinas's opinion about where and when the philosopher proves God's existence. Hence, my questions have an urgency for Owens that they do not have for me. For Owens the questions pose a challenge to the metaphysical interpretation itself. They ask whether the *viae* should be read metaphysically. For me the questions ask how the established metaphysical reading is compatible with the camouflage and with knowing God as subsistent *esse* later.

The desperate situation faced by Owens, in my opinion, leads him to produce exegeses of unsurpassed nuance that place him high among the great Thomistic commentators. So, even though I will not be asking the same questions faced by Owens, I will at least note the answers to the questions that he faced and I will use them when appropriate.

Why Not the *De Ente* Reasoning?

In my opinion, a plausible reply to this question begins by recalling that it is Aquinas, the theologian, who is philosophizing here. As a philosopher, Aquinas is following the canons of Aristotelian scientific procedure of investigating first the *an sit*, then the *quid sit*: that it is, then what it is.[2] As a theologian, he is committed to explaining to his fellows the content of divine revelation. That theological vocation is expressed poignantly in *SCG*: "I have set myself the task of making known, as far as my limited powers will allow, the truth that the Catholic faith professes, and of setting aside the errors that are opposed to it."[3] Hence, while a philosopher might be content to deal with the *an sit* of God by giving the *De Ente* proof, a theologian in fidelity to his vocation might want to multiply the arguments so that where one fails another works. Accordingly, Aquinas runs the *De Ente* reasoning in many different contexts and he indicates the accidentality of *esse* by other means then the *duplex operatio*.

By showing that the *De Ente* reasoning works in various venues, Aquinas shows that natural reason can reach God from practically anything. Remember, even motion participates in the *ratio entis*. Natural reason takes no esoteric path to God. Everything proclaims God. In other words, by garbing

2. For a description of this procedure, see Ashley, *The Way toward Wisdom*, 61–71. For Aquinas's different understanding of the *An sit* question, see my concluding chapter, note 10.
3. *SCG* I.2, *Assumpta* (trans. Pegis, 1:62).

his *De Ente* reasoning in the proofs of others, Aquinas is not intending to camouflage his reasoning. Rather, Aquinas is intending to show that God's existence is a secure point of natural reason by showing that multiple application points for his metaphysics of *esse* exist.

An admission of this strategy seems to be contained in *De Ver.*, q. 10, a. 12. The article is devoted to whether God's existence is known through itself to the human mind just as the first principles of demonstration are not able not to be known. Aquinas replies that because God's existence is not self-evident to us, it must be demonstrated. This is the same context as the *viae*. But in his reply to the tenth objection of the second set, Aquinas makes the following remark on demonstrative knowledge of God: "God is known not only in the works which proceed from His justice, but also in His other works. Hence, granted that someone does not know Him as just, it does not follow that he does not know Him at all. Nor it is possible for anyone to know none of His works, since being in general [*ens commune*], which cannot be unknown, is His work."[4] *Ens commune* is another Thomistic moniker for the subject of metaphysics. As *De Ver.*, q. 1, a. 1, argued, it is a nongeneric intelligibility and so encompasses everything. Hence, if one instance of *ens commune* is unknown, then another one will be and God can be known as the cause of that. This adaptive procedure would be the very strategy Aquinas is following in his *viae* to God. The strategy would be geared to show that natural reason inescapably affirms the existence of God because some effect of God, that is some instance of *ens commune*, is unavoidable.

So that is why Aquinas could be presenting the *De Ente* reasoning through the wording of others. This manner of writing has nothing to do with camouflaging the *De Ente* reasoning but with showcasing it in order to make a theological point: natural reason can know God from his effects. Nor is Aquinas interested in claiming that the historical authors proved God. In fact the case can be made that when Aquinas ascribes creation to Aristotle, it is not the historical Aristotle that he has in mind.[5] No, the focus of the strategy is not how pagans prove God; the focus is how the *De Ente* reasoning can be begun from any one of a multitude of effects.

---

4. Trans. McGlynn, 2:71.
5. See John F. X. Knasas, "Aquinas' Ascriptions of Creation to Aristotle," *Angelicum* 73, no. 4 (1996): 487–506.

The Later Proof of God as Subsistent *esse*

There is another issue that the metaphysical interpreter of Aquinas's *viae* often encounters. If the *viae* are interpreted in line with Aquinas's metaphysics, then no matter how their conclusions are named, the conclusions should always be understood as subsistent *esse*. The previous readings of the *viae* illustrate the point. The unmoved mover, first efficient cause, first intelligence, and greatest being, are various guises of subsistent *esse* as it is reached from some nature that has *esse*. What causes a question to arise is that only subsequently, for example, in *ST* I, q. 3, a. 4, and *SCG* I.22, does Aquinas deal with the identity of essence and *esse* in God. Why would Aquinas do that if he has reached God as subsistent *esse* in the *viae*?

Again, this question has two meanings depending upon the context in which it is asked. If one already knows that Aquinas's desired philosophical approach to God is metaphysical, then the question becomes one of understanding why he would repeat something we should already know. On the other hand, if one is still arguing that the *viae* are metaphysical, then Aquinas's later treatment of the identity of essence and *esse* in God constitutes an objection to the metaphysical interpretation of the *viae*. The second context is the one in which Joseph Owens is facing this question. As I mentioned, I find his exegeses to be models of textual commentary. So, for those not inclined to my approach to the *viae* in terms of Aquinas's opinion of where and when the philosopher proves God's existence, I recommend a study of Owens's articles.[6]

---

6. In the case of the *Summa Theologiae*, Owens, "Actuality in the *Prima Via*," 200, notes two things. First, in the second argument at I, q. 3, a. 4, for the identity of essence and existence in God, Aquinas recalls from a. 1 that in God there is nothing potential, "in Deo nihil sit potentiale." The first article said it this way: "impossibile est igitur quod in Deo sit aliquid in potentiale." The talk of act and potency indicates as a basis for this claim the previous *prima via*. Owens observes that Aquinas could not claim God to be absolute actuality from the *prima via* unless, like Aristotle, Aquinas used the eternity of motion in the *prima via* or unless the *prima via* is using *actus* in Aquinas's basic metaphysical sense of *esse*. Of course, the *prima via* of *ST* does not use the eternity of motion as a stage in rising to the unmoved mover. Hence, the total lack of potentiality must mean that Aquinas is thinking about actuality in terms of existence. Second, Owens notes that when Aquinas gives his second proof that God's essence is his existence at *ST* I, q. 3, a. 4, Aquinas's understanding of actuality in terms of having *esse* is brought up as if it had been presupposed all along: "This is not referred back to any previous proof in the *Summa Theologiae*. It is mentioned as if it is something that has to be everywhere understood" (ibid.). I would add that there is some precedent in the Thomistic texts for Aquinas using

The first context, however, is the one in which I face the question. So for me the issue is how to reconcile God as subsistent existence in the *viae* of both *Summae* and the apparent repetition of that thesis in Aquinas's later argument for the identity of essence and *esse* in God. In other words, because the *viae* are metaphysical, Aquinas concludes to God as subsistent *esse*; why, then, does Aquinas say God is subsistent *esse* only later?

Is not the answer found by recalling that it is Aquinas the theologian who is dealing with Aristotle's *an sit* question? By crafting *viae* that present his *De Ente* reasoning in a multiplicity of guises, Aquinas has effectively prevented himself from "saying" that God is subsistent *esse*. A straightforward presentation of the *De Ente* reasoning, as perhaps a philosopher would give or as Aquinas himself provided in the *De Ente*, would have allowed Aquinas to "say" God is subsistent *esse*.

Aquinas's theological strategy effectively creates the opening for saying that God is subsistent *esse*. A philosopher explicitly using the *De Ente* reasoning would both know and have said that God is subsistent *esse*. Hence, in turning from the *an sit* question to God's simplicity, the philosopher would not bother to bring up the possibility of an essence/*esse* distinction in God. Aquinas, however, has not yet had the occasion to "say" that God is subsistent *esse*. Hence, there is an understandable appropriateness in Aquinas making that claim explicitly in *ST* I, q. 3.

---

a term with a very specific meaning and Aquinas not always calling attention to that specific meaning. Consider the discussion of "soul" in the *prima pars*. The reader goes a long while before learning that Aquinas is specifically meaning by "soul" an Aristotelian substantial form. In "Immobility and Existence," 225, Owens makes an astute observation about *SCG* I.22, the parallel text to *ST* I, q. 3, a. 4. Owens notes that Aquinas is not arguing that pure act must be *esse*. Aquinas is arguing that pure act already understood as *esse* cannot have an essence other than it. This strategy would indicate that act has been understood in terms of *esse* all along. Owens remarks: "In the course of the subsequent reasoning [from chap. 13] no query was framed in terms of proving that the entirely immobile movement was subsistent existence. Rather, the query was framed in terms of lack of any difference between essence or quiddity and existence in God. The conclusion as first expressed is that God has no essence that is not his existence: 'Deus igitur non habet essentiam quae non sit suum esse' (*CG*, I, 22, *Ostensum*). Does not this read as though the divine existence is taken as established, here by the argument from the possible and the necessary, and the query is whether any essence is there in addition to the existence? When the argument from pure actuality as demonstrated through motion is reached, the framework of the reasoning can hardly be regarded as changed. The conclusion accordingly is worded: 'Non igitur Dei essentia est aliud quam suum esse' (*CG*, I, 22, *Amplius esse*)."

The Existential Interpretation and God's Nominal Definition

Another Thomistic concern with reading the *viae* in the light of Aquinas's metaphysics of *actus essendi* is that it has us using God's proper name and not a "nominal definition." At the end of *SCG* I.22 Aquinas equates subsistent *esse* with God's proper name "I am who am" as revealed to Moses. Moreover, unlike nominal definitions, a proper name signifies the nature or essence of a thing. Hence, when the *viae* reach their conclusion of unmoved mover, first efficient cause, necessary being *per se*, etc., understood as subsistent *esse* and the premise "God is subsistent *esse*" is added to conclude to God, the premise appears to appeal, not to a nominal definition of God, but to an essence-revealing proper name. At that point the *viae* would be *propter quid*. *Propter quid* demonstrations use the essence of the cause as their middle term. The problem is that the *viae* were supposed to be *quia* demonstrations, but now they are combinations of both types.

In reply, the objector is failing to realize that what can be a proper name in relation to itself (*quoad se*) can be only a nominal definition in relation to us (*quoad nos*). To understand this distinction, it is necessary to consider Aquinas's doctrine of "formed intentions" that I referenced in my chapter 4 reply to Kenny. Formed intentions of essence and existence present these two items outside the contexts of the *prima* and *secunda operationes* in which they were originally apprehended. In the case of essence, the formed intention enables us to fantasize wild combinations of essence that would be impossible if we stayed in the context of the *prima operatio*. In the case of existence, the formed intention of *esse* enables us to think existence without having it made present to us. The formed intention of *esse* is an existence-neutral sense of *esse*. In this case, we both know and do not know existence.

In my Kenny response I also detailed how from a multitude of formed intentions of individual *esses*, we intellect *esse commune*, or *esse formale*. This object is a common sense of *esse*. Of it too, the intellect can produce a formed intention. Moreover, as I explained, suitably modified by the negating, or dividing, capacity of the second operation, *esse commune* can be used to get some grasp of the divine quiddity. We can see Aquinas himself going from *esse commune* to God when in *ST* I, q. 4, a. 3 he argues from the perfection of *esse commune* to the perfection of God as subsistent *esse*.

Because we understand subsistent existence in terms of a formed intention of existence that does not present what we are conceiving, for us the understanding of subsistent existence is just nominal and does not reveal the essence of God. For us, *ipsum esse subsistens* is *both* a nominal definition and the most proper name of God.

My point is that the definition of God as subsistent existence is ultimately understood by us through this existence-neutral formed intention of existence. The point means that we have only a nominal sense of subsistent *esse*, a sense of subsistent *esse* that fails to present it or to show it. Hence, the premise "God is subsistent *esse*" does not "show" us the divine quiddity. It can be brought into the metaphysical reasoning for God without changing or derailing the reasoning from *quia* to *propter quid*.

The Existential Interpretation of the *viae* Is Too Complicated

Does not the existential interpretation of Aquinas's *viae* make them so exotic that the *viae* become inaccessible to ordinary people? Is not Aquinas's metaphysics just an academic creation only in the minds of those who have had a course in Thomistic metaphysics? My first reaction is to ask if the physical, or natural philosophy, interpretation is less complicated. When you consider the *SCG* elaborations of the proof from motion, the answer to this question seems to be that it is a draw. There is enough difficulty to go around. So the objection proves too much and should be withdrawn. I want to argue, nevertheless, that the central ideas of Aquinas's metaphysics are alive and well in the minds of ordinary people, even though they are unaware of it. Hence, the existential interpretations of the Aquinas's *viae* are nearer than one would at first think.

This may sound like a Kantian theme. For Immanuel Kant there is the synthetic *a priori* of the mind before our conscious experience. The synthetic *a priori* accounts for the experience that we are having; for example, it accounts for objects in space and time, causes for what happens, substances for accidents. But Aquinas's metaphysics is prior to human awareness in a way other than Kant's sense of the *a priori*. As I will explain, for Aquinas the human mind can function in an *a posteriori* manner so spontaneously and automatically that the mind's workings stay below the level of consciousness. So in going from the explicit to the implicit in philosophy, we are not necessarily going to the *a priori*. I want to illustrate this implicitness first with respect to the thing/*esse* distinction and the causal implications thereof and second with respect to the *ratio entis*.

I want to begin by reflecting upon *SCG* III.38. This chapter falls in Aquinas's canvasing of a list of possible candidates for human happiness. He has already eliminated from that list pleasures, honors, glory, riches, power, bodily goods, and moral virtue. In III.38 he wonders if human happiness might consist in the general knowledge of God possessed by most people. In my opinion, the text of III.38 contains a puzzle that can only be solved by my proposed thesis.

At the beginning of III.38, Aquinas describes an ordinary knowledge of God possessed by all mature human beings. This ordinary knowledge of God is *a posteriori* and appears to recount a primitive version of the teleological argument. It runs as follows:

> What seems indeed to be true, that man can immediately reach some sort of knowledge of God by natural reason. For, when men see that things in nature run according to a definite order, and that ordering does not occur without an orderer, they perceive in most cases that there is some orderer of the things that we see. But who or what kind of being, or whether there is but one orderer of nature, is not yet grasped immediately in this general consideration.... But this knowledge admits of a mixture of many errors. Some people have believed that there is no other orderer of worldly things than the celestial bodies, and so they said that the celestial bodies are gods. Other people pushed it further, to the very elements and the things generated from them, thinking that motion and the natural functions which these elements have are not present in them as the effect of some other orderer, but that other things are ordered by them. Still other people, believing that human acts are not subject to any ordering, other than human, have said that men who order others are gods. And so, this knowledge of God is not enough for felicity.[7]

Aquinas concedes that the argument has many shortcomings. For example, Aquinas notes that one does not yet grasp who or what is this orderer or if the orderer is one or many. On the strength of this argument, some identify the orderer with the heavenly bodies, the elements, or other human beings. Does Aquinas's concession contradict his thesis that men are knowing God?

7. *SCG* III.38, *Inquirendum* (trans. Bourke, 3.1:125–26).

None of the characterizations of the orderer are remotely similar to the God of Aquinas's religious belief who is spiritual, unique, and nonhuman. Would it not have been clearer for Aquinas to say that men fail to attain knowledge of God? In other words, when a physicist discovers a new particle, he does not proclaim it as "God." And if he did, we would think him strange. Hence, is not Aquinas odd to attribute man's knowledge of God to man's knowledge of the elements? In fact on another occasion, Aquinas is uncompromising, if not uncharacteristically cruel, in his dismissal of David of Dinant's identification of God with matter.[8]

I can also point out that elsewhere at *ST* I, q. 44, a. 2, Aquinas says that when philosophers correctly reasoned from the elements, they reached a "universal cause" still far below the "most universal cause," God. Later when considering substantial transmutations, philosophers, like Aristotle, went further to the heavens. That conclusion, however, was still to arrive at only a "more universal cause," not the most universal cause, God. My point is that if philosophers, in Aquinas's opinion, fail to reach God from the elements or in the heavens, how can Aquinas say that ordinary people do it?

Returning to *SCG*, it is important to realize that Aquinas does not say that men reach something "like" God. Aquinas's assertion is unqualified. Men reach God, even though they take what they reach and identify it with the mentioned nondivine instances. Consequently, when next in III.39 Aquinas introduces philosophical demonstrations to remove the errors, the removal does not consist in moving on to a higher being than those mentioned. Rather, the corrections consist in purifying through removal of the errors, what the general reasoning had reached.

On the other hand, there is another sort of knowledge of God, higher than the foregoing, and we may acquire it through demonstration. A closer approach to a proper knowledge of Him is effected through this kind, for many things are set apart from Him, through demonstration, whose removal enables Him to be understood in distinction from other beings. In fact, demonstration shows that God is immutable, eternal, incorporeal, altogether simple, one, and other such things which we have shown about God in Book One.

---

8. "The third error is that of David of Dinant, who most stupidly [*stultissime*] taught that God was primary matter." *ST* I, q. 3, a. 8, co. (trans. Pegis, 1:35).

So, some explanation of how the conclusion of Aquinas's reasoning at *SCG* I.38 can be so wrong and still be right is required.

According to Aquinas, the errors in man's ordinary knowledge of God are set aside by demonstration. The backward reference is important. Early in *SCG* I, Aquinas reserves these points of demonstration to the last part of philosophy to be learned, namely, to metaphysics. At I.4 he says, "In order to know the things that the reason can investigate concerning God, a knowledge of many things must already be possessed. For almost all of philosophy is directed towards the knowledge of God, and that is why metaphysics which deals with divine things, is the last part of philosophy to be learned."[9] In I.3, naturally knowable truth about God includes the knowledge of his existence: "But there are some truths which the natural reason also is able to reach. Such that God exists, that He is one, and the like." This assignment should mean that the ordinary knowledge of God is in some way metaphysical. Only as metaphysical could it successfully reach God, albeit imperfectly, as Aquinas claims. But can one possibly regard ordinary individuals to be in possession of Aquinas's central metaphysical idea of *esse*?

The answer depends upon access to the data that provokes this idea. What are the data? The setting up of things in various multiplicities is the standard procedure for the discernment of the thing's acts. For example, because I find the water both hot and cold, I come to discern the various temperatures as acts of the water that in itself is temperature-neutral. Moreover, I come to understand each of the instances as a composition of the water plus some temperature. Likewise, because I can find Tom both pale and ruddy, I come to discern the complexions as acts of Tom who in himself is complexion-neutral. But for Aquinas things are found not only in temperature and complexion multiplicities but also in existential multiplicities.

Aquinas is an immediate realist in his understanding of sensation. Sensation provides not an image, a representation, a picture of the real thing but the real thing itself. Consequently, the hot water and the pale Tom do not just really exist, in my sensation, they also cognitionally exist. What is implied by this doubling of reality? Is it not the following? For a reality to exist cognitionally also means that the reality of itself cannot be real. Likewise if the water of itself were hot, then the water would become impervious to gen-

---

9. Trans. Pegis, 1:67.

uinely taking on any other temperature. That the water does truly take on other temperatures means that the water of itself is not temperatured. One might say that of itself the water is temperature-neutral. The various temperatures are then attributes that come to the water and modify it. The same type of thinking will hold for a reality that cognitionally exists. The only way in which something real could also cognitionally exist is by being of itself existence-neutral. If the thing of itself is real, then it becomes impervious to existing in another way. Real existence should, then, be understood as an attribute that comes to the thing just as the hot temperature is eventually understood as an attribute that comes to the water.

It is the presentation of some individual thing in an existential multiplicity that drives the mind to understand the thing to be in itself existence-neutral and to understand the thing's real existence to mean an attribute that the thing has in order to be a reality, or in Aquinas's Latin, an *ens*. The answer to the above question reduces to an answer to this question: is the mentioned existential multiplicity available to the ordinary person? I think so. No ordinary person doubts a real world in sensation. No ordinary person questions the distinction between remembering their beloved in a memory versus being in the beloved's presence. Even though modern philosophy has run away from the immediate presence of the real in sensation, ordinary people continue to live according to that marvelous truth. Furthermore, ordinary people have sufficient presence of mind that none lack an awareness of their own sensation. Hence, they not only know real things, they know that they know real things. In other words, ordinary people not only sense real things, they also are aware that they sense real things. In short, there is every reason to think that the intellect apprehends the notion of being in the sense of *habens esse*. The data are sufficiently available for the intellect to be led to the metaphysical distinction between a thing and its *esse*, even if our awareness is elsewhere.

Upon a grasp of the composition, cannot the intellect go on to grasp the conclusion that the *esse* is caused? One conscious outcrop of this activity is Leibniz's question of why there is something rather than nothing. As Heidegger points out at the very start of his *Introduction to Metaphysics*, the question steals upon us in moments of despair, rejoicing, and boredom. Looked at Thomistically, Heidegger's remark makes sense. Common to these moods is the shutting down of our plans and designs so that we are left simply in the presence of things. But that hovering of things in our awareness bespeaks, as explained, an instability in existents that prompts Leibniz's question. Aquinas's metaphysics is as near as the sense realism of ordinary experience.

But if this is how people can get it so right, how can they get it so wrong? I now move to my second claim (above) that Aquinas regards as implicit knowledge not only the thing/*esse* distinction and its causal implication: in addition, the data that provokes the thing/*esse* distinction occurs in a larger field. This larger field is an intelligible object, a commonality. Between things really and cognitionally existing, Aquinas sees something the same. Both instances in some way exist. Hence, as noted, *ens* can be used of real things and of cognitional items like propositions, and *esse* can be duplex for *in re* and *in anima*. This commonality is a result of the fact that our cognition is never so sunk into real things that it loses all awareness of itself. Hence, Aquinas often, for example, at *De Ver.*, q. 1, a. 1, co., and the opening of *De Ente*, describes the notion of being by the real natures, the items *in re*, that are its focus and are said to be divided by the ten categories of Aristotle. Cognition is, however, a way of being a being and so the focus of the notion of being, the *ratio entis*, does not express its true extent. The extending of the notion of being into cognition suffices, however, to distinguish the notion from *ens mobile*, the subject of natural philosophy. Sensible items are the sole extension of *ens mobile*.

Importantly, Aquinas emphasizes that the notion of being is a nongeneric intelligibility. Unlike a genus, the *ratio entis* does not suffer division by differences brought in from outside its meaning. Being is divided, for example, into the real natures of the various categories by the natures making explicit what is implicit in being.[10] This thinking about the notion of being gives being a striking richness. As I have argued elsewhere, it is the key to much of Aquinas's philosophical psychology.[11] For example, as intelligibly rich, being

---

10. "Yet, in this sense, some predicates may be said to add to being inasmuch as they express a mode of being [*exprimunt ipsius modum*] not expressed by the term being." *De Ver.*, q. 1, a. 1, co. (trans. Mulligan, 1:5). At *De Ver.*, q. 21, a. 1, co., Aquinas says that a genus contains its differences implicitly but potentially: "Animal is limited by man because what is contained in the notion of man determinately and actually, is only implicitly and, as it were, potentially [*implicite et quasi potentialiter*] contained in the notion of animal" (trans. Schmidt, 3:5). This remark implies that the notion of being contains its differences implicitly but actually. See also James F. Anderson, *The Bond of Being: An Essay on Analogy and Existence* (New York: Greenwood Press, 1969), 256.

11. *Being and Some Twentieth-Century Thomists*, chap. 8.

automatically excites the will into its first act of volition. Being leaves us really free in the face of individual beings which as individuals are goods but not the good. Finally, its heightened presence in humans insofar as humans are intellectors of being creates an obligation to exercise our freedom in relation to ourselves and others in a respectful and solicitous way.

While ordinary people may not be self-aware of the intellection of being, ordinary people certainly experience yearning, freedom, and obligation. These experiences can be taken as telltale signs of the intellection of being in their minds. Aquinas explains how we can be intellectors and not even know it. At *SCG* III.26, Aquinas writes that it is not strange that humans act for sensual pleasures rather than intellectual ones insofar as most humans lack intellectual experience. For this lack Aquinas appeals to his abstractionist epistemology.[12] He says that external things are better known because human cognition begins from sensible things. One would be wrong to interpret Aquinas's remarks to mean that the workings of the intellect are totally absent or that these workings have no experienced effects. Though our attention is focused on sensible things, our intellection has gone on to grasp commonalities of which we are still unaware but with the above conscious psychic effects.

What has implicit intellection of the notion of being to do with ordinary people so poorly reasoning to God? The already abstracted notion of being can also play tricks in our conscious life. It can create *faux* epiphanies of itself. In this case an instance of being, due to certain superficialities, can become associated with the notion of being and acquire a value out of all proportion to the truth. This *faux*ing can happen in our awareness of spatially gargantuan things and minute things. For example, it can happen that to contemplate the heavens in our minds, we profile the heavens, we objectify them, by hanging them up and against the already abstracted notion of being. Just as there is the physical sky up and against which the clock tower is profiled, so too the already abstracted notion of being is an intellectual sky against which things can be objectified. In their own way, minutiae can become overly associat-

---

12. "Nor do more persons seek the pleasure that is associated with knowing rather than the knowledge. Rather, there are more people who seek sensual pleasures than intellectual knowledge and its accompanying pleasure, because things that are external stand out as better known, since human knowledge starts from sensible objects [*quia ea quae exterius sunt, magis nota pluribus existunt, eo quod a sensibilibus incipit humana cognitio*]." *SCG* III.26, *Non autem* (trans. Bourke, 3.1:109–10).

ed with being. To visually contemplate something small every other thing is swept away. This can leave the minute alone with being.

These two cognitive situations can result in the physically great and small taking on all the truth of being. For example, because of the causal implications in the notion of being, the great and the small can take on religious overtones. To the Native American on horseback in the Western plains, the mountain is something mystical; he unknowingly mixes the experience of the mountain with his intellection of being. The scientist's insistence that the mountain is just a heap of basalt particles is so focused on minutiae that the association of the mountain with being is lost. Yet if the scientist is not careful, being can break through in the scientist's consideration of minutiae. For in contemplating the small, everything else is removed from our attention. The result is that the small stands alone with being. Because of that cognitive association, the small can become invested with the preciousness of being itself. Hence, the reverential and awe-filled remark of that popularizer of current science, Carl Sagan, that we are all "star stuff." It is interesting to recall that in *SCG* III.38, Aquinas himself describes ordinary people's errors about God in terms of the great and the small. Aquinas mentions that some call God the heavens and other call God the elements.

So my conclusion is that a meditation upon *SCG* III.38 indicates that Aquinas did not regard the basic notions of his metaphysics to be so much the product of an academic laboratory that they could not be understood as present in the minds of ordinary people. Moreover, he did not regard this metaphysics as so clearly present in the minds of ordinary people that it was exempt from *faux*izing. This implicit presence of *a posteriori* metaphysical knowledge explains why Aquinas regards this knowledge of God by ordinary people to be so correct but also so wrong. It is ironic, however, that the notion of being in whose intellection lies our natural dignity is the very thing than can cause so much error.

Conclusion

Does Aquinas Contribute to Cosmological Reasoning?

In his *The Cosmological Argument from Plato to Leibniz*, William Lane Craig analyzes the first three of the *quinque viae*. He interprets the *prima via* as an Aristotelian physical argument; the other two involve Aquinas's notion of *actus essendi*. Craig does not think that *actus essendi* is original to Aquinas, but posits that it is a borrowing from the Arabs. Hence, Craig concludes that other than providing model summarizations, Aquinas adds little of substance to the tradition of cosmological reasoning.[1]

Has this book, then, been in vain? Has Aquinas nothing distinctive to contribute to the tradition of cosmological reasoning except good summaries of the thought of others? Actually Aquinas himself would be the first person to claim that he is not doing something original. This supposed lack of originality is especially true with Aquinas's treatment of Aristotle. As far as I know, the only criticism that Aquinas makes of Aristotle's speculative thought is the latter's opinion that the world was eternal.

Even that criticism is tempered. Aristotle knows that there is no strict demonstration of the world's eternity because Aristotle already knows that things can come into being in a way other than through motion. Things can have as their cause a *principium essendi*. In other words, Aristotle knows what Aquinas called *esse*.[2] Hence, Aristotle used the world's eternity only as a *sup-*

---

1. Craig, *The Cosmological Argument from Plato to Leibniz*, 195–96.
2. For a listing of the many texts in which Aquinas ascribes to Aristotle a knowledge of creation

positio in his proof for God. The supposition of the world's eternity made the proof more efficacious. What caused Aristotle to think that the world was in fact eternal was the record of human observations of the heavens. Apparently, that record sufficed to convince Aristotle that the eternity of the world was more than a possibility but a fact.[3]

Until that point, however, there is no daylight between Aristotle and Aquinas's metaphysics. In other words, Craig is correct. Aquinas did not present himself as an innovator on Aristotle. Nevertheless, the Aristotle that Aquinas is content to express is a metaphysician of *actus essendi*. Most would take that fact to be indicative of great innovation on Aquinas's part.[4] Yet, others will insist on speaking of "Aristotelian existentialism."

In his *Praeambula Fidei: Thomism and the God of the Philosophers*, Ralph McInerny gives four reasons for the presence in Aristotle of the real distinction between essence and existence. First, "If Aristotle identified essence and existence, natural substances would exist necessarily; but natural substances are the vary paradigm of contingent being: therefore ... ? The minimum conclusion is that, if to be contingent involves a distinction between essence and existence, then it looks as if Aristotle held this, however, implicitly."[5] Second, we know from the *Posterior Analytics* that Aristotle explicitly acknowledges the entitative distinction. Aristotle distinguishes the questions *an sit* (whether it is) and *quid sit* (what it is). McInerny then quotes from Aquinas's commentary that the existence/essence distinction is the basis for these two questions.[6] Third, McInerny reviews *Metaphysics* III.3 on being and one as

---

and of *esse*, see Mark Johnson, "Did St. Thomas Attribute a Doctrine of Creation to Aristotle?," *The New Scholasticism* 63, no. 2 (1989): 129–55. Johnson corrects Etienne Gilson's opinion that Aquinas never ascribed a doctrine of creation to Aristotle. See Etienne Gilson, *The Spirit of Medieval Philosophy* (New York: Charles Scribner's Sons, 1940), 438n4.

3. In Aquinas's *Disputed Questions on Spiritual Creatures*, a. 5, co., he presents Aristotle as wrongly arguing to spiritual substances from the eternity of motion. Earlier at *SCG* II.91, *Praeterea*, Aquinas offered the same argument but noted human observations of the heavens over many generations. Evidently, Aquinas saw the observation record as swaying Aristotle to assert the eternity of motion even though Aquinas said that Aristotle knew that the eternity of motion could not be proved strictly.

4. For example, Joseph Owens, "Aquinas as Aristotelian Commentator," in *Aquinas on the Existence of God*, 1–19.

5. Ralph McInerny, *Preambula Fidei: Thomism and the God of the Philosophers* (Washington, D.C.: The Catholic University of America Press, 2006), 296.

6. Ibid., 297.

Conclusion 307

not being genera. He then turns to *Metaphysics* IV.2 and Aquinas's commentary thereof. What does "being" mean? It is taken from existence and so is something as it were constituted by the principles of the essence. Hence, the *ratio entis* "has an account that is drawn from the fact that it exists," and so "being" signifies the same thing as the term imposed from essence, such as the term "man."[7] This third reason seems to define existence as nothing more than the fact of hylomorphic composites. So perhaps not surprisingly, McInerny finishes with a fourth reason drawn from David Twetten. According to McInerny's summary, Twetten argues that "actually to be" a material thing needs more than matter and form. Twetten's main points are as follows. Matter is potency to be. Form, though act, is actual only in matter; form needs a cause to come to be in matter and to continue in matter. Consequently, neither will matter and form together account for a thing actually to be. Hence, "since 'actually to be' must be accounted for, there must be some component that accounts for it that is really distinct from form and matter."[8]

I do not find these four reasons conclusive for an Aristotelian existentialism. As a preface to my replies, McInerny's previous statement about *esse* should be borne in mind: "When it is, *esse* is first recognized as the actual inherence of the form in matter—it is not the matter, not the form, not the combination or them, but, so to say, their combining. For the natural thing to exist is for the matter to be actuated by a form."[9] It is difficult to understand how this view of *esse* is compatible with that of Aquinas in *SCG* II.54. In the context of distinguishing the matter/form composition from the essence/*esse* composition, Aquinas regards the matter/form composition as constituting a changeable substance but not yet a being (*ens*). To attain the status of a being, the substance so composed must in turn be composed with *esse*. Hence, there is a twofold composition in material beings. In this text, *esse* is not the inherence of form in matter. That inherence gives you only a possible which is yet to be made actual by composition with a further act, *esse*.

It is difficult to see in McInerny's understanding of *esse* anything more than the fact view of existence. Such a notion of existence leads to the thinnest understanding of existence and so to the weakest sense of the essence/

---

7. Ibid., 302.
8. Ibid., 303n19.
9. Ibid., 144. Also, "But *esse* we might say is only the actuation of form and has no reality apart from that function" (ibid., 143).

existence distinction. Are we not back to the lack of difference between the possible thalers and the actual thalers? The actual thalers are just the possible ones realized. If this understanding of *esse* is what McInerny's four reasons are after, then the reasons are much ado about nothing. Finally, in none of the texts of the Latin Aristotle referenced by McInerny does the Latin Aristotle mention *esse* or *actus essendi*. *Esse* talk is brought in by Aquinas in his commentary on the Latin Aristotle.

In sum, if *esse* means form in matter, then all that McInerny's arguments are doing is saving the term *esse*, but they are not saving the idea, especially as expressed in *SCG* II.54. He can speak about Aristotelian existentialism but what he is speaking about continues to appear as Aristotelian essentialism. In other words, McInerny could be considered a proponent of Craig's opinion that Aquinas has nothing philosophically new to offer.

To the first reason, the argument that identifying the essence and existence of corruptibles would make them incorruptibles is working with a sense of existence different than McInerny's. It is working with the same sense of existence that Aquinas's calls *esse* when in *De Ente*, chap. 4, he argues that intelligibly merging it with a thing would make that thing unique. At that point in the *De Ente*, *esse* is as known as a distinct act, if not yet known as a really distinct act. As I have mentioned in previous chapters, there are other effects of this intelligible merging. One of them is the incorruptibility of which McInerny speaks. But in all these cases, we are not understanding *esse* as McInerny understands *esse*, namely as form in matter.

Talk of identifying essence and existence in McInerny's case becomes second-order talk for first-order talk of a substance that is its form. Likewise, talk of a thing losing existence becomes second-order talk for first-order talk of a hylomorphic substance losing its form. It is difficult to see how any of this moves beyond the hylomorphic substance that has not received its *esse* and so is not yet a being. As I noted in chapter 3, Peter Geach seems more honest and so admits: "Aquinas's doctrine of *esse* really adds nothing over and above his doctrine of form."

To the second reason, another way exists to read Aristotle's *an sit/quid sit* questions. Joseph Owens points out that by the *an sit* question Aristotle simply wants to know if what we are investigating is not an absurdity or contradiction, such as a centaur or a goat-stag. Aristotle wants to know if the item is a being in the most general sense of the word. Actual existence in the real world is not the issue, though actual existence, for example of the eclipse, is relevant for establishing the possibility of the item. With Aquinas actual existence is the concern of the *an sit* question as is indicated in the *De Ente* by our ability to know what a man or a phoenix is and be ignorant that they exist.[10] In other words, Aquinas brings these Aristotelian questions back into his context of the *duplex operatio* that I described in chapter 2.

To the third reason, I would repeat what I said at the end of chapter 4. Understanding *esse* as a distinct act does not ruin predicating being essentially. One can argue the point in two ways. Both ways elaborate data seen within the context of metaphysical judgment. First, *esse* is a *sui generis actus*. Unlike garden-variety attributes, which are subsequent and posterior to their subjects, *esse* is an attribute basic and fundamental to its subject. Hence, like the hole of the donut, *esse* is both inside its subject and outside. Insofar as *esse* can be considered inside, then it can ground predication that is essential. Calling a thing a being will continue to describe what the thing is. Second, as thoroughly existence-neutral, the subject of *esse* is an absolute passive potency for the *esse*. Form plays a special role in this set up of the subject. As Aquinas says in *SCG* II.54, form is the *principium essendi* insofar as form is the *complementum* of the substance whose act is *esse*. Hence, through the disposition of form, *esse* is as necessary to the thing as its essential constituents are necessary. In this way also being (*ens*) can be predicated essentially.

To the fourth reason, I believe that Twetten is correct to point out an instability in hylomorphic composites. This instability implies something. Does it imply some component in the thing, distinct from the matter and form, that accounts for the thing actually to be? I do not see it. First, I do not see it textually or philosophically. Where does Twetten's assembled argument occur in the texts either of Aristotle or Aquinas? The closest text that comes to

---

10. "The question *an est* [in Aristotle] inquires merely if something is able to have the general character of being, and so does not indicate a combination of mutually exclusive notions, like a centaur or a goat-stag. If, like a centaur or a goat-stag, it is not even a being, there is no possibility of asking the further question 'What is it?' . . . For St. Thomas, on the other hand, one can know what a thing is without knowing that it is in reality. The question *an est* refers here to the real existence of the thing. One can know what a phoenix is, or a mountain of gold, or what an eclipse is, without knowing whether any of these actually exist in the real world. For Aristotle, the *an est* is not at all asking if the thing exists in reality, but only if it is free from internal contradiction, if it is a being in the most general sense of the word." Joseph Owens, "The Accidental and Essential Character of Being in the Doctrine of St. Thomas Aquinas," in *St. Thomas and the Existence of God* (ed. Catan), 59.

mind is the *De Principiis Naturae*. I looked at this text in chapter 7. All that Aquinas gets out of the matter/form composition, and I believe correctly, is the need for an efficient cause that is the generator that causes the thing by bringing about the form to be in matter. The efficient cause is not a further component of the substance distinct from the matter and form. Elsewhere Aquinas argues for a sustainer of the form in matter, but Aquinas does that from the eternity of generators back into the past. Again, the sustainer is not a component of the substance. It is an ungenerable and incorruptible body that Aquinas identifies with a celestial sphere. Nothing of Aquinas's distinctive *actus* sense of the thing's existence is reached from hylomorphism. Should not one take seriously Aquinas's assertions that the *secunda operatio respicit esse rei* in order to appreciate philosophically *actus essendi*?

This discussion of Aristotelian existentialism is valuable for replying to Craig's opinion that Aquinas has nothing new to offer cosmological reasoning. Aristotelian existentialism is not an existentialism in the Thomistic sense. It does not regard *esse* as a distinctive *actus*. Rather, *esse* is second-order talk for hylomorphic talk. *Esse* means in first order a form/matter composition. The proof of that thesis would surely validate Craig. The disproof would nonvalidate Craig. In my opinion, that is just what happens when the reasons for Aristotelian existentialism are tested.

A reader might call to mind the medieval image of the wax nose of Aristotle. The point of the image was to fit one's ideas to the text of Aristotle rather than to Aristotle, the historical man. So many of Aquinas's claims about Aristotle are actually claims about Aristotle's texts as seen through the lens of Aquinas's own metaphysics. As I mentioned above, the text of the Latin Aristotle fails to mention the terms *esse* and *actus essendi*. What the texts contain is terminology that will sound like what Aquinas means by these terms if the hermeneutics is through Aquinas's metaphysics.[11] No medieval is lying, if no medieval is speaking about the historical Aristotle.

Finally, I think that enough has been said also to distinguish Aquinas from Avicenna. For the Latin Avicenna, the possible thing with its *esse proprium* loses its passive potency for caused existence. Hence, *esse* from God does

11. For an analysis of Aquinas's central claim that Aristotle expressly says (*expresse dicit*) that the heavens have not only a cause of their motion but also a cause of their *esse* (*In II Meta.*, l. 2, nn. 294–98), see John F. X. Knasas, "Aquinas's Ascription of Creation to Aristotle," *Angelicum* 73, no. 4 (1996): 487–506.

not quite complete it. *Esse* from God appears superfluous and "superadded." Aquinas's *De Ente* discussion of the absolutely considered essence as *abstrahit ad quolibet esse* is a completely new discussion. It is crucial philosophically. The consideration of a thing as existence-neutral is the *sine qua non* for judgment going on to grasp the *esse rei* as an *actus* that is *profundius* and *magis intimum*.

Classic Cosmological Reasoning and Aquinas's *De Ente* Reasoning

To conclude, it is appropriate to revisit Leibniz's *a posteriori* arguments and to compare them to Aquinas. Both thinkers focus on the existence of a thing, but, in my opinion, Aquinas's focus extends to a far greater depth. To Leibniz's credit, he adopts the "V" model for what happens. The model implies some kind of distinction between a thing and its existence. Without that model it is difficult to understand a happening as more than a brute fact. Hume savaged the idea that simply what happens has a cause.[12] The Aristotelian gloss of a happening as the matter acquiring form or the substance acquiring an accident is an understanding that Hume missed. It offers resources to know an efficient cause. In Aristotle's case, however, the cause could be a mover only, not a creator. Also, the infinite power of the mover could only be concluded to from the eternity of motion.

In his *De Ente* Aquinas applied this thinking that what belongs to a thing is caused to the thing's *sui generis* accident of *esse*. As the act of all form, *esse* is a nonformal act that, if subsistent, would be all perfect. Also as prior to the substance of which it is the act, it immediately demands a creator that is subsistent *esse*.

Leibniz's "V" model is in some way an acknowledgment of the thinking of Aristotle and Aquinas. The model, however, is far from developed. The biggest indicator of the underdevelopment is Leibniz's treatment of the contingent relation between the thing and its existence. The treatment is by the principle of sufficient reason (PSR). The crux of the principle is the intolerability of *de facto* togetherness. We can call that togetherness "contingency." The items are merely touching. Two plates on a rack, two books on a shelf,

12. For a discussion of Hume, see Knasas, *Being and Some Twentieth-Century Thomists*, 216–21.

two beads on a string would be examples. No acknowledgment of stratification is necessary. It is never quite clear, then, why contingency requires a cause.

Both Aristotle and Aquinas bring out the need for a cause. They, however, make no mention of the PSR. They appeal to a subject/attribute analysis of situations. For example, the book is the subject, its touching the other is the attribute. Attributes are essentially dependent items. They are not totally dependent upon their subjects which are attribute-neutral. Hence, the attribute is dependent upon a cause. In short, the discernment of attributes gets the idea of dependency going; the attribute-neutrality of the subject *qua* subject extends the dependency to a cause.

Perhaps this thinking could be made implicit to the PSR. The *de facto* togetherness of the subject and attribute on which the PSR focuses would then correspond to the above remark on the attribute neutrality of the subject. Such an interpretation would save the PSR, but the PSR would lose its status as a principle. The principle would become: what belongs to a thing, that is, an accident, is caused.

Also, Leibniz gives no explanation of the "V" model as it applies to existence. He just assumes that as the thing's motion and shape are distinct from the thing, so too is the existence. This hurried conception will come back to haunt him and others. The conception is wide open to the whole discussion about whether existence is a predicate of its own. Aquinas's presentation of *esse* is much more studied. A brief summary of the presentation is as follows. The key is the data with which Aquinas begins. Real things cognitionally exist in sensation. Such is Aquinas's sense realism. Every morning when we open our eyes, we double the existence of the world. For real things to exist cognitionally also, real things of themselves cannot be real. Somewhat similarly, if the hot coffee is also cold, then the hot coffee of itself cannot be hot. These situations lead us to appreciate various neutralities. The thing both really and cognitionally existing is existence-neutral. As Aquinas remarked in this *De Ente*, it abstracts from every *esse*. The coffee is temperature-neutral.

The grasp of the thing's real existence as *actus essendi*, or *esse*, follows. Just as appreciating the coffee as temperature-neutral leads to understanding its hot temperature as something the coffee has, that is, as an attribute or accident, so too appreciating the thing as existence-neutral disposes us to regard its real existence as an attribute also. Moreover, because the thing has been understood as existence-neutral, then the attribute of its real existence is understood as basic and fundamental to the thing.

In his idea of *esse* Aquinas is considering the existence of the thing in a way completely foreign to its consideration in analytic debates. As the act of all form, *esse* adds, but it does not add something finite and determinate; hence the persistent erroneous disposition to equate the existence of the thing with the fact of the thing. Also, as an act fundamental and basic to a thing of itself existence-neutral, *esse* permits existential propositions to be subject/predicate without generating incoherencies like tautologies or self-contradictions. It is somewhat surprising to note that for all of his ability to see twelve senses of existence in Aquinas, Kenny misses the *actus essendi* sense.[13]

Leibniz's arguments continue by dealing with an infinite regress of causes back into the past. There is no disjunction as far as I can see. As such Leibniz's reasoning is similar to that of the Aristotelian natural philosopher who explains motion by a self-mover and then explains the self-mover by its generator *ad infinitum*. This path of Leibniz's reasoning again indicates that for all the use of the "V" model and the application of the model to the existence of a thing, Leibniz has little appreciation of Aquinas's priority of existence. An appreciation of the priority of existence would have opened a much more direct path to the necessary being.

Finally, the lack of nuance continues in Leibniz's understanding of the necessary being. Its identity with its existence means that it somehow accounts for its existence. A *de facto* togetherness of thing and existence is overcome in this way in the necessary being. Leibniz's thinking is implying that there is at least conceptually something prior to existence. The Thomistic challenge to Leibniz is to elaborate a nature that is existence positive prior to having *esse*. What could this something be? Prior to having *esse*, is not every nature existence-neutral? Did not Leibniz's famous question "Why is there something rather than nothing?" at least inchoately affirm the priority of existence? Hence, Aquinas's understanding of necessary being as subsistent *esse* is more consistent. It does not open up a whole new metaphysics as Leibniz's conception of necessary being appears to do.

In conclusion, in one twentieth-century interpretation of Aquinas, Aqui-

---

13. Kenny, *Aquinas on Being*, chap. 10.

nas appears to have thought through the meaning of the existence as an act in far greater depth than Leibniz and with far greater consistency than the analytics. That past interpretation is called Thomistic Existentialism. In that interpretation, Aquinas's efforts to understand existence payoff in a more cogent cosmological argument for God than the classic form. This more cogent argument, properly understood, is also central to all of Aquinas's God proofs. In these ways, I have tried to show that both secular thinkers and Thomists engaged in cosmological argument debate would profit by a reconsideration of Thomistic Existentialism.

SELECTED BIBLIOGRAPHY

Adams, Marilyn McCord, and Robert Merrihew Adams, eds. *The Problem of Evil*. Oxford: Oxford University Press, 1990.
Adams, Robert Merrihew. *Leibniz: Determinist, Theist, Idealist*. Oxford: Oxford University Press, 1994.
Albertson, J. S. "The *Esse* of Accidents according to St. Thomas." *The Modern Schoolman* 30, no. 4 (1953): 265–78.
Anderson, James. *The Bond of Being: An Essay on Analogy and Existence*. New York: Greenwood Press, 1969.
Aquinas, Thomas. *Commentary on Aristotle's De Anima*. Translated by Kenelm Foster and Silvester Humphries. Notre Dame, Ind.: Dumb Ox Books, 1994.
———. *Commentary on Aristotle's Physics*. Translated by Richard J. Blackwell et al. New Haven, Conn.: Yale University Press, 1963.
———. *Commentary on the Metaphysics of Aristotle*. Translated by John P. Rowan. Notre Dame, Ind.: Dumb Ox Books, 1995.
———. *Compendium of Theology*. Translated by Cyril Vollert. St. Louis, Mo.: Herder, 1947.
———. *De Principiis Naturae*. Edited by John J. Pauson. Fribourg: Société Philosophique, 1950.
———. *Disputed Questions on Truth*, vol. 1: *Questions I–IX*. Translated by Robert W. Mulligan, Chicago: Regnery, 1952.
———. *Disputed Questions on Truth*, vol. 2: *Questions X–XX*. Translated by James V. McGlynn. Chicago: Regnery, 1953.
———. *Disputed Questions on Truth*, vol. 3: *Questions XXI–XXIX*. Translated by Robert W. Schmidt. Chicago: Regnery, 1954.
———. *Expositio super Librum Boethii de Trinitate*. Edited by Bruno Decker. Leiden: Brill, 1959.
———. *Faith, Reason and Theology: Commentary on the* De Trinitate *of Boethius, Questions 1–4*. Translated by Armand Maurer. Toronto: Pontifical Institute of Mediaeval Studies, 1987.

———. *In Aristotelis Librum de Anima Commentarium*. Edited by Angelus M. Pirotta. Rome: Marietti, 1936.

———. *In Duodecim Libros Metaphysicorum Aristotelis Expositio*. Edited by M. R. Cathala and Raymundus M. Spiazzi. Rome: Marietti, 1950.

———. *In Octo Libros Physicorum Aristotelis Expositio*. Edited by P. M. Maggiolo. Rome: Marietti, 1954.

———. *Liber de Veritate Catholicae Fidei contra Errores Infidelium seu "Summa Contra Gentiles."* Edited by Ceslaus Pera, Petrus Marc, and Petrus Caramello. Rome: Marietti, 1961.

———. *On Being and Essence*. Translated by Armand Maurer. Toronto: Pontifical Institute of Mediaeval Studies, 1968.

———. *On Interpretation*. Translated by Jean T. Oesterle. Milwaukee, Wis.: Marquette University Press, 1962.

———. *On the Division and Methods of the Sciences: Commentary on the* De Trinitate *of Boethius, Questions 5 and 6*. Translated by Armand Maurer. Toronto: Pontifical Institute of Mediaeval Studies, 1963.

———. *Opusculum De Ente et Essentia*. Turin: Marietti, 1957.

———. *Quaestiones Disputatae de Anima*. Edited by James H. Robb. Toronto: Pontifical Institute of Mediaeval Studies, 1968.

———. *Quaestiones Disputatae de Malo*. Edited by P. Bazzi. In *Quaestiones Disputatae*, edited by Raymundus Spiazzi, vol. II. Rome: Marietti, 1965.

———. *Quaestiones Disputatae de Potentia Dei*. Edited by Paulus M. Pession. In *Quaestiones Disputatae*, edited by Raymundus Spiazzi, vol. II. Rome: Marietti, 1965.

———. *Quaestiones Disputatae de Veritate*. Edited by R. Spiazzi. In *Quaestiones Disputatae*, edited by Spiazzi, vol. I. Rome: Marietti, 1964.

———. *Quaestiones Quodlibetales*. Edited by R. Spiazzi. Rome: Marietti, 1949.

———. *Scriptum super Libros Sententiarum Magistri Petri Lombardi Episcopi Parisiensis*. Vols. 1–2 edited by Pierre Mandonnet. Paris: P. Lethielleux, 1929. Vols. 3–4 edited by Maria Fabianus Moos. Paris: P. Lethielleux, 1933–47.

———. *Summa Contra Gentiles*, vol. 1: *God*. Translated by Anton C. Pegis. Notre Dame, Ind.: University of Notre Dame Press, 1975.

———. *Summa Contra Gentiles*, vol. 2: *Creation*. Translated by James Anderson. Notre Dame, Ind.: University of Notre Dame Press, 1975.

———. *Summa Contra Gentiles*, vol. 3: *Providence*. Translated by Vernon J. Bourke. Notre Dame, Ind.: University of Notre Dame Press, 1975.

———. *Summa Contra Gentiles*, vol. 4: *Salvation*. Translated by Charles O'Neil. Notre Dame, Ind.: University of Notre Dame Press, 1975.

———. *Summa Theologiae*. Edited by the Ottawa Institute of Mediaeval Studies. Ottawa: Collège Dominicain d'Ottawa, 1941.

Ashley, Benedict. *The Way toward Wisdom: An Interdisciplinary and Intercultural Introduction to Metaphysics*. Notre Dame, Ind.: University of Notre Dame Press, 2006.

Averroes. *Tahāfut al Tahāfut.* Translated by Simon Van den Bergh. London: University Press, Oxford, 1954.
Avicenna. *Metaphysica.* In *Opera Omnia.* Venice, 1508.
——. *Metaphysices Compendium.* Edited by Nematallah Carame. Rome: Pontifical Institute of Mediaeval Studies, 1926.
Ayer, Alfred Jules. *Language, Truth and Logic.* New York: Dover, 1952.
Banez, Dominic. *The Primacy of Existence in Thomas Aquinas.* Chicago: Regnery, 1966.
Baisnée, Jules A. "St. Thomas Aquinas's Proofs of the Existence of God Presented in Their Chronological Order." In *Philosophical Studies in Honor of the Very Reverend Ignatius Smith, O.P.*, edited by John K. Ryan, 29–64. Westminster, Md.: Newman Press, 1952.
Barnes, Jonathan. *The Ontological Argument.* London: St. Martin's Press, 1972.
Bobik, Joseph. *Aquinas on Being and Essence.* Notre Dame, Ind.: University of Notre Dame Press, 1970.
Boyle, Leonard. *The Setting of the Summa Theologiae of Saint Thomas.* Toronto: Pontifical Institute of Mediaeval Studies, 1982.
Brown, Barry. *Accidental Being: A Study in the Metaphysics of St. Thomas Aquinas.* Lanham, Md.: University Press of America, 1986.
Burrill, Donald R., ed. *The Cosmological Arguments, A Spectrum of Opinion.* Garden City, N.Y.: Doubleday, 1967.
Cahalan, John. "On the Proving of Causal Propositions." *The Modern Schoolman* 44, no. 2 (1967): 129–67.
——. "Remarks on Father Owens's 'The Causal Proposition Revisited.'" *The Modern Schoolman* 44, no. 2 (1967): 152–60.
Catan, John R., ed. *St. Thomas Aquinas on the Existence of God: The Collected Papers of Joseph Owens.* Albany: State University of New York Press, 1980.
——, ed. *Aristotle: The Collected Papers of Joseph Owens.* Albany: State University of New York Press, 1981.
Clarke, William Norris. "Aseity (*Aseitas*)." In *New Catholic Encyclopedia*, 1:946. New York: McGraw-Hill, 1967.
Collins, James. *A History of Modern European Philosophy.* Milwaukee, Wis.: Bruce Publishing, 1954.
Copleston, Fredrick. *A History of Philosophy.* Westminster, Md.: Newman Press, 1960.
——. *Aquinas.* Baltimore, Md.: Penguin, 1961.
Craig, William Lane. *The Cosmological Argument from Plato to Leibniz.* London: Macmillan Press, 1980.
Cunningham, Francis A. "Averroes vs. Avicenna on Being." *The New Scholasticism* 48, no. 2 (1974): 185–218.
Curley, E. M. "The Root of Contingency." In *Leibniz: A Collection of Critical Essays*, edited by Harry G. Frankfurt, 83–96. Notre Dame, Ind.: University of Notre Dame Press, 1976.
Davies, Brian. "Aquinas, God, and Being." *The Monist* 80, no. 4 (1997): 500–520.

———. "The Action of God." In *Mind, Method, and Morality: Essays in Honour of Anthony Kenny*, edited by John Cottingham and Peter Hacker, 165–84. Oxford: Oxford University Press, 2010.

Decaen, Christopher A. "The Viability of Aristotelian-Thomistic Color Realism." *The Thomist* 65, no. 2 (2001): 179–222.

Dewan, Lawrence. "Saint Thomas, Joseph Owens, and the Real Distinction between Being and Essence." *The Modern Schoolman* 61, no. 3 (1984): 145–55.

———. "Discussion of Anthony Kenny's *Aquinas on Being*," *Nova et Vetera* (English Edition) 3, no. 2 (2005): 335–400.

Dummett, Michael. *Frege, Philosophy of Language*. Cambridge, Mass.: Harvard University Press, 1981.

Edwards, Paul. "The Cosmological Argument." In *The Cosmological Arguments, A Spectrum of Opinion*, edited by David Burrill, 101–24. Garden City, N.Y.: Doubleday, 1967.

Gale, Richard M., and Alexander R. Pruss. "A New Cosmological Argument." *Religious Studies* 35, no. 4 (1999): 461–76.

Garrigou-Lagrange, Reginald. *God: His Existence and His Nature*. Translated by Dom Bede Rose. St. Louis, Mo.: Herder, 1939.

Geach, Peter. *Three Philosophers*. Oxford: Basil Blackwell, 1961.

———. *God and Soul*. London: Routledge and Kegan Paul, 1978.

Gilson, Etienne. *The Spirit of Medieval Philosophy*. New York: Charles Scribner's Sons, 1940.

———. "La preuve du '*De Ente et Essentia*.'" *Doctor Communis* 3, no. 2 (1950): 257–60.

———. *Being and Some Philosophers*. Toronto: Pontifical Institute of Mediaeval Studies, 1952.

———. *The Elements of Christian Philosophy*. New York: Doubleday, 1960.

———. "Trois leçons sur le problème de l'existence de Dieu." *Divinitas* 1 (1961): 23–87.

———. *Le Thomisme*. 6th edition. Paris: J. Vrin, 1972 (1962).

———. *Christian Philosophy*. Translated by Armand Maurer. Toronto: Pontifical Institute of Mediaeval Studies, 1993.

———. *The Christian Philosophy of St. Thomas Aquinas*. Translated by L. K. Shook. Notre Dame, Ind.: University of Notre Dame Press, 1994.

Gurr, John. *The Principle of Sufficient Reason in Some Scholastic Systems 1750–1900*. Milwaukee, Wis.: Marquette University Press, 1959.

Haldane, Elizabeth S., and G. R. T. Ross. *The Philosophical Works of Descartes*. Mineola, N.Y.: Dover, 1955.

Hawkins, D. J. B. "Sufficient Reason, Principle of." In *New Catholic Encyclopedia*, 3:777–78. New York: McGraw-Hill, 1967.

Heidegger, Martin. *Being and Time*. Translated by John Macquarie and Edward Robinson. New York: Harper and Row, 1962.

———. *Identity and Difference*. Translated by Joan Stambaugh. New York: Harper and Row, 1969.

———. *The Basic Problems of Phenomenology*. Translated by Albert Hofstadter. Bloomington: Indiana University Press, 1988.

Henle, Robert J. *Method in Metaphysics*. Milwaukee, Wis.: Marquette University Press, 1980.

Husserl, Edmund. *Cartesian Meditations: An Introduction to Phenomenology*. Translated by Dorion Cairns. The Hague: Martinus Nijhoff, 1964.

———. *Ideas: General Introduction to Pure Phenomenology*. Translated by W. R. Boyce Gibson. New York: Collier Books, 1972.

Johnson, Mark. "Did St. Thomas Attribute a Doctrine of Creation to Aristotle?" *The New Scholasticism* 63, no. 2 (1989): 129–55.

Kant, Immanuel. *Critique of Pure Reason*. Translated by Norman Kemp Smith. New York: St. Martin's Press, 1965.

Kenny, Anthony. *The Five Ways: St. Thomas Aquinas' Proofs of God's Existence*. New York: Schocken Books, 1969.

———. *Aquinas on Being*. Oxford: Clarendon Press, 2002.

Kerr, Gaven. *Aquinas's Way to God: The Proof in the De Ente et Essentia*. Oxford: Oxford University Press, 2015.

Kirn, Arthur G., ed. *G. B. Phelan: Selected Papers*. Toronto: Pontifical Institute of Mediaeval Studies, 1967.

Klima, Gyula. "On Kenny on Aquinas on Being." *International Philosophical Quarterly* 44, no. 4 (2004): 567–80.

Knasas, John F. X. "Making Sense of the *Tertia Via*." *The New Scholasticism* 54, no. 4 (1980): 476–511.

———. "Thomistic Existentialism and the Silence of the *Quinque Viae*." *The Modern Schoolman* 63, no. 3 (1986): 157–71.

———. "Does Gilson Theologize Thomistic Metaphysics?." In *Thomistic Papers V*, edited by Thomas A. Russman, 3–24. Houston, Tex.: Center for Thomistic Studies, 1990.

———. "Materiality and Aquinas' Natural Philosophy: A Reply to Johnson." *The Modern Schoolman* 68, no. 3 (1991): 251–54.

———. "Transcendental Thomism and *De Veritate* I, 9." In *Thomistic Papers VI*, edited by John F. X. Knasas, 229–52. Houston, Tex.: Center for Thomistic Studies, 1994.

———. "A Heideggerian Critique of Aquinas and a Gilsonian Reply." *The Thomist* 58, no. 3 (1994): 415–39.

———. "Aquinas' Ascriptions of Creation to Aristotle." *Angelicum* 73, no. 4 (1996): 487–506.

———. "*Contra* Spinoza: Aquinas on God's Free Will." *American Catholic Philosophical Quarterly* 76, no. 3 (2002): 417–30.

———. *Being and Some Twentieth-Century Thomists*. New York: Fordham University Press, 2003.

———. "Haldane's Analytic Thomism and Aquinas's *Actus Essendi*." In *Analytical Thomism: Traditions in Dialogue*, edited by Craig Paterson and Matthew S. Pugh, 233–51. Burlington, Vt.: Ashgate, 2006.

———. *Thomism and Tolerance*. Scranton, Penn.: Scranton University Press, 2011.
———. *Aquinas and the Cry of Rachel: Thomistic Reflections on the Problem of Evil*. Washington, D.C.: The Catholic University Press of America, 2014.
Koons, Robert C. "A New Look at the Cosmological Argument." *American Philosophical Quarterly* 34, no. 2 (1997): 193–210.
Krapiec, Mieczyslaw Albert. *Metaphysics: An Outline of the History of Being*. Translated by Theresa Sandok. New York: Peter Lang, 1991.
Kretzmann, Norman. *The Metaphysics of Theism: Aquinas's Natural Theology in Summa Contra Gentiles I*. Oxford: Clarendon Press, 1997.
Langan, Thomas. *The Meaning of Heidegger*. New York: Columbia University Press, 1966.
Lonergan, Bernard J. F. "*Insight*: Preface to a Discussion." *Proceedings of the American Catholic Philosophical Association* 32 (1958): 71–81.
MacDonald, Scott. "The *Esse/Essentia* Argument in Aquinas' *De ente et essentia*." *The Journal of the History of Philosophy* 22, no. 2 (1984): 157–72.
———. "Aquinas's Parasitic Cosmological Argument." *Medieval Philosophy and Theology* 1 (1991): 119–55.
Maritain, Jacques. *The Dream of Descartes*. Translated by Mabelle L. Andison. New York: Philosophical Library, 1944.
———. *The Degrees of Knowledge*. Translated by Gerald B. Phelan. New York: Charles Scribner's Sons, 1959.
———. *Existence and the Existent*. Translated by Lewis Galantiere and Gerald B. Phelan. New York: Vintage, 1966.
Maurer, Armand. "St. Thomas and Eternal Truths." *Mediaeval Studies* 32 (1970): 91–107.
———. *About Beauty: A Thomistic Interpretation*. Houston, Tex.: Center for Thomistic Studies, 1983.
———. "Dialectic in the *De Ente et Essentia* of St. Thomas Aquinas," in *Mélanges offerts au Père L. E. Boyle à l'occasion de son 75e anniversaire*, edited by J. Hamesse, 573–83. Louvain-le-Neuve: F.I.D.E.M. Publications, 1998.
McCool, Gerald A. *From Unity to Pluralism: The Internal Evolution of Thomism*. New York: Fordham University Press, 1999.
McInerny, Ralph M. *A History of Western Philosophy*. Notre Dame, Ind.: University of Notre Dame Press, 1970.
———. *Being and Predication*. Washington, D.C.: The Catholic University of America Press, 1986.
———. *Praeambula Fidei: Thomism and the God of the Philosophers*. Washington, D.C.: The Catholic University of America Press, 2006.
McKeon, Richard, ed. *The Basic Works of Aristotle*. New York: Random House, 1970.
McLaughlin, Thomas J. "Aristotelian Mover-Causality and the Principle of Inertia." *International Philosophical Quarterly* 38, no. 2 (1998): 137–51.
Miller, Barry. "The Contingency Argument." *The Monist* 54, no. 3 (1970): 359–73.
———. *The Fullness of Being: A New Paradigm for Existence*. Notre Dame, Ind.: University of Notre Dame Press, 2002.

Miyakawa, Toshiyuki. "The Value and the Meaning of the *Tertia Via* of St. Thomas Aquinas." *Aquinas* 6, no. 2 (1963): 239–95.
O'Brien, Thomas C. *Metaphysics and the Existence of God*. Washington, D.C.: Thomist Press, 1960.
O'Callaghan, John. "Concepts, Mirrors, and Signification: Response to Deely." *American Catholic Philosophical Quarterly* 84, no. 1 (2010): 133–62.
O'Donaghue, Dermot. "An Analysis of the *Tertia Via* of St. Thomas Aquinas." *The Irish Theological Quarterly* 20 (1953): 129–51.
Owens, Joseph. "The Causal Proposition—Principle or Conclusion?" *The Modern Schoolman* 32, nos. 2–4 (1955): 159–71, 257–70, 323–39.
———. "Common Nature: A Point of Comparison between Thomistic and Scotistic Metaphysics." *Mediaeval Studies* 19 (1957): 1–14.
———. *The Doctrine of Being in the Aristotelian Metaphysics*. Toronto: Pontifical Institute of Mediaeval Studies, 1963.
———. "Aquinas and the Proof from the 'Physics.'" *Mediaeval Studies* 28 (1966): 119–50.
———. "The Causal Proposition Revisited." *The Modern Schoolman* 44, no. 2 (1967): 143–51.
———. "The Range of Existence," *Proceedings of the Seventh Inter-American Congress of Philosophy*, vol. 1. Québec: Les Presses de L'Université Laval, 1967.
———. *St. Thomas and the Future of Metaphysics*. Milwaukee, Wis.: Marquette University Press, 1973.
———. "Aquinas: 'Darkness of Ignorance' in the Most Refined Notion of God." *The Southwestern Journal of Philosophy* 5, no. 2 (1974): 93–110.
———. "The Accidental and Essential Character of Being in the Doctrine of St. Thomas Aquinas." In *Collected Papers* (ed. Catan), 52–96.
———. "Actuality in the *Prima Via*." In *Aquinas: Collected Papers* (ed. Catan), 192–207.
———. "Aquinas and the Five Ways." In *Aquinas: Collected Papers* (ed. Catan), 132–41.
———. "Aquinas as Aristotelian Commentator." In *Aquinas: Collected Papers* (ed. Catan), 1–19.
———. "Immobility and Existence for Aquinas." In *Aquinas: Collected Papers* (ed. Catan), 208–27.
———. "Judgment and Truth in Aquinas." In *Aquinas: Collected Papers* (ed. Catan), 34–51.
———. "The Starting Point of the *Prima Via*." In *Aquinas: Collected Papers* (ed. Catan), 169–91.
———. *St. Thomas Aquinas on the Existence of God: The Collected Papers of Joseph Owens*. Edited by John R. Catan. Albany: State University of New York Press, 1980.
———. "Aristotle: Cognition a Way of Being." In *Aristotle: The Collected Papers of Joseph Owens*, edited by John R. Catan, 74–89. Albany: State University of New York Press, 1981.
———. *An Elementary Christian Metaphysics*. Houston, Tex.: Center for Thomistic Studies, 1985.

———. *An Interpretation of Existence*. Houston, Tex.: Center for Thomistic Studies, 1985.
———. "Aquinas' Distinction at *De ente et essentia* 4, 119–123." *Mediaeval Studies* 48 (1986): 264–87.
———. *Cognition: An Epistemological Inquiry*. Houston, Tex.: Center for Thomistic Studies, 1992.
Paterson, Craig, and Matthew S. Pugh, eds. *Analytical Thomism: Traditions in Dialogue*. Burlington, Vt.: Ashgate, 2006.
Patt, Walter. "Aquinas's Real Distinction and Some Interpretations." *The New Scholasticism* 62, no. 1 (1988): 1–29.
Pears, D. F., and J. F. Thomson. *Is Existence a Predicate?* London: Aquin Press, 1963.
Pegis, Anton, ed. *The Basic Writings of St. Thomas Aquinas*. New York: Random House, 1945.
Penelhum, Terence. "Divine Necessity." In *The Cosmological Arguments: A Spectrum of Opinion*, edited by David R. Burrill, 143–61.
———. "Divine Goodness and the Problem of Evil." In *The Problem of Evil*, edited by McCord Adams and Merrihew Adams, 69–82. Oxford: Oxford University Press, 1990.
Penfield, Wilfred. *The Mystery of the Mind: A Critical Study of Consciousness and the Human Brain*. Princeton, N.J.: Princeton University Press, 1978.
Phelan, Gerald B. "*Verum sequitur Esse Rerum*." In *G. B. Phelan: Selected Papers*, edited by Arthur G. Kirn. Toronto: Pontifical Institute of Mediaeval Studies, 1967.
Plantinga, Alvin. "Necessary Being." *The Cosmological Arguments: A Spectrum of Opinion*, edited by David R. Burrill, 125–41. Garden City, N.Y.: Doubleday, 1967.
Pruss, Alexander R. "The Leibnizian Cosmological Argument." In *The Blackwell Companion to Natural Theology*, edited by William Lane Craig and J. P. Moreland, 24–99. Oxford: Wiley-Blackwell, 2009.
Quinn, John. *The Thomism of Etienne Gilson*. Villanova, Penn.: Villanova University Press, 1971.
———. "The Third Way to God: A New Approach." *The Thomist* 42, no. 1 (1978): 50–68.
Reichenbach, Bruce. *The Cosmological Argument: A Reassessment*. Springfield, Ill.: Charles C. Thomas, 1972.
———. *Evil and a Good God*. New York: Fordham University Press, 1982.
Rowe, William. *The Cosmological Argument*. Princeton, N.J.: Princeton University Press, 1975.
Russell, Bertrand. *Why I Am Not a Christian and Other Essays on Religion and Related Subjects*. London: Simon and Schuster, 1957.
Russman, Thomas A., ed. *Thomistic Papers V*. Houston, Tex.: Center for Thomistic Studies, 1990.
Ryan, John K., ed. *Philosophical Studies in Honor of the Very Reverend Ignatius Smith, O.P.* Westminster, Md.: Newman Press, 1952.
Shanley, Brian J. "Analytic Thomism." *The Thomist* 63, no. 1 (1999): 125–37.

Selected Bibliography 323

Siger de Brabant. *Quaestiones in Metaphysicam.* Edited by Armand Maurer. Louvain-La-Neuve: Éditions de l'Institut Supérieur de Philosophie, 1983.

Sillem, Edward. *Ways of Thinking about God. Thomas Aquinas and the Modern Mind.* New York: Sheed and Ward, 1961.

Smart, J. J. C. "The Existence of God." In *The Cosmological Arguments, A Spectrum of Opinion,* edited by Donald R. Burrill, 255–78. Garden City, N.Y.: Doubleday, 1967.

Smith, Gerard. "Avicenna and the Possibles." *The New Scholasticism* 17, no. 4 (1943): 340–57.

Smith, Vincent. "The Prime Mover: Physical and Metaphysical Considerations." *Proceedings of the American Catholic Philosophical Association* 28 (1954): 78–94.

———. *The General Science of Nature.* Milwaukee, Wis.: Bruce Publishing, 1958.

Sokolowski, Robert. *Introduction to Phenomenology.* Cambridge: Cambridge University Press, 2000.

Thomson, Iain. "Ontotheology? Understanding Heidegger's *Destruktion* of Metaphysics." *International Journal of Philosophical Studies* 8, no. 3 (2000): 297–327.

Van Steenberghen, Fernand. *Thomas Aquinas and Radical Aristotelianism.* Washington, D.C.: The Catholic University of America Press, 1980.

Weiner, Philip P. *Leibniz Selections.* New York: Charles Scribner's Sons, 1951.

Weisheipl, James. *Friar Thomas D'Aquino: His Life, Thought, and Work.* Garden City, N.Y.: Doubleday, 1974.

Westphal, Merold. "Aquinas and Onto-theology." *American Catholic Philosophical Quarterly* 80, no. 2 (2006): 173–92.

Williams, C. J. F. *Being, Identity, and Truth.* Oxford: Clarendon, 1992.

Wippel, John F. "Aquinas' Route to the Real Distinction." *The Thomist* 43, no. 2 (1979): 279–95.

———. *The Metaphysical Thought of Thomas Aquinas: From Finite Being to Uncreated Being.* Washington, D.C.: The Catholic University of America Press, 2000.

INDEX

Absolute consideration: as first operation, 41–45; modality, 63–67, 261; singular essence, 49–52
Actus essendi. See Esse.
Adams, Robert Merrihew: Leibniz on existence, 23–25
Albertson, J. S., 207
Anderson, James, 302n10
Aquinas, Thomas: analogous conceptualization, 168; concluding comparison with Leibniz, 311–14; division of sciences, 186–88; *esse commune* and *esse formale*, 126n45; fallacy of composition, 153; first physical cause, 195; formed intention of existence, 121–25; God and evil, 155–61; infinite regress, 154, 194, 225n10; metaphysics and God, 175–88; metaphysics and cognitive soul, 183; metaphysics and motion, 213–15; negation and modifying *esse commune* to represent *esse subsistens*, 126–29; ordinary knowledge of God, 298–304; participation, 286; scope of explanation, 150–52; singular essence vs universal essence, 49; *suppositio* of motion's eternity, 232
Ashley, Benedict, 2n1, 180n11; physical God proof, 198

Avicenna; essence as relative passive potency in Latin Avicenna, 104, 310–11
Ayer, Alfred Jules, 133–35

Baisnée, Jules A., 117n1
Barnes, Jonathan, 142n13
Being (*ens*): non-generic, 88, 302; derived from *esse*, 33n4; fauxing, 303–4
Bobik, Joseph, infinite regress, 61n35
Boyle, Leonard, 249n2
Brown, Barry, 207

Caputo, Joseph: Heidegger as transcendental thinker, 163n53
Cahallan, John C.: critique of Owens on causal proposition, 96–99
Chance, 246
Classic Cosmological Reasoning, 1
Collins, James: Kant reply, 22
Copleston, Fredrick: 173n1; infinity of past causes, 194n7; Kant reply, 22
Curley, E. M., 25n25

Davies, Brian: critique of *esse* as attribute, 114–18
Decan, Christopher A., 145n22

De Ente reasoning: robust version, 189–215; too complicated, 297; universal application, 292–293; without unicity argument, 87, 282
Descartes, René: *causa sui*, 17n10; sense illusions, 144n20
Dewan, Lawrence: real distinction and efficient causality, 93–96
Dream possibility, 147–48
Dummett, Michael, 140
Duplex operatio intellectus: general nature of, 39–46; metaphysical application, 46–54; negation and the second operation, 129; other interpretations, 54–59

Esse: as analogous, 168; analytic debates on existence, 139–43; as *vivere*, 114; causality, 59–63; diversification of as *esse formale*, 88, 127, 205; for accidents, 205–210; form as cause of, 99–105; meaning of, 33–38; priority, 36; real distinction, 81–85; sense realism, 51–52; three senses of, 57
Esse subsistens: as unique, creator and conserver, 62–63; as *per se notum*, 130; as God, 159, 294; nominal definition, 196
Eternity of motion: Aquinas on Aristotle; Aquinas's *suppositio*, 232; proofs, 233

Feser, Edward, 85n34
Formed intentions, 122; *speciositas*, 280

Gale, Richard M., Principle of Sufficient Reason, 26n26
Geach, Peter: *esse* as form, 106–14
Gilson, Etienne: De Ente argument 69–77; judgment, 40n16; meaning of being, 43n25
God. *See Esse subsistens*.
Gurr, John, Principle of Sufficient Reason, 26n26

Hawkins, D. J. B., Principle of Sufficient Reason, 26n26
Heidegger, Martin: ontotheology, 161–69; Being as a priori, 162n53; sense realism, 167n61
Henle, Robert: Thomistic Existentialism, 2n1; meaning of judgment, 40n16
Husserl, Edmund: perceptual intentionality, 52n39, 145

Inertia, 255
Infinite regress, 60–63, 154, 258; of generators, 194, 225n10

Kant, Immanuel: classic, 1; cosmological critique, 21; ontological critique, 18–20; apriority of space, 148–49
Kenny, Anthony: identity of cause problem, 61, 220n5; infinite regress, 227n11; man/phoenix argument, 119–30; meaning of "*est*," 59; metaphysical analysis of motion, 220n4, 222n7; *omne quod movetur* principle, 223n8, 224n9, 225n10; teleology, 269–72; twelve senses of existence, 313
Kerr, Gavin, 29n29, 52n40, 53n41, 85n34
Koons, Robert C., new cosmological proof, 26n26
Krapiec, Albert, 107n34
Kretzmann, Norman, 229n12, 230n13

Langan, Thomas, 167n61
Leibniz, Gottfried Wilhelm: cosmological proofs, 10–17; concluding comparison with Aquinas, 311–14

McCool, Gerald, 2n1
MacDonald, Scott: real *essentia/esse* distinction, 90–93; Aquinas's motion proof, 237–41
McInerny, Ralph; Aristotelian Existen-

tialism, 2n1, 306–10; *In Meta* trans., 184n20
McLaughlin, Thomas J., 219n3
Maritain, Jacques: Kant reply, 22; Thomistic Existentialism, 2
Maurer, Armand A.: beauty, 280n7; *De Ente* argument, 77–81; eternal truths, 59, 111n15
Miller, Barry, 138
Miyakawa, Toshiyuki, 260n11

O'Brien, Thomas C.: Gilson as theologizer, 71n7; *tertia via*, 260n11
O'Callaghan, John: formal signs, 44n26
O'Donaghue, Dermot, 261n13
Owens, Joseph, 306n4; *An sit/quid sit* questions, 309n10; as Thomistic commentator, 190–91l; cognitional reception of form, 52n39; efficiency in separate substance, 181; *esse* as vivere, 114; Five Ways, 173n1; judgmentally grasped *esse* as conceptualizable, 71n8; later subsistent *esse* proof, 294n6; meaning of judgment, 40n17; "phenomenology," 39; philosophical roles for *negatio*, 129n55; theological prompt for *esse*, 73; Thomistic Existentialism, 2n1

Patt, Walter, 82n32
Penelhum, Terence M., 173n1; existence and God as *per se notum*, 139; reconstituted cosmological critique, 22; scope of explanation, 149–52
Phelan, Gerald B., 40n16
Plantinga, Alvin, 135–38
Possibility: kinds of, 63
Prima via, 25–56
Principle of Noncontradiction, 65–67
Pruss, Alexander: modality, 64n60, 66n62, 67n64; Principle of Sufficient Reason, 26n26, 144n19

Quinta via, 268–72
Quarta via, 266–67
Quinn, John; judgmental *esse* as the concrete reality, 55; first physical cause, 196n9, 199–201

Reichenbach, Bruce: causality, 98n70: Kant reply, 22n16; logical necessity, 265n19
Rowe, William: critique of PSR, 27–28

Secunda via, 256–59
Sense realism, 143–49
Sense relativities, 145–47
Smart, J. J. C.: reconstructed cosmological critique, 22.
Smith, Vincent: physical God proof, 196–98
Spinoza, Baruch; infinite substance, 17

Tertia via, 259–66
Thomistic Existentialism, 2–5; too complicated, 297
Thomistic *magister*, 249–50
Twetten, David: argument for *esse*, 307, 309–10

Van Steenberghen, Fernand, 235n20

Weisheipl, James A., 249n1
Westphal, Merold, 169n65
Willimas, C. J. F., 139n5
Wippel, John F.: *ex nihilo*, 277n2; Gilson as theologizer, 71n7; inertia, 255n7; infinite regress, 61n35; judgmental *esse* as facticity, 56–59; *prima via*, 254n6; *quarta via*, 267n11; real *essentia/esse* distinction, 85–89; *secunda via*, 257n9

Thomistic Existentialism and Cosmological Reasoning was designed in Adobe Garamond and composed by Kachergis Book Design of Pittsboro, North Carolina. It was printed on 60-pound Maple Eggshell Cream and bound by Maple Press of York, Pennsylvania.

www.ingramcontent.com/pod-product-compliance
Lightning Source LLC
Chambersburg PA
CBHW020314010526
44107CB00054B/1838